Installing and Configuring Windows Server 2025

A practical guide to management and optimization of Windows Server environment

Bekim Dauti

www.bpbonline.com

First Edition 2025

ISBN: 978-93-65894-295

LIMITS OF LIABILITY AND DISCLAIMER OF WARRANTY

Distributors:

BPB PUBLICATIONS
20, Ansari Road, Darya Ganj
New Delhi-110002
Ph: 23254990/23254991

DECCAN AGENCIES
4-3-329, Bank Street,
Hyderabad-500195
Ph: 24756967/24756400

MICRO MEDIA
Shop No. 5, Mahendra Chambers,
150 DN Rd. Next to Capital Cinema,
V.T. (C.S.T.) Station, MUMBAI-400 001
Ph: 22078296/22078297

Published by Manish Jain for BPB Publications, 20 Ansari Road, Darya Ganj, New Delhi-110002 and Printed by him at Manipal Technologies, Manipal

www.bpbonline.com

Dedicated to

"To our planet Earth, the home that sustains us all.
May this book inspire a deeper commitment to preserving and protecting the environment for future generations."

About the Author

Bekim Dauti is a dedicated computer technology expert with a bachelor's degree in informatics from the University of Tirana, a master's in information technology from UMGC Europe, and a doctorate in computer science from Aspen University. Bekim is a Cisco Certified Academy Instructor (CCAI) and a Microsoft Certified Trainer (MCT) specializing in server administration, computer networking, and training.

With over two and a half decades of experience, Bekim has authored nearly 20 books and numerous articles in reputable publications such as PC World Albanian and CIO Albanian. Certifications from ECDL, Certiport, CompTIA, Cisco, Microsoft, and Sun Microsystems validate his expertise.

Bekim is a Microsoft Certified Trainer at TeKnowledge and the founder of InfoTech Academy and Dautti. He also maintains a blog, "Bekim Dauti's Blog," where he shares his insights on technology. Bekim is grateful for his family's support.

Acknowledgement

I want to express my heartfelt gratitude to my parents and family for their unwavering love, support, and encouragement—this book would not have been possible without them. Their sacrifices and guidance were a constant source of motivation throughout this journey. To my colleagues at TeKnowledge and Dautti, thank you for your continuous support and belief in me. I am also profoundly grateful to BPB Publications for their expert guidance in bringing this book to life. The revision of this book was a long and rewarding process, made even more valuable by the contributions of reviewers, technical experts, and editors. Above all, I thank god for granting me life, health, and the opportunity to contribute to the sharing of knowledge. I also pray that god rewards my family, friends, colleagues, and all those who supported me throughout this endeavor. Finally, I wish peace, health, and blessings to every reader.

Preface

Windows Server 2025 is the server operating system developed by Microsoft as part of the Windows NT family of operating systems. This book is designed to get you started with Windows Server 2025. At the same time, this book aims to introduce you to the roles that Windows Server 2025 supports. In addition, the book teaches you how to install roles using the Add Roles and Features Wizard and Windows PowerShell cmdlets. Furthermore, the book provides instructions for configuring client/server network services using various graphical user interface (GUI) wizards, tools, and Windows PowerShell cmdlets.

The book begins with an introduction to computer networks and Windows Server 2025. Then, it continues with the installation and post-installation tasks of Windows Server 2025. You will then move on to more advanced aspects of working with Windows Server 2025, such as installing roles and configuring client/server network services like AD DS, DNS, DHCP, WDS, PDS, WSUS, Web Server, Hyper-V, and other essential network services. The book also explores new and advanced features On-Premises Server Hotpatching with Azure Arc, next-generation Active Directory and SMB enhancements, improved storage performance with NVMe SSDs and better SAN integration, and robust in-place upgrades for streamlined version updates. Next, with the help of real-world examples, you will get to grips with the fundamentals of Windows Server 2025, which will help you solve complex tasks the easy way. Later, the book also shows you maintenance and troubleshooting tasks, where, with the help of best practices, you can easily manage Windows Server 2025. By the end of this book, you will have the knowledge required to administer and manage Windows Server environments.

Chapter 1: Understanding Network Components - This chapter aims to provide a comprehensive introduction to networking within Windows Server 2025 environments. It begins with the historical context of the Birth of the Internet. It progresses to modern computer networks, covering essential topics such as network components, architecture, topologies, IP addressing, and subnets. The goal is to equip IT professionals with a solid understanding of network fundamentals crucial for effective management and optimization. Additionally, the chapter discusses the role of Network Operating Systems (NOS) and emerging technology trends. To illustrate practical implementation, it concludes with a hands-on example demonstrating Hyper-V configuration in Windows 11 Pro using Settings and Windows PowerShell, offering actionable insights for real-world scenarios.

Chapter 2: Introduction to Windows Server 2025 - This chapter will provide a comprehensive understanding of server hardware and its critical components, such as the processor, memory, storage, and network interfaces. You will be introduced to Windows Server 2025 while learning the hardware fundamentals. This introduction will cover key details, including its release timeline, the various editions available, notable new features, and the system requirements for successful deployment. The chapter will conclude with a practical hands-on activity, where you will download both Windows Server 2025 and the Windows Admin Center. This exercise will reinforce your understanding by allowing you to apply the concepts discussed in a real-world scenario.

Chapter 3: Windows Server 2025 Installation - This chapter will guide you through the installation process of Windows Server 2025. Before initiating the installation, you will learn about partition schemes, boot options, and installation methods. Familiarizing yourself with these concepts will provide a solid foundation for smoothly installing Windows Server 2025. Additionally, you will set up the virtual switch and virtual machine (VM) within the Hyper-V Client, utilizing the ISO image you acquired in Chapter 2, which introduced you to Windows Server 2025. These tasks have been thoughtfully designed to be interactive and engaging, ensuring that you quickly grasp the process of installing Windows Server 2025. Moreover, this chapter incorporates new and improved technologies in Windows Server 2025, offering enhanced performance, security, and management capabilities to streamline your server setup experience.

Chapter 4: Initial Configuration of Windows Server 2025 - This chapter aims to provide clear explanations and instructions for post-installation tasks and the initial configuration of Windows Server 2025. The post-installation tasks section will cover essential topics such as managing devices and drivers, Plug and Play, IRQ, DMA, interrupts, driver signing, registry and services, registry entries, service accounts, and dependencies. The initial configuration section will offer step-by-step instructions for hands-on exercises, including setting up the IP address, changing the time zone, activating Windows Server 2025, and many more tasks in an understandable and straightforward format. The goal is to guide you through the process and demonstrate how to perform these tasks step by step, ensuring you have a solid foundation for effectively managing and configuring Windows Server 2025.

Chapter 5: Installing Roles Using Server Manager and PowerShell - The primary objective of this chapter is to provide comprehensive guidance on installing roles in Windows Server 2025. This is achieved through detailed, step-by-step instructions and clear explanations on using the Add Roles and Features Wizard in Server Manager and PowerShell to install various roles such as Active Directory Domain Services (AD DS), Domain Name System

(DNS), Dynamic Host Configuration Protocol (DHCP), Hyper-V, Internet Information Services (IIS), Print and Document Services (PDS), Remote Access, Remote Desktop Services (RDS), and Windows Server Update Services (WSUS). Additionally, this chapter aims to help readers understand the purpose of each role and configure them to meet their organization's specific needs. By the end of this chapter, readers will have acquired the necessary skills and knowledge to install roles effectively and customize their Windows Server 2025 efficiently, allowing them to tailor it to their organizational requirements.

Chapter 6: Azure Arc On-Premises Hotpatching - The primary objective of this chapter is to provide comprehensive guidance on implementing On-Premises Server Hotpatching with Azure Arc in Windows Server 2025. This is achieved through step-by-step instructions and clear explanations on configuring Azure Arc for hotpatching, implementing hotpatching policies and schedules, and monitoring and managing hotpatching updates. Additionally, this chapter aims to help readers understand the benefits of hotpatching, best practices for deployment, and real-world use cases. By the end of this chapter, readers will have gained the necessary skills and knowledge to effectively implement hotpatching, enhance security and minimize downtime in their on-premises server environments.

Chapter 7: Next-Generation Active Directory and SMB Enhancements - The primary objective of this chapter is to provide an in-depth understanding of the evolution and advancements in Active Directory (AD) and Server Message Block (SMB) protocols in Windows Server 2025. This chapter will guide you through detailed explanations and practical examples of the new features and enhancements in Active Directory Domain Services (AD DS) and the SMB protocol. By the end of this chapter, readers will have gained the knowledge and skills to implement and optimize AD and SMB in Windows Server 2025, focusing on enhanced security, improved performance, and scalability. You will be equipped to effectively manage authentication, access control, and file sharing in your organization's infrastructure, whether upgrading from a previous version or deploying new capabilities.

Chapter 8: Configuring Windows Server 2025 Services - This chapter equips readers with the knowledge and skills to configure and manage client/server network services in Windows Server 2025 using Windows PowerShell cmdlets. Readers will learn to efficiently set up and manage critical services, including DHCP, Active Directory Domain Services (AD DS), DNS, virtual machines, and web servers, to meet the demands of dynamic infrastructure environments. Additionally, the chapter covers configuring print servers, Windows Deployment Services (WDS), Virtual Private Networks (VPNs), Remote Desktop Services (RDS) users, and Windows Server Update Services (WSUS) to enhance operations and provide secure, centralized management. Through practical, step-by-step instructions and PowerShell automation, readers will gain hands-on experience and develop the expertise to effectively manage these essential network services in a modern and hybrid server environment.

Chapter 9: Enhancing Storage with NVMe SSDs and SAN - This chapter's primary objective is to guide readers in enhancing storage performance in Windows Server 2025. It provides step-by-step instructions on deploying and optimizing NVMe SSDs, integrating SAN solutions, and fine-tuning storage performance. The chapter also covers advanced topics like storage virtualization and Software-Defined Storage (SDS), offering practical insights for scalable, high-performance storage. By the end, readers will be equipped to implement modern storage solutions and maximize Windows Server 2025's storage capabilities.

Chapter 10: In-Place Upgrades for Version Updates - This chapter's primary objective is to guide readers in performing robust in-place upgrades for streamlined version updates in Windows Server 2025. It provides step-by-step instructions on understanding the benefits and prerequisites, planning and executing the upgrade, and preparing the environment. The chapter also covers advanced topics like validating compatibility, resolving issues, managing dependencies, mitigating risks, and ensuring data integrity. Additionally, it offers practical insights into fine-tuning and optimizing the upgraded environment. By the end, readers will be equipped to implement successful in-place upgrades and maximize the efficiency and performance of their Windows Server 2025 environments.

Chapter 11: Tuning Windows Server 2025 for Peak Performance - The primary objective of this chapter is to equip system administrators with the knowledge and skills necessary to optimize the performance of Windows Server 2025. It focuses on key areas such as understanding the role of server hardware components and making informed decisions when selecting and configuring hardware for maximum performance. The chapter also delves into using powerful tools like Windows Admin Center and Performance Monitor to efficiently track and assess server performance metrics. Additionally, it highlights the critical role that logs and alerts play in maintaining system health, guiding administrators through configuring them for real-time issue detection and resolution. By adhering to the best practices and techniques outlined, readers can ensure their Windows Server 2025 environments consistently operate at peak efficiency, with robust monitoring and management capabilities in place.

Chapter 12: Maintaining and Troubleshooting Windows Server 2025 - This chapter aims to equip readers with a thorough understanding of key tasks related to troubleshooting, updating, monitoring, and maintaining Windows Server 2025. It introduces practical strategies to make these essential activities more manageable. The chapter explores the server startup process, advanced boot options, and Safe Mode as critical tools for diagnosing issues. Additionally, it covers creating and implementing backup and restoring disaster recovery plans and updating Windows Server 2025 to ensure system security and stability. The Event Viewer is highlighted as an invaluable tool for monitoring system logs and diagnosing errors, helping to reduce server downtime and prevent potential financial impacts. By the end, readers will have a firm grasp of these concepts and the confidence to apply them effectively in real-world server management scenarios.

Appendix A: Navigating Microsoft Certifications - This appendix aims to thoroughly understand Microsoft certifications, specifically in the context of Windows Server 2025. It will cover the fundamentals of certificates and certifications, detail the skills assessed in the certification exams, and offer practical tips for adequate exam preparation. Additionally, the chapter will equip professionals with the necessary resources to succeed in these certification exams and achieve the Microsoft Certified Professional (MCP) status. The ultimate goal is to guide professionals toward a successful career in Microsoft technologies by leveraging the latest advancements in Windows Server 2025.

Appendix B: Review and Solutions - This appendix is dedicated to answering the questions raised throughout the book, which are part of the dedicated Questions section in each chapter. Its purpose is to provide valuable insights and clarity to readers struggling with specific concepts or topics. The answers in this appendix are carefully crafted to help readers deepen their understanding of the material and ensure they have a solid grasp of the main ideas and concepts discussed in the book. By reviewing the answers provided here, readers can resolve any uncertainties they may have encountered and strengthen their comprehension of the subject matter. Whether you want to revisit key points, clarify specific concepts, or reinforce your knowledge, this appendix is an essential resource for enhancing your understanding of the content covered in the book.

Coloured Images

Please follow the link to download the
Coloured Images of the book:

https://rebrand.ly/v1nshne

We have code bundles from our rich catalogue of books and videos available at **https://github.com/bpbpublications**. Check them out!

Errata

We take immense pride in our work at BPB Publications and follow best practices to ensure the accuracy of our content to provide with an indulging reading experience to our subscribers. Our readers are our mirrors, and we use their inputs to reflect and improve upon human errors, if any, that may have occurred during the publishing processes involved. To let us maintain the quality and help us reach out to any readers who might be having difficulties due to any unforeseen errors, please write to us at :

errata@bpbonline.com

Your support, suggestions and feedbacks are highly appreciated by the BPB Publications' Family.

Piracy

If you come across any illegal copies of our works in any form on the internet, we would be grateful if you would provide us with the location address or website name. Please contact us at **business@bpbonline.com** with a link to the material.

If you are interested in becoming an author

If there is a topic that you have expertise in, and you are interested in either writing or contributing to a book, please visit **www.bpbonline.com**. We have worked with thousands of developers and tech professionals, just like you, to help them share their insights with the global tech community. You can make a general application, apply for a specific hot topic that we are recruiting an author for, or submit your own idea.

Reviews

Please leave a review. Once you have read and used this book, why not leave a review on the site that you purchased it from? Potential readers can then see and use your unbiased opinion to make purchase decisions. We at BPB can understand what you think about our products, and our authors can see your feedback on their book. Thank you!

For more information about BPB, please visit **www.bpbonline.com**.

Join our book's Discord space

Join the book's Discord Workspace for Latest updates, Offers, Tech happenings around the world, New Release and Sessions with the Authors:

https://discord.bpbonline.com

Table of Contents

How can we hope to make the world a better place when, on New Year's Eve alone, cities worldwide spend millions on fireworks displays that cause significant air pollution?
Isn't it time we reflect and take steps to protect our planet?

- Bekim Dauti

Chapter 1

Understanding Network Components

Introduction

This chapter is a foundational introduction to the core elements of network infrastructure, tailored explicitly for IT professionals working with Windows Server environments. As part of the esteemed Windows NT series, Windows Server 2025 continues the legacy of its predecessors by delivering enhanced security, versatility, and stability. Noteworthy advancements include seamless integration with hybrid deployments through Windows Server 2025 Datacenter Azure, reflecting Microsoft's commitment to meeting the evolving demands of modern network environments. Understanding the role of Windows Server within network architecture is paramount, and this chapter begins by providing a detailed overview of essential network concepts. The *Computer Network Overview* section delves into critical terms such as hosts, nodes, peer-to-peer, and clients/servers, ensuring a solid grounding in network fundamentals.

Additionally, you will gain insights into general concepts, including clients, servers, **Network Operating Systems (NOSs)**, hardware, software, and networking architectures. By explaining these fundamental concepts in accessible language, we aim to equip IT professionals with the knowledge to navigate and understand network components in Windows Server environments. This comprehensive exploration lays the groundwork for effective network management and optimization in Windows Server 2025 environments.

Structure

In this chapter, we will cover the following topics:

- Birth of the Internet
- Computer networks
- Network components
- Network architectures
- Network topologies
- IP address and subnets
- Network Operating System
- Technology trends

Objectives

This chapter aims to provide a comprehensive introduction to networking within Windows Server 2025 environments. It begins with the historical context of the birth of the Internet. It progresses to modern computer networks, covering essential topics such as network components, architecture, topologies, IP addressing, and subnets. The goal is to equip IT professionals with a solid understanding of network fundamentals crucial for effective management and optimization. Additionally, the chapter discusses the role of NOS and emerging technology trends. To illustrate practical implementation, it concludes with a hands-on example demonstrating Hyper-V configuration in Windows 11 Pro using Settings and Windows PowerShell, offering actionable insights for real-world scenarios.

Birth of the Internet

The Internet, a cornerstone of modern communication, began with the US government's initiative to create a reliable and resilient communication network through the **Defense Advanced Research Projects Agency** (**DARPA**). This initiative led to developing two distinct projects: ARPANET, designed for research needs, and MILNET, focused on military operations. By 1985, the Internet had emerged as a different entity, marking the end of ARPANET's era with the adage, *Every new beginning is some beginning's end.*

On October 24, 1995, the **Federal Networking Council** (**FNC**) adopted a resolution defining the **Internet** as a global information system with three key characteristics:

- It is logically connected by a globally unique address space based on the **Internet Protocol** (**IP**).
- It supports communication through the TCP/IP protocol suite and compatible protocols.

- It provides accessible high-level services in communications and related Infrastructure.

As network technologies evolved, the need to connect an increasing number of computers across various locations became paramount. This necessity drove the development of precise terminologies and concepts in computer networking, resulting in diverse network topologies, architectures, and components.

Technological advancements have continued to shape the Internet's landscape in recent years, significantly impacting various sectors. Windows Server 2025 exemplifies these advancements, offering enhanced security, versatility, and seamless hybrid deployment capabilities through Windows Server 2025 Datacenter: Azure Edition. These features are essential for modern network environments, enabling efficient management and network infrastructure optimization.

Windows Server 2025 supports the latest internet applications and services, integrating advanced technologies such as AI and machine learning to enhance performance and security. Understanding the evolution of the Internet and its current capabilities is crucial for IT professionals, as it underscores the importance of mastering network fundamentals, topologies, architectures, and components. This knowledge is vital for leveraging the full potential of modern NOS like Windows Server 2025.

Note: For a comprehensive overview of the Internet's history, visit the Internet Society's webpage at https://www.internetsociety.org/internet/history-internet/. This resource covers significant milestones, developments, and contributions of various individuals and organizations, offering valuable insights into the Internet's evolution and global impact.

Computer networks

The intention of this section is not to compare computer networks and network components but rather to define a computer network and expound upon its components. Without delving into intricate academic or professional explanations, a **computer network** can be defined as a system that connects two or more computers to share resources. This fundamental definition shows that a pair of computers is the minimum requirement for constructing a network. Factors such as network coverage, accessibility of services, and the purpose of network servers contribute to determining the different types of computer networks. Various networks can be classified as follows:

- **Personal area network (PAN):** A PAN connects devices within an individual's workspace, enabling data transmission and reception. A notable example is the **wireless personal area network (WPAN)**, which employs Bluetooth technology to interconnect devices. Recent advancements include Bluetooth 5.0, which offers improved range, speed, and data capacity, enhancing device interoperability and efficiency.

- **Local area network (LAN):** A LAN connects devices within a specific area, such as a floor or a building, facilitating data exchange. A **wireless local area network (WLAN)** exemplifies a LAN, utilizing radio waves for interconnection. The most prevalent technology in WLANs is Wi-Fi, which now includes Wi-Fi 6 (802.11ax) and the emerging Wi-Fi 6E, operating on the 6 GHz band. These advancements provide higher speeds, lower latency, and increased capacity, essential for modern high-density environments.
- **Campus area network (CAN):** A CAN interconnects multiple LANs within a limited geographical area, such as a university campus or corporate premises. This extended LAN supports connectivity across various buildings. Modern CANs leverage **fiber-optic backbones and high-speed Ethernet** to ensure robust, scalable, high-performance networks supporting advanced applications and services.
- **Metropolitan area network (MAN):** A MAN connects LANs within a town, city, or metropolitan area, encompassing a more extensive geographical scope than a CAN. MANs often use technologies like **Metro Ethernet and 5G networks** to deliver high-speed data exchange and connectivity. These technologies enable efficient urban network infrastructures, supporting innovative city initiatives and widespread IoT deployments.
- **Wide area network (WAN):** A WAN extends across vast geographical areas, facilitating data transfer between MANs. The Internet is the quintessential example of a WAN, connecting networks globally and enabling worldwide communication and information exchange. Modern WANs increasingly utilize technologies like **Software-Defined Wide Area Networking (SD-WAN)** to optimize traffic management, enhance security, and improve performance over large distances.

Recent technological advancements in computer networking have significantly enhanced the capabilities and efficiency of these network types. For instance, integrating AI and machine learning in network management systems allows for predictive analytics and automated optimizations, ensuring higher reliability and performance. Additionally, the adoption of edge computing enables data processing closer to the source, reducing latency and improving real-time data handling.

Understanding these various network types and their **components** is crucial for IT professionals, as it enables the design and management of efficient, scalable, and secure network infrastructures. This knowledge is particularly relevant in modern **operating systems (OSs)** like Windows Server 2025, which support these advanced networking technologies and applications.

Network components

Once the fundamental concepts of a computer network are understood, identifying its various elements becomes more straightforward. These elements include computers, the networking medium, networking devices, and the resources utilized within the network, as depicted in *Figure 1.1*.

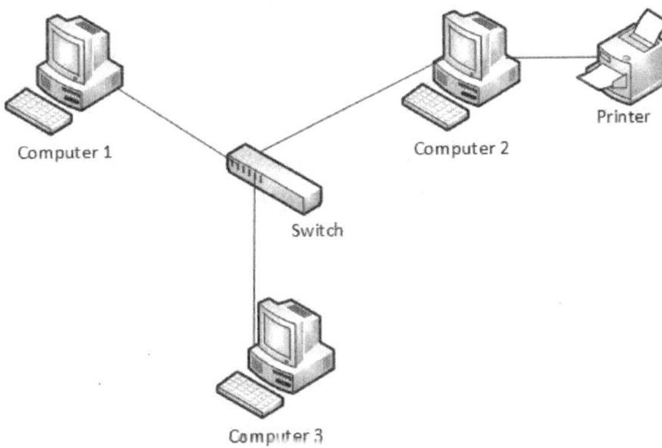

***Figure 1.1:** The computer network and network components*

In modern network environments, computers are typically interconnected through network devices, such as switches, using advanced networking media. While traditional twisted pair cables (Ethernet) are still common, there has been a significant shift towards fiber-optic cables for higher bandwidth and more extended-distance communication. Wireless technologies like Wi-Fi 6 and the upcoming Wi-Fi 6E are becoming prevalent, offering enhanced speed, capacity, and reliability.

Substantial advancements have also been made in networking devices. Modern switches, often called smart or managed switches, now include **quality of service** (**QoS**), advanced security measures, and integration with network management software. These features are crucial for maintaining optimal network performance and security in increasingly complex environments.

OSs that facilitate resource sharing have also evolved. With Windows Server 2025 and Windows 11, IT professionals can leverage advanced features for resource management, such as enhanced virtualization through Hyper-V, improved file-sharing capabilities with the latest SMB protocol versions, and integrated cloud services for hybrid deployments.

For instance, within a Windows Server 2025 network, resources such as files, printers, and applications can be shared efficiently across connected devices. The integration with Azure services allows for seamless cloud backup and disaster recovery solutions, ensuring data integrity and availability. Additionally, AI and machine learning advancements integrated into these OSs facilitate predictive maintenance and automated optimizations, further enhancing network performance and reliability.

Hosts and nodes

By examining the computer network shown in *Figure 1.1*, we can identify computers 1 to 3 as hosts, the switch as a node, and the printer as a peripheral device. While this description might seem straightforward, it's essential to distinguish between **hosts and nodes** to understand their specific roles within a network.

At first glance, hosts and nodes might appear interchangeable but have distinct meanings. In computer networks, a node is a broad term for any device connected to the network. However, not all nodes have network interfaces with assigned IP addresses. The IP address is crucial for locating a node within the network, enabling data transmission, and accessing network services. This specific attribute is what distinguishes a host from a node.

A host is any device with a network interface and an assigned IP address. It uses this address to communicate with other devices and utilize network services. Hence, while all hosts are nodes, not all nodes qualify as hosts.

To further illustrate this distinction, consider *Figure 1.2*, which depicts a network with clients, servers, and a router identified as hosts. In contrast, the switch is classified as a node within the same network.

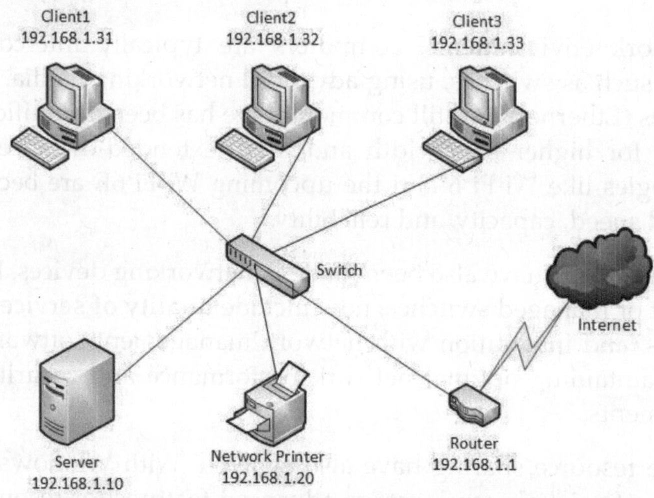

Figure 1.2: *The hosts and nodes in a computer network*

Recent advancements in network technology have further refined these distinctions. Modern hosts, such as computers running Windows Server 2025, leverage advanced IP addressing schemes, including IPv6, to accommodate the growing number of connected devices. These hosts can also utilize **network interface cards (NICs)** with advanced features such as offloading, which improves network performance by reducing the processing load on the host's CPU.

Network switches, while traditionally considered nodes, have also evolved. Contemporary switches are often equipped with Layer 3 capabilities, enabling them to perform routing functions and support more advanced network management tasks. These switches can also integrate with **software-defined networking (SDN)** solutions, providing greater flexibility and control over network traffic.

Note: In computer networking, hosts and nodes are distinct terms. All hosts are nodes, but not all nodes are hosts. Hosts have network interfaces with assigned IP addresses for communication and service access. In contrast, network nodes may have IP addresses used primarily for management purposes.

Clients and servers

Within the computer network illustrated in *Figure 1.2*, computers labeled 1 to 3 functions as clients, while the central server is identified as the server entity. The switch and router operate as nodes, and the network printer is a peripheral device. In this context, **clients** are responsible for initiating requests to access resources within the network, whereas **servers** are designed to provide these services. Specifically, servers respond to access requests by delivering the requested services. Hence, the term **server** originates from its role in serving the needs of its clients.

This distinction between clients and servers is fundamental to understanding their roles and responsibilities within a computer network. Clients actively seek resources or services, while servers fulfill those requests, ensuring efficient service delivery.

Recent advancements in computer networking have refined and revolutionized these roles. Modern servers, especially those running Windows Server 2025, are equipped with advanced virtualization technologies like Hyper-V. These technologies efficiently allocate resources and provide scalable services, instilling trust in their reliability. Moreover, these servers are seamlessly integrated with cloud platforms, creating hybrid environments that enhance flexibility and resource management.

On the other hand, clients have evolved to support a wide range of devices, including desktop computers, laptops, tablets, and smartphones, all of which access network resources. With advancements in networking technology, clients now benefit from higher-speed connections through Wi-Fi 6 and Ethernet over fiber-optic cabling, providing faster and more reliable access to network services.

Grasping the differentiation between clients and servers is fundamental and empowering for IT professionals. It forms the bedrock of modern computer networks, enabling them to effectively design, implement, and manage network infrastructures. This understanding allows them to leverage the latest technological enhancements, ensuring their organization's needs are met with precision and control.

Network interface

As shown in *Figure 1.3*, a **network interface** refers to hardware components such as a network card or LAN port on various network devices. Its primary function is facilitating connection and communication between clients, servers, peripheral devices, and other network equipment. The network interface plays a dual role in the computer network, acting as both a passive and active component.

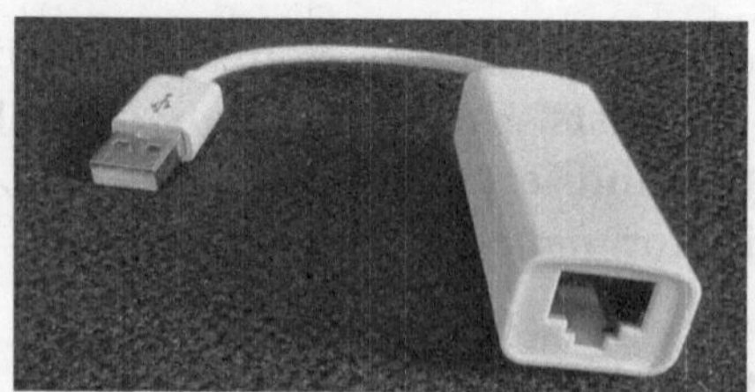

Figure 1.3: USB network interface

In its passive role, the network interface serves as a connector, allowing devices to connect to the network physically. It provides the necessary ports and connectors to establish a link between the device and the network infrastructure. This passive function enables the transmission of data packets to and from the connected device.

The network interface actively handles the translation and management of data packets. Modern network interfaces, especially those integrated into advanced network devices, support high-speed data transfer rates and protocols, including Ethernet, Wi-Fi, and advanced wireless standards like Wi-Fi 6E.

Recent technological advancements have significantly enhanced the capabilities of network interfaces. For instance, NICs now support features like hardware-based encryption, improving network security without compromising performance. Additionally, integrating SDN capabilities allows for more flexible and dynamic network management, enabling automated real-time adjustments to network configurations.

Understanding the dual role of network interfaces is crucial for IT professionals. By leveraging these components' passive and active functions, they can design and manage robust network infrastructures that meet the demands of modern organizational environments. The continuous evolution of network interface technology ensures that networks can support the increasing data transfer needs and advanced applications of today's digital landscape.

Peripheral devices

Peripheral devices encompass a variety of hardware components, including printers, scanners, and storage devices, that offer client resources via LAN or as shared devices on a network. These devices play both passive and active roles within the computer network.

In their passive role, peripheral devices provide resources or services to clients without actively participating in network management or control. For example, a printer may accept print jobs from client devices and produce physical copies without actively managing network traffic. Similarly, scanners allow clients to scan documents without actively controlling network operations.

However, specific peripheral devices, such as **storage area networks (SANs)** and **network-attached storage (NAS)** systems, take on active roles in the network. These devices actively manage and control network data storage and retrieval operations, offering centralized and efficient storage solutions.

Recent advancements in peripheral devices have further enhanced their capabilities and integration within computer networks. Modern printers, for instance, support wireless connectivity options such as **Wi-Fi Direct** and **cloud printing** services, enabling seamless printing from various devices across the network. Advanced scanners now feature automatic document feeders, high-speed scanning capabilities, and integration with document management systems, streamlining document processing workflows in networked environments.

Similarly, SANs and NAS systems have evolved to offer higher storage capacities, faster data transfer speeds, and enhanced data protection features such as **Redundant Array of Independent Disks (RAID)** configurations and encryption. Integration with cloud storage platforms allows for hybrid storage solutions, providing flexibility and scalability to meet the growing demands of modern organizations.

Understanding the roles and capabilities of peripheral devices is essential for IT professionals tasked with designing and managing network infrastructures. By leveraging these devices' passive and active functionalities, they can optimize resource utilization, enhance productivity, and ensure seamless operation of networked environments.

Shared apps and data

Shared applications and data are essential components of modern computer networks. They represent the presence of applications and shared files accessible to network users. Typically hosted by servers, these components facilitate user collaboration, productivity, and resource sharing.

While applications and shared data primarily serve as passive resources within the network, the server responsible for hosting these services is active in network management and control. In their passive role, applications and shared data are available for users to access and utilize without direct involvement in network administration.

On the other hand, the server hosting these services plays a crucial active role in the network ecosystem. It actively manages and controls the availability, delivery, and security of applications and shared data, ensuring optimal performance and reliability. The server handles client requests efficiently, processes data, and implements security measures to safeguard sensitive information.

Recent advancements in server technology have enhanced the capabilities and efficiency of hosting shared applications and data. Modern servers, powered by advanced processors and optimized storage solutions, offer improved performance, scalability, and reliability. Virtualization technologies, such as containerization and server virtualization, enable flexible deployment and management of applications across the network infrastructure.

Furthermore, cloud computing services have revolutionized shared applications and data hosting, providing on-demand access to scalable resources and eliminating the need for extensive on-premises infrastructure. Cloud-based solutions offer enhanced flexibility, agility, and cost-effectiveness, enabling organizations to adapt quickly to changing business requirements.

Understanding the roles of shared applications, data, and the servers hosting them is crucial for IT professionals designing, implementing, and managing network infrastructures. By effectively leveraging these components, IT professionals can optimize resource utilization, enhance collaboration, and ensure the seamless operation of networked environments in today's dynamic business landscape.

Hubs and switches

Hubs and **switches** play crucial roles in Ethernet communication technology. They serve as central points in computer networks and facilitate efficient communication between devices. While both are essential components, they differ significantly in functionality and efficiency.

Hubs, often considered essential connectivity devices, are passive components in the network infrastructure. They allow multiple devices to connect and share the same network segment. However, hubs lack intelligence and do not actively manage or control network traffic. Instead, they indiscriminately replicate incoming data packets and broadcast them to all connected devices, leading to network congestion and inefficient data transmission.

On the other hand, switches (as depicted in *Figure 1.4*) are active devices that play a proactive role in network management. Unlike hubs, switches make intelligent forwarding decisions based on the data packets' destination **Media Access Control** (**MAC**) addresses. By maintaining a table of MAC addresses and associated port connections, switches can selectively forward packets to the appropriate devices, effectively reducing network congestion and optimizing data transmission efficiency.

***Figure 1.4:** Cisco switch*

Recent advancements in switch technology have further enhanced their capabilities and efficiency. Modern switches feature advanced algorithms and hardware acceleration, enabling high-speed packet forwarding and low-latency operation. Additionally, integrating SDN principles allows for dynamic network provisioning and management, optimizing network performance and adaptability to changing traffic patterns.

Moreover, emerging technologies such as **network programmability** and **intent-based networking (IBN)** are revolutionizing switch management and configuration. These advancements enable IT professionals to automate network operations, streamline troubleshooting, and ensure consistent policy enforcement across the network infrastructure.

Understanding the differences between hubs and switches and their respective roles in network communication is essential for IT professionals designing, implementing, and managing modern network infrastructures. By leveraging switches' capabilities and adopting best practices in network design and management, IT professionals can optimize network performance, enhance security, and meet the evolving demands of today's digital landscape.

Routers

Figure 1.5 depicts **routers**, which are integral components of computer networks. They facilitate the efficient bidirectional transfer of data packets between LANs and the Internet. As active participants in network operations, routers play a pivotal role in ensuring seamless communication across diverse network environments.

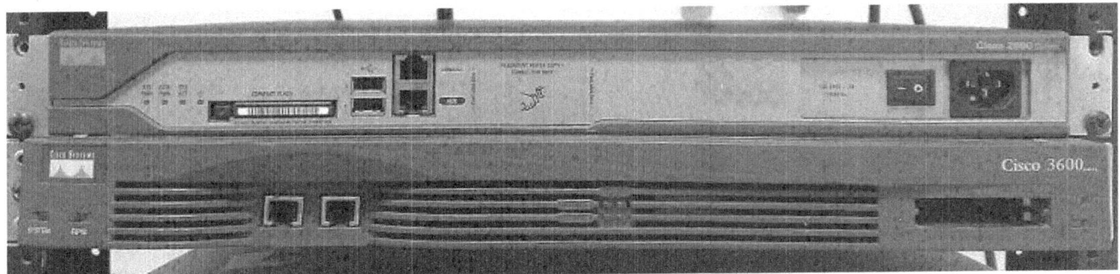

***Figure 1.5:** Cisco routers*

Responsible for directing data packets from their source to their destination, routers employ sophisticated routing algorithms to analyze network addresses and determine the most optimal path for data transmission. This process, known as routing, involves making intelligent decisions based on network topology and routing protocols, ensuring timely and accurate data delivery.

Recent advancements in router technology have led to significant improvements in routing efficiency and network performance. Modern routers feature advanced packet processing capabilities, hardware acceleration, and support for emerging routing protocols, enabling faster data forwarding and reduced latency.

Moreover, integrating SDN principles has revolutionized router management and configuration. SDN allows for centralized network control, dynamic traffic engineering, and programmable routing policies, enhancing agility and adaptability in network operations.

In addition to facilitating Internet connectivity, routers provide network segmentation by dividing LANs into smaller subnets. This segmentation enhances security, performance, and network management by controlling data flow and isolating network segments for specific purposes or user groups.

Furthermore, routers are crucial in enforcing QoS policies, prioritizing critical network traffic, and ensuring consistent performance for essential applications and services. With the growing complexity of modern network environments, routers continue to evolve to meet the demands of emerging technologies and dynamic business requirements.

Understanding router capabilities and functionalities is essential for IT professionals who design, implement, and manage network infrastructures. By leveraging modern routers' advanced features and capabilities, IT professionals can optimize network performance, enhance security, and ensure seamless connectivity for users and applications in today's digital landscape.

Firewall

A **firewall**, as depicted in *Figure 1.6*, is a pivotal network component essential for fortifying the security of modern network infrastructures. Acting as a **digital sentinel**, the firewall monitors and regulates incoming and outgoing network traffic based on predefined security policies.

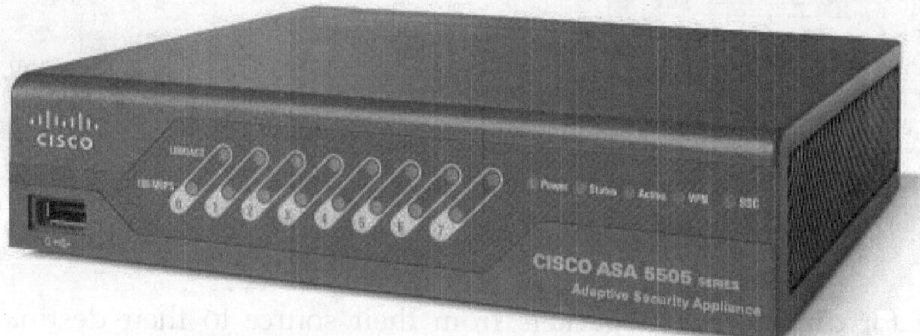

Figure 1.6: Cisco firewall

A firewall functions as the digital equivalent of a vigilant security officer stationed at an organization's main gate. Just as a security officer scrutinizes individuals entering or leaving premises, the firewall meticulously inspects and controls network traffic flow as a barrier against unauthorized access and potential threats.

Recent advancements in firewall technology have introduced innovative features and capabilities to enhance network security. Modern firewalls incorporate state-of-the-art **intrusion detection and prevention systems (IDPS)**, threat intelligence feeds, and advanced machine learning algorithms to identify and thwart sophisticated cyber threats in real-time.

Moreover, **next-generation firewalls (NGFWs)** leverage **deep packet inspection (DPI)** and application-aware filtering to analyze network traffic at a granular level, enabling precise identification and mitigation of emerging threats and malicious activities.

By enforcing stringent security rules and policies, firewalls play a crucial role in safeguarding networks from unauthorized access attempts, data breaches, and cyber-attacks. They serve as the first line of defense, preventing unauthorized or potentially harmful traffic from infiltrating the network perimeter while facilitating seamless and secure communication for legitimate users and applications.

Understanding the details of firewall technology and deployment strategies is paramount for IT professionals designing, implementing, and managing network security architectures. By leveraging the advanced capabilities of modern firewalls and adopting best practices in cybersecurity, IT professionals can fortify network defenses, mitigate risks, and ensure the integrity and confidentiality of sensitive information in today's dynamic threat landscape.

Networking mediums

Various networking mediums play essential roles in facilitating data transfer and communication, catering to diverse requirements and scenarios within modern network environments. These mediums encompass physical (cable-based) and wave-based (wireless) communications, each offering distinct advantages and characteristics.

- **Metallic mediums:** Copper wires in twisted pairs and coaxial cables serve as foundational metallic mediums for transmitting electrical impulses. These mediums leverage metal's conductive properties and facilitate reliable and cost-effective wired connections suitable for various network applications.
- **Glass mediums:** Fiber optic cables represent cutting-edge glass mediums for transmitting light pulses. Comprising glass fibers that transmit data through the reflection and refraction of light signals, fiber optics offer high-speed and long-distance transmission capabilities. This technology has revolutionized data transmission, enabling the rapid exchange of large volumes of data over vast distances with minimal signal degradation.
- **Air mediums:** Wave-based communication utilizes air mediums to transmit signals wirelessly across different frequencies within the electromagnetic spectrum. Wireless communication technologies, such as radio waves, microwaves, or other frequencies, enable data transfer without needing physical cables. These air mediums provide flexibility and mobility in data transfer, empowering users to access network resources and communicate seamlessly from various locations.

Recent advancements in networking mediums have led to significant improvements in data transfer speeds, reliability, and scalability. Emerging technologies, such as 5G wireless networks and advanced fiber optic infrastructure, promise even greater bandwidth capacities and lower latency, supporting the growing demands of modern applications and services.

Understanding the characteristics and advantages of different networking mediums is crucial for IT professionals designing, implementing, and managing network infrastructures. By effectively leveraging these mediums' capabilities, IT professionals can optimize network performance, enhance scalability, and ensure seamless connectivity for users and devices in today's dynamic digital landscape.

Network architectures

Computer network architectures are pivotal in enabling seamless communication and collaboration among networked devices, shaping the foundation of modern network infrastructures. While different types of computer networks classify networks based on geographical coverage, network architectures focus on the design principles and frameworks that govern communication within a network ecosystem. Let us take a look at them:

- **Peer-to-peer (P2P) architecture:** In a P2P architecture, network communication operates on a distributed framework, eliminating the need for dedicated servers. Instead, communication occurs directly between peer computers, which function as clients and servers. This decentralized approach fosters equality among peer computers, each with equal permissions and responsibilities. Recent advancements in P2P technology have introduced enhanced peer discovery mechanisms and decentralized protocols, enabling efficient resource sharing and collaboration across distributed networks.

- **Client/server architecture:** Client / server architecture revolves around the client-server relationship, where clients request services from centralized servers. This architecture facilitates the sharing of network services, with clients sending requests to servers using predefined protocols. Modern client / server architectures leverage scalable server infrastructures, load-balancing mechanisms, and distributed computing technologies to ensure high availability, fault tolerance, and optimal performance. Additionally, server virtualization and cloud computing advancements have revolutionized client / server architectures, enabling dynamic resource allocation and on-demand scalability to meet evolving business needs.

Understanding network architectures is essential for IT professionals who design, implement, and manage network infrastructures. While P2P and client / server architectures represent fundamental computer networking models, hybrid approaches combining elements from both paradigms are increasingly prevalent in modern network designs. These hybrid architectures offer the flexibility to address specific requirements and optimize performance across diverse network environments.

Key considerations, such as scalability, security, and service requirements, influence the choice of architecture. Scalability assessments ensure the network can accommodate increased demands and adapt to evolving user needs. Security considerations encompass robust authentication mechanisms, data encryption, and intrusion detection systems to safeguard against cyber threats. Furthermore, aligning the architecture with the nature of services and resources within the network ensures optimal performance and resource utilization.

By carefully evaluating these factors and leveraging advancements in networking technology, IT professionals can design resilient, efficient, and secure network architectures that support the evolving needs of modern businesses and ensure seamless connectivity for users and applications.

Peer-to-peer applications

P2P networking facilitates efficient and decentralized file sharing, empowering users to exchange digital content seamlessly across distributed networks. At the heart of P2P networking are peer applications, commonly called **P2P Applications (P2P apps)**, designed to facilitate collaborative file sharing among connected peers.

- **Consider the following scenario:** When utilizing a P2P app to download a file from the Internet, the file is acquired in fragments or chunks from multiple peer computers connected to the same P2P network through the application. Simultaneously, the file stored on your computer is uploaded to peers who are currently downloading the same file. This P2P exchange fosters a dynamic network environment, enabling bidirectional communication and promoting the exchange and sharing of files among peers in a decentralized manner.

P2P networking represents a paradigm shift in file sharing, harnessing participating peers' collective resources and bandwidth to optimize data transfer efficiency. Unlike traditional client/server architectures, where file distribution relies on centralized servers, P2P networks distribute the workload across interconnected peers, enhancing scalability and resilience. Recent advancements in P2P technology have introduced sophisticated algorithms for peer discovery, content indexing, and data replication, further improving network performance and reliability.

However, it is essential to acknowledge that P2P networks also present challenges and considerations, particularly regarding copyright infringement and the unauthorized sharing of copyrighted materials. Addressing these concerns requires robust regulatory frameworks, digital rights management mechanisms, and proactive enforcement measures to promote responsible and lawful usage of P2P networks.

By understanding the principles and functionalities of P2P networking, IT professionals can leverage this innovative technology to facilitate secure and efficient file sharing within organizational networks while mitigating potential risks and ensuring compliance with legal and regulatory requirements.

Network topologies

In addition to classifying computer networks based on their types, another crucial aspect is their **topology**, which defines network components' structural layout and interconnections. Topology is pivotal in shaping network architecture and functionality, offering insights into how data flows and communicates within the network ecosystem. There are two primary types of network topologies: physical topology and logical topology, each serving distinct purposes:

- **Physical topology**: Physical topology refers to network components' tangible arrangement and placement within a computer network. That encompasses the physical layout of computers, peripheral devices, data transmission cables, and network devices such as switches and routers. Common physical topologies include bus, ring, star, extended star, hierarchical, and mesh configurations, each tailored to specific requirements and environments. Recent advancements in physical topology design have introduced innovations such as modular cabling systems, high-speed fiber optics, and compact network devices, enhancing scalability, flexibility, and performance in modern network infrastructures.
- **Logical topology:** Conversely, logical topology focuses on the communication pathways and protocols governing data transmission between network components. It describes how data accesses the transmission medium, routing paths, and communication protocols for efficient data exchange. Vital elements of logical topology include hostnames, IP addresses, and communication protocols such as TCP/IP and Ethernet. Recent developments in logical topology design have emphasized protocols for virtual networking, SDN, and **network function virtualization (NFV)**, enabling dynamic and programmable network architectures that adapt to changing demands and workloads.

Understanding physical and logical topologies is essential for IT professionals designing, implementing, and managing network infrastructures. Physical topology insights aid in optimizing the physical layout of devices, identifying potential points of failure, and ensuring robustness and reliability in network infrastructure. Meanwhile, understanding logical topology facilitates efficient data flow, troubleshooting network issues, and implementing security measures to safeguard data integrity and confidentiality.

By leveraging advancements in physical and logical topology design, IT professionals can create resilient, scalable, and agile network architectures that meet the evolving needs of modern businesses and ensure seamless connectivity for users and applications.

Note: Integrating physical and logical topologies provides a comprehensive grasp of a computer network's structure and functionality. Network administrators can adeptly design and manage networks by considering both aspects, resulting in seamless operation and optimal performance. This holistic approach ensures that networks are structured and configured to align with the organization's requirements, facilitating efficient device communication and maximizing resource utilization.

Types of physical topologies

Understanding the physical topology of computer networks is essential for grasping their structural layout and communication pathways. Physical topologies visualize how network components are physically interconnected, shaping data transmission and network performance. Let us delve into the critical physical topologies:

- **Bus topology:** In a bus topology, devices connect to a shared communication channel, resembling a linear structure. Data transmitted by one device is broadcast to all others on the bus, with each device determining if it's the intended recipient. While simple to set up, bus topologies can encounter issues with signal reflection and network disruption if the cable fails.
- **Ring topology:** In a ring topology, devices form a closed loop, with data circulating unidirectionally from one device to the next until it reaches its destination. Dual-ring networks utilizing optical fiber enhance reliability by establishing redundant paths to reroute data in case of cable breaks or failures.
- **Star topology:** Star topologies feature devices independently linked to a central hub or switch, streamlining communication through centralized routing. This configuration offers simplified management and fault isolation, with twisted pair cables commonly used for cost-effective connectivity.
- **Extended star topology:** Combining elements of star and bus topologies, extended star configurations interconnect multiple star networks via a shared bus. This design facilitates scalability and fault tolerance, allowing network expansion while mitigating disruptions.
- **Hierarchical topology:** Hierarchical topologies organize networks into multiple levels, each featuring interconnected star topologies. Centralized control points facilitate efficient resource management and data distribution, ensuring scalability and fault tolerance.
- **Mesh topology:** Mesh topologies establish direct point-to-point connections between every device, offering robustness and reliability. Common in WANs, mesh topologies enable seamless communication across geographically dispersed LANs, though their implementation can be resource-intensive.

Understanding these physical topologies equips network professionals with the knowledge to design resilient and efficient networks tailored to organizational needs.

IP addresses and subnets

In computer networking, effective communication hinges on assigning IP addresses to individual devices. These addresses serve as unique identifiers, allowing seamless interaction within the network. Typically, IP addresses are allocated to a device's NIC, enabling it to participate in network activities.

Two prominent IP addressing technologies, IPv4 and IPv6, shape the landscape of modern networking. While IPv4 has long been the backbone of internet communication, the emergence of IPv6 heralds significant advancements in addressing capabilities.

Internet Protocol version 4

In computer networking **Internet Protocol version 4** (**IPv4**) remains a cornerstone of Internet communication, defining the structure of IP addressing. Recognized by the **Internet Engineering Task Force** (**IETF**) in RFC 791, IPv4 addresses serve as fundamental components within network architectures.

An IPv4 address, encapsulating a 32-bit logical entity, is a core element of computer networks, facilitating the identification and communication of devices. With approximately 4.3 billion unique addresses available, IPv4 addresses are structured into four segments, or octets, each comprising 8 bits. This segmentation, delineated by decimal points, enables clear interpretation and configuration of addresses (for example, 192.168.1.1).

Despite its foundational role, IPv4 faces challenges stemming from its finite address space, intensifying as the demand for IP addresses surges in the digital age. To address this constraint, the transition to IPv6, the next iteration of IP addressing, assumes paramount importance.

IPv4 remains a cornerstone of contemporary networking, facilitating seamless data exchange across the digital landscape. However, the imperative transition to IPv6 looms significantly, promising enhanced scalability and resilience in the face of escalating connectivity demands. By embracing IPv6 alongside IPv4, network professionals can chart a course toward a robust and future-ready networking paradigm.

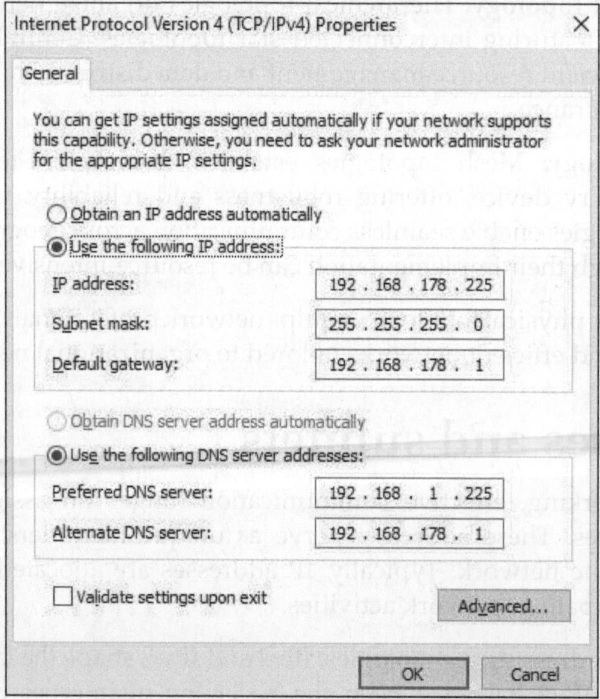

Figure 1.7: The manually assigned IPv4 address in Windows Server 2025

Internet Protocol version 6

In contemporary computer networking **Internet Protocol version 6 (IPv6)** represents a significant advancement in IP addressing technology, providing a robust framework for Internet communication. Established in the IETF publication RFC 2460, IPv6 introduces transformative enhancements over its predecessor, IPv4.

IPv6 features a 128-bit address structure, divided into eight hextets, each comprising 16 bits. This expanded address format, discernible by colons separating hextets, facilitates allocating a staggering number of unique addresses. For instance, an IPv6 address may appear as follows: **`2001:0DB8:85A3:0000:0000:8A2E:0370:7334`**.

With its expansive address space, IPv6 can accommodate approximately 340 undecillion addresses, offering an abundance of available IPv6 addresses. This vast pool of addresses ensures scalability and alleviates concerns regarding address exhaustion, a prominent challenge in IPv4 networks.

While IPv6 presents compelling advantages in addressing the limitations of IPv4, widespread adoption encounters obstacles, including legacy system compatibility and infrastructure readiness. However, as organizations transition to IPv6-compatible networks, the benefits of enhanced scalability, improved security features, and streamlined network management become increasingly apparent.

IPv6 embodies technological innovation, empowering network administrators to embrace a future-proof addressing protocol capable of meeting the evolving demands of modern networking landscapes. Its advanced features, such as hierarchical addressing and enhanced support for mobile devices and **Internet of Things (IoT)** ecosystems, position IPv6 as a cornerstone of next-generation network architectures.

IPv6 represents a pivotal evolution in IP addressing technology, heralding a new era of connectivity and innovation in computer networking. By embracing IPv6 alongside IPv4 and leveraging its expansive address space and advanced capabilities, organizations can forge resilient, future-ready network infrastructures capable of supporting the burgeoning array of digital services and devices. Refer to the following figure:

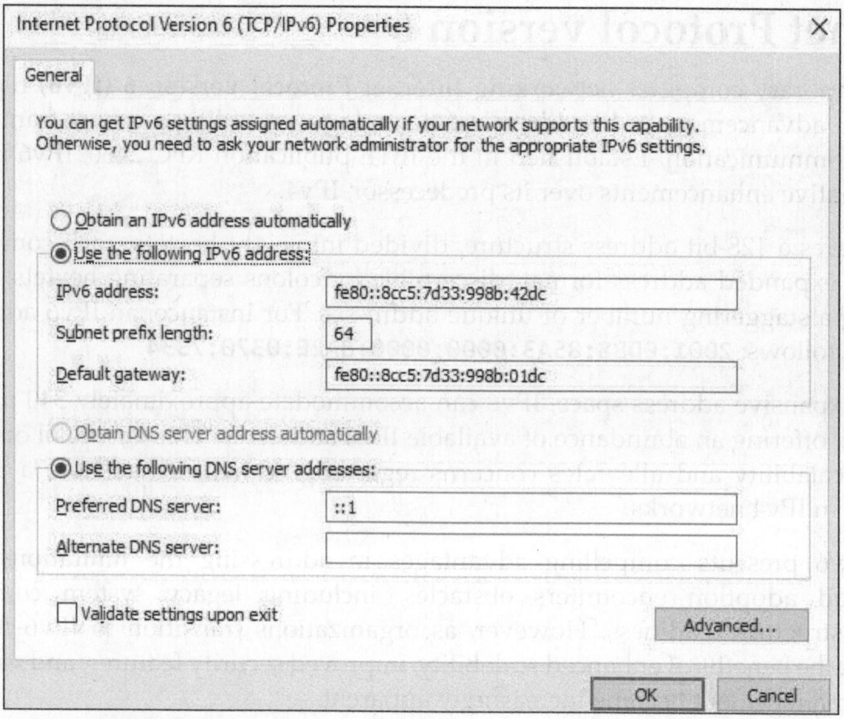

***Figure 1.8:** The manually assigned IPv6 address in Windows Server 2025*

Subnets

In contemporary computer networking, **subnets** remain indispensable tools for optimizing network management and enhancing efficiency. Subnetting, a foundational concept, involves partitioning a more extensive network into smaller, logically segregated segments, known as subnetworks or subnets. Organizations can achieve granular control over network resources and streamline data traffic management by implementing subnetting alongside IP addressing.

The subnet mask is at the core of subnetting, a critical component that facilitates network segmentation and delineates the boundaries of individual subnets. By combining the subnet mask with the IPv4 address, network administrators can ascertain each subnet's network address, host address, and broadcast address, enabling precise communication and resource allocation within the network.

While historically rooted in the classful addressing system delineated in the Internet Engineering Task Force's RFC 791, modern networking practices have evolved to embrace more flexible and scalable addressing schemes. While the classful system categorized IP addresses into predefined classes—A, B, C, D, and E—modern networks often eschew rigid class boundaries in favor of **Classless Inter-Domain Routing (CIDR)** and **Variable Length Subnet Masking (VLSM)** methodologies. These advancements afford more excellent subnet design and allocation flexibility, empowering network architects to tailor subnet sizes to specific organizational requirements.

Despite the prominence of CIDR and VLSM, understanding the foundational principles of the classful addressing system remains pertinent in networking education. Classes A, B, and C, characterized by their distinct bit-length prefixes, continue to inform network architecture design and subnet allocation strategies. Moreover, classes D and E, reserved for specialized applications such as multicasting and research, underscore the versatility of the IP addressing framework in accommodating diverse networking paradigms.

In today's dynamic networking landscape, subnetting remains a cornerstone of network design and optimization. By embracing contemporary subnetting methodologies and adapting to evolving standards, organizations can fortify their networks against scalability challenges and ensure seamless communication across diverse network environments.

Subnetting remains a fundamental technique in modern networking, empowering organizations to achieve optimal resource utilization and robust network performance. By leveraging subnetting alongside advanced addressing methodologies, network administrators can confidently navigate the complexities of network design, laying the groundwork for resilient and agile network infrastructures. Refer to the following table:

Classes of IPv4	Default subnet masks
A	255.0.0.0
B	255.255.0.0
C	255.255.255.0

Table 1.1: *The IPv4 default subnet masks*

Note: For a deeper understanding of IPv4 addressing technology, including insights into address space depletion and network categorization based on address space, consider exploring the comprehensive resource available at https://blogs.igalia.com/dpino/2017/05/25/ipv4-exhaustion/. This insightful blog post delves into the intricacies of IPv4 exhaustion and offers valuable perspectives on navigating contemporary networking challenges.

Network Operating System

Like a computer, a server relies on an **operating system** (**OS**) to function effectively within a network environment. Specifically, a **Network Operating System** (**NOS**) is specialized software designed to manage, administer, and optimize network resources. In addition to traditional functions like file and application sharing, modern NOS solutions encompass user management, access control, configuration management, and service provisioning.

The NOS landscape has evolved significantly in recent years with advancements in server and client OSs. While traditional server platforms like Windows Server, Linux Server, and macOS Server continue to excel in offering comprehensive network services, notable enhancements in client OS versions such as Windows 11, Linux Ubuntu, and macOS have expanded their capabilities to include robust networking functionalities.

Today, these client OS versions boast sophisticated networking features, empowering them to serve as viable alternatives for deploying network services. Modern client OSes can handle diverse networking tasks efficiently and reliably, from file sharing and printer management to web hosting and remote access.

As a result, the definition of NOS has broadened to encompass both traditional server platforms and advanced client OSs. This evolution reflects the dynamic nature of computer networking, where the boundaries between server and client environments continue to blur, ushering in a new era of versatile and adaptable network management solutions.

Windows Server

Windows Server, pioneered by Microsoft, debuted in the early 1990s with Windows NT 3.5 and has since undergone numerous iterations. Initially, it featured a **graphical user interface (GUI)** akin to standard Windows OSs. However, with the advent of Windows Server 2008, Microsoft introduced the Server Core edition, a **command line interface (CLI)** based OS, providing administrators greater flexibility and efficiency in managing server resources.

Throughout its evolution, Windows Server has adapted to the changing landscape of computing, transitioning exclusively to a 64-bit architecture starting from Windows Server 2012. This shift reflects the industry's move towards 64-bit computing, enabling enhanced performance, scalability, and support for larger memory capacities.

One of the hallmark features of Windows Server is its robust file system support. While the **New Technology File System (NTFS)** has long been the native file system, introducing the **Resilient File System (ReFS)** with Windows Server 2012 marked a significant milestone. Engineered for resilience and optimized for network-intensive workloads, ReFS expands the capabilities of Windows Server, offering improved data integrity and fault tolerance for modern network environments.

In addition to its traditional role in on-premises environments, Windows Server has emerged as a cornerstone in cloud computing infrastructures. Its seamless integration with virtualization technologies enables organizations to harness the power of **virtual machines (VMs)** in **Infrastructure as a Service (IaaS)** environment, unlocking unparalleled flexibility, scalability, and resource utilization.

Windows Server is preferred for organizations seeking a reliable, feature-rich platform to deliver network services to Windows and non-Windows systems. Its adaptability to diverse computing environments underscores its enduring relevance in meeting the evolving demands of modern IT landscapes. Refer to the following figure:

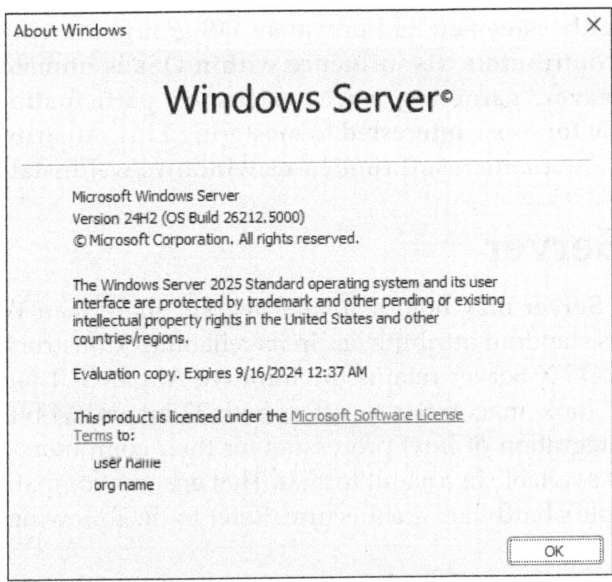

Figure 1.9: *Windows Server 2025 Standard*

Note: For a comprehensive overview of ReFS, visit https://docs.microsoft.com/en-us/windows-server/storage/refs/refs-overview.

Linux Server

The **Linux** OS traces its origins to Linus Torvalds' aspiration to refine MINIX's capabilities in the early 1990s. Rather than refining MINIX, Torvalds created a new OS dubbed Linux. The GNU GPL project subsequently handled the licensing of this new OS. Over time, the Linux penguin emerged as the iconic symbol of the OS. Various events, including the publication of the first Linux booklet and the founding of Linux-themed magazines, played pivotal roles in fostering the global Linux community, now one of the largest volunteer communities worldwide.

In the contemporary landscape, Linux servers enjoy widespread adoption, driven by their steadfast focus on security and commitment to open-source principles. Powering numerous web servers and supercomputers worldwide, Linux is a pillar of reliability and innovation. Its robust security features and the collaborative ethos of open-source development have propelled its popularity. Consequently, Linux has emerged as the preferred solution for server applications, offering unmatched stability, flexibility, and the ability to tailor solutions to specific needs. Refer to the following figure:

Figure 1.10: *Ubuntu Server*

Note: Linux is a highly esteemed and prevalent OS group, drawing a vast community of volunteers and contributors. Its influence within OSs is unmatched, with no other technological endeavor garnering such extensive participation. Comprehensive guidance is available for those interested in mastering Linux distributions on Windows Server 2019 at https://docs.microsoft.com/en-us/windows/wsl/install-on-server.

Mac OS X Server

Though **Mac OS X Server** may hold a smaller market share than Windows Server and Linux Server OSs, its standout attribute lies in its reliability. Constructed upon a modified Unix OS base, Mac OS X Server retains the intuitive Apple GUI familiar to Mac users. Like Windows and Linux, macOS Server offers both 32-bit and 64-bit versions. However, owing to Apple's integration of Intel processors for their computers and servers, macOS Server is exclusively available in a 64-bit format. That ensures compatibility and enhanced performance on Apple's hardware architecture. Refer to the following figure:

Figure 1.11: *MacOS X Server*

Note: In the past, Apple shifted from Mac OS X Server to macOS Server, distributed via the App Store. However, as of April 2022, even macOS Server has been discontinued. Nonetheless, customers with macOS Servers can still download and utilize the software on macOS Monterey. For additional details regarding macOS Servers, please visit https://support.apple.com/guide/server/welcome/mac.

Technology trends

We are currently entrenched in the IoT era, where the Internet profoundly influences our daily routines and professional endeavors. This paradigm shift has taken concepts once confined to science fiction and turned them into tangible realities. The swift pace of technological advancement has fostered an environment in perpetual flux, demanding adaptation to this new digital reality. Within the realm of computer networks, several noteworthy trends have emerged:

- **Enhanced security** stands as the paramount concern for enterprise networks. With an uptick in users and the escalating sophistication of cyber threats, there's an urgent need for fortified security measures.

- **Escalating bandwidth demands rank** as the immediate priority following security enhancements. The surge in data traffic exerts substantial strain on networks, necessitating expanded bandwidth to manage the burgeoning load effectively.
- **Software-defined networks (SDNs)** are gaining traction, particularly within enterprise circles. SDNs offer multiplexing capabilities, optimizing performance by efficiently utilizing multiple physical links for data transmission.
- **Video communication** has upended remote interaction, rendering it more engaging and opening avenues for online collaboration and entertainment.
- **Online collaboration**, including video communication, fosters collective endeavors, drawing together businesses, educational institutions, and individuals.
- **Bring Your Own Devices (BYOD)** is a prevailing network trend that permits users to utilize personal devices to access business data, affording them freedom, flexibility, and expanded opportunities while interfacing with resources.
- **Cloud computing** has redefined how we access and store data, reshaping the internet landscape. From enterprises to individuals, cloud computing furnishes on-demand services securely and cost-effectively, accessible from any device, anywhere worldwide.

These trends epitomize the ongoing evolution of computer networks, propelled by imperatives for fortified security, expanded bandwidth, innovative communication modalities, collaborative utilities, and the adaptability conferred by cloud computing. Embracing and harnessing these trends empowers organizations and individuals to thrive amid the dynamic technological milieu.

Conclusion

In conclusion, this chapter has provided an extensive overview of computer networks, covering various types such as PAN, LAN, CAN, MAN, and WAN. It introduced essential network components like hosts, nodes, clients, and servers and explored network architecture, topology, IP addressing, subnetting, and NOSs. Discussions included the differences between P2P and client/server networks and physical and logical topologies. Additionally, the chapter delved into IPv4 and IPv6 addressing technologies and elucidated the IPv4 classes from A to E. The chapter concluded with a practical exercise on enabling Hyper-V Client using Settings and Windows PowerShell, laying the groundwork for the subsequent chapter's exploration of server hardware and the functionalities of Windows Server 2025. This comprehensive coverage prepares readers for the evolving landscape of computer networks, emphasizing the advancements and features of Windows Server 2025.

Exercise 1.1: Enabling Hyper-V using Settings

Windows 11 Pro incorporates a functionality known as Hyper-V Client, enabling virtualization capabilities. Initially introduced alongside Windows Server 2008, Microsoft's Hyper-V succeeds Windows Virtual PC. With time, Hyper-V has garnered recognition among system administrators, emerging as a formidable competitor to VMware within the virtualization platform arena. It provides various services facilitating the creation and administrating of VMs and their associated resources. Users can follow the steps outlined within the Settings menu to activate the Hyper-V Client feature in Windows 11 Pro.

1. Click the Start button and then Settings within the All Apps section of the Start menu.
2. In the **Settings** navigation menu, click Apps and select Optional features from the list.
3. Scroll to the bottom and select More Windows features from the Related settings section.
4. The Windows Features window opens, allowing you to Turn Windows features on or off. Then, search for **Hyper-V** and click its check box. Ensure that both Hyper-V Management Tools and Hyper-V Platform are checked, as shown in *Figure 1.12*:

Figure 1.12: Enabling Hyper-V Client using Settings.

5. Click on the OK button. Shortly after that, Windows Features will begin applying changes. Once completed, Windows Features displays the message **Windows completed the requested changes.**
6. Click the Restart Now button to restart the computer.

Exercise 1.2: Enabling Hyper-V using PowerShell

This exercise involves enabling the Hyper-V Client feature on Windows 11 Pro using Windows PowerShell. To accomplish this, follow the provided instructions:

1. Right-click the Start button, select **Terminal (Admin)** from the administrator's menu, and select Terminal (Admin).
2. The User Account Control window opens to confirm whether you want to allow that application to change your device. Click on the Yes button shortly after the Windows PowerShell window opens.
3. In Windows PowerShell, enter the following cmdlet and press *Enter*. Refer to *Figure 1.13*.

   ```
   Enable-WindowsOptionalFeature -Online -FeatureName Microsoft-Hyper-V -All
   ```

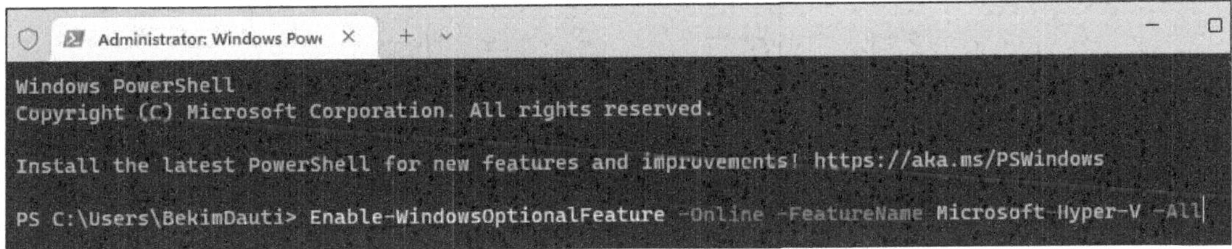

Figure 1.13: *Installing Hyper-V Client using the Windows PowerShell*

4. Shortly after the execution of the cmdlet, the installation of the Hyper-V Client will begin. Once completed, enter the following cmdlet to reboot the computer:

   ```
   Restart-Computer -ComputerName ComputerName -Force
   ```

Questions

1. Explain, using your terminology, what constitutes a computer network.
2. Identify and name as many types of computer networks as you can.
3. Enumerate the various types of network components you are familiar with.
4. Highlight three critical differences between IPv4 and IPv6 addressing technologies.
5. Define a NOS using your own words.

Join our book's Discord space

Join the book's Discord Workspace for Latest updates, Offers, Tech happenings around the world, New Release and Sessions with the Authors:

https://discord.bpbonline.com

CHAPTER 2
Introduction to Windows Server 2025

Introduction

This chapter will delve into Windows Server 2025, Microsoft's latest evolution in server operating systems. Before exploring the specifics of Windows Server 2025, it is essential first to understand the distinct hardware characteristics that differentiate servers from standard PCs—a vital factor for businesses. We will begin by examining the unique attributes of server hardware and software, clarifying how they differ from those found in personal computers. Following that, we will provide an overview of Windows Server 2025, including its release timeline, available editions, and the introduction of enhanced cloud integration through Azure Arc capabilities. A comparison with its predecessor, Windows Server 2022, will be made to highlight this version's key improvements and new features. Administrators need to be familiar with both the minimum and recommended system requirements to ensure a smooth and efficient deployment of Windows Server 2025. These requirements will be discussed to aid in making well-informed decisions for server setup and deployment. A step-by-step guide will be provided for downloading Windows Server 2025 and Windows Admin Center, offering practical insights on acquiring and preparing the necessary tools for effective implementation.

Structure

In this chapter, we will cover the following topics:

- Understanding server hardware and its specifics
- Overview of Windows Server 2025
- Editions of Windows Server 2025
- Comparing Windows Server versions
- System requirements
- New features in Windows Server 2025

Objectives

This chapter aims to equip you with a comprehensive understanding of server hardware and its critical components, such as the processor, memory, storage, and network interfaces. You will be introduced to Windows Server 2025 while learning about the hardware fundamentals. This introduction will cover key details, including its release timeline, the various editions available, notable new features, and the system requirements needed for successful deployment. The chapter will conclude with a practical hands-on activity, where you will download both Windows Server 2025 and the Windows Admin Center. This exercise will reinforce your understanding by allowing you to apply the concepts discussed in a real-world scenario.

Understanding server hardware and its specifics

While servers and personal computers share similar components—such as hardware and software—their roles and requirements differ significantly. Servers are designed to handle more demanding tasks, requiring more powerful hardware and specialized software to efficiently provide network services to multiple clients. This distinction in hardware and software between PCs and servers is crucial for understanding their respective roles. In a business setting, individual users primarily use personal computers as workstations. In contrast, servers function as the network's backbone, delivering services such as file storage, databases, and applications. As a result, server hardware must be highly reliable and built for continuous operation. For example, a database server must have substantial memory and storage capacity to perform efficiently. Key components such as the processor, memory, storage, and network interface play a vital role in determining the server's overall performance, making their quality and robustness critical to maintaining seamless network services.

Four key hardware components

To ensure optimal server performance across a range of workloads, it is critical to routinely evaluate and monitor a server's four key hardware components: the processor, memory, disk, and network interface. Proactive assessment helps identify and mitigate potential bottlenecks, ensuring that the server operates efficiently under both standard and demanding conditions. Let us take a look at them:

- The **processor**, or **central processing unit** (**CPU**), as shown in *Figure 2.1*, is the core of the server's operations, akin to the *brain* of the system. It manages all computational and data processing tasks. Leading manufacturers such as Intel and AMD design processors for both personal computers and servers, with modern processors adopting a 64-bit architecture. This architecture allows for greater data throughput per communication session between the processor and RAM—64 bits compared to 32 bits in older, 32-bit systems—resulting in more efficient and high-capacity data exchange, which significantly enhances server performance and responsiveness. For instance, in a Windows Server 2022 environment, a 64-bit system processes double the amount of data as its 32-bit counterpart, making it better suited for handling large-scale workloads and computations.

***Figure 2.1:** A processor in a server's motherboard*

Note: When evaluating Windows Server 2025's processing capabilities, it is important to highlight that the 64-bit edition can manage twice the data volume of the 32-bit edition of the same operating system. That means that, when deployed on the same hardware, the 64-bit edition of Windows Server 2025 provides a significant advantage in processing more extensive data sets, resulting in enhanced performance and improved capacity for handling complex computational tasks.

- **Random access memory** (**RAM**), illustrated in *Figure 2.2*, serves as the server's working memory, which is vital for the smooth operation of both the server's operating system and the applications running on it. Adequate RAM ensures that the server can efficiently handle multiple tasks simultaneously, reducing latency and improving system responsiveness. In environments where resource-intensive applications are in use, increasing the RAM capacity directly boosts the server's ability to manage heavier workloads, ultimately improving performance. For example, a database server with high RAM capacity will efficiently manage concurrent data processing requests without overloading the system.

Figure 2.2: *RAM modules in a server's motherboard*

- The **disk subsystem**, presented in *Figure 2.3*, is composed of multiple disks and is responsible for the permanent storage of data. In server environments, efficient read/write operations are crucial to achieving high performance. Selecting disks with fast read/write capabilities, configuring disk arrays (such as RAID) for enhanced performance and redundancy, and utilizing caching mechanisms can significantly improve the speed at which data is read from or written to the disk. For example, servers utilizing **solid state drives (SSDs)** benefit from faster data access speeds than traditional **hard disk drives (HDDs)**, improving performance in data-intensive applications like virtual machines or high-traffic web servers.

Figure 2.3: *SSD disks in a server*

- Lastly, the **network interface** enables the server to connect to a **local area network (LAN)** and the Internet, facilitating communication between the server and users.

The speed of the server's network connection directly affects data transfer rates. Servers with high-speed network interfaces can handle larger volumes of data, reduce transmission delays, and ensure smoother data exchanges between internal networks and the cloud or external clients. For example, a web server with a high-bandwidth network interface will provide faster load times for web applications and reduce latency for end users, especially when handling high traffic. Refer to the following figure:

Figure 2.4: *Network interfaces on a server*

By regularly monitoring these key hardware components, IT professionals can identify potential performance issues early, allowing them to take corrective actions to maintain server efficiency and reliability under varied operational conditions.

Server size and form factor

In addition to the critical hardware components discussed earlier, a server's size and form factor play vital roles in its performance and application. A server's size pertains to the dimensions of its physical hardware, while the **form factor** refers to its overall design, layout, and structure. Understanding these factors can significantly influence deployment decisions and operational efficiency.

For instance, as illustrated in *Figure 2.5*, rack-mountable servers are engineered for installation within standard server racks. This design is particularly advantageous in on-premises data centers or server rooms where space is at a premium. These servers typically support multiple units stacked in a single rack, maximizing space utilization while allowing for effective cooling and cable management. An example of this setup is seen in enterprise environments where numerous servers are required to handle high traffic and data loads.

Figure 2.5: *A rack-mountable server*

In contrast, **blade servers** utilize a modular approach, where individual blades are inserted into a chassis. This design, also optimized for rack mounting, significantly enhances both space and power efficiency, making it an ideal choice for large-scale data centers and supercomputing environments. Blade servers minimize cabling and can share power and cooling resources within the chassis, which is particularly beneficial when scaling operations. For example, in a research facility where computational tasks demand high performance, blade servers can be deployed to handle parallel processing efficiently without consuming excessive physical space.

Tower servers, on the other hand, depicted in *Figure 2.6*, function as standalone units that operate vertically. They are often employed in **Small Office/Home Office (SOHO)** environments or for testing purposes where limited IT infrastructure is needed. Due to their design, tower servers are easy to transport and set up, making them suitable for businesses that do not require the density of rack-mounted systems. For instance, a small business may use a tower server to run local applications and store data without the need for extensive server room setups.

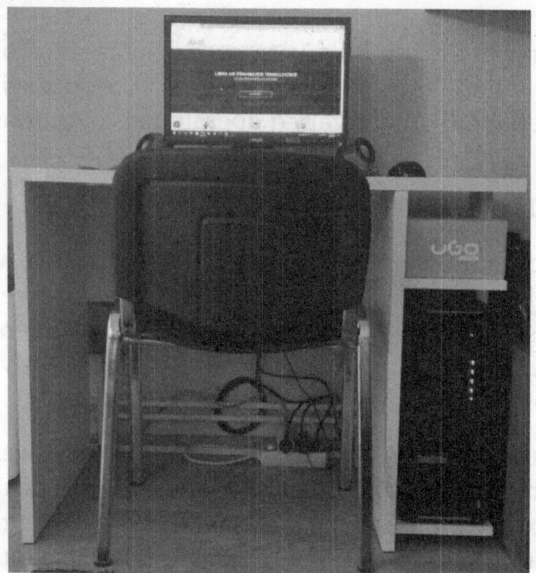

Figure 2.6: *The tower server under the desk*

Understanding the various server sizes and form factors is essential for IT professionals in selecting the appropriate hardware for specific operational needs. Organizations can effectively tailor their infrastructure to optimize space, power efficiency, and overall performance by evaluating the physical dimensions and design configurations of different server types, ensuring that their server environment aligns with their operational requirements.

Overview of Windows Server 2025

Over the last 30 years since the launch of Windows NT, Microsoft has showcased an exceptional ability to adapt its Windows Server operating systems to meet the ever-changing demands of network services. This adaptability is reflected in the timeline of Windows Server development, which highlights significant advancements in server technology. As illustrated in *Table 2.1*, this journey can be segmented into several distinct eras:

Server for the masses era 1996-2000	Enterprise era 2000 - 2008	Datacenter era 2009 - 2013	Cloud for the masses era 2016 -present
Windows NT Server 3.5 Windows NT Server 4.0	Windows 2000 Server Windows Server 2003	Windows Server 2008 Windows Server 2012	Windows Server 2016 Windows Server 2022 Windows Server 2022 Windows Server 2025

Table 2.1: *Windows Server's timeline*

- **Server for the masses era (1996-2000):** This initial phase focused on making server technology accessible to a broader audience.
- **Enterprise era (2000-2008):** During this time, Microsoft concentrated on enhancing features tailored for large organizations, emphasizing advanced management and security functionalities.
- **Datacenter era (2009-2013):** This era was characterized by resource optimization and improvements in virtualization capabilities, which are crucial for modern data centers.
- **Cloud for the masses era (2016-present):** The current phase emphasizes cloud integration, empowering organizations to utilize cloud services for greater scalability and operational flexibility.

The latest version, Windows Server 2025, represents a significant evolution within this lineage. As depicted in *Figure 2.7*, it features a revamped Start menu and desktop environment. Windows Server 2025 was announced on January 26, and while it is currently in preview, general availability is anticipated this fall. While earlier versions like Windows Server 2016, 2019, and 2022 were based on the Windows 10 codebase, Windows Server 2025 is built on Windows 11's architecture, utilizing the October 2023 Update (version 23H2). A key difference is that Windows Server 2025 does not require TPM 2.0, providing organizations with more excellent deployment options and flexibility.

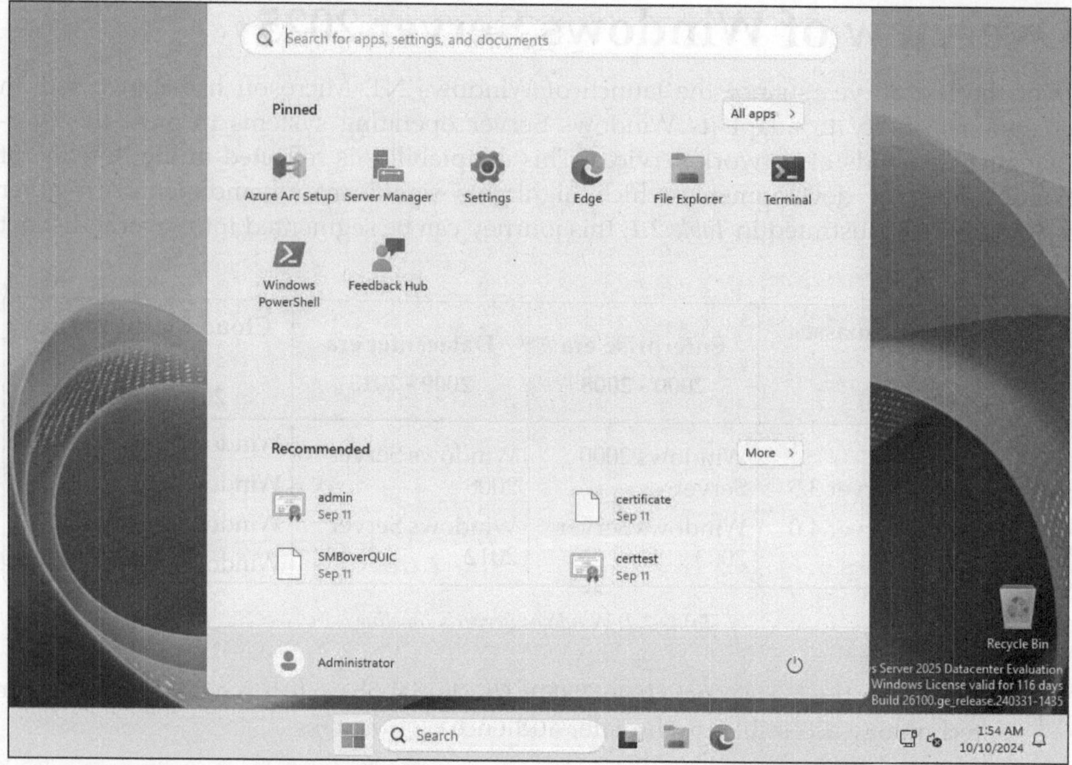

***Figure 2.7**: Start menu and desktop in Windows Server 2025*

The continuous evolution of Windows Server illustrates Microsoft's commitment to meeting the diverse needs of businesses and IT professionals. Windows Server 2025 not only builds on the legacy of its predecessors but also introduces modern features that facilitate advanced cloud integration and operational efficiency, ensuring that organizations can effectively manage complex network environments.

Cloud-oriented Windows Server

In the current landscape dominated by cloud computing, server operating systems must possess cloud-capable features. This shift began with the release of Windows Server 2016, which Microsoft aptly branded as **Windows Server for the cloud**. The focus on cloud capabilities has intensified with each subsequent version, particularly with Windows Server 2022. This latest iteration enhances security, flexibility, and support for hybrid deployments, primarily through new features found in the Windows Server 2025 Datacenter Azure edition. Each version, including Windows Server 2025, has introduced critical features such as System Insights, hybrid cloud tools, and improved security functionalities, including the Storage Migration Service and support for Kubernetes. Microsoft has consistently evolved Windows Server to bolster security, connectivity, Azure integration, application platform capabilities, and storage management.

Building on this robust foundation, Windows Server 2025 brings a host of new features tailored to meet the demands of modern cloud environments. One notable enhancement is in **Active Directory Domain Services** (**AD DS**), which now supports a larger 32k database page size. This improvement boosts scalability and optimizes data handling for multi-valued attributes. Schema updates expand AD's capabilities, allowing administrators to repair objects with missing core attributes efficiently. The introduction of SMB over QUIC significantly enhances file-sharing performance and security across all server editions.

Furthermore, Windows Server 2025 innovates with hotpatching capabilities, which allow for the seamless application of security patches without necessitating server restarts. This functionality minimizes downtime and is crucial for maintaining operational continuity. The operating system also leverages AI-driven management optimizations, providing administrators with proactive insights and enhancing operational efficiency. These advancements highlight Microsoft's dedication to delivering a server operating system that sets new benchmarks for performance, security, and manageability in today's IT environment, further solidifying its leadership in cloud computing innovation.

Note: In addition to the Remote Server Administration Tools (RSAT), Microsoft has unveiled the Windows Admin Center, a modern server management tool that features an interface akin to that of Azure. This innovative tool seamlessly enables managing multiple servers, providing IT administrators with a streamlined experience. After installing Windows Server 2025 and accessing the desktop environment, users will encounter the Windows Admin Center dialog box, which facilitates intuitive server management. This powerful tool is available for free and can be easily downloaded from the official Microsoft website at Windows Admin Center: https://www.microsoft.com/en-us/windows-server/windows-admin-center. With its capabilities, Windows Admin Center significantly enhances server management efficiency and simplifies the administrative process for IT professionals.

Editions of Windows Server 2025

Similar to its predecessors, Windows Server 2016 and Windows Server 2019, Windows Server 2025 presents a variety of editions designed to meet the distinct needs of different enterprises. The available editions for Windows Server 2025 include the following:

- **Datacenter edition:** Ideal for expansive virtualization and cloud environments, this edition supports unlimited virtual instances while offering a comprehensive suite of advanced features tailored for large-scale operations.
- **Standard edition:** This edition is geared towards smaller organizations that operate with fewer virtual instances. It encompasses all essential server functionalities required for effective and efficient operation in less demanding environments.
- **Azure edition (for VM evaluation only):** This edition is tailored specifically for testing and evaluating Windows Server in Azure virtual machines. It allows

organizations to explore its capabilities within a cloud context, ensuring a better understanding of its potential for deployment.

- **Annual channel for container host:** Focused on managing container workloads, this edition streamlines the deployment and administration of containerized applications, making it an optimal choice for businesses utilizing modern development practices.

These various editions of Windows Server 2025 are designed to accommodate a wide array of enterprise requirements, ensuring that organizations—regardless of their size and infrastructure complexities—can select the version that best aligns with their specific operational needs.

Comparing Windows Server versions

At first glance, Windows Server 2025 and Windows Server 2022 may seem quite alike; however, a detailed examination uncovers significant improvements and innovative features in Windows Server 2025. This section will highlight the key differences between these two operating systems, underscoring the most important enhancements.

When comparing Windows Server 2025 with Windows Server 2022, several noteworthy upgrades come to light:

- **AD DS enhancements:** Windows Server 2025 introduces a larger 32k database page size for **Active Directory** (**AD**), significantly boosting scalability. Additionally, new schema updates expand AD functionality, enabling enterprise administrators to repair objects with missing core attributes efficiently. In contrast, Windows Server 2022 primarily focused on improving AD management and schema flexibility.

- **SMB over QUIC:** In Windows Server 2025, **Server Message Block** (**SMB**) can be configured to use **Quick UDP Internet Connections** (**QUIC**) across all editions, which enhances both file-sharing performance and security. Windows Server 2022, on the other hand, only introduced initial support for SMB over QUIC.

- **Security enhancements:** Windows Server 2025 includes advanced security features such as hypervisor-based code integrity, improved secure-core server capabilities, and hardware-enforced stack protection. The default support for TLS 1.3 further enhances network security. While Windows Server 2022 did improve security protocols, including secured-core server support, it lacked the comprehensive features found in the latest version.

- **Hotpatching support:** A standout feature in Windows Server 2025 is its hot patching capabilities, which allow updates to be applied without downtime. Windows Server 2022 continued to support robust update management tools but lacked this seamless update feature.

- **AI-based management:** Windows Server 2025 introduces advanced management capabilities enhanced by AI-driven optimizations, improving overall operational efficiency. In contrast, Windows Server 2022 laid the groundwork with initial AI-driven management tools.
- **Platform flexibility:** The latest version focuses on dynamic routing and improved management of service accounts, whereas Windows Server 2022 introduced **Dynamic Source Routing** (**DSR**) and improved virtualized time zones.
- **Windows Admin Center enhancements:** Windows Server 2025 features enhanced management tools, including automated extension lifecycle management and customizable views for virtual machine information. Windows Server 2022 supported improved Windows Admin Center tools but did not offer the same level of functionality.
- **Kubernetes support:** With advancements in container management, Windows Server 2025 enhances support for Kubernetes environments, allowing for more robust container orchestration. While Windows Server 2022 provided initial Kubernetes support, it lacked the depth of enhancements found in its successor.

Organizations can decide which version best fits their needs by understanding the distinctions between Windows Server 2025 and Windows Server 2022. Next, we will delve into these operating systems' minimum and recommended system requirements.

System requirements

Before exploring the details of the minimum and recommended system requirements for Windows Server 2025, it is essential to grasp their importance. The minimum requirements refer to the hardware specifications necessary to successfully install the operating system, while the recommended requirements outline the hardware needed to achieve an optimal user experience. Understanding these distinctions allows IT professionals to make informed decisions about hardware selection based on the specific services they plan to deploy.

According to Microsoft's documentation, Windows Server 2025 maintains the exact minimum hardware requirements as its predecessor, Windows Server 2022. This consistency implies that organizations can continue utilizing existing hardware that meets the specifications set forth for Windows Server 2022, ensuring a seamless transition to the new version without necessitating immediate hardware upgrades. By recognizing these requirements, IT teams can effectively plan their infrastructure to support the enhanced features and functionalities of Windows Server 2025 while ensuring reliability and performance in their deployments.

Minimum and recommended system requirements

Before examining the specific system requirements for Windows Server 2025, it is important to distinguish between the minimum and recommended hardware specifications. The minimum requirements are designed to enable the basic installation and functionality of the operating system, while the recommended specifications aim to deliver optimal performance and user experience. Comprehending these distinctions is vital for selecting the hardware that aligns with the intended applications and workloads. According to Microsoft's documentation, the hardware requirements for Windows Server 2025 are consistent with those of its earlier versions.

Here are the minimum system requirements:

- **Processor**: A 1.4 GHz 64-bit processor.
- **RAM**: 512 MB (2 GB for installations utilizing the Desktop Experience option).
- **Disk space**: 32 GB of available space.
- **Network**: An Ethernet adapter capable of a minimum throughput of 1 Gigabit.
- **Graphics device and monitor**: A device capable of Super VGA (1024 x 768) resolution or higher.
- **Other hardware**: A DVD drive for installations from DVD media, along with a keyboard, mouse (or a compatible pointing device), TPM, and internet access.

The recommended hardware requirements are as follows:

- **Processor**: A 2.0 GHz 64-bit processor or higher.
- **RAM**: 32 GB or more.
- **Disk space**: A 256 GB SSD and a 1 TB HDD combination.
- **Network**: At least one Gigabit Ethernet network interface card (NIC).
- **Graphics device and monitor**: A device capable of Super VGA (1024 x 768) resolution or higher.
- **Other hardware**: A DVD drive, keyboard, mouse (or a compatible pointing device), TPM, and internet access.

This overview highlights the minimum and recommended hardware requirements for Windows Server 2025, demonstrating its continuity with previous versions while ensuring robust performance suited for modern server environments. A thorough understanding of these requirements is essential for making informed hardware investment decisions that cater to your server deployment objectives. The following section will explore the new features and enhancements in Windows Server 2025.

New features in Windows Server 2025

While Windows Server 2025 retains many standard features from its predecessor, Windows Server 2022, it brings a host of significant innovations and enhancements. Among these improvements are several new features that enhance the overall functionality and performance of Windows Server 2025. Let us take a look at them:

- **Arc-enabled hotpatching:** Previously exclusive to Windows Server 2022 Datacenter: Azure Edition (Core) virtual machines, hotpatching now extends its capabilities to both Standard and Datacenter editions of Windows Server 2025, including support for virtual machines and various cloud environments. This feature allows server administrators to apply updates without rebooting the server or disrupting ongoing processes. An Azure Arc subscription is required to utilize hotpatching.
- **Next-generation AD:** Windows Server 2025 introduces support for 32k page-sized AD databases, a substantial upgrade from the 8k page databases supported by Windows Server 2000. This next-gen AD enhances replication processes and introduces a new functional-level forest and domain. While detailed documentation is still emerging, Microsoft has indicated that to take advantage of the 32k page database feature, all domain controllers within a forest must support this capability, necessitating a migration to the new functional level.
- **Security enhancements:** Windows Server 2025 further strengthens the security landscape by incorporating Kerberos keys for local user accounts, expanding beyond previous limitations that applied only to domain controllers. In a move away from legacy protocols, the Mailslot communication method used in Windows Server Active Directory for decades will be eliminated, as it fails to meet modern security standards. This change emphasizes the shift toward more secure communication protocols.
- **Improved storage performance:** Microsoft claims a remarkable 90% increase in **Input/Output Operations Per Second** (**IOPS**) for storage performance, achieved through enhancements related to Native **Non-Volatile Memory Express** (**NVME**) SSDs. Storage Replica has also seen significant improvements, with compression capabilities now available across all editions of Windows Server. Additionally, new functionalities have been introduced for data deduplication and Storage Spaces, further optimizing storage management.
- **Enhanced Hyper-V capabilities:** Hyper-V in Windows Server 2025 now supports virtual machines with up to 1,792 virtual processors and 29.7 terabytes of RAM, significantly boosting virtualized workloads. A notable addition is GPU partitioning (GPU-P), enabling the sharing of a GPU across multiple virtual machines while supporting Live Migration and failover clustering. However, this feature requires specific hardware, including servers supporting SR-IOV and equipped with AMD Milan processors or Intel Sapphire Rapids CPUs.

These advancements in Windows Server 2025 enhance the system's operational capabilities and position it as a robust platform for modern enterprise needs, ensuring that organizations can leverage the latest technology to drive efficiency and security in their IT environments.

Conclusion

This chapter provided an in-depth exploration of Windows Server 2025, the latest iteration of Microsoft's Network Operating System (NOS) within the Windows NT family. We commenced by emphasizing the significance of server hardware and its various components, illustrating how they contribute to optimizing server performance. Following this foundation, we offered a detailed overview of Windows Server 2025, including its release timeline and a comparative analysis with its predecessor, Windows Server 2022. Furthermore, we outlined the critical minimum and recommended system requirements and discussed essential factors that system administrators should consider when deploying Windows Server 2025.

Moreover, this chapter highlighted several innovative features introduced in Windows Server 2025, such as arc-enabled hotpatching, a next-generation AD, enhanced security measures, improved storage performance, and advanced Hyper-V capabilities. These enhancements enrich the user experience, facilitate seamless integration with cloud services, and strengthen overall system security. To solidify the learning experience, we concluded with a practical exercise that guides readers through downloading Windows Server 2025 and the Windows Admin Center, laying the groundwork for the installation process to be detailed in the subsequent chapter. This thorough approach ensures that readers are well-equipped to harness the powerful capabilities of Windows Server 2025 in their IT environments.

Exercise 2.1: Downloading Windows Server 2025

This book is organized around a project framework, with the exercises in this chapter building upon the concepts covered in *Chapter 1, Understanding Network Components*. To download Windows Server 2025 on your Windows 11 computer, please follow these steps:

1. Press the **Windows key + R** to open the **Run** dialog box.
2. Type **Microsoft-edge:** into the dialog and hit *Enter*.
3. Once **Microsoft Edge** opens, click on the **address bar**, enter **https://www.microsoft.com/en-us/evalcenter**, and press *Enter*.
4. On the **Evaluation Center** page, locate the horizontal menu at the top, click on **Windows Server**, and then select the **Windows Server** option. From the available list of Windows Server versions, choose **Windows Server 2025**, as illustrated in *Figure 2.8*.

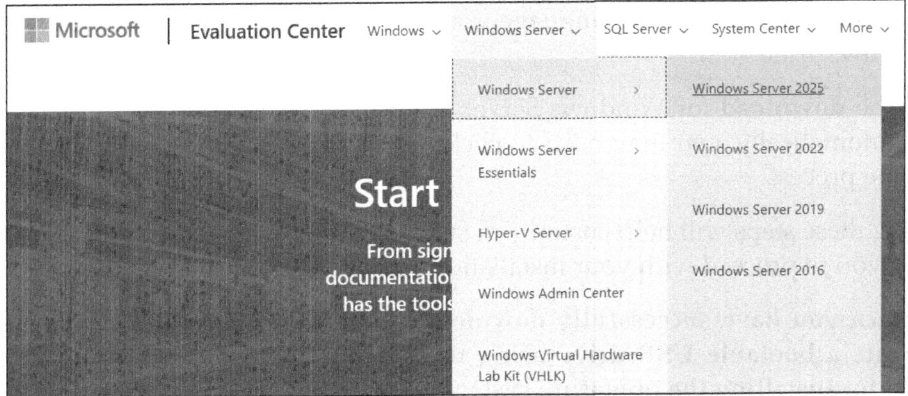

Figure 2.8: *Selecting Windows Server 2025 from the list*

5. In the **Get Started for Free** section on the Windows Server 2025 page, opt for **Download the ISO** as your product experience.
6. Complete the **registration form** as shown in *Figure 2.9*, then click **Continue**.

Evaluate Windows Server 2025

Microsoft Windows Server 2025 prepares you for tomorrow while delivering the security, performance, and flexibility you need today. Be more productive with easier networking, faster storage, and hybrid cloud capabilities that adapt to your needs. Get ahead of what's next with forward-looking security, and AI-ready compute.

Resources

- Release notes and system requirements
- Microsoft Tech Community: Windows Server
- Windows Server technical documentation

**Participation in this trial comes at no cost for the 180 day duration of the trial. Once the 180 day trial period expires, the trial instance will deactivate. No additional costs will be incurred at the end of the trial period. Customers can purchase a license and convert the license to full product after the trial period. Trial descriptions accurate as of November 2024 and are subject to change in the future.*

Register for your free trial today

Complete the form below.

* First name

* Last name

* Email

* Company name

* Country/Region
Country/region *

* Company size
Company size

* Job role

* Phone
Country Code *

Questions/Comments

Download now

Figure 2.9: *Registering for the free trial to evaluate Windows Server 2025*

7. Choose your **preferred language** from the **dropdown menu** and click **Download Now**.

8. The **download** for Windows Server 2025 should start shortly. If it doesn't begin automatically, you may need to click the **Download** button manually to initiate the process.

Following these steps will help ensure you successfully download Windows Server 2025, allowing you to proceed with your installation and evaluation.

Note: Once you have successfully downloaded Windows Server 2025, the next step is to create a bootable USB drive using the ISO file you obtained. This process is essential for installing the operating system on your server. If you are unfamiliar with creating a bootable USB drive, you can find detailed instructions by visiting Lifewire's guide: https://www.lifewire.com/how-to-burn-an-iso-file-to-a-USB-drive-2619270. This resource provides a step-by-step approach, ensuring that you can easily and effectively prepare your USB drive for installation, which is a critical part of the setup process.

Exercise 2.2: Downloading Windows Admin Center

To download Windows Admin Center on your Windows 11 computer, follow these straightforward steps:

1. To download **Windows Admin Center** on your **Windows 11** computer, follow these straightforward steps:

2. Launch **Microsoft Edge** and navigate to the official download page at **https://www.microsoft.com/en-us/windows-server/windows-admin-center**.

3. locate and click the **Download Windows Admin Center** button on the Windows Admin Center webpage, as illustrated in *Figure 2.10*.

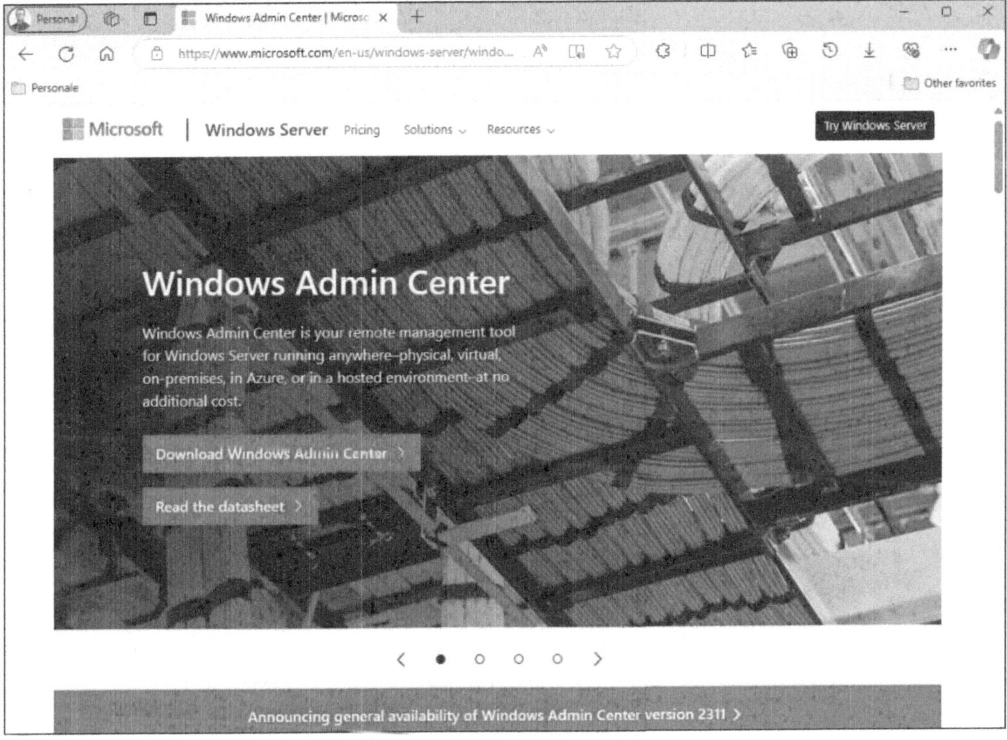

Figure 2.10: *Windows Admin Center download site*

4. A prompt will appear, giving you the option to either **Open** or **Save** the file to your device.
5. After the download, proceed with the installation by following the instructions in the **Windows Admin Center Setup** wizard.

This process ensures you have the tools to manage and administer your Windows Server environment efficiently.

Questions

1. Identify a server's four key hardware components and describe their respective functions.
2. Can you outline the various eras of Windows Server along with the corresponding versions released during each period?
3. What is meant by minimum system requirements in the context of operating systems?
4. Name three notable features introduced in Windows Server 2025.
5. What aspects of Windows Server 2025 do you find most appealing or beneficial?

Join our book's Discord space

Join the book's Discord Workspace for Latest updates, Offers, Tech happenings around the world, New Release and Sessions with the Authors:

https://discord.bpbonline.com

CHAPTER 3
Windows Server 2025 Installation

Introduction

Up to this point, you have successfully navigated the first two chapters, which introduced various network components, server hardware, and accessing Windows Server 2025. Additionally, you have acquired and installed Windows Server 2025 and Windows Admin Center and configured the Hyper-V Client. Now, it is essential to deepen your engagement by becoming familiar with partition schemes, boot options, and installation choices while also comprehending the detailed instructions for installing Windows Server 2025. This chapter is meticulously organized, offering step-by-step instructions and clear visuals that ensure a smooth installation process and efficient setup of Windows Server 2025. Moreover, it provides valuable tips for a swift and effective installation. As before, practical exercises are included, but this time in greater quantity, allowing for more hands-on experience. The topics covered in this chapter involve getting to know partition schemes, understanding boot options, exploring various installation methods, and familiarizing yourself with the installation options available in Windows Server 2025.

Structure

The chapter covers the following topics:

- Getting to know partition schemes
- Boot option

- Getting to know installation methods
- Getting to know installation options

Objectives

As previously mentioned, this chapter will guide you through the installation process of Windows Server 2025. Before initiating the installation, you will learn about partition schemes, boot options, and installation methods. Familiarizing yourself with these concepts will provide a solid foundation for smoothly installing Windows Server 2025. Additionally, you will set up the virtual switch and **virtual machine** (**VM**) within the Hyper-V Client, utilizing the ISO image you acquired in the previous chapter, which introduced you to Windows Server 2025. These tasks have been thoughtfully designed to be interactive and engaging, ensuring that you quickly grasp the process of installing Windows Server 2025. Moreover, this chapter incorporates new and improved technologies in Windows Server 2025, offering enhanced performance, security, and management capabilities to streamline your server setup experience.

Getting to know partition schemes

Understanding disk partitioning is a crucial aspect of server management. A **disk partition** is a method to logically divide a disk, enabling the operating system to manage its data efficiently. The **partition scheme**, however, refers to the specific strategy used to segment the disk into distinct sections. Typically, computers and servers employ two primary types of partition schemes. Let us look at these schemes in more detail:

- **Master Boot Record** (**MBR**) is a **legacy partition scheme**, often regarded as a legacy boot option. It operates within a disk sector size of 512 bytes and allows for a maximum of four primary partitions, three primary, and one extended partition. Creating up to 26 logical partitions within the extended partition is possible. MBR uses **Logical Block Addressing** (**LBA**) to support disk sizes up to 2 **terabytes** (**TB**). It has been widely utilized as a partition scheme for platforms requiring multi-boot capabilities, enabling multiple operating systems to be installed on a single disk.

- **GUID Partition Table** (**GPT**) is a more **advanced and modern partition scheme** that overcomes the limitations of MBR. GPT employs a **Global Unique Identifier** (**GUID**), a 128-bit number used by Microsoft to identify various resources uniquely. GPT supports block sizes starting at 512 bytes and can go higher, with the most common default being 4,000 or 4,096 bytes. Each partition entry in GPT is 128 bytes. GPT is integral to the **Unified Extensible Firmware Interface** (**UEFI**) standard, which replaces the outdated **basic input/output system** (**BIOS**) and supports modern hardware. Notably, GPT offers fault tolerance and can handle up to 18 **exabytes** (**EB**) of disk storage, accommodating up to 128 partitions per disk.

Windows Server 2025 incorporates new and improved technologies, enhancing performance, security, and management capabilities. One notable feature is the improved **Storage Spaces Direct** (**S2D**), which provides greater flexibility and reliability in managing disk partitions. S2D allows for creating highly available and scalable storage solutions, making the most of the latest hardware innovations, and ensuring a robust and efficient server environment.

Boot option

The **boot option** is a critical configuration setting that determines the method or source used to initiate the operating system on a computer. It specifies the device from which the computer should begin the boot process, including options such as the hard drive, DVD, USB, or network connection. Modifying the boot option allows you to start the computer from a different source, install a new operating system, or troubleshoot issues with the current operating system. Understanding and managing these options are key to maintaining system functionality.

Once you have entered the UEFI, you will find various available boot options. Presently, some of the commonly utilized boot options include:

- **Bootable DVD**: Using a bootable DVD is common for installation media. First, insert the DVD into the DVD drive before entering the UEFI. Once inside the UEFI, set the DVD as the primary boot option, save the modifications, and exit the UEFI.
- **USB flash drive**: When utilizing a USB flash drive, ensure it has a minimum capacity of 8 GB. Before accessing the UEFI, connect the bootable USB drive to the computer. Designate the USB drive as the first boot option within the UEFI settings, save the changes, and exit the UEFI.
- **Network booting**: Network booting is employed when installing Windows Server 2025 via a network connection. First, network booting should be enabled within the UEFI settings. Then, specify network booting as the primary boot option. Lastly, save the adjustments and exit the UEFI.

Windows Server 2025 incorporates new and improved technologies, enhancing performance, security, and management capabilities. One notable feature is the improved Secure Boot, which ensures that only trusted software is loaded during the boot process, providing additional security and integrity for your server environment.

Note: To create a bootable USB flash drive for Windows Server 2025, you can use the Windows USB/DVD Download Tool or Rufus. You can obtain the Windows USB/DVD Download Tool from the official Microsoft website: https://www.microsoft.com/en-GB/download/details.aspx?id=56485 and Rufus can be obtained from https://rufus.ie/en/.

Advanced startup options

In Windows Server 2025, the traditional *F8* key for accessing advanced startup options has been replaced with a more streamlined approach. You can now utilize the advanced startup options to recover the server operating system. This modern method provides a more intuitive and efficient way to manage recovery tasks. To access these options, follow these steps:

1. Click the **Start** button on the **desktop**.
2. From the **Start Menu**, select the **Settings app** icon.
3. Locate and click the **System** option on the **Settings** app screen.
4. From the list of options, select the **Recovery** option.
5. On the right-hand side of the screen, click the **Restart Now** button within the **Recovery options** section, as illustrated in *Figure 3.1*:

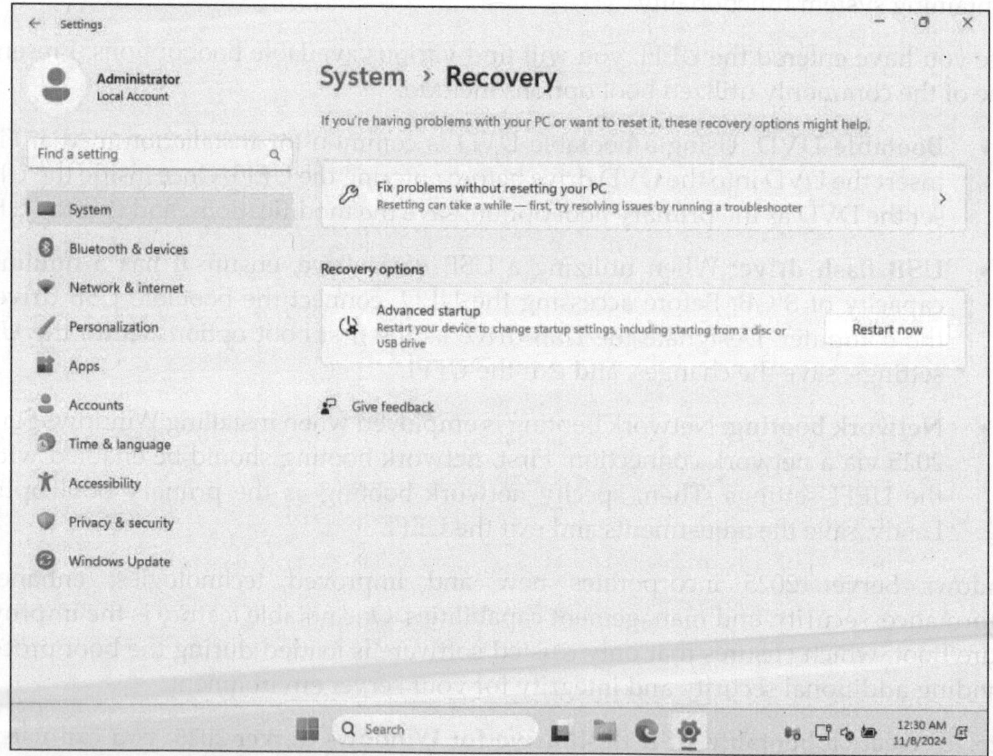

Figure 3.1*: Navigating to advanced options in Windows Server 2025*

6. A dialog box will appear, prompting you to save your work. Click the **Restart Now** button again to confirm. Choose the **reason** and click **Continue**.
7. Select **Troubleshoot** from the **Choose an option** screen after the system restarts.

8. On the **Advanced Options** screen, as shown in *Figure 3.2*, you can select various options to recover or repair your server OS.

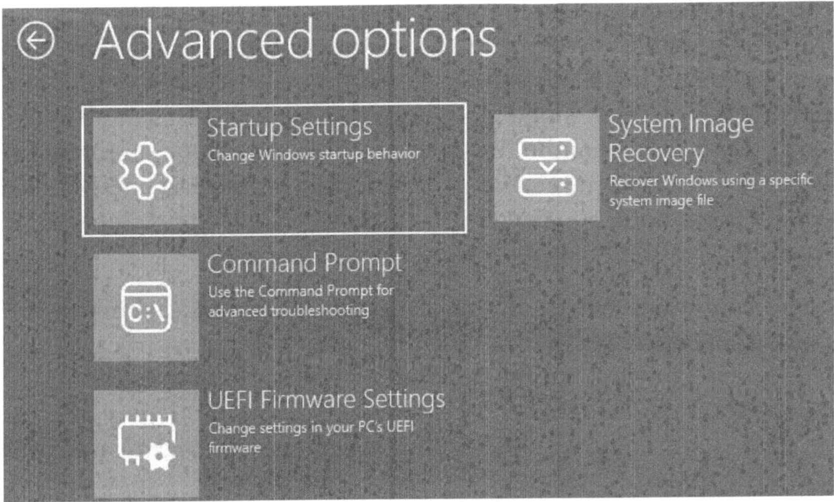

***Figure 3.2**: Advanced startup options in Windows Server 2025*

Getting to know installation methods

When installing Windows Server 2025, there are several methods to choose from. Selecting a specific process will depend on the deployment environment in which you intend to install Windows Server 2025. Here are the available methods:

- **Clean installation**: This method involves replacing the existing operating system on a hard disk with the new Windows Server 2025. It requires **user interaction**, although it may involve fewer steps than an upgrade.
- **Upgrade**: The upgrade method involves replacing the current operating system with Windows Server 2025 while preserving files and settings. This type of installation is known as an in-place upgrade, as it is performed on the same machine. Before proceeding with the upgrade, it is recommended that all important files and settings be backed up. You can perform an in-place upgrade if the server runs **Windows Server 2022, 2019, 2016, or 2012 R2**. Notably, Windows Server 2025 introduces the capability to directly upgrade from Windows Server 2012 R2 without running an intermediate upgrade, thus simplifying the transition process.
- **Migration**: This method involves transferring roles, features, applications, settings, and network services from an old server to a new server. The new server must have Windows Server 2025 installed to perform a migration. Before migrating, it is essential to ensure the existing applications are compatible with Windows Server 2025. The **Windows Server Migration Tool (WSMT)** can assist in the migration process, or you can use the appropriate cmdlets to migrate the necessary services.

- **Network installation (using MDT)***:* Organizations deploying multiple servers can benefit from using the **Microsoft Deployment Toolkit (MDT)**. Microsoft has deprecated **Windows Deployment Services (WDS)** in Windows Server 2025, so MDT is now the recommended tool for network installations. MDT must be downloaded and installed on a server to automate deployments of both desktops and servers. An unattended network installation is an automated installation method that requires minimal user interaction and can be performed using MDT. This type of installation is facilitated by an answer file and an XML file containing installation prompts. You can create an answer file using Notepad or find sample answer files available for download from the Internet.

- **Cloud installation***:* This method leverages the cloud capabilities of **Windows Server 2025 Datacenter: Azure Edition**. It allows seamless integration with Azure services, providing enhanced scalability, security, and management features. This installation option is ideal for organizations looking to deploy and manage their VMs in a cloud environment, taking advantage of the latest advancements in cloud technology.

Note: An unattended installation is a network installation option that automates the deployment process, requiring minimal user interaction. This method is ideal for deploying multiple servers in enterprise environments. Although Microsoft has deprecated WDS in Windows 11 and Windows Server 2025, the Windows Assessment and Deployment Kit (ADK) and MDT offer robust alternatives for automating installations. These tools are available for download from the following links: ADK from https://learn.microsoft.com/en-us/windows-hardware/get-started/adk-install and MDT from https://www.microsoft.com/en-us/download/details.aspx?id=54259.

These various installation methods provide flexibility and cater to different deployment scenarios when installing Windows Server 2025. Additionally, Windows Server 2025 introduces enhanced features and improved technologies, ensuring a more efficient and secure installation process.

Getting to know installation options

In the preceding section, you were introduced to various installation methods for Windows Server 2025. Now, let us shift our focus to the diverse installation options available. It is crucial to comprehend the distinction between installation methods and options to ensure a successful installation of Windows Server 2025 or any operating system. Windows Server 2025 presents three distinct installation options, and the choice of option will impact the availability of roles and features. Therefore, it is imperative to carefully consider the following options before deciding:

- **Desktop experience***:* This installation option includes all the features of Windows Server 2025. However, your hardware must fully meet the minimum system requirements to utilize the **graphical user interface (GUI)** fully.

- **Server core:** Microsoft recommends this option as it utilizes fewer hardware resources and enhances security. Roles and features can be installed on the local server using **Windows PowerShell** or remotely through **Server Manager**.
- **Nano Server**: An alternative to Server Core, Nano Server offers greater efficiency in terms of updates and reboots, and it has a smaller server image size, allowing more disk space for other purposes. Nano Server prioritizes enhanced security and improved performance. However, it has limitations: it only supports 64-bit applications and cannot function as a standalone server. Instead, it must operate within another host as a container. Nano Server lacks local login access and can only be managed remotely. It is often regarded as a "set and forget" installation option.
- **Containers**: Windows Server 2025 supports containers, offering a lightweight and isolated application environment. These containers encompass the complete **Windows APIs and system services**, making them ideal for consistent application deployment and management across various environments. They enhance scalability, security, and efficiency, facilitating rapid application deployment and streamlined management.

These installation options provide flexibility and cater to different deployment scenarios when installing Windows Server 2025. Additionally, Windows Server 2025 introduces enhanced features and improved technologies, ensuring a more efficient and secure installation process.

Conclusion

In this chapter, we have covered the installation process of Windows Server 2025. Before the installation, you gained insights into partition schemes, boot options, and installation methods. These methods, including clean installation, in-place upgrade, migration, network installation via MDT, and cloud deployment of Windows Server 2025 on VMs, cater to various scenarios such as installing on new or existing servers, upgrading from previous versions of Windows Server, migrating services to Windows Server 2025, and deploying it in an automated manner within an enterprise network.

Furthermore, we explored the installation options: Desktop Experience, Server Core, Nano Server, and Containers. Each option has its characteristics and suitability, depending on your specific requirements. To reinforce your understanding, hands-on exercises were included, such as setting up virtual switches and VMs in Hyper-V Client and performing a Windows Server 2025 installation.

This chapter presents all the information necessary to prepare you for the upcoming chapter, which will explore post-installation tasks in Windows Server 2025 In the next chapter, you will explore the initial configuration tasks of Windows Server 2025, including managing devices and drivers, reviewing the registry and service status, and configuring the server.

Exercise 3.1: Setting up Virtual Switches in Hyper-V Client

A switch is a fundamental component in computer networking at the layer 2 level. It connects computers and other devices within a **local area network (LAN)**, whether in a home or workplace environment. Additionally, switches can be employed to expand networks and accommodate more devices. These switches possess multiple physical ports, known as switch ports, where network cables are inserted to establish connections and construct the network infrastructure. Switches utilize a star physical topology and a logical bus topology to facilitate forwarding frames between computers.

There are two main categories of switch types: unmanaged and managed. Unmanaged switches function independently without configuration options, while managed switches offer more control and administration capabilities.

Furthermore, virtual networks, like physical networks requiring computers to connect, require virtual switches to link VMs. Hyper-V, a virtualization platform, provides three types of virtual switches:

- **External switch***:* This type connects to a physical network adapter, enabling VMs to access and communicate with the external physical network and connect to other devices and resources.
- **Internal switch:** This type operates exclusively within the confines of the physical server. It facilitates communication between the VMs and the physical server itself. However, it does not provide direct access to the external physical network or other devices outside the server.
- **Private switch***:* This type is isolated and accessible only to the VMs residing within the physical server. It creates a private network environment exclusively for communication between the VMs within the server without external network connectivity.

By utilizing these different types of virtual switches, administrators can establish the desired level of connectivity and isolation for their virtualized environments, enabling effective communication and network management for the VMs.

To create a virtual switch on the Hyper-V Client in Windows Server 2025, follow these steps:

1. Click the **Start** button in **Windows 11** to open the **Start** menu.
2. Search for **Hyper-V Manager** in the **Start** menu and **launch** it.
3. Once **Hyper-V Manager** is open, click **Virtual Switch Manager...** in the **Actions** pane on the right side of the **Hyper-V Manager**, as shown in *Figure 3.3*:

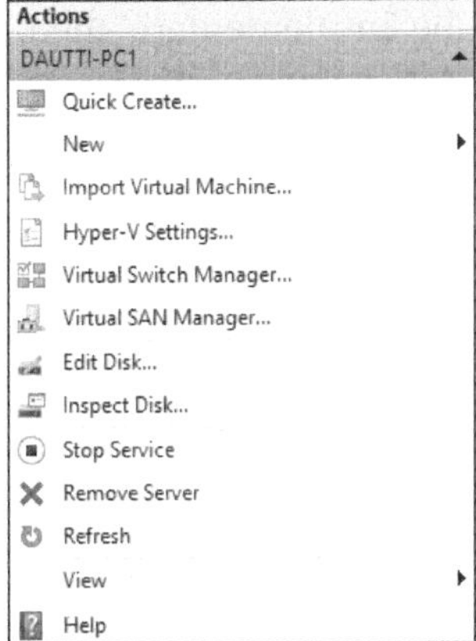

Figure 3.3: *Selecting Virtual Switch Manager in the Actions pane of Hyper-V Manager*

4. In the **Virtual Switch Manager** window, select **External Virtual Switch** and click **Create Virtual Switch**.
5. Name the virtual switch **Internet**, select the **network adapter** you want to use and click **Apply**, as shown in *Figure 3.4*:

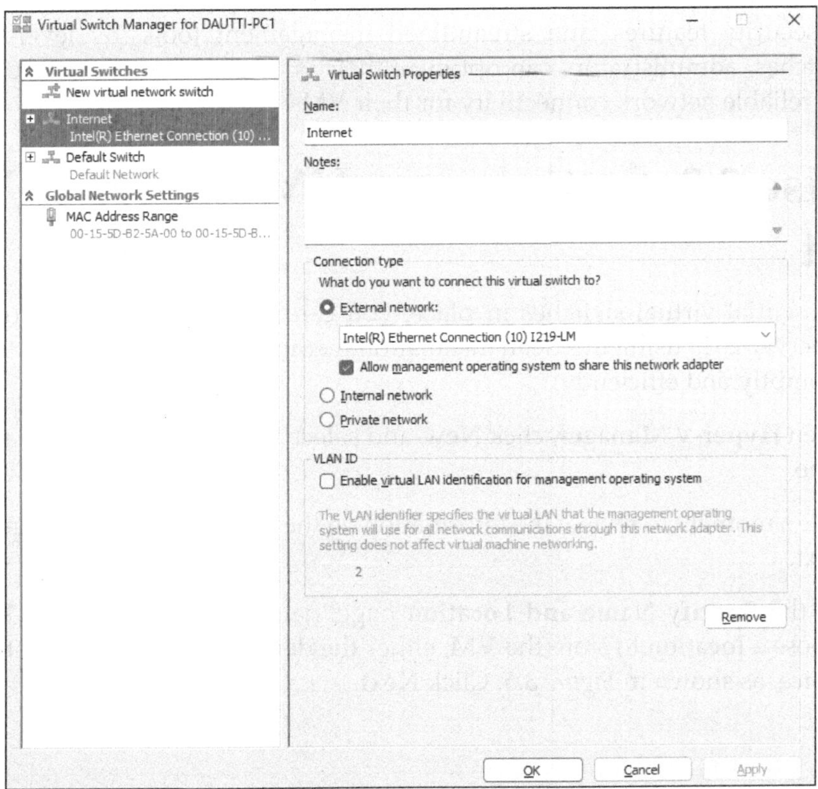

Figure 3.4: *Setting up the External virtual switch in Virtual Switch Manager*

6. Wait for the changes to be implemented, then select the new **virtual network switch** in the **Virtual Switches** pane.
7. Choose **Internal Virtual Switch** and click **Create Virtual Switch**.
8. Name the virtual switch **Intranet**, select **Internal network** as the connection type, then click **OK**.

After completing these steps, you will observe two virtual switches configured in the Hyper-V Manager: Internet and Intranet. The Internet virtual switch will facilitate communication between the physical server and the VMs. In contrast, the Intranet virtual switch will be exclusively utilized for communication among the VMs.

Configuring these virtual switches creates distinct communication pathways within the Hyper-V environment. The Internet switch facilitates connectivity between the VMs and the external network, enabling them to access and interact with external resources by leveraging the Internet connection. Conversely, the Intranet switch is dedicated to seamless communication and interaction exclusively among the VMs within the server. This segregation of roles allows for efficient management of the networking aspects of your virtualized environment, ensuring secure and effective data exchange.

Windows Server 2025 enhances these capabilities with improved network performance, advanced security features, and streamlined management tools. By leveraging these virtual switches, administrators can optimize their virtualized infrastructure, providing robust and reliable network connectivity for their VMs.

Exercise 3.2: Setting up a VM in Hyper-V Client

With the essential virtual switches in place, you can now create the VM for installing Windows Server 2025 using the clean installation method. Follow these steps to configure the VM promptly and efficiently:

1. Open **Hyper-V Manager**, click **New,** and select **Virtual Machine** from the **Actions** pane.
2. Take a moment to review the information on the **Before You Begin** page, then click **Next**.
3. On the **Specify Name and Location** page, name the VM `WinSrv2k25-DC1` and choose a **location** to store the **VM**, either the default location or a location of your choice, as shown in *Figure 3.5*. Click **Next**.

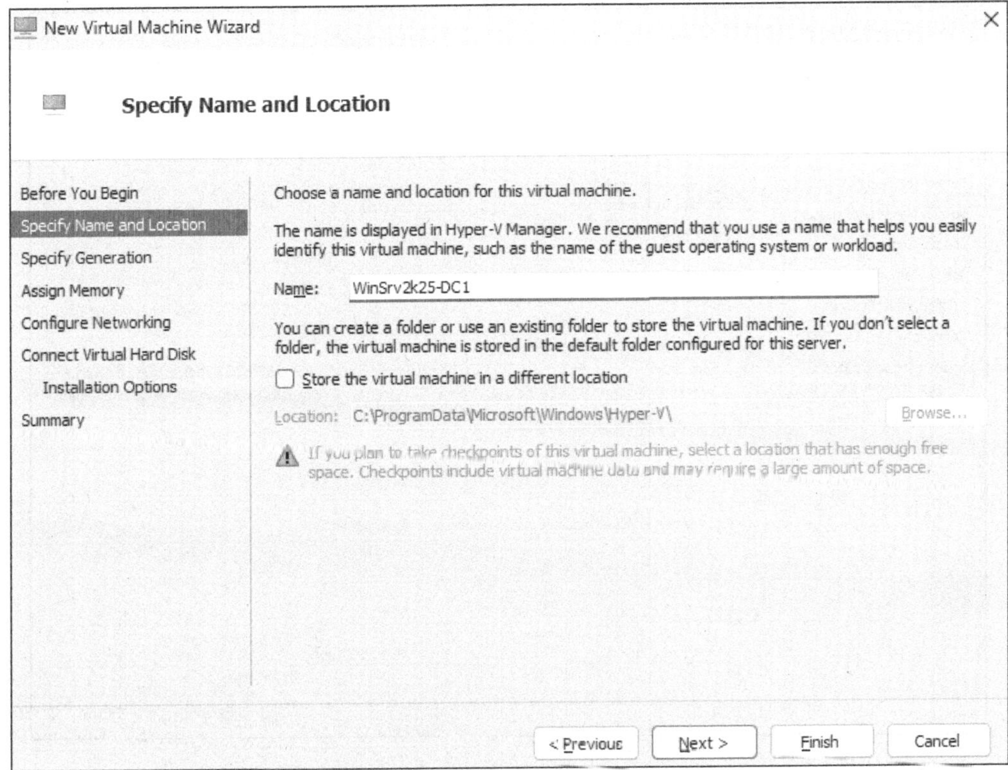

***Figure 3.5:** Specifying the name and location of the VM*

4. On the **Specify Generation** page, ensure the **Generation 1** option is selected (as this is a test environment), then click **Next**.

5. On the **Assign Memory** page, enter **4096** for the **Startup Memory** value and keep **Use Dynamic Memory** selected. Then click **Next**.

6. Choose the **Internet** virtual switch on the **Configure Networking** page and click **Next**.

7. On the **Connect Virtual Hard Disk** page, keep the virtual hard disk's default name (**`.vhdx`**) and set the disk size to **35 GB**. Keep the default location and click **Next** when finished.

8. On the ***Installation Options*** page, choose **Install** an operating system from a bootable CD/DVD-ROM, then select the **Image file (`.iso`)** option. Next, click **Browse** to locate the *Windows Server 2025 evaluation* .iso file you downloaded. Click **Next** when done.

9. Review the information in the **Description** section, as shown in *Figure 3.6*, to ensure everything is correct, then click **Finish** on the **Completing the New Virtual Machine Wizard** page.

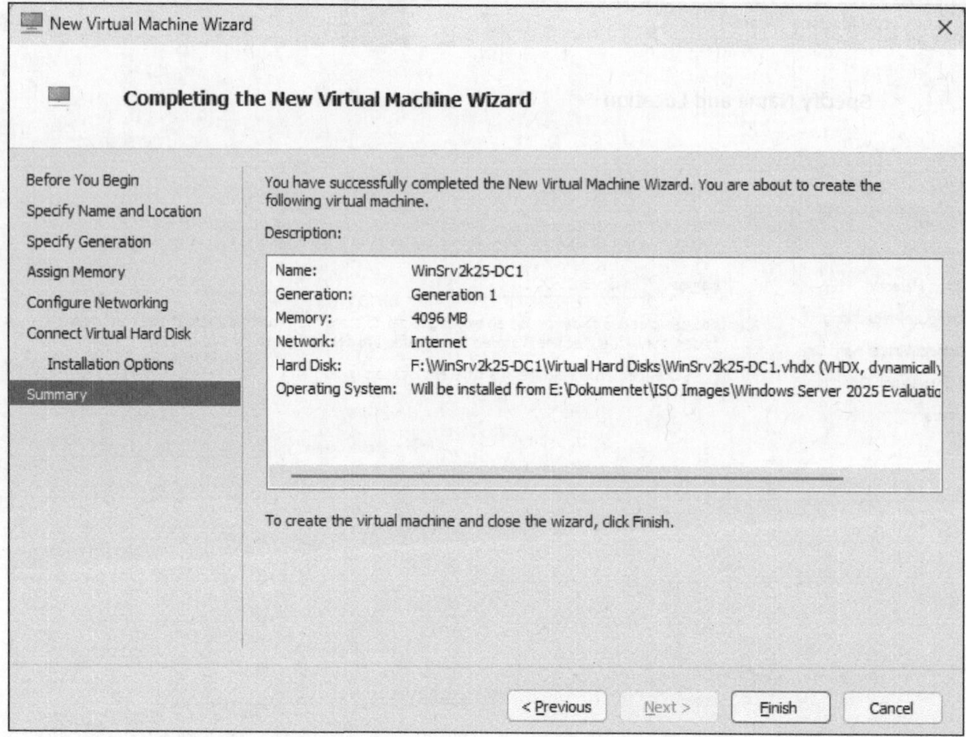

Figure 3.6: Reviewing the entries in Completing the New Virtual Machine Wizard page

Before installing Windows Server 2025, some essential tasks must be completed to ensure a smooth installation process. Firstly, it is necessary to turn off the **Checkpoint** feature in Hyper-V, which creates restore points or snapshots of VMs. Disabling Checkpoints ensures that previous snapshots or restore points do not interfere with installation.

A new network adapter must be added to the VM where Windows Server 2025 will be installed. This network adapter will be connected to the **Internet** virtual switch, which facilitates communication between VMs and is like an organization's LAN. Connecting the VM to the **Internet** virtual switch enables it to establish network connectivity and communicate with other VMs within the virtual environment.

These steps ensure that the installation of Windows Server 2025 proceeds smoothly, without any interference from previous Checkpoints, and allow the VM to connect to the "Internet" virtual switch for efficient communication with other VMs.

To turn off Checkpoints and add a new network adapter to the VM, follow these steps:

1. In the **Virtual Machines** pane of the **Hyper-V Manager**, right-click on *WinSrv2k25_DC1* and select **Settings**.
2. In the *VM's Settings* window, navigate to the **Management** section and select **Checkpoints**, as shown in *Figure 3.7*:

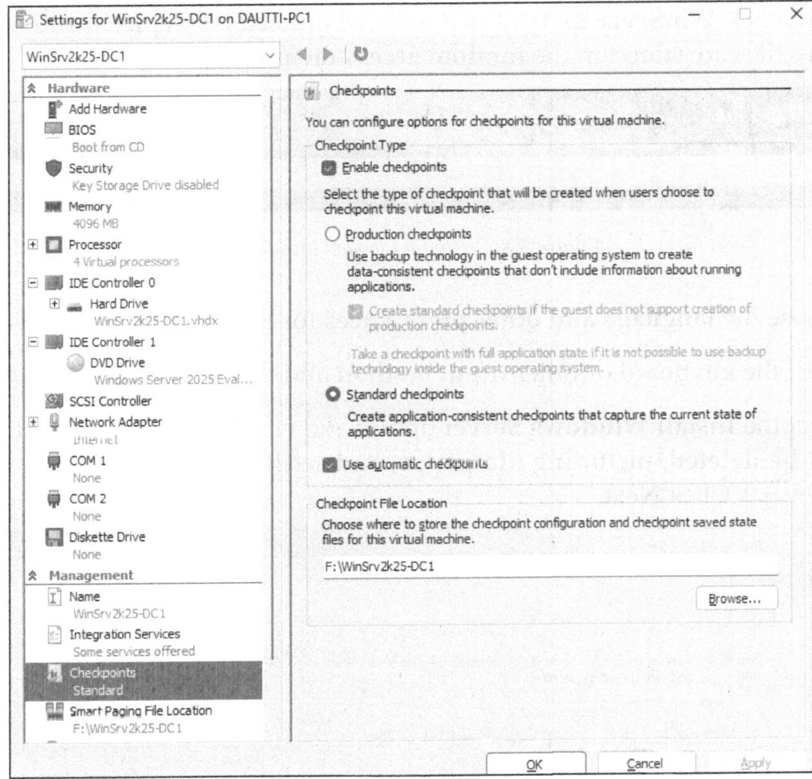

Figure 3.7: Turning off Checkpoints and adding a new network adapter

3. Within the same **Management** section, uncheck the **Enable checkpoints** box. Then click the **Apply** button.
4. At the top of the **Settings** window, go to the **Hardware** section and select **Add Hardware**. From the list, choose **Network Adapter**, and then click the **Add** button.
5. Select **Intranet** as the **virtual switch** for this network adapter and click **OK**.

By following these steps, you will ensure that the installation of Windows Server 2025 proceeds without any interference from previous Checkpoints and that the VM is connected to the **Intranet** virtual switch for efficient communication with other VMs.

Exercise 3.3: Performing Windows Server 2025 installation

Once all the necessary steps have been completed, it is time to install Windows Server 2025. To perform a clean installation, please follow these steps:

1. In the **Virtual Machines** pane of the **Hyper-V Manager**, right-click on **WinSrv2k25_DC1** and select **Start**.

2. Right-click **WinSrv2k25_DC1** and select **Connect**. As depicted in *Figure 3.8*, the setup files are stored in the **random access memory (RAM)**.

Figure 3.8: Setup files loaded into RAM

3. Choose the **language and other preferences** for the **installation**, then click **Next**.
4. Select the **keyboard** or other **input method** and then click **Next**.
5. Select the **Install Windows Server** option and ensure that **I agree that everything will be deleted, including files, apps, and settings** box, is **checked**, as shown in *Figure 3.9*. Click **Next**.

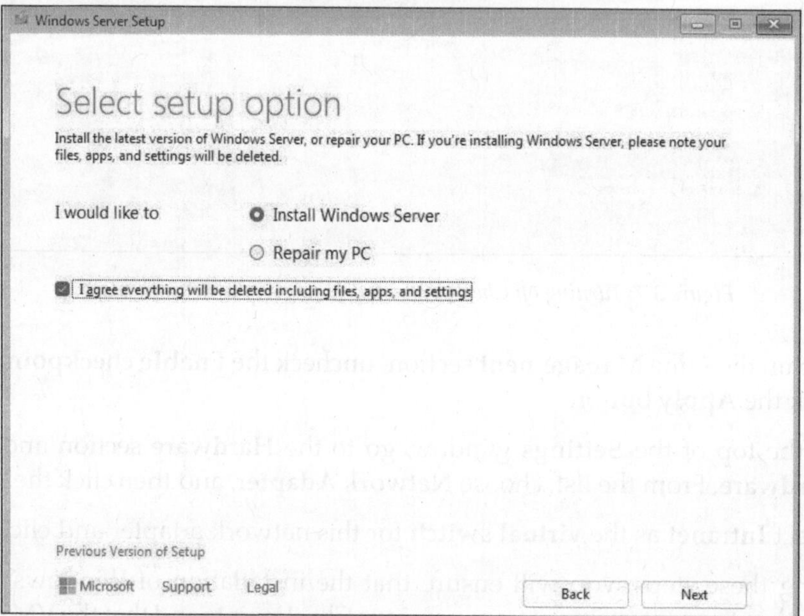

Figure 3.9: Setting up Windows Server 2025

6. Please take the time to **read** the **applicable notices and license terms** before clicking **Accept**.
7. Choose a **disk** or **partition** to install **Windows Server 2025**. Click **Next**.
8. Click the **Install** button on the **Windows Server Setup** wizard's **Ready to Install** page.
9. **Windows Setup** will begin **installing Windows Server 2025**. You can sit back and relax during this process.

10. After the server restarts a few times and the installation is complete, set up an administrator's password and click **Finish**, as shown in *Figure 3.10*:

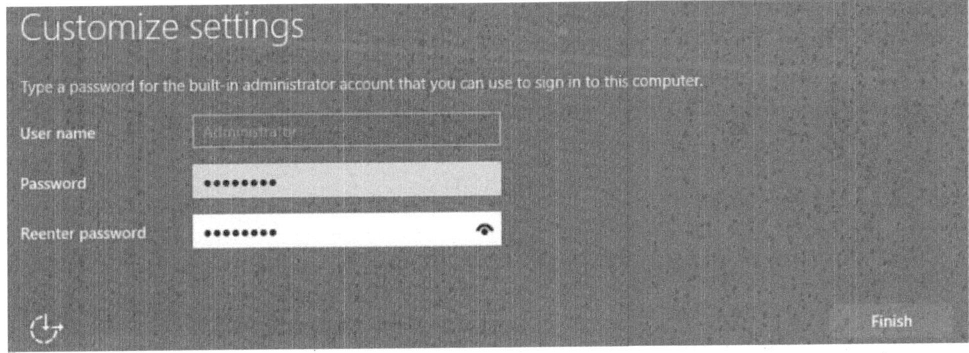

***Figure 3.10:** Configuring the Administrator password*

11. Press *Ctrl* + *Alt* + *Delete* to unlock the system. Enter the **administrator password** and press *Enter* to log in for the first time.
12. Select your **preferred choice** in the **Send diagnostic data to Microsoft** section and click **Accept**.
13. Congratulations! You have successfully installed Windows Server 2025, as shown in *Figure 3.11*:

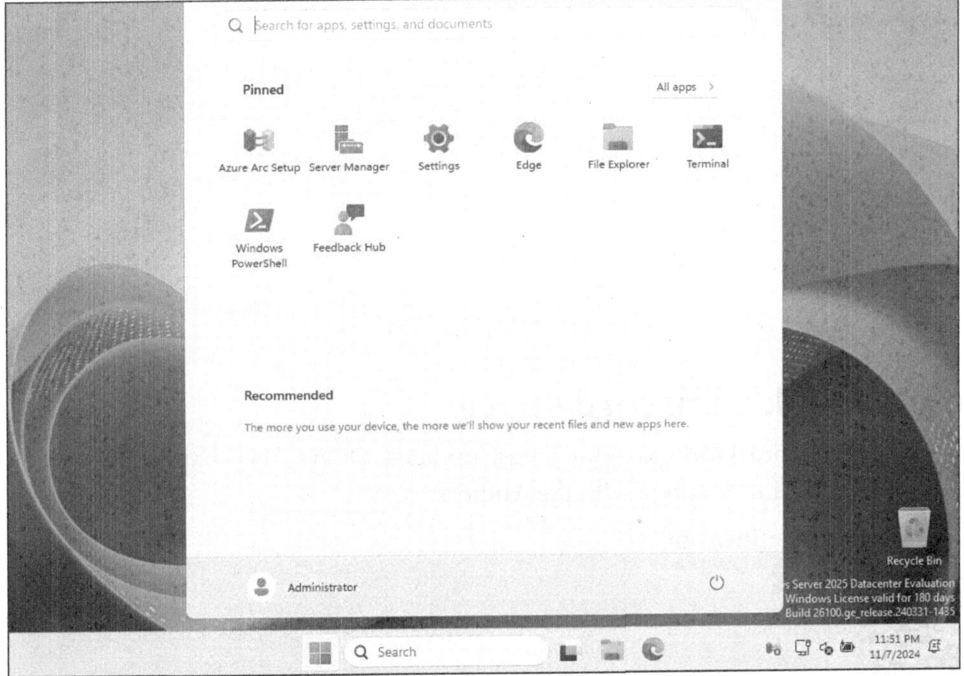

***Figure 3.11:** Windows Server 2025 Start menu and Desktop interface*

With Windows Server 2025 now installed, you are ready to explore its new features and capabilities. This powerful operating system offers enhanced security, improved performance, and advanced management tools, making it an ideal choice for modern enterprise environments. As you proceed to the next chapter, you will delve into post-installation tasks and configurations to optimize your server for your specific needs. Enjoy the journey of mastering Windows Server 2025!

Questions

1. What are the two primary partition schemes typically used in computers and servers?
2. What is the boot option?
3. Can you provide the names of installation methods?
4. What installation options should be considered before installing Windows Server 2025?
5. What is the purpose of a virtual switch in Hyper-V?

Join our book's Discord space

Join the book's Discord Workspace for Latest updates, Offers, Tech happenings around the world, New Release and Sessions with the Authors:

https://discord.bpbonline.com

Chapter 4
Initial Configuration of Windows Server 2025

Introduction

This is a gentle reminder that the book is structured around the **Installing and Configuring Windows Server 2025** project. So far, this book has introduced you to network components, explained what Windows Server is, and guided you through the installation of Windows Server 2025. After installing the server, the next step is to configure its services. However, before diving into this task, you will need to learn about the initial configuration tasks of Windows Server 2025, such as managing devices and drivers, checking the registry and service status, and configuring the server. Just like the previous chapters, this chapter will provide detailed instructions and practical exercises to help you understand and perform various aspects of the initial configuration of Windows Server 2025. This includes configuring the server's name, remote access settings, IP address, time zone, server updates, and more. The goal is to guide you through the process and demonstrate how to do it step by step.

Structure

The chapter will cover the following topics:

- Overview of devices and device drivers
- PnP, IRQ, DMA, interrupts, and driver verification

- Understanding the registry and services
- Describing registry entries, service accounts, and dependencies
- Initial configuration of Windows Server 2025

Objectives

This chapter aims to provide clear explanations and instructions for post-installation tasks and the initial configuration of Windows Server 2025. The post-installation tasks section will cover essential topics such as managing devices and drivers, **Plug and Play (PnP)**, IRQ, DMA, interrupts, driver signing, registry and services, registry entries, service accounts, and dependencies. The initial configuration section will offer step-by-step instructions for hands-on exercises, including setting up the IP address, changing the time zone, activating Windows Server 2025, and many more tasks in an understandable and straightforward format. The goal is to guide you through the process and demonstrate how to perform these tasks step by step, ensuring you have a solid foundation for effectively managing and configuring Windows Server 2025.

Overview of devices and device drivers

Exploring the interaction between computer hardware and software is fascinating because hardware encompasses more than just physical components; the operating system is a collection of programmed instructions. For the operating system to communicate with the physical components, it requires a translator known as a device driver. The device driver manages and operates the hardware, which can be obtained through installation media or downloaded from the manufacturer's website.

Suppose you recently purchased a device that did not include installation media with a device driver. That is okay because modern operating systems like Windows 10 and 11 support PnP. However, when working with Windows Server 2025, you will likely need to download the device driver from the manufacturer's website.

Since this book focuses on Windows Server 2025, the Settings app is the new administrative console for managing devices. The legacy applet used to work with device drivers is **Device Manager**. It is essential to remember that in Device Manager, depending on the status of the device driver, there are additional representations aside from the standard presentation of device drivers. Let us examine the various statuses of the device driver in Device Manager, as illustrated in *Figure 4.1:*

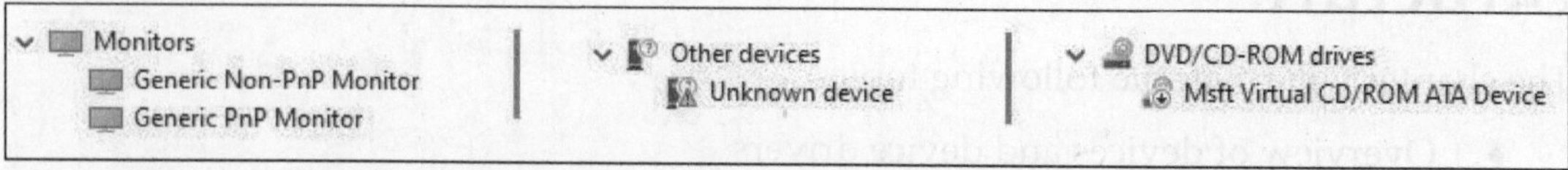

Figure 4.1: *Various statuses of device drivers in Device Manager*

If we refer to the exact figure and analyze the statuses of the device drivers from the left-hand side to the right-hand side, we encounter the following situations:

- If a device driver's status is **Generic**, an alternative driver has been installed instead of the appropriate one.
- If there is a **black exclamation mark on a yellow triangle**, it means either the device driver is missing, or the installed device driver is unsuitable.
- If there is a **black downward arrow**, it means the device is disabled.

PnP, IRQ, DMA, interrupts, and driver verification

A **computer system** is composed of hardware and software, with the operating system requiring system resources to manage the hardware components such as the CPU, memory, disk, input/output devices, and network connections. System resources refer to the various hardware and software components utilized to perform tasks and provide services within a computer system. These resources can be broadly categorized into two types: **hardware resources** and **software resources**. For example, **Interrupt Request (IRQ)** and **Direct Memory Access (DMA)** are essential system resources that the operating system must manage to efficiently utilize computer hardware, along with I/O ports and memory addresses. The following will explore these concepts in greater detail:

- **PnP** originated from a collaboration between Intel and Microsoft. This technology has significantly simplified the process of working with devices and drivers. With PnP, connecting a device to a computer becomes seamless; the Windows operating system detects the device as soon as it is plugged in. The device driver is then installed from the Driver Store, which in Windows Server 2025 is located at **`C:\Windows\System32\DriverStore`**.
- As illustrated in *Figure 4.2*, an IRQ is a signal sent by a device through communication channels to the computer's processor, indicating that it requires attention to perform a task. In modern computers, an IRQ is represented by a numerical value between 0 and 31.

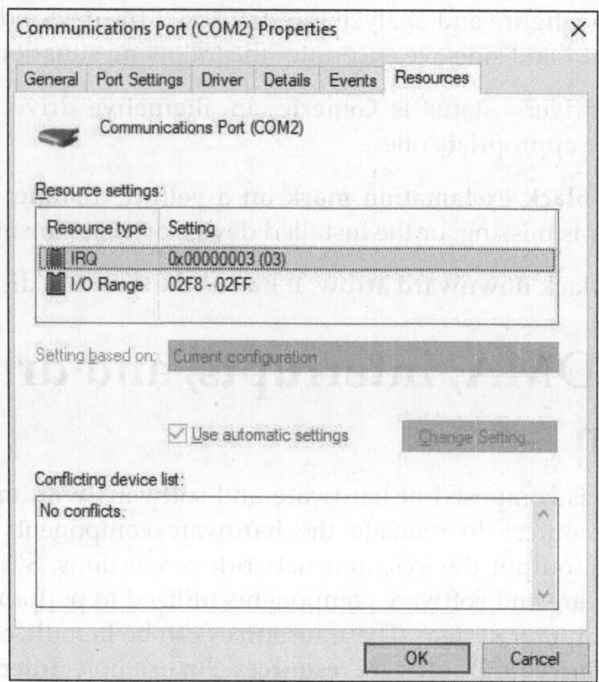

***Figure 4.2:** A Communications Port (COM2) IRQ settings*

- **DMA** is a technique for transferring data between devices and the computer's memory without the direct involvement of the CPU. This method is beneficial for devices quickly transmitting large amounts of data, such as disk drives, network adapters, and video cards. In Windows Server 2025, DMA is assigned a value between 0 and 8.
- **Driver signing** involves adding a digital signature to device drivers to ensure their authenticity and integrity, as illustrated in *Figure 4.3*. This digital signature acts as a unique identifier attached to the driver package, verifying that it has not been altered since it was signed. Additionally, the signature confirms that Microsoft has tested and approved the driver package, reducing the risk of reliability and security issues during installation.

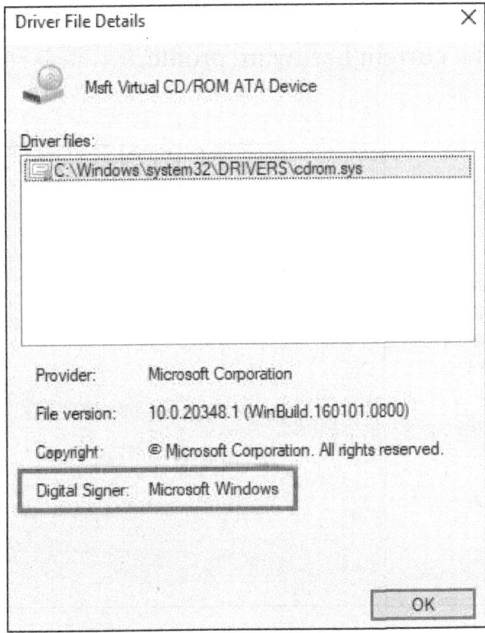

Figure 4.3: *Digitally signed driver*

Understanding the registry and services

The **Windows Registry** and **Windows services** are fundamental components of the Windows operating system. The Windows Registry is a hierarchical database that stores the Windows OS's configuration settings and system information. It is a critical element of the Windows environment, containing details about installed hardware, software, and user preferences. The registry is organized into five primary hives, or HKEYs, as illustrated in *Figure 4.4*. These hives are divided into subkeys and values that can be accessed and modified using the Registry Editor tool. The registry plays a pivotal role in the operation of Windows, and any changes can significantly impact the operating system's behavior and installed applications. These hives follow the standard Windows file path syntax, separated by a backslash, and Windows Server 2025 includes the following five hives:

- **HKEY_CLASSES_ROOT:** Stores details about installed applications and their file extensions.
- **HKEY_CURRENT_USER:** Contains information related to the currently logged-in user.
- **HKEY_LOCAL_MACHINE:** Holds information specific to the local computer, including hardware and software configuration settings.
- **HKEY_USERS:** Contains information about the profiles of all currently logged-in users.

- **HKEY_CURRENT_CONFIG:** Stores information collected during the boot process, such as the current hardware profile.

Refer to *Figure 4.4:*

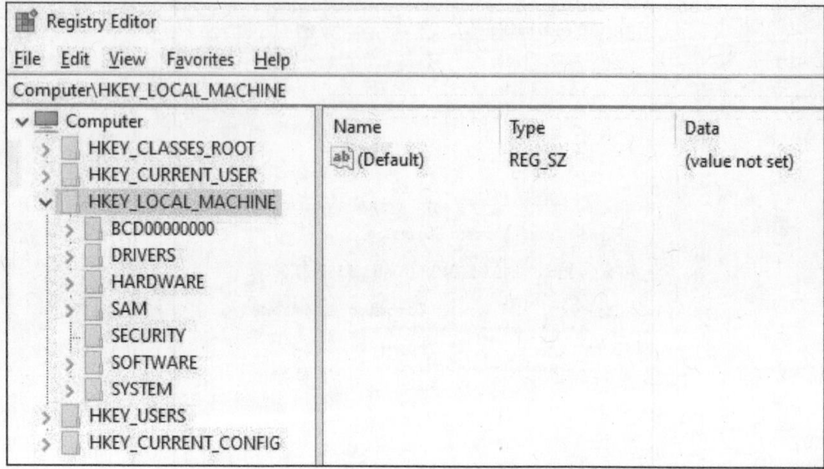

Figure 4.4: *Windows Registry in Windows Server 2025*

In Windows Server 2025, the Windows Registry remains a critical component for managing the configuration settings and system information, ensuring the operating system functions efficiently and reliably. Additionally, Windows Server 2025 introduces enhanced features and improved technologies to streamline registry management and automation further.

Windows services explained

In any computer system, background programs or services (*Figure 4.5*) operate behind the scenes to support applications and network services. These services can be managed using the **Services Control Manager**, which allows you to start, stop, restart, or pause them. When accessing services through the Services Control Manager, you will notice that each service has a startup type, which can be one of several options. For example, there are four different startup types for services:

- **Automatic:** The service automatically starts when the operating system boots up.
- **Automatic (Delayed Start):** The service will start approximately two minutes after all other marked-as-automatic services have started.
- **Manual:** The service must be started by a user or other dependent services.
- **Disabled:** The service cannot be started by the operating system, a user, or dependent services.

Refer to *Figure 4.5:*

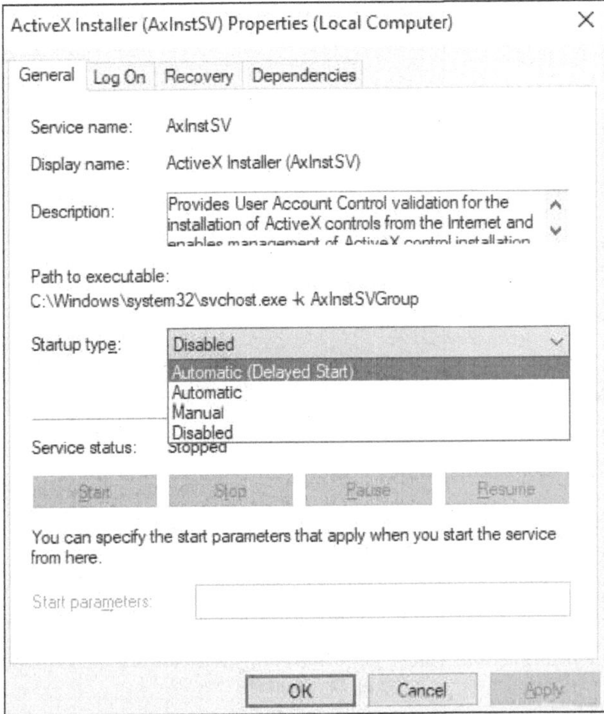

Figure 4.5: *Windows Service startup types*

In Windows Server 2025, these startup types remain crucial for managing service behavior and performance, ensuring the system operates efficiently and reliably. Additionally, Windows Server 2025 introduces enhanced features and technologies to streamline service management and automation further.

Describing registry entries, service accounts, and dependencies

You may need to create a new registry key or value when making changes or adding new features to a Windows Server. A registry entry can represent a specific setting or configuration value for a component or application installed on the system. Information stored in a registry entry can include file paths, program settings, user preferences, and system configurations. Registry entries are organized into a hierarchical structure, with each entry organized into a key containing one or more subkeys and values. As shown in *Figure 4.6*, Windows Registry entries can be added, modified, or deleted using the Registry Editor tool or through programmatic interfaces provided by the Windows API. However, it is essential to be cautious when working with Windows Registry entries, as any changes can significantly impact the operating system's behavior and installed applications. In

Windows Server 2025, the Windows Registry remains critical for managing configuration settings and system information, ensuring the operating system functions efficiently and reliably.

Refer to *Figure 4.6:*

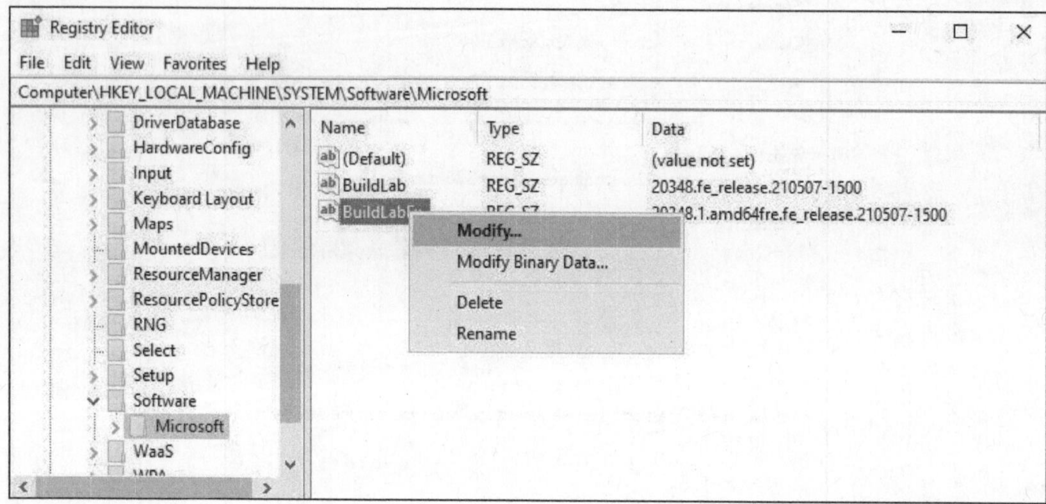

Figure 4.6: *Various actions can be performed on entries within the Windows Registry*

Additionally, **Windows services**, as illustrated in *Figure 4.7*, utilize service accounts, either native Windows Server accounts or user-created accounts, to manage running services. These service accounts enable services to access local and network resources, providing necessary security and authentication. Each service can use a different service account, and you can choose from various types of service accounts, such as built-in system accounts or user-created accounts with specific permissions. In Windows Server 2025, there are several native accounts available for services to run, as follows:

- **Local System:** This is a built-in account in Windows Server with the highest privileges and access to system resources. Often referred to as a superuser account, it has more power than any user account, including administrative accounts.
- **NT Authority\LocalService:** Another built-in account in Windows Server that runs system services and some applications with limited privileges, equivalent to those of a regular user account in the "Users" group.
- **NT Authority\NetworkService:** This built-in account in Windows Server runs system services and some applications with more privileges than the LocalService account but fewer privileges than the Local System account.

Refer to *Figure 4.7:*

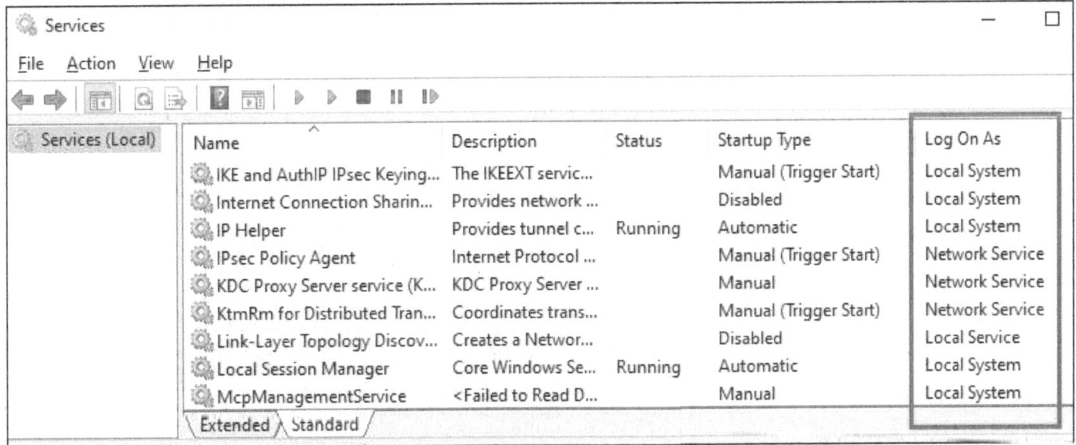

Figure 4.7: *Several built-in systems accounts in Windows Server 2025*

In Windows Server 2025, these service accounts remain crucial for managing service behavior and performance, ensuring the system operates efficiently and reliably.

Initial configuration of Windows Server 2025

Performing a server's initial configuration is a critical task that impacts its functional state before it assumes any roles. Based on experience, the initial configuration should begin with setting up the IP address, changing the time zone, and activating Windows Server 2025. Following this, it is necessary to check for updates, change the default server name, join the domain, and enable Remote Desktop. These steps ensure the server is configured correctly and ready to fulfill its intended role within the IT infrastructure.

In Windows Server 2025, two tools can be used to perform the initial configuration:

- **Server manager:** This Windows Server tool provides a centralized interface for managing servers, their roles, and features. It allows administrators to perform various management tasks, such as adding or removing server roles and features, configuring settings, and monitoring server performance. Server Manager has been included in Windows Server versions since Windows Server 2008 and is designed to simplify server management for administrators. For example, when logging into Windows Server 2025, Server Manager, depicted in *Figure 4.8,* will automatically start and will continue to do so unless the configuration is changed.

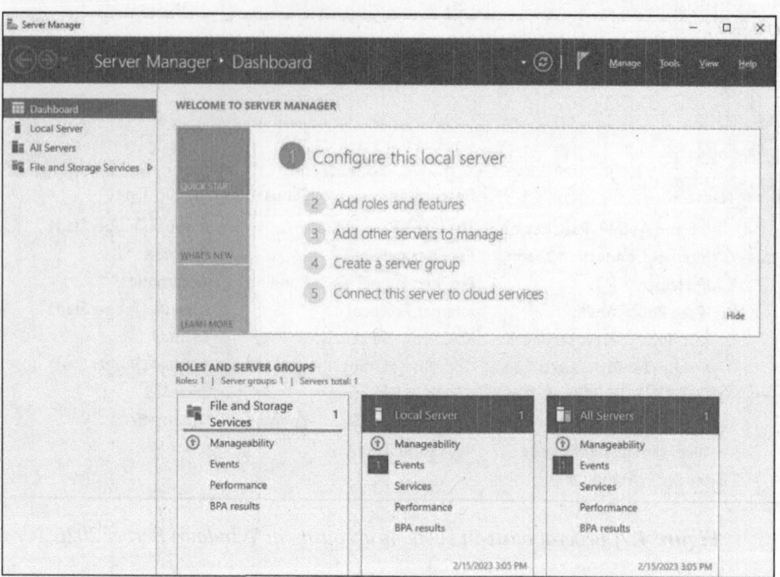

Figure 4.8: Server Manager in Windows Server 2025

- **Server Configuration** is a Windows Server **command-line** (**CMD**) tool that can perform essential Server Configuration tasks on a Server Core installation option. This tool provides a straightforward menu-driven interface, enabling administrators to configure various settings such as network settings, domain membership, and Windows Update settings. The tool is designed to simplify Server Configuration on Server Core installations, which do not include a **graphical user interface** (**GUI**). As illustrated in *Figure 4.9*, Server Configuration is available on all Windows Server editions and can be accessed from the command prompt by running the **`SConfig.cmd`** command.

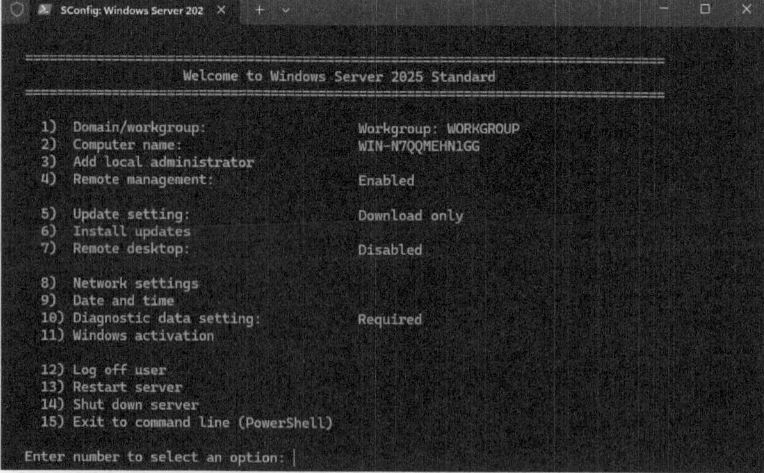

Figure 4.9: Server Configuration in Windows Server 2025

Conclusion

In this chapter, you explored various tasks that must be completed after installing Windows Server 2025, including managing device drivers, registries, and services. You also learned about the organization of hardware components within a computer system and the role of device drivers. Additionally, you gained insights into system resources, the Windows Server registry, and services. You became familiar with using the Registry Editor (regedit) to perform basic activities on the Windows Registry, such as adding, modifying, and deleting keys. Finally, you were introduced to the concept of initial Server Configuration and performed post-installation tasks as an exercise.

The next chapter will look at **Active Directory Domain Services** (**AD DS**) in Windows Server 2025, providing a comprehensive understanding of its features and functionalities.

Exercise 4.1: Device Manager access

To open Device Manager from the administrator's menu, follow these steps:

1. Right-click on the **Start** button to open the **administrator's menu.**
2. From the **administrator's menu**, choose **Device Manager**.
3. The **Device Manager** window will open soon, as shown in *Figure 4.10*:

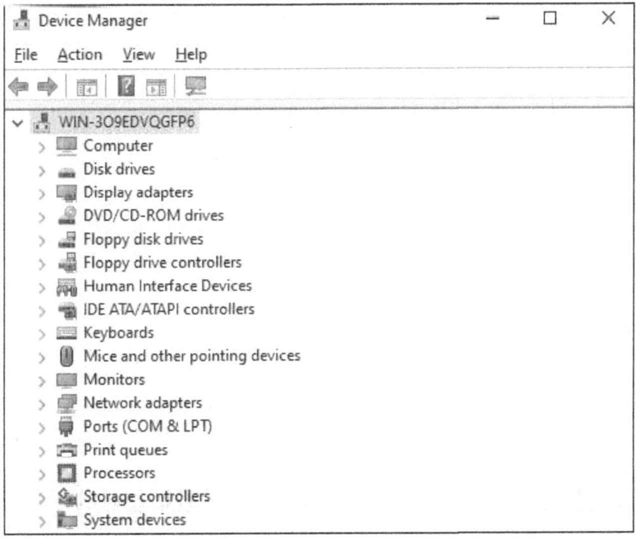

Figure 4.10: *Device Manager in Windows Server 2025*

Note: In addition to right-clicking on the Start button to access the administrator's menu, you can also use the Windows key + X combination. Similarly, you can use the Windows key + I combination to open Windows Settings. For example, open Device Manager or enter `devmgmt.msc` in the Run dialog box.

If you encounter technical difficulties with a device driver, there are several troubleshooting options available:

- **Updating the driver:** You can update the driver automatically or manually browse the server for the appropriate driver software.
- **Rolling back the driver:** If the current driver is causing issues, you can roll back to a previous version.
- **Disabling the driver:** You can disable the driver if the driver is causing significant problems, such as server instability.
- **Uninstalling the driver:** If you have identified the correct driver from the device manufacturer, you can uninstall the current driver.

  Refer to *Figure 4.11*:

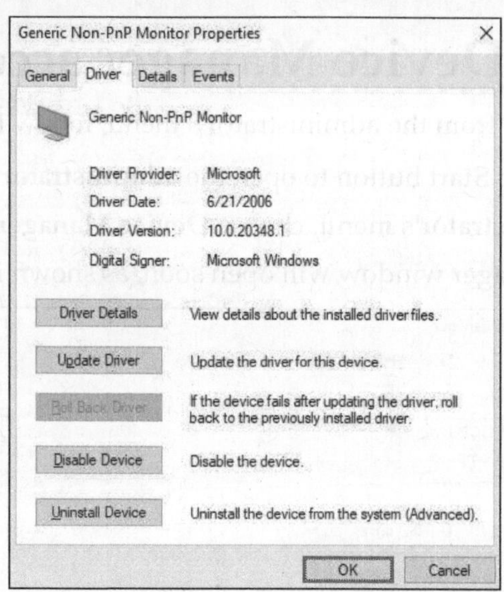

Figure 4.11: *Troubleshooting device drivers using Device Manager*

Windows Server 2025's troubleshooting steps remain essential for maintaining system stability and performance.

Exercise 4.2: Configuring Server with Server Manager and Sconfig.cmd

This exercise aims to guide you through the initial setup of Windows Server 2025 using two methods: **Server Manager** and **Server Configuration**. It is essential to note that, depending on the tool being used, you must access it and follow the outlined procedures. For instance, when using Server Manager, you must select **Local Server** from the panel on the left-hand side.

Changing the server's name using Server Manager

To change the server's name, as shown in *Figure 4.12*, follow these instructions:

1. After opening **Server Manager** and selecting **Local Server**, click the link for the **computer name** in the **server's properties**.
2. Select the **Change** button in the **System Properties** window.
3. Click on the **Computer name** text box highlighted in the **Computer Name/Domain Change** window.
4. In the **Computer Name/Domain Changes** window, erase the current computer name, type in the **new server's name**, and click **OK**.

Refer to *Figure 4.12:*

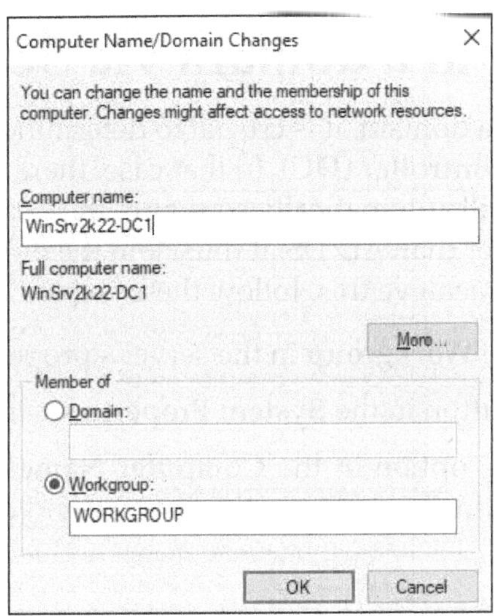

Figure 4.12: *Changing the name of the server using Server Manager*

5. Confirm that you want to restart the server to activate the changes by clicking **OK**.
6. Choose the Close button in the **System Properties** window.
7. Finally, click **Restart Now** in the **Microsoft Windows** dialog box.

Changing the server's name using the Server Configuration

To change the server's name, as shown in *Figure 4.13*, follow these instructions:

1. Type "**2**" in the **Server Configuration** menu prompt and hit *Enter*.
2. Input the **new server's name** and press *Enter*.

Refer to *Figure 4.13:*

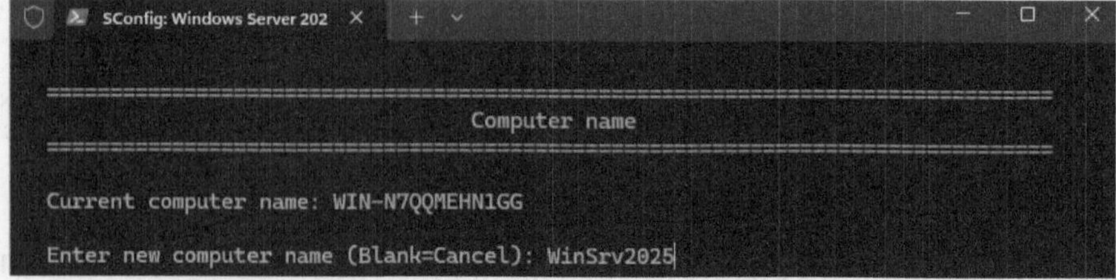

Figure 4.13: *Changing the name of the server using Server Configuration*

3. Click **Yes** in the **Restart** dialog box to restart the server.
4. The server will **restart** to implement the changes made to the **server's name**.

Joining a server to a domain via Server Manager

Before adding the server to a domain, it is crucial to determine its role. Suppose the server is designated as a **domain controller** (**DC**). In that case, there is no need to join a domain, as adding the AD DS role will automatically configure the server as a DC. However, if the server is assigned a role other than AD DS, it must join the domain as a member server, as illustrated in *Figure 4.14*. To achieve this, follow these steps:

1. Click the link for the **Workgroup** in the server's properties.
2. Click the **Change** button in the **System Properties** window.
3. Select the "**domain:**" option in the **Computer Name/Domain Changes** window, enter your organization's domain in the textbox, and click **OK**.

   Refer to *Figure 4.14:*

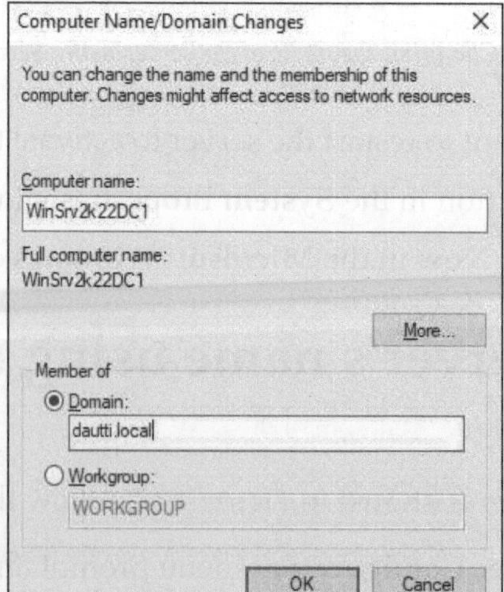

Figure 4.14: *Joining a domain using Server Manager*

4. In the **Windows Security** window, provide the name and password of an account with permission to join the domain, then click **OK**.
5. The **Computer Name/Domain Changes** dialog box will welcome the server to the organization's domain. Click **OK** to close it.
6. Click **OK** to confirm that the server needs to be **restarted** to apply these changes.
7. Click the **Close** button in the **System Properties** window.
8. Click **Restart Now** in the **Microsoft Windows** dialog box.

Joining a server to a domain via Server Configuration

To join a server to a domain, follow these steps as shown in *Figure 4.15*:

1. On the **Server Configuration** menu, select option "**1**" and press *Enter*.
2. Enter "**D**" to join the organization's domain and press *Enter*.
3. Type the **organization's domain** and press *Enter*.

Refer to *Figure 4.15:*

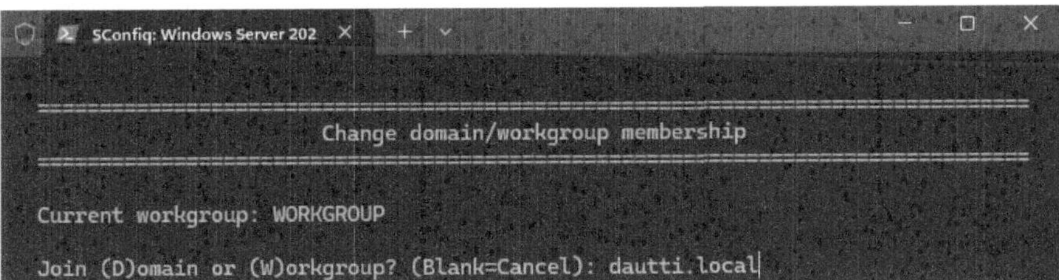

***Figure 4.15:** Joining a domain using Server Configuration*

4. Enter the **username** authorized to join the domain and press *Enter*.
5. Type the **password** for the authorized user and press *Enter*.
6. In the **Change Computer Name** dialog box, select **No** when asked to change the server's name.

Enabling Remote Desktop using Server Manager

To enable Remote Desktop, as shown in *Figure 4.16*, follow these steps:

1. Click the link for the **Remote Desktop** in the **server's properties**.
2. Click on the **Remote** tab in the **System Properties** dialog box.
3. Choose the **Allow remote connections to this computer** option in the **System Properties** window.

4. The **Remote Desktop Connection** dialog box will notify you that the **Remote Desktop firewall exception** will be activated. Press **OK** to close it.

   Refer to *Figure 4.16:*

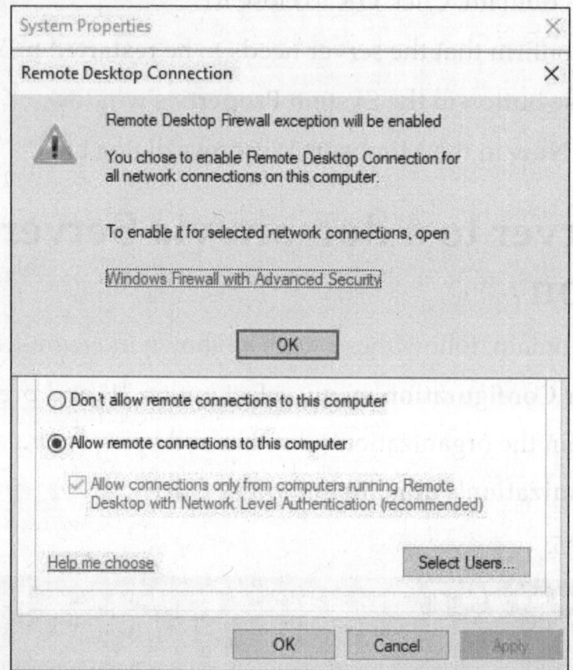

Figure 4.16: Enabling Remote Desktop using Server Manager

5. Click the **Select Users...** button to add **Remote Desktop** users.
6. In the **Remote Desktop Users** window, select **users or groups** from your **AD DS** and click the **Add** button to add them. Once you have finished adding users, press **OK** to close the window.
7. Finally, click **OK** to close the **System Properties** window.

Enabling Remote Desktop using Server Configuration

To enable Remote Desktop, follow these steps as shown in *Figure 4.17*:

1. Access the **Server Configuration** menu prompt and choose option 7 by typing "**7**" and pressing *Enter*.
2. Activate Remote Desktop by typing "**E**" and pressing *Enter*.
3. Choose a more secure access option by typing "**1**" and pressing *Enter*.

Refer to *Figure 4.17:*

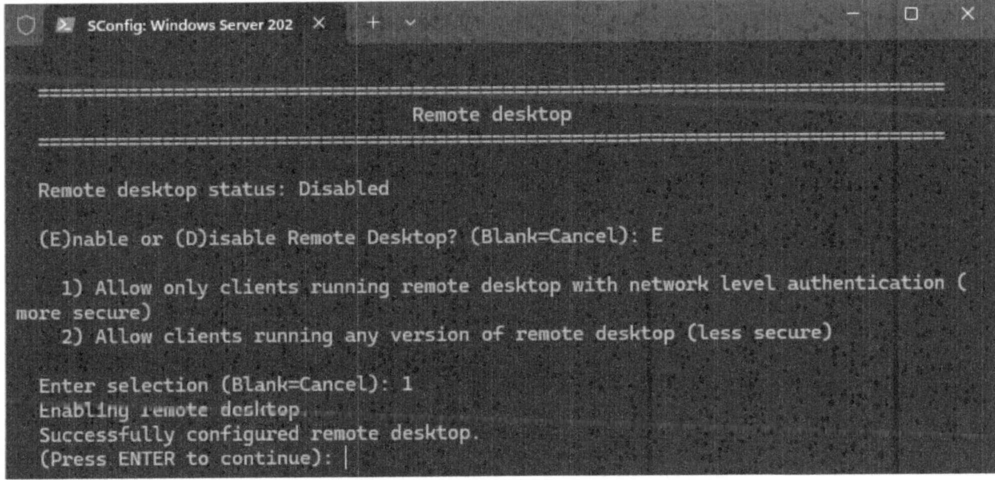

Figure 4.17: *Enabling Remote Desktop using Server Configuration*

4. In the **Remote Desktop** dialog box, click **OK** to verify that Remote Desktop is now enabled.

Setting up the IP address using Server Manager

To configure the IP address as shown in *Figure 4.18*, follow these steps:

1. Click the link for the **Ethernet** in the **server's properties**.
2. Right-click on the **Ethernet** setting of the server in the **Network Connections** window, then choose **Properties**.
3. Select **Internet Protocol Version 4 (TCP/IPv4)** in the **Ethernet Properties** window and click the **Properties** button.
4. In the **Internet Protocol Version 4 (TCP/IPv4) Properties** window, choose the **Use the following IP address** option and fill in the IP address, subnet mask, and default gateway fields. Also, select the **Use the following DNS server addresses** option and supply the **Preferred and Alternate DNS** server fields. Finally, click **OK** to save the changes.

Refer to the following *Figure 4.18:*

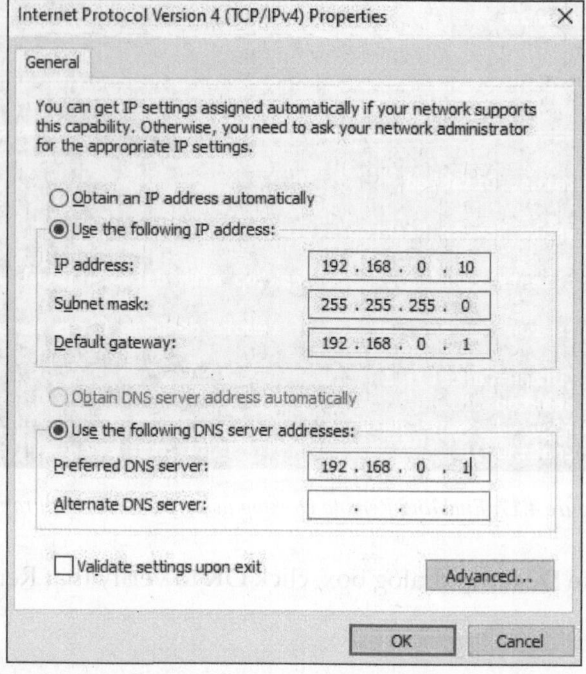

Figure 4.18: Setting up the IP address using Server Manager

5. Click on the **Close** button to exit the **Ethernet Properties** window.

6. Finally, click the **Close** button (the red X) in the upper-right corner to close the **Network Connections** window.

Setting up the IP address using Server Configuration

To configure the IP address for a network adapter, as shown in *Figure 4.19*, perform the following steps:

1. Access the **Server Configuration** menu and select option "8".

2. Specify the **network adapter number** you want to configure the IP address and hit *Enter*.

3. Enter "**1**" in the submenu to set the **network adapter address**, then press *Enter*.

4. Type "**S**" to select a **static IP address**, then press *Enter*.

5. Enter the **static IP address** and press *Enter*.

6. Enter the **subnet mask** and press *Enter*.
7. Enter the **default gateway** and press *Enter*.

   Refer to *Figure 4.19:*

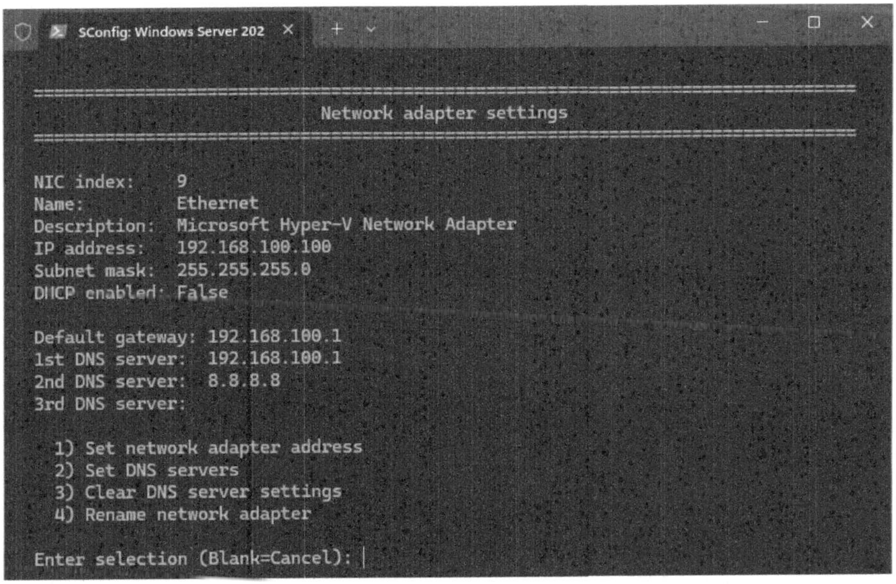

```
SConfig: Windows Server 202

==========================================================================
                         Network adapter settings
==========================================================================

NIC index:     9
Name:          Ethernet
Description:   Microsoft Hyper-V Network Adapter
IP address:    192.168.100.100
Subnet mask:   255.255.255.0
DHCP enabled:  False

Default gateway: 192.168.100.1
1st DNS server:  192.168.100.1
2nd DNS server:  8.8.8.8
3rd DNS server:

  1) Set network adapter address
  2) Set DNS servers
  3) Clear DNS server settings
  4) Rename network adapter

Enter selection (Blank=Cancel):
```

Figure 4.19: *Setting up the IP address using Server Configuration*

8. Enter "**2**" in the submenu to set the **DNS servers**, and press *Enter*.
9. Enter the **new preferred DNS server** and press *Enter*.
10. Click **OK** in the **Network Settings** dialog box to close it.
11. Enter the **alternate DNS server** and press *Enter*.
12. Enter "**4**" in the **submenu** to exit and return to the **main menu**.

Checking for updates using Server Manager

To check for updates, follow these steps as shown in *Figure 4.20*:

1. Click the link for the **last check for updates** in the **server's properties**.
2. The available updates (if any) are listed in the **Settings** window on the right-hand side of the **Windows Update** section. If updates are ready for installation, click the **Install Now** button.

Refer to *Figure 4.20:*

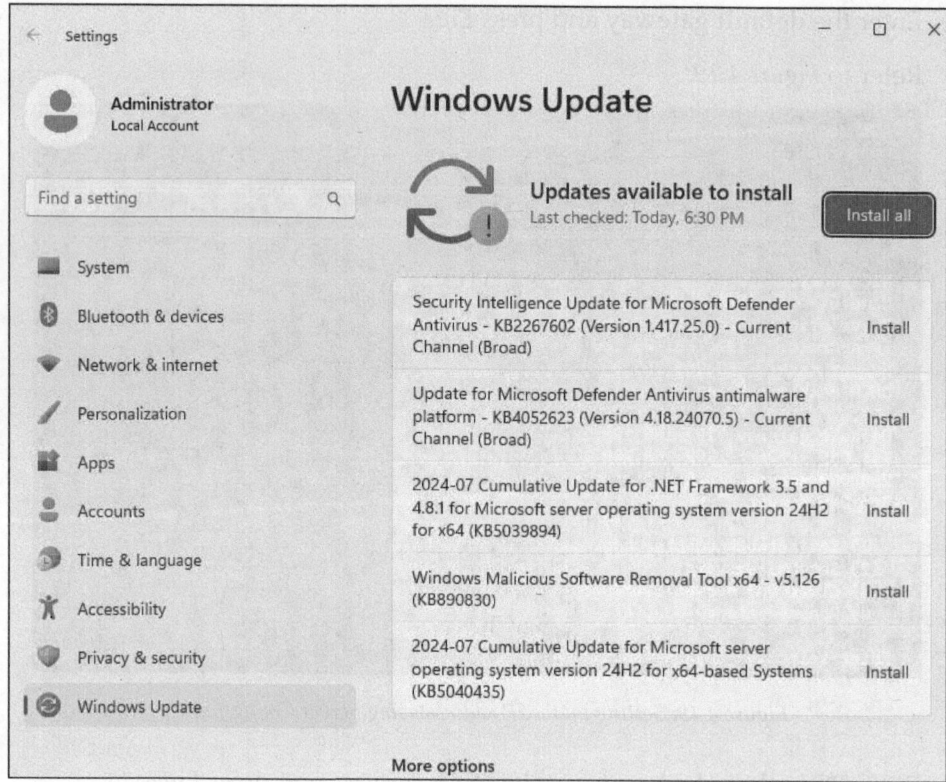

Figure 4.20: *Checking for updates using Server Manager*

3. Note that installing updates may take some time. Once the installation is **complete**, you may need to **restart the server** for the updates to take effect.

Checking for updates using Server Configuration

To check for updates, follow these steps shown in *Figure 4.21:*

1. Select option "**6**" in the **Server Configuration** menu prompt and press *Enter*.
2. Choose how you want to set the updates: **(1) Automatic, (2) Download, (3) Manual**, or **(5) Opt-in to Microsoft Update**. Then press *Enter*.
3. Wait while **Windows Update** searches for updates.
4. If updates are found, choose whether to install **all of them (A), none of them (N)**, or a **single one (S)**, then press *Enter*.

   Refer to the following *Figure 4.21:*

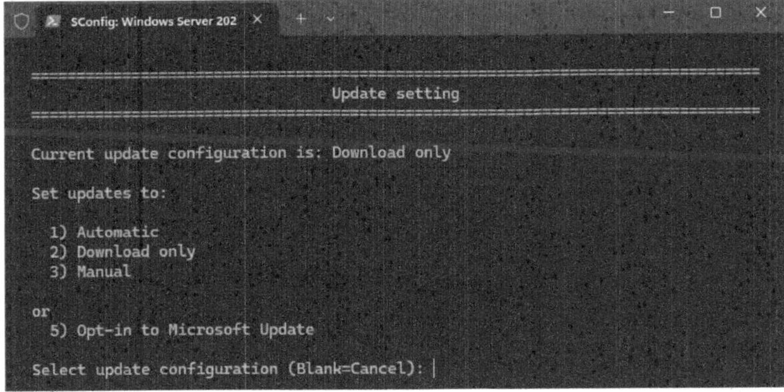

***Figure 4.21:** Checking for updates using Server Configuration*

5. After the updates are **downloaded**, they will be **installed automatically**. If prompted, click **Yes** to restart the server.

Changing the Time Zone using Server Manager

To adjust the time zone, follow these steps as shown in *Figure 4.22*:

1. Click the link for the **Time zone** in the **server's properties**.
2. Click the **Change time zone…** button in the **Date and Time** window.
3. Select your **time zone** from the drop-down list in the **Time Zone Settings** window.

   Refer to *Figure 4.22:*

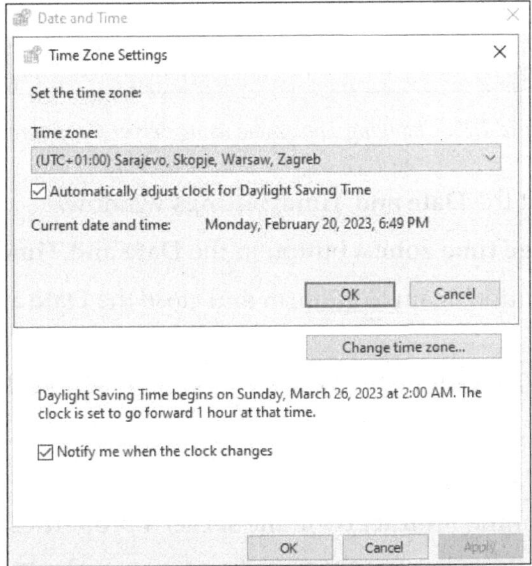

***Figure 4.22:** Changing Time Zone using Server Manager*

4. Close the **Time Zone Settings** window by clicking the **OK** button.
5. To complete the process, click **OK** again to close the **Date and Time** window.

Changing the Time Zone using Server Configuration

To change the time zone, do the following steps as illustrated in *Figure 4.23*:

1. Select "**9**" and press *Enter* in the Server Configuration menu prompt.
2. Click the **Change date and time...** button in the **Date and Time** window.
3. Choose the **Date or Time** section to adjust the time and date as needed.

   Refer to *Figure 4.23:*

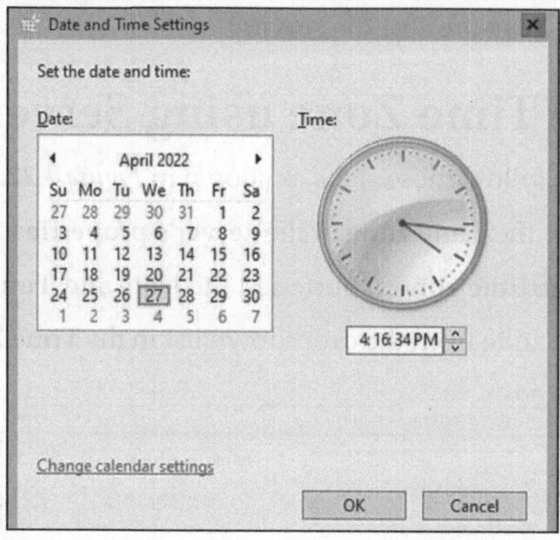

Figure 4.23: *Changing Time Zone using Server Configuration*

4. Click **OK** to exit the **Date and Time Settings** window.
5. Click the **Change time zone...** button in the **Date and Time** window.
6. Click the **OK** button again to confirm and close the **Date and Time** window.

Activating Windows Server using Server Manager

To activate your Windows Server 2025 (Desktop Experience) like the example shown in *Figure 4.24*, try with the following instructions:

1. Click the link for the **Product ID** in the **server's properties**.
2. Enter your **Windows Server 2025 product key** into the **Product key** text box and click **Next**.

Refer to *Figure 4.24:*

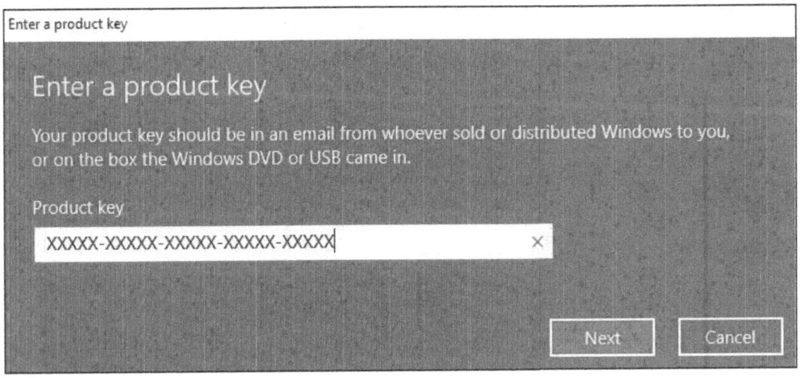

Figure 4.24: *Activating Windows Server 2025 using Server Manager*

3. **Microsoft's Activation Server** will **verify** the product key you entered. If **confirmed**, click **Next** in the **Activate Windows** window.
4. Once activation is complete, click **Close** to close the **Thank you for activating** window.

Activating Windows Server using Server Manager

To activate Windows Server 2025 (Server Core), as in *Figure 4.25*, follow these steps:

1. Select "**11**" in the **Server Configuration** menu prompt and press **Enter**.
2. Select option "**3**" in the sub-menu to install the product key and press *Enter*.

   Refer to *Figure 4.25:*

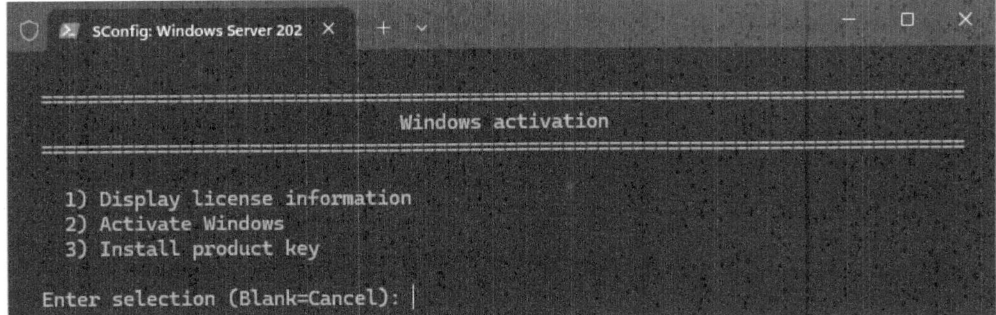

Figure 4.25: *Activating Windows Server 2025 using Server Configuration*

3. Enter the product key for **Windows Server 2025 (Server Core)** and press *Enter*.
4. Choose the option "**2**" in the sub-menu to activate Windows and press *Enter*.

5. Wait briefly until **Windows Server 2025 (Server Core)** is started, and then close the activation window by entering **Exit**.

In Windows Server 2025, these initial configuration steps remain crucial for ensuring that the server operates efficiently and reliably.

Questions

1. What are device drivers?
2. What is Windows Registry?
3. What is Windows service?
4. Why is initial configuration essential for Windows Server?
5. Which tools can you use to run the initial configuration in Windows Server 2025?

CHAPTER 5
Installing Roles Using Server Manager and PowerShell

Introduction

Welcome to this chapter on installing roles in Windows Server 2025. This chapter provides comprehensive, step-by-step instructions on installing roles using the Add Roles and Features Wizard available in the Server Manager of Windows Server 2025 and PowerShell. Roles are a set of features that enable the server to perform specific tasks, and by installing these roles, you can tailor your server to meet your organization's requirements. This chapter covers the roles available in Windows Server 2025, how to use the Add Roles and Features Wizard, and what additional features you may need to select for the role to function correctly. Additionally, the guidance provided in this chapter helps you configure the role to meet your organization's specific needs. The exercises in this chapter include instructions on installing **Active Directory Domain Services** (**AD DS**), **Domain Name System** (**DNS**), **Dynamic Host Configuration Protocol** (**DHCP**), Hyper-V, **Internet Information Services** (**IIS**), **Print and Document Services** (**PDS**), **Remote Access, Remote Desktop Services** (**RDS**), and **Windows Server Update Services** (**WSUS**), using both Server Manager and PowerShell. By including PowerShell, the installation process becomes even more accessible and flexible, allowing you to choose the method that best suits your preferences and expertise. This chapter aims to provide an easy and efficient way to install roles in Windows Server 2025. Whether you prefer using Server Manager or PowerShell, you can customize your server to meet your organizational needs.

Structure

The chapter will cover the following topics:

- Understanding role, role service, and feature
- Understanding the Active Directory Domain Service role
- Exercise 5.1: Adding AD DS role
- Understanding the Domain Name System role
- Exercise 5.2: Adding DNS Server role
- Exploring the DHCP Role
- Exercise 5.3: Adding DHCP Server role
- Understanding Hyper-V
- Exercise 5.4: Adding Hyper-V role
- Use of a Web Server role
- Exercise 5.5: Adding Web Server role
- Getting to know the Print and Document Services role
- Exercise 5.6: Adding PDS role
- Unique features of the Remote Access role
- Exercise 5.7: Adding Remote Access role
- Need for a Remote Desktop Services role
- Exercise 5.8: Adding Remote Desktop Service role
- Understanding Windows Server Update Services role
- Exercise 5.9: Adding Windows Server Update Services role

Objectives

The primary objective of this chapter is to provide comprehensive guidance on installing roles in Windows Server 2025. This is achieved through detailed, step-by-step instructions and clear explanations on using the Add Roles and Features Wizard in Server Manager and PowerShell to install various roles such as AD DS, DNS, DHCP, Hyper-V, IIS, PDS, Remote Access, RDS, and WSUS. Additionally, this chapter aims to help readers understand the purpose of each role and configure them to meet their organization's specific needs. By the end of this chapter, readers will have acquired the necessary skills and knowledge to install roles effectively and customize their Windows Server 2025 efficiently, allowing them to tailor it to their organizational requirements.

Understanding role, role service, and feature

Understanding the server's intended function is crucial to correctly adding a role within an organization's IT infrastructure. In Windows Server 2025, a server role defines the server's primary function. Ideally, a server should have a single primary role, although it can perform multiple roles if necessary. Therefore, when adding a role to the server, selecting the appropriate hardware based on the server's intended function is essential.

In addition to adding roles, there are instances when role services need to be added to enhance the functionality of the role. Role services are supplementary features that provide additional capabilities to a role. For example, suppose an organization requires an Internet print server. In that case, it will add the PDS role to the server and then include Internet Printing as a role service to augment its functionality.

Furthermore, server features are added to support specific functions. For instance, the .NET Framework 3.5 feature may need to be installed to support the added role or the **IP Address Management (IPAM)** feature may be required to support the DHCP or DNS roles within the organization's network infrastructure. Additionally, adding a WINS server alongside DNS may be necessary to resolve issues arising from NetBIOS name resolution in routed environments. These are just a few examples of situations where server features may need to be added.

Understanding the Active Directory Domain Services role

AD DS is a crucial component of the Windows Server **operating system** (**OS**), introduced by Microsoft in 2000. Before the release of Windows 2000 Server, the primary mechanism for managing Windows-based networks was the **Primary Domain Controller** (**PDC**) and **Backup Domain Controller** (**BDC**) architecture of Windows NT. AD DS was designed to replace this outdated architecture, providing a more efficient, scalable, and secure way of managing networks.

AD DS is a distributed database that stores objects such as users, computers, peripheral devices, and network services in a hierarchical, structured, and secure format. These objects are uniquely identified by their names and attributes, making them easily searchable and manageable. The network topology of AD DS is divided into domains, forests, and trees, each representing a logical network division.

AD DS's most significant benefit is its ability to provide **Organizational Units (OUs)**, allowing administrators to manage objects more efficiently. **Group Policies (GP)** can be applied to these OUs, simplifying the management and configuration of settings across multiple objects. Additionally, AD DS supports the delegation of administrative control, enabling administrators to delegate specific tasks to non-administrative users, thereby enhancing network management security.

AD DS utilizes several protocols to perform its functions, including:

- **Lightweight Directory Access Protocol (LDAP):** Used to access directory services data.
- **Kerberos:** Provides a mechanism for authenticating users and servers on the network.
- **Domain Name System:** Translates domain names into IP addresses.

In Windows Server 2025, AD DS continues to be a vital component, with enhanced features and improved technologies to further streamline network management and ensure that your server operates efficiently and securely.

Active Directory consoles

As previously explained, **Active Directory** (**AD**) is a system that provides centralized management for various services, simplifying administrative tasks by offering a unified platform for managing different aspects of its services. In **Microsoft Management Console (MMC)**, several administrative consoles, also known as snap-ins, can be used to manage AD services. The following will explore these snap-ins in greater detail:

- **Active Directory Administrative Center (`dsac.exe`):** As shown in *Figure 5.1*, this is the primary administrative console, providing a **graphical user interface** (**GUI**) for managing Windows Server's directory services. It offers a convenient way to perform administrative tasks related to user management, computer management, OUs, and other relevant information.

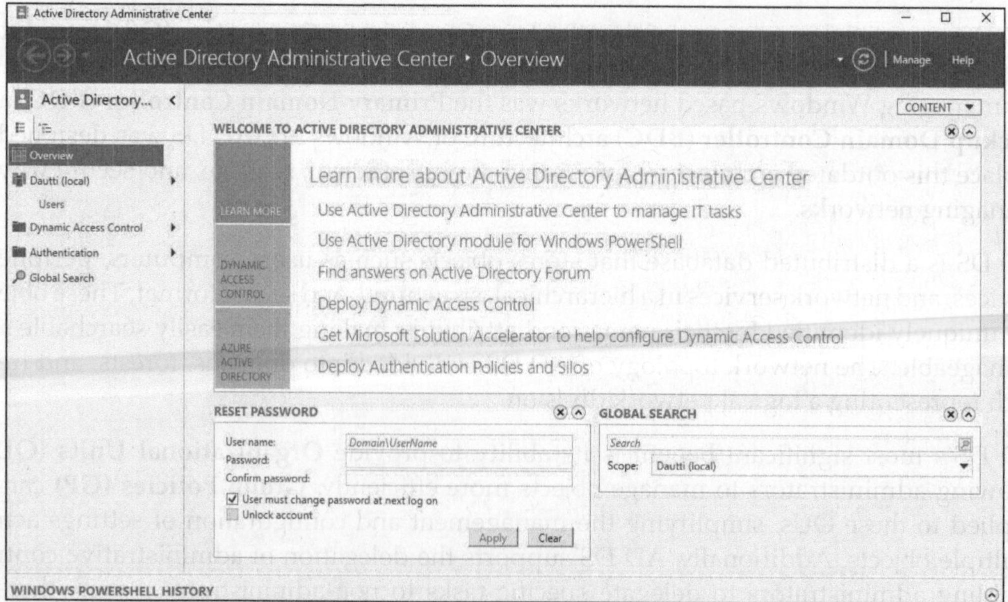

Figure 5.1. The Active Directory Administrative Center in Windows Server 2025

- **Active Directory Users and Computers (`dsa.msc`):** This administrative console is specifically designed to manage users, computers, OUs, and related information. It provides comprehensive tools and options to efficiently handle user accounts, group memberships, computer objects, and other AD-related operations.
- **Active Directory Domains and Trusts (`domain.msc`):** This console manages domains, trusts, and associated information. It allows administrators to configure trust relationships between domains, manage domain properties, and perform tasks related to domain management.
- **Active Directory Sites and Services (`dssite.msc`):** This console manages replication and services between different sites in an AD environment. It enables administrators to control the replication of directory data between **domain controllers** (**DCs**) located on various sites, ensuring efficient data synchronization and availability.
- **Active Directory Module for Windows PowerShell:** In addition to graphical consoles, this module provides a **command-line interface** (**CLI**) for managing Windows Server's directory services. Typically installed using the Add Roles and Features Wizard, as shown in *Figure 5.2*, it offers a set of cmdlets (commands) that allow administrators to perform various administrative tasks efficiently through scripting or direct command execution.

In Windows Server 2025, these tools remain essential for efficient and reliable management of directory services.

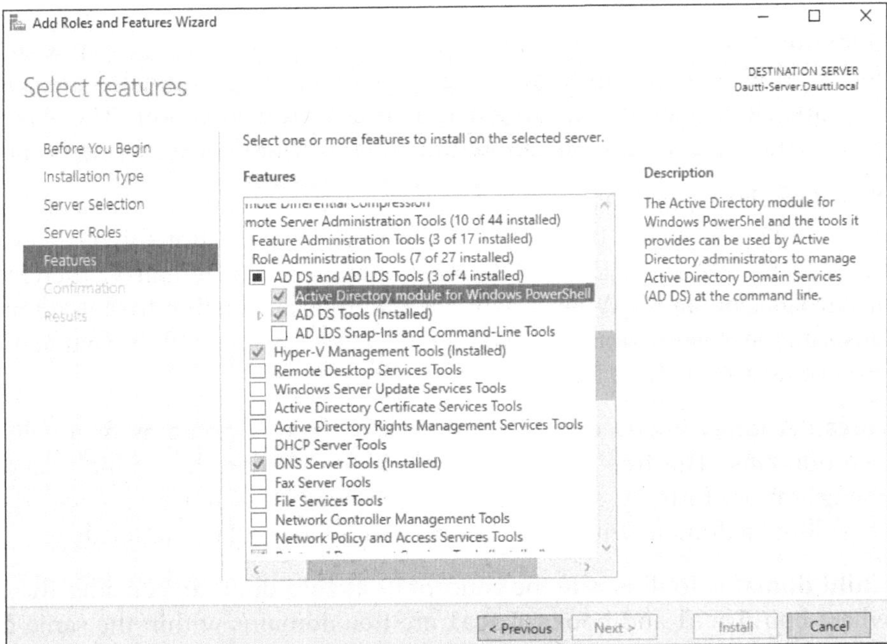

Figure 5.2: *Adding Active Directory module for Windows Powershell in Windows Server 2025*

These administrative consoles in the MMC provide administrators with diverse options for managing different aspects of AD services, including user and computer management, domain and trust administration, site and service management, and PowerShell-based administration.

AD structure

AD is a powerful and flexible directory service provided by Microsoft, serving as the backbone of many enterprise networks. It offers a centralized and secure way to manage and organize resources such as users, computers, and network services. AD utilizes a hierarchical structure consisting of forests, trees, and domains to efficiently manage and control access to network resources. Understanding this structure is crucial for effectively configuring, securing, and maintaining an AD environment. Within this structure, various components such as DCs, trust relationships, replication, and schema play essential roles in ensuring seamless authentication, data synchronization, and efficient management of network resources. Let us look into these components to understand how AD functions and empowers organizations to streamline network operations:

- **Domain controller:** A DC server securely authenticates users to access an organization's network resources. In the past, there were PDCs and BDCs in Windows NT, where each domain had one PDC and other DCs acted as backups. However, in Windows Server 2025, the concepts of primary and backup are no longer used. Instead, DCs are identified by numbers, such as DC1 and DC2, to indicate their order.
- **Domain:** A domain is a logical grouping of users, computers, peripheral devices, and network services. In terms of network architecture, domains are centralized network environments where a DC handles authentication. The AD DS role powers the DC and authentication functions in Windows Server-based networks.
- **Tree domain:** In an AD structure, multiple domains can be organized into a tree domain. Domains in a tree are interconnected through transitive trust, meaning that if Domain A trusts Domain B and Domain B trusts Domain C, then Domain A also trusts Domain C. When a new domain joins an existing tree, it automatically trusts all the existing domains. Configuring a new domain within a tree is done by promoting a server to a DC.
- **Forest:** A forest in AD consists of one or more tree domains or a collection of tree domains. The tree domains within a forest share a common schema and configuration, forming a contiguous namespace. This means the tree domain is considered a domain within the forest, creating a circular relationship.
- **Child domain:** To illustrate the concept of a child domain, consider the example where `bpb.local` and `books.local` are tree domains within the same forest. In this scenario, `bpb.local` is the root domain and represents the entire forest. The

domain **`marketing.bpb.local`** is a child domain of the **`bpb.local`** tree domain. This establishes a parent-child relationship, similar to a tree data structure, where the root domain is at the top and child domains branch out from it. This hierarchical structure allows for efficient organization and management of resources within the AD environment. The parent-child relationship ensures that child domains inherit certain properties and trust relationships from their parent domains. For example, if **`bpb.local`** trusts another domain, **`books.local`**, then **`marketing.bpb.local`** will also trust **`books.local`** due to the inherited trust relationship. This transitive trust mechanism simplifies the management of trust relationships and enhances security within the forest. By organizing domains into a hierarchical structure with parent and child domains, AD provides a scalable and flexible way to manage network resources, user accounts, and security policies across an organization.

- **Flexible Single Master Operation (FSMO) roles:** When the AD DS role is installed, and a server is promoted to a DC, AD DS automatically assigns FSMO roles. The first two roles, the master schema and domain naming master, are forest-wide operations. The remaining three roles, **relative identifier** (**RID**), PDC emulator, and infrastructure master, are specific to the tree domain. The master schema and domain naming master manage AD's schema, ensuring only one unique domain exists within the forest. The RID assigns **security identifiers** (**SIDs**) to DCs, the PDC emulator handles password updates, and the infrastructure master tracks changes to other domain objects.
- **Trust relationships:** Trust relationships exist between computers, DCs, and domains in AD. When a computer joins a domain, its local **Security Account Manager** (**SAM**) trusts the AD's authentication mechanism, Kerberos, on a DC. This means that user authentication occurs through a DC on the network, not locally on the computer's SAM. Similarly, the authentication mechanism of each tree domain trusts the authentication mechanisms of other trusted tree domains within the forest. For example, the **`bpb.local`** domain authenticates users from the **`user.local`** domain, and this authentication is accepted by the **`books.local`** domain because they are part of the same forest, with **`bpb.local`** as the root domain.
- **Forest Functional Level (FFL) and Domain Functional Level (DFL):** The FFL determines which versions of Windows Server can be used in the DCs of the entire forest, and it also enables specific capabilities across all domains within the forest. On the other hand, the DFL controls the versions of Windows Server that can be run on the DCs of a specific domain and enables capabilities within that domain only. In the context of Windows Server 2025, it is recommended that the DFL and FFL be set to at least Windows Server 2016 to ensure compatibility and take advantage of the features and improvements offered by newer versions of Windows Server. It is worth noting that the DFL and FFL can be raised to Windows Server 2025 to leverage the latest features and enhancements.

In Windows Server 2025, AD DS continues to be a vital component, with enhanced features and improved technologies to further streamline network management, ensuring that your server operates efficiently and securely.

Note: Please be aware that Windows Server 2025 introduces its own functional level. The highest available functional level is Windows Server 2025.

- Referring back to the previous example, the domain **`bpb.local`** serves as both a forest and a root domain simultaneously. Within this forest, **`bpb.local`** and **`books.local`** are tree domains. Additionally, the **`bpb.local`** tree domain other than **`marketing.bpb.local`** child domain contains another child domain named **`programming.bpb.local`**. The child and tree domains share a **common namespace**. This arrangement is known as a **contiguous namespace**. To better understand namespaces, one can draw a parallel with **Uniform Resource Locators (URLs)**, which are unique web addresses used to locate websites on a Web Server.
- In AD, there are **physical and logical topologies**. A **domain** represents the **logical topology**, defining the organization and structure of objects within the domain. Conversely, a **site** represents the **physical location** of a computer network within a specific domain. Sites in the AD infrastructure reflect the actual **physical topology**.
- **Replication** is a crucial process in an AD infrastructure. It involves synchronizing the standard directory partition across all DCs in a forest. Replication ensures that changes made to the directory data in one DC are propagated to other DCs, maintaining consistency and data availability. **Replication topology** refers to the communication paths through which replication data travels between DCs.
- In AD, **objects**, **classes**, and **attributes** are essential components that define the schema. A class represents the object type, while an attribute represents the characteristics or properties of the object. AD stores objects identified by their classes and attributes. The **schema** acts as a blueprint or model that establishes rules and structures for the types of objects stored in AD. **Replication** also ensures that the schema remains synchronized among all DCs in the forest, allowing consistent object definitions and operations throughout the AD environment.

In Windows Server 2025, these processes and structures remain vital for efficient and reliable management of network resources.

Note: A server that has become part of a domain within an organization's network is called a member server.

Exercise 5.1: Adding AD DS role

This exercise outlines the procedure for adding an AD DS role using Server Manager and PowerShell.

Adding AD DS role using Server Manager

To begin the process of adding an AD DS role in Windows Server 2025 using Server Manager, follow these steps:

1. Open **Server Manager** from the Start menu and click the **Add Roles and Features** link.
2. Click the **Next** button on the **Before you Begin** page of the Add Roles and Features Wizard.
3. Accept the default settings on the **Select Installation Type** page and click **Next**.
4. Accept the default settings on the **Select Destination Server** page and click **Next**.
5. Choose the **Active Directory Domain Services**, as shown in *Figure 5.3*, role from the **Select Server Roles** page list. When the **Add Features required for AD DS** window appears, click the **Add Features** button. Then, click the **Next** button to continue adding the AD DS role.

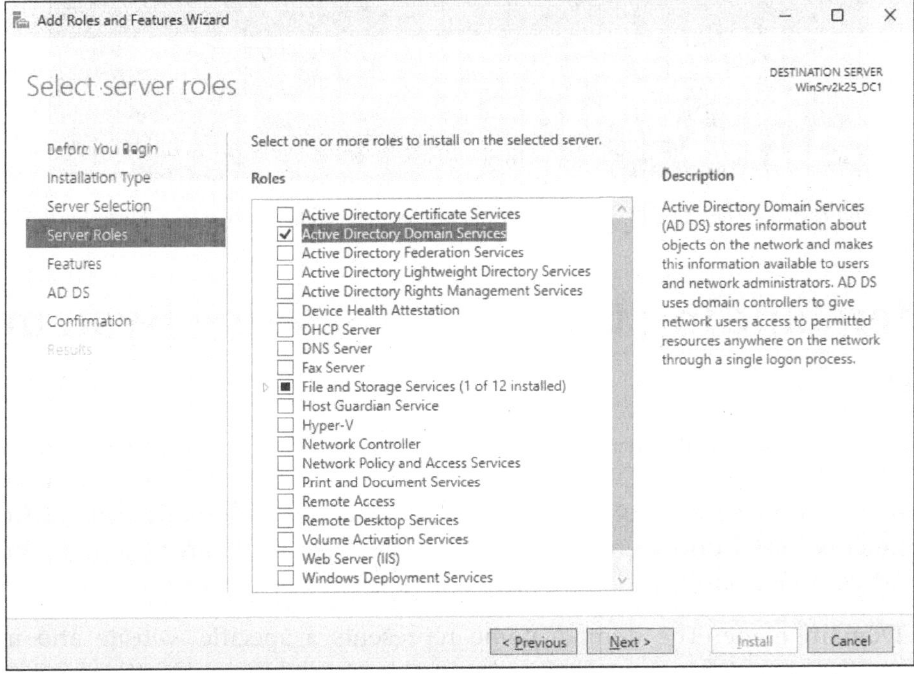

Figure 5.3: *Installing AD DS role in Windows Server 2025 using Server Manager*

6. Accept the default settings on the **Select Features** page and click the **Next** button to proceed.
7. Click the **Next** button on the **Active Directory Domain Services** page.
8. Review the options on the page and click the **Install** button.

The installation process for confirming installation selections for the AD DS role will begin, as indicated by the progress bar shown in *Figure 5.3*. Once the installation is complete, click the **Close** button to exit the Add Roles and Features Wizard.Adding AD DS role using Windows PowerShell.

To begin the process of adding an AD DS role in Windows Server 2025 using Windows PowerShell, follow these steps:

1. Launch **Windows PowerShell** by right-clicking on the **Start** button.
2. Within the Windows PowerShell interface, input the provided cmdlet and then press *Enter*:

```
Install-WindowsFeature AD-Domain-Services -IncludeManagementTools
```

3. The installation of the AD DS role will commence shortly, as depicted in *Figure 5.4:*

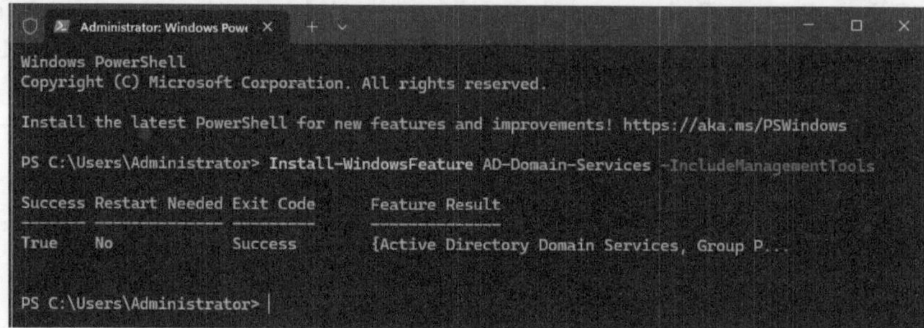

Figure 5.4: Installing AD DS role in Windows Server 2025 using Windows PowerShell

Understanding the Domain Name System Role

The DNS is a protocol that converts domain names into IP addresses, thereby controlling the name resolution process. DNS has existed since the ARPANET era, but it became a standard with the publication of the first DNS specifications in the early 1980s as **Requests for Comments** (**RFC**) documents. The DNS architecture is hierarchical and consists of three main components:

- **Domain name:** The domain name represents a specific website and includes multiple parts known as labels, separated by periods (e.g., *Dautti.com*).
- **Domain namespace:** This hierarchical naming system organizes the DNS database into zones. Each zone represents a different level of the domain hierarchy, such as the root domain, **top-level domains** (**TLDs**), **second-level domains** (**SLDs**), subdomains, and hostnames.
- **Name server:** The name server plays a crucial role in the DNS system. It is a network server that handles queries sent to a directory service. For example, when

a query is made with a domain name, the name server responds by mapping the domain name to the correct IP address, allowing the client to connect with the desired website.

Understanding the DNS architecture is essential for comprehending how the Internet's addressing system functions and enables seamless communication between websites and devices. In Windows Server 2025, DNS continues to be a vital component, with enhanced features and improved technologies to streamline name resolution further and ensure efficient network operations.

DNS zones

To fully understand the DNS architecture, it is essential to examine its zones. DNS zones are fundamental components that contribute to the overall structure and functionality of the system. A DNS zone is a hierarchical structure within the DNS namespace that facilitates the organization and management of DNS information. It allows for dividing the DNS namespace into separate zones, each responsible for storing information about specific domains or subdomains. Within the DNS architecture, three primary types of zones exist, each serving a particular purpose:

- **Primary zone:** The primary zone is the authoritative source for a particular DNS domain. It stores a complete and direct copy of the DNS database, including all the zone records. Changes made to the primary zone are propagated to other DNS servers, ensuring consistent and up-to-date information for the domain.

- **Secondary zone:** The secondary zone is a backup to the primary zone. It contains a replicated copy of the primary zone's DNS database. The secondary zone is not editable; it aims to provide redundancy and fault tolerance. When the primary zone becomes unavailable, the secondary zone can step in and handle DNS queries, ensuring continuity of service.

- **Stub zone:** A stub zone is conceptually similar to a secondary zone but with one notable difference. Unlike a secondary zone, it does not store a complete copy of the DNS database. Instead, it contains essential information to identify and locate the authoritative DNS servers for a specific domain. The stub zone acts as a reference point for DNS resolution, directing queries to the authoritative DNS servers for further processing.

By offering these different zone types, DNS allows for efficient management, replication, and fault tolerance within the DNS. Primary zones ensure authoritative control, while secondary and stub zones provide redundancy and distributed resolution capabilities. In Windows Server 2025, these DNS zone types remain crucial in maintaining a robust and reliable DNS infrastructure. Additionally, Windows Server 2025 introduces enhanced features and improved technologies to streamline DNS management further and ensure seamless network operations.

Understanding how DNS works

DNS is supported by a database that employs a distributed client/server architecture, where network hosts represent the servers' names. Consequently, DNS uses a distributed structure in which the recursive resolver acts as an intermediary between your browser and the DNS infrastructure. The resolver undertakes actions involving root servers, TLDs, and domain name servers to translate the domain name into its associated IP address. This systematic process enables your browser to communicate with the intended Web Server and retrieve the requested content. The following steps describe how DNS works:

1. **Initiate request:** Type **`www.dautti.com`** in your browser's address bar and hit *Enter*. Your computer's browser initiates a request to access the website **www.dautti.com**.

2. **Recursive resolver:** The first server your browser encounters is the **recursive resolver.** This resolver is usually provided by your **internet service provider (ISP)** and handles the request on your behalf.

3. **Root servers:** The recursive resolver then contacts the **root servers**, which are spread across different locations worldwide. These root servers contain crucial information about TLDs, such as *.com*.

4. **DNS information:** The root servers provide the necessary DNS information to the recursive resolver, enabling it to proceed with the **resolution process**.

5. **Domain name server:** Once the recursive resolver receives the information from the root servers, it contacts the domain name server responsible for *dautti.com*. The recursive resolver seeks to determine the IP address associated with the **domain name** by leveraging the DNS's local DNS database.

6. **IP address communication:** After obtaining the **Web Server's IP address**, the recursive resolver communicates it back to your computer's browser. Now equipped with the correct IP address, your browser can connect with the Web Server and access its content.

In Windows Server 2025, DNS continues to be a vital component, with enhanced features and improved technologies to streamline name resolution further and ensure efficient network operations.

Components of name resolution

Several components and configurations are vital in ensuring efficient name resolution and smooth communication within networks. These elements work together to provide a seamless experience for users:

- **Hosts and lmhosts files:** These files are essential for local device name resolution. Stored in the **`C:\Windows\system32\drivers\etc`** directory, they contain mappings of **IP addresses to hostnames** (in the hosts file) and **IP addresses to computer names** (in the `lmhosts` file). They are manually edited and used for **DNS** and **NetBIOS** name resolution, respectively.

- **Hostname:** A **hostname** is a unique logical identifier assigned to a device in a network. It represents the device's name and is used for internal communication within a **local area network** (**LAN**). The hostname is crucial for accurately locating and addressing machines.
- **Authoritative DNS servers:** These servers are responsible for holding the **DNS records** of a specific domain. System administrators can configure these servers manually or rely on dynamic updates from other DNS servers. **Authoritative DNS** ensures the accuracy and reliability of domain-related information.
- **Non-authoritative DNS servers:** These servers store cached information obtained from previous **DNS lookups**. This cache holds frequently accessed **domain records**, allowing for faster name resolution by eliminating the need to query authoritative servers repeatedly.
- **Windows Internet Naming Service (WINS) servers:** Utilized in Windows networks, WINS servers **map IP addresses** to **NetBIOS names**. They play a critical role when devices connect to shared folders or printers, facilitating seamless communication by resolving **NetBIOS names to corresponding IP addresses**.
- **Universal Naming Convention (UNC):** This is a standard method for identifying network shares in Unix systems. It uses a syntax with double backslashes (\\) preceding the server's name, followed by the specific folder or resource (e.g., `\\hostname\folder`). UNC simplifies the process of accessing and sharing files across Unix-based networks.

By leveraging these components and configurations, networks can achieve efficient name resolution, enabling devices to locate and communicate with each other effectively. In Windows Server 2025, these components continue to play a crucial role in maintaining a robust and reliable network infrastructure.

Note: There is a significant distinction between a domain and a domain name. A domain refers to the logical arrangement of users, servers, devices, and resources within a specific group of such elements in a network. Conversely, a domain name denotes the logical naming system that governs the Internet, encompassing Web Servers and websites.

Exercise 5.2: Adding DNS Server role

This exercise outlines the procedure for adding a DNS Server role using Server Manager and PowerShell.

Adding DNS Server role using Server Manager

To begin the process of adding a DNS Server role in Windows Server 2025 using Server Manager, follow these steps:

1. Open **Server Manager** from the Start menu and click the **Add Roles and Features** link.
2. Click the **Next** button on the **Before you Begin page** of the Add Roles and Features Wizard.
3. Accept the default settings on the **Select Installation Type** page and click **Next**.
4. Accept the default settings on the **Select Destination Server** page and click **Next**.
5. Choose the **DNS Server** role, as in *Figure 5.5*, from the **Select Server Roles** page list. When the **Add Features** required for the DNS window appears, click the **Add Features** button. Then, click the **Next** button to continue adding the DNS Server role.

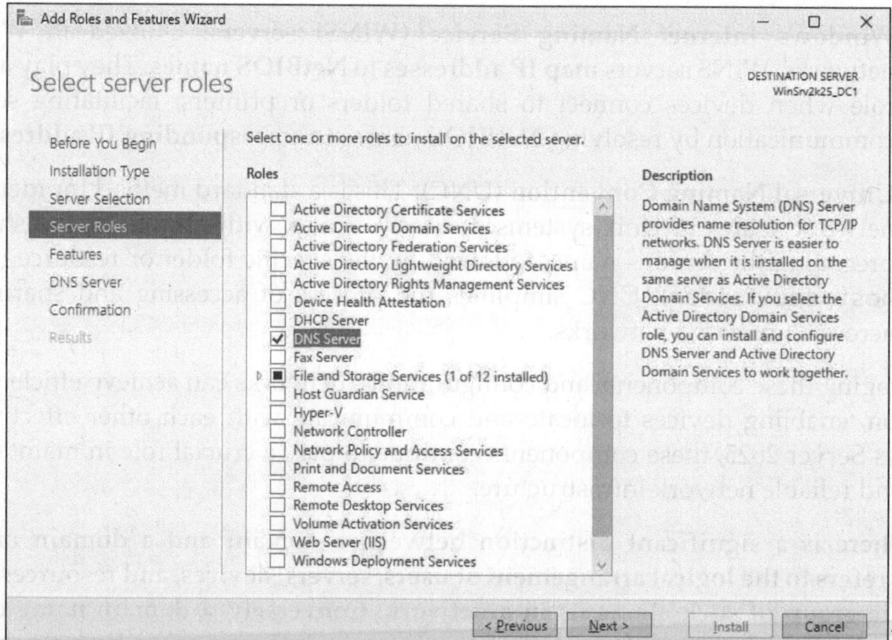

Figure 5.5: Installing DNS Server role in Windows Server 2025 using Server Manager

1. Accept the default settings on the **Select Features** page and click the **Next** button to proceed.
2. On the **DNS Server** page, click the **Next** button.
3. Review the options on the **Confirm installation selections** page and click the **Install** button.

4. The installation process for the DNS Server role will begin, as indicated by the progress bar shown in *Figure 5.5*. Once the installation is complete, click the **Close** button to exit the Add Roles and Features Wizard.

Adding DNS Server role using Windows PowerShell

To begin the process of adding a DNS Server role in Windows Server 2025 using Windows PowerShell, follow these steps:

1. Launch **Windows PowerShell** by right-clicking on the **Start** button.
2. Within the Windows PowerShell interface, input the provided cmdlet and then press *Enter*:

   ```
   Install-WindowsFeature DNS -IncludeManagementTools
   ```

3. The installation of the DNS Server role will commence shortly, as depicted in *Figure 5.6*:

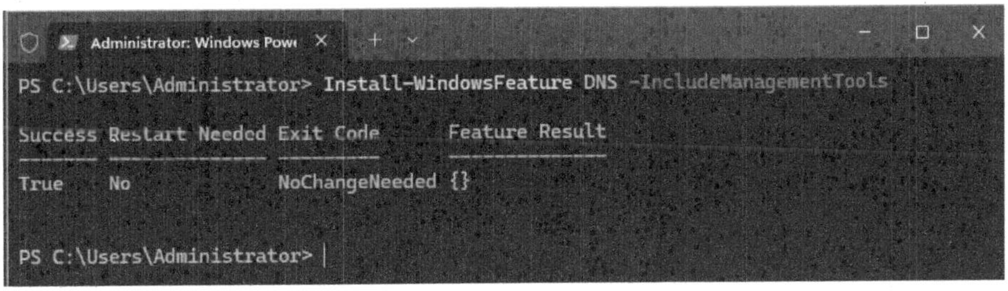

```
PS C:\Users\Administrator> Install-WindowsFeature DNS -IncludeManagementTools

Success Restart Needed Exit Code      Feature Result
------- -------------- ---------      --------------
True    No             NoChangeNeeded {}

PS C:\Users\Administrator> |
```

Figure 5.6: *Installing DNS Server role in Windows Server 2025 using Windows PowerShell*

Exploring the DHCP role

The DHCP is a network service that automatically assigns IP addresses to devices within a network. In a client/server architecture, DHCP operates by having clients request IP addresses and servers respond with the requested services. In this context, a DHCP service is called a DHCP server.

This section focuses on DHCP servers, which dynamically assign IPv4 addresses to devices. Typically, these IP addresses are allocated from a designated pool within the DHCP server. The assigned IP addresses have a predetermined lease period and are referred to as leased IP addresses. Once the lease expires, the DHCP client must request another IPv4 address, which may sometimes result in reassigning the same IP address. This process is known as IP address renewal.

The presence of a DHCP server significantly simplifies and expedites the IP address assignment process for network administrators. In Windows Server 2025, DHCP continues to be a vital component, with enhanced features and improved technologies to streamline IPAM further and ensure efficient network operations.

DHCP explained

The **Discovery, Offer, Request, and Acknowledgment** (**DORA**) process outlines the functioning of DHCP. It unfolds as follows:

- **Discovery:** When a computer is powered on and its OS boots up, the DHCP client service broadcasts a `DHCPDISCOVER` message requesting an IP address. This broadcast aims to locate a DHCP server within the **local area network** (**LAN**). If a DHCP server is available, it accepts the DHCPDISCOVER message from the client and reserves an IP address.
- **Offer:** In response to the client's request, the DHCP server sends a `DHCPOFFER` message. This message contains the allocated IP address and additional information, such as the subnet mask, default gateway, lease time, and the DHCP server's IP address.
- **Request:** Upon receiving the DHCPOFFER message, the client sends a `DHCPREQUEST` message to the DHCP server, confirming its interest in the offered IP address. This step ensures the client formally requests the IP address it intends to use.
- **Acknowledgment:** Once the DHCPREQUEST message reaches the DHCP server, it initiates an acknowledgment process. The server responds to the client with a `DHCPACK` message, which includes the requested elements mentioned earlier. This DHCPACK message marks the DHCP server's completion of the IP address assignment to the DHCP client.

The DORA process provides a systematic and standardized approach for DHCP to allocate IP addresses efficiently within a computer network. In Windows Server 2025, DHCP continues to be a vital component, with enhanced features and improved technologies to streamline IPAM further and ensure efficient network operations.

Exercise 5.3: Adding DHCP Server role

This exercise outlines the procedure for adding a DHCP Server role using Server Manager and PowerShell.

Adding DHCP Server role using Server Manager

To begin the process of adding a DHCP Server role in Windows Server 2025 using Server Manager, follow these steps:

1. Open **Server Manager** from the Start menu and click the **Add Roles and Features** link.

2. Click the **Next** button on the **Before you Begin page** of the Add Roles and Features Wizard.

3. Accept the default settings on the **Select Installation Type** page and click **Next**.

4. Accept the default settings on the **Select Destination Server** page and click **Next**.

5. Choose the **DHCP Server** role (*Figure 5.7*) from the **Select Server Roles** page list. When the **Add Features** required for the DHCP window appears, click the **Add Features** button. Then, click the **Next** button to continue adding the DHCP Server role.

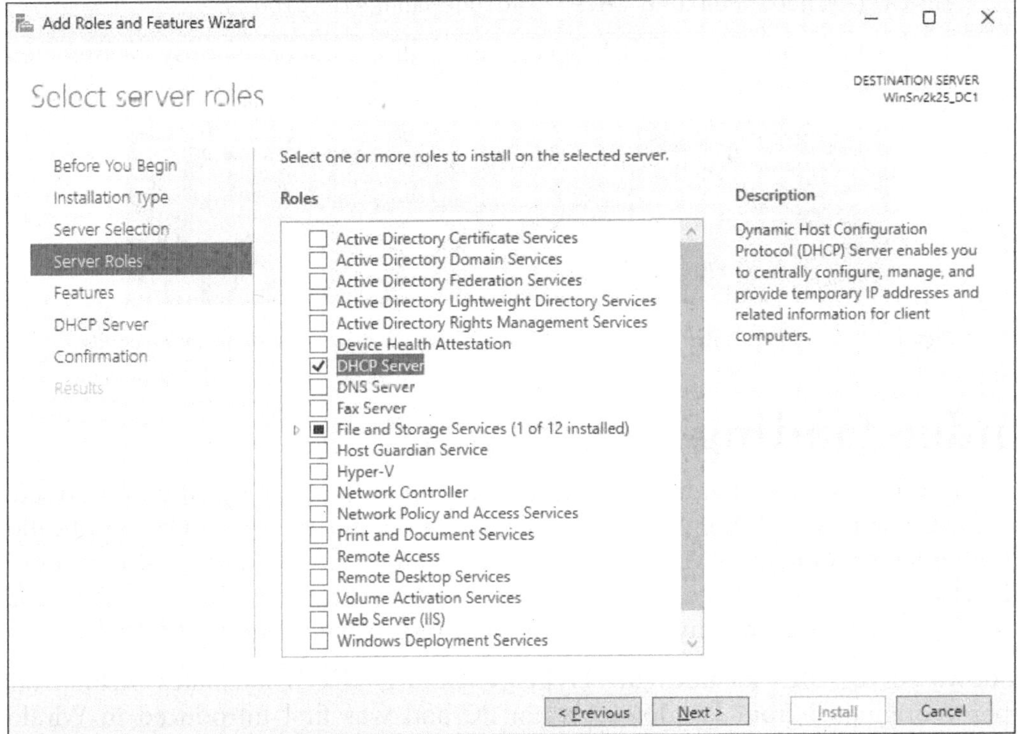

Figure 5.7: *Installing DHCP Server role in Windows Server 2025 using Server Manager*

6. Accept the default settings on the **Select Features** page and click the **Next** button to proceed.

7. On the DHCP Server page, click the **Next** button.

8. Review the options on the **Confirm installation selections** page and click the **Install** button.

9. The installation process for the DHCP Server role will begin, as indicated by the progress bar shown in *Figure 5.7*. Once the installation is complete, click the **Close** button to exit the Add Roles and Features Wizard.

Adding DHCP Server role using Windows PowerShell

To begin the process of adding a DHCP Server role in Windows Server 2025 using Windows PowerShell, follow these steps:

1. Launch **Windows PowerShell** by right-clicking on the **Start** button.
2. Within the Windows PowerShell interface, input the provided cmdlet and then press *Enter*:

```
Install-WindowsFeature DHCP -IncludeManagementTools
```

3. The installation of the DHCP Server role will commence shortly, as depicted in *Figure 5.8*:

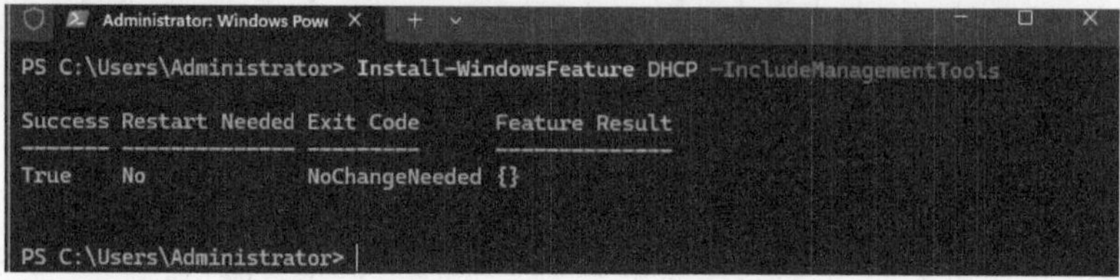

Figure 5.8: *Installing DHCP Server role in Windows Server 2025 using Windows PowerShell*

Understanding Hyper-V

To gain a technical understanding of **virtualization** and the technology involved in setting up a **virtual machine** (**VM**), we can explore how it allows us to run OSs, applications, and other tools within the VM. Virtualization also extends to configuring storage devices and network resources. Instead of operating multiple physical servers, virtualization consolidates them into one physical server, enabling efficient resource utilization.

Windows Server 2025 includes the **Hyper-V** feature, which facilitates virtualization. Hyper-V originated from Windows Virtual PC and was first introduced in Windows Server 2008. Since then, it has garnered attention from system administrators, establishing itself as a prominent contender in the virtualization platform market, competing with VMware. From a technical standpoint, Hyper-V provides services that enable the creation and management of VMs and their associated resources.

In Windows Server 2025, Hyper-V is a vital component, with enhanced features and technologies to further streamline virtualization and ensure efficient resource management.

Modes of virtualization

In today's virtualized environments, there are three commonly used modes of virtualization:

- **Fully virtualized mode:** This mode enables the secure execution of one or more OSs in isolation on a single physical server. In this mode, the guest OSs cannot be recompiled; instead, they utilize the resources of the host OS. It provides a complete virtual environment for each OS instance.

- **Para-virtualized mode:** In this mode, a computer within a computer is created, where an OS is installed without simulating the hardware. Instead, it offers an **application programming interface (API)** that allows the guest OS to be recompiled. This mode requires modifications to the guest OS and the virtualization software to achieve efficient communication.
- **Containerization mode:** This mode involves **containers**, which are self-contained packages comprising the runtime environment, system tools, and necessary settings to run the application code. Containers provide an isolated environment for applications, allowing them to run consistently across different systems without needing full OS virtualization. This mode offers lightweight and efficient application deployment.

These three **virtualization modes** cater to diverse needs and use cases in virtualized environments, offering flexibility and optimization based on the specific requirements of applications and systems. In Windows Server 2025, these virtualization modes continue to play a pivotal role in maintaining a robust and reliable virtual infrastructure. Enhanced features and improved technologies in Windows Server 2025 further streamline virtualization, ensuring efficient resource management and seamless operations.

Architecture of Hyper-V

The Hyper-V architecture in Windows Server 2025 follows a **hierarchical structure**, with the hypervisor serving as the central element that forms the foundation of the Hyper-V virtual platform. The hypervisor resides at the root level and directly interacts with the underlying hardware, managing and controlling the virtualization environment.

Within this architecture, the **root component** creates branch OSs as isolated execution environments. These branch OSs operate within a logical isolation unit without direct access to the underlying hardware. They are designed to host guest OSs and provide a secure and isolated environment for their execution.

Specific components known as the **virtualization service provider (VSP)** and **Virtualization Service Consumer (VSC)** facilitate communication between the root component and the branch OSs. These components utilize logical channels called the **Virtual Machine Bus (VMBus)** to establish communication pathways. The VMBus enables efficient and secure communication between the hypervisor and the branch OSs, allowing coordinated operations and resource sharing.

Overall, the Hyper-V architecture employs a hierarchical structure with the hypervisor at the root, branch OSs for isolated execution, and communication facilitated by VSP, VSC, and the VMBus. This architecture enables the efficient management and operation of virtualized environments within the Hyper-V virtual platform.

Nesting the virtualization

Nested virtualization refers to the capability of running a VM within another VM. This means that the host machine's hardware allows the execution of Hyper-V from within a VM, enabling the creation and management of additional VMs within this nested setup.

While nested virtualization may seem unusual, it has gained support and recognition since Windows Server 2016. Microsoft has introduced features and enhancements to facilitate nested virtualization, making it a viable option for specific use cases. To better grasp and manage this concept, you can think of running Hyper-V from the guest OS in the same manner as it runs from the host OS. This approach allows for effectively nesting one instance of Hyper-V within another, enabling multiple **virtualization layers**.

Setting up nested virtualization in Windows Server 2025 is straightforward using Windows PowerShell. Begin by right-clicking the Start button and selecting Windows PowerShell (Administrator) from the admin menu. Once in the PowerShell window, execute the following commands:

```
Set-VMProcessor -VMName <YourVMName> -ExposeVirtualizationExtensions $true
```

This command enables the guest VM to expose the necessary virtualization extensions, allowing it to run Hyper-V.

```
Get-VMNetworkAdapter -VMName <YourVMName> | Set-VMNetworkAdapter
-MacAddressSpoofing On
```

This command enables MAC address spoofing on the VM's network adapter, which is required for networking functionality in a nested virtualization scenario.

By utilizing nested virtualization, you can explore scenarios where running VMs within VMs becomes essential. This approach enables testing, development, and experimentation within a controlled virtual environment. While not commonly employed in everyday scenarios, nested virtualization provides flexibility and versatility for specific use cases, expanding the possibilities of virtualized environments.

Prerequisite for virtualization

To utilize Hyper-V, the server's processors must support **virtualization**. This means the physical server's processor must be equipped with **virtualization technology (VT)**. Therefore, it is essential that the hosting machine is equipped with an **Intel or AMD processor** that has Intel VT or **AMD Virtualization** enabled.

Enabling VT on the processor allows for efficient and secure execution of VMs. It provides the necessary hardware-level support for virtualization, enabling software like Hyper-V to create and manage VMs effectively.

Having processors with VT or AMD Virtualization support is a fundamental requirement for deploying and utilizing Hyper-V and other virtualization platforms. It ensures the smooth operation and optimal performance of virtualized environments.

Exercise 5.4: Adding Hyper-V role

This exercise outlines the procedure for adding a Hyper-V role using Server Manager and PowerShell.

Adding Hyper-V role using Server Manager

To begin the process of adding a Hyper-V role in Windows Server 2025 using Server Manager, follow these steps:

1. Open **Server Manager** from the Start menu and click the **Add Roles and Features** link.
2. Click the **Next** button on the **Before you Begin page** of the Add Roles and Features Wizard.
3. Accept the default settings on the **Select Installation Type** page and click **Next**.
4. Accept the default settings on the **Select Destination Server** page and click **Next**.
5. Choose the **Hyper-V** role, depicted in *Figure 5.9*, from the **Select Server roles** page list. When the Add Features required for the Hyper-V window appears, click the **Add Features** button. Then, click the **Next** button to continue adding the Hyper-V role.

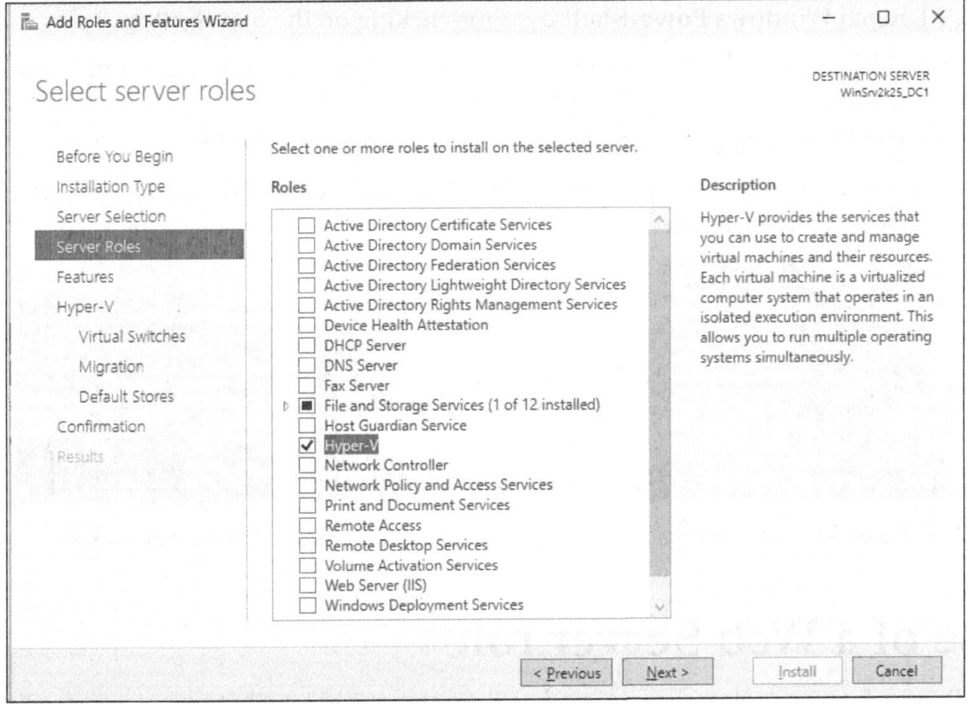

Figure 5.9: *Installing Hyper-V role in Windows Server 2025 using Server Manager*

6. Accept the default settings on the **Select Features** page and click the **Next** button to proceed.
7. On the Hyper-V page, click the **Next** button.
8. On the **Create virtual switches** page, reserve a network adapter that the virtual switch will use, and then click the **Next** button.
9. Accept the defaults on the VM migration page and click the **Next** button to move forward.
10. Accept the defaults on the **Default stores** page and click the **Next** button.
11. Review the options on the **Confirm installation selections** page and click the **Install** button.
12. The installation process for the Hyper-V role will begin, as indicated by the progress bar shown in *Figure 5.9*. Once the installation is complete, click the **Close** button to exit the Add Roles and Features Wizard. Afterward, **restart** the server to complete the installation of the Hyper-V role.

Adding Hyper-V role using Windows PowerShell

To begin the process of adding a Hyper-V role in Windows Server 2025 using Windows PowerShell, follow these steps:

1. Launch **Windows PowerShell** by right-clicking on the Start button.
2. Within the Windows PowerShell interface, input the provided cmdlet and then press *Enter*:

```
Install-WindowsFeature Hyper-V -IncludeManagementTools
```

3. The installation of the **Hyper-V** role will commence shortly, as depicted in *Figure 5.10*. Afterward, **restart** the server to complete the installation of the **Hyper-V** role.

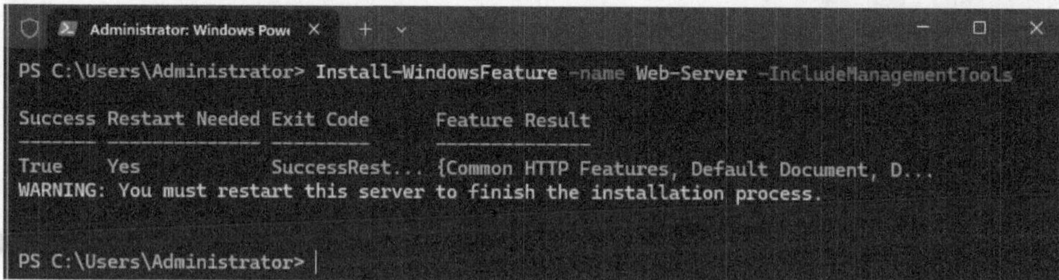

Figure 5.10: *Installing Hyper-V role in Windows Server 2025 using Windows PowerShell*

Use of a Web Server role

A **web service** is a network service that operates within web technology, facilitating communication between a web browser and a Web Server through the request/response paradigm. Typically, web services function over the Internet, utilizing the **Hypertext Transfer Protocol** (**HTTP**) as the communication protocol. To gain a comprehensive understanding of web services, it is essential to familiarize oneself with IIS, the **World Wide Web (WWW)**, and **File Transfer Protocol (FTP)**.

IIS, developed by Microsoft, is a robust and scalable Web Server for hosting web applications. It supports various communication protocols, including HTTP, HTTPS, FTP, FTPS, SMTP, and NNTP, enabling seamless interaction between web browsers and the Web Server. Microsoft introduced a scripting technology known as **Active Server Pages (ASP)** to allow dynamic content on the server side.

With the release of IIS version 10, Microsoft has significantly emphasized enhancing security. This includes support for scripts with longer execution times, adopting the **HTTP/2 protocol**, and implementing **TLS 1.3** for improved encryption. Additionally, Microsoft introduced the **Microsoft Edge** browser based on the Chromium engine, which offers improved compatibility and performance. Noteworthy features introduced in IIS 10 for Windows Server 2025 include upgraded **server-side cipher** suite negotiation for **HTTP/3**, **PowerShell cmdlets** for IIS administration, **wildcard host headers**, and other enhancements. These improvements have contributed to enhanced performance and strengthened security within IIS.

Understanding the concepts of IIS, WWW, and FTP, along with the advancements in IIS 10, provides valuable insights into the operation, capabilities, and security measures of web services within the web technology landscape.

Web elements and technologies

Understanding the intricacies of web technology and its various internet services is essential in today's digital landscape. One common source of confusion is the distinction between the Internet and the WWW. While the Internet is a vast network connecting computers globally, the WWW represents just one of the many services operating within this network. In this context, it becomes crucial to grasp concepts such as web services, IIS, FTP, web directories, sites, hardware and software ports, as well as security measures like **Secure Sockets Layer (SSL)** and **certificates**. This comprehensive understanding will enable us to navigate the web effectively, develop robust web applications, and ensure secure communication between browsers and Web Servers. Now, let us look into the intricacies of these concepts to gain a holistic view of web technology and its underlying mechanisms:

- **Internet versus WWW:** The confusion between the Internet and the WWW is common. Many people mistakenly perceive the WWW as synonymous with the Internet itself, but in reality, the WWW is just one of the numerous Internet services accessible through the HTTP protocol. It comprises electronic documents created with **Hypertext Markup Language (HTML)** and is a platform for accessing and navigating web pages.

- **File Transfer Protocol:** FTP is a specific internet service primarily used for transferring files between computers over the Internet. It finds extensive applications in corporate networks for sending and receiving corporate data. FTP is commonly employed on websites and Web Servers to upload and download files. It operates on a client/server network architecture, establishing sessions through **port 21** and transferring data through **port 20**.
- **Web directory in IIS:** In the IIS context, a web directory represents a website associated with an application pool. A web directory encompasses multiple applications, each supported by a dedicated worker process within the application pool. This separation ensures that if a specific web application encounters issues, it does not impact the functionality of other applications running in different application pools.
- **Website:** A website is a collection of web pages grouped to present content on the intranet or Internet through web services. While HTML is commonly used to structure web pages and design websites, various scripting languages introduce dynamic content to specific websites. For example, by adding the **Web Server** role in Windows Server 2025, the automatic creation of a default website, representing a single web page website, occurs.
- **Hardware and software ports:** Hardware ports are physical interfaces in computers, peripheral devices, or network devices that facilitate communication and management. Conversely, software ports, also known as application ports, serve as logical endpoints where applications on a server communicate with other applications within a LAN, WAN, or the Internet. For instance, Web Servers utilize **port 80** for the **HTTP protocol** and **port 443** for the **HTTPS protocol**.
- **Secure Sockets Layer (SSL):** SSL is a communication technology that encrypts the communication channel between a Web Server and a browser, typically over the HTTPS protocol on port 443. SSL ensures the secure transmission of data between the server and the browser. In this secure infrastructure, certificates are crucial in encrypting all transmitted data. Certificates, often issued by a **certificate authority (CA)**, are used by both the website and the browser to establish a secure session for browser-to-server or server-to-server communications.
- **Digital certificates:** Digital certificates secure the communication channel between websites and browsers. They are electronic documents that enable secure data exchange over the Internet. Certificate authorities are trusted entities that issue these certificates. The secure web infrastructure commonly employs a **public key infrastructure (PKI)**, which utilizes certificates to validate the ownership of public keys and establish secure connections.

In Windows Server 2025, these concepts are crucial in maintaining a robust and reliable web infrastructure.

Exercise 5.5: Adding Web Server role

This exercise outlines the procedure for adding a **Web Server (IIS)** role using Server Manager and PowerShell.

Adding Web Server role using Server Manager

To begin the process of adding a Web Server (IIS) role in Windows Server 2025 using Server Manager, follow these steps:

1. Open **Server Manager** from the Start menu and click the **Add Roles and Features** link.
2. Click the **Next** button before you begin **Adding Roles and Features Wizard** page.
3. Accept the default settings on the **Select Installation Type** page and click **Next**.
4. Accept the default settings on the **Select Destination Server** page and click **Next**.
5. Choose the **Web Server** role, illustrated in *Figure 5.11*, from the **Select Server roles** page list. When the **Add Features** required for the Web Server window appears, click the **Add Features** button. Then, click the **Next** button to continue adding the Web Server role.

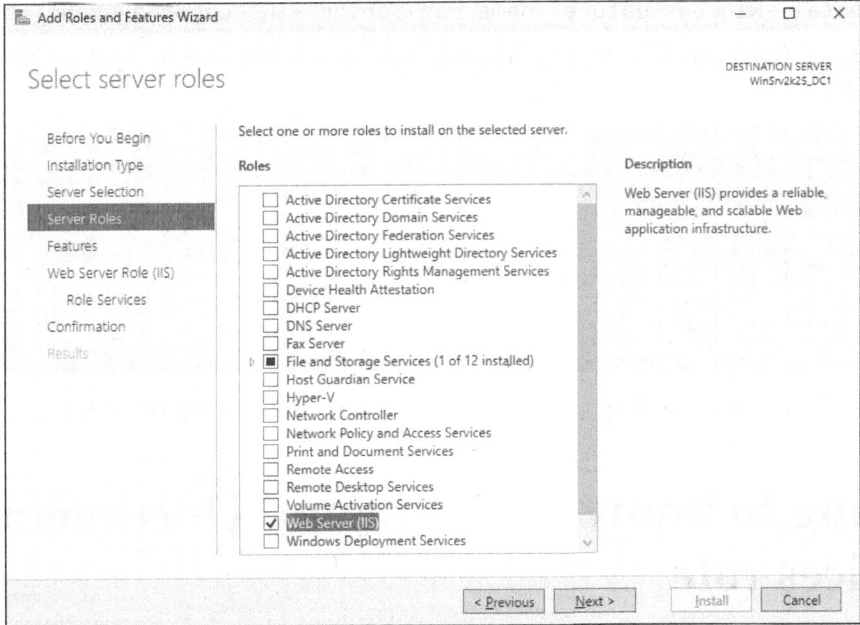

***Figure 5.11:** Installing Web Server (IIS) role in Windows Server 2025 using Server Manager*

6. Accept the default settings on the **Select Features** page and click the **Next** button to proceed.

7. On the **Web Server** page, click on the **Next** button.
8. On the **Select role services** page, select the **role services** to install for the Web Server (IIS) role and click the **Next** button.
9. Review the options on the **Confirm installation selections** page and click the **Install** button.
10. The installation process for the Web Server role will begin, as indicated by the progress bar shown in *Figure 5.11*. Once the installation is complete, click the **Close** button to exit the Add Roles and Features Wizard.

Adding Web Server role using Windows PowerShell

To begin the process of adding a Web Server (IIS) role in Windows Server 2025 using Windows PowerShell, follow these steps:

1. Launch **Windows PowerShell** by right-clicking on the **Start** button.
2. Within the Windows PowerShell interface, input the provided cmdlet and then press *Enter*:

```
Install-WindowsFeature -name Web-Server -IncludeManagementTools
```

3. The installation of the Web Server role will commence shortly, as depicted in *Figure 5.12*:

```
Administrator: Windows Powe
PS C:\Users\Administrator> Install-WindowsFeature Hyper-V -IncludeManagementTools

Success Restart Needed Exit Code      Feature Result
------- -------------- ---------      --------------
True    Yes            SuccessRest... {Hyper-V, Hyper-V Module for Windows Power...
WARNING: You must restart this server to finish the installation process.

PS C:\Users\Administrator>
```

Figure 5.12: *Installing Web Server (IIS) role in Windows Server 2025 using Windows PowerShell*

Getting to know the Print and Document Services role

PDS is a comprehensive network-based solution that extends beyond traditional printing capabilities. In addition to facilitating centralized printing across a network, PDS offers a document scanning feature. This scanning service allows users to conveniently receive scanned documents from a network scanner and efficiently send them to **share network resources**.

PDS is typically integrated as a role within Windows Server 2025, enhancing its functionality. Organizations can streamline their printing and document management processes by incorporating PDS into the server environment, achieving greater efficiency and productivity. Users can leverage the **centralized printing** capability to send print jobs from various network-connected devices, simplifying the printing workflow.

Furthermore, PDS's document scanning service enables users to digitize physical documents and seamlessly transmit them to designated network destinations. This functionality facilitates document sharing, collaboration, and archival, reducing reliance on physical paper documents.

PDS is a versatile solution that combines **network printing and document scanning capabilities**. By integrating PDS as a role in Windows Server 2025, organizations can optimize their printing and document management workflows, improving efficiency and promoting a digital-centric approach to information handling.

PDS role services

PDS extends its capabilities beyond basic printing and scanning by offering various role services. These services provide administrators and users with comprehensive tools to effectively manage printing queues, enable Internet-based printing, facilitate client-side printing, and ensure compatibility with non-Windows OSs. This comprehensive approach enhances the flexibility and versatility of the printing infrastructure, catering to the diverse needs of organizations and promoting efficient document management. These role services are explained as follows:

- **Print server role service:** This role empowers administrators to manage printing queues and effectively deploy and migrate **print servers**. By utilizing the print server role, organizations can efficiently handle print jobs and ensure smooth operations across the network.
- **Internet Printing role service:** This service enables the establishment of a **website** that allows users to **print over the Internet**. This feature provides convenient remote printing capabilities, enabling users to submit print jobs from their devices and have them processed by the network printer.
- **Line Printer Daemon (LPD) service role:** This service enables Unix-based computers and non-Windows OSs to leverage the **Line Printer Remote (LPR)** protocol for printing. By incorporating LPD, organizations can ensure compatibility and allow printing functionality across diverse computing environments, promoting seamless **cross-platform printing**.

In Windows Server 2025, these role services continue to play a crucial role in maintaining a robust and reliable printing infrastructure.

Printer and printing concepts

The following points explore various concepts related to printers and printing, providing a comprehensive understanding of the topic:

- **Local printer:** As the name implies, a local printer is **physically connected** to a computer through the parallel or **USB port** (printer port). Its primary purpose is to serve the computer to which it is connected. However, if the host computer shares the printer, it can also provide printing services to other computers on the network.

- **Network printer:** In contrast, a network printer is a **dedicated computer network printer** offering printing services. It utilizes an **Ethernet** or **Wi-Fi** interface and can be accessed simultaneously by multiple devices connected to the same network. Network printers can even be accessed over the Internet, depending on the network setup.

- **Printer pooling:** Printer pooling is a **feature** in Windows Server 2025 that allows configuring two or more physical printers into a single logical printer. The printers installed on the print server must be nearly identical or compatible with the same print driver. From the client's perspective (the front end), even though multiple physical network printers exist in the background, they appear as a **single printer**. This logical pooling of printers helps balance the workload and enhances usability, providing users with efficient printing capabilities.

- **Web printing:** Web printing is a concept that integrates printing with web browsers for easier understanding and accessibility. To set up web printing in an organization's network, the PDS role and **Internet Printing** as a role service must be added. Additionally, the **Web Server (IIS)** role is required.

- **Managing print jobs:** Like local and network printing, web printing also includes methods for managing print jobs. Users can control print jobs through **web printing management tools** accessible via a web browser, just like when managing a local or network printer. For example, by entering `http://servername/printers` in the browser's address bar and selecting the printer, users can access a web interface displaying a list of printable jobs. However, it is essential to note that before utilizing web printing, the Internet Printing role services must be added to the server, in addition to the PDS role.

By exploring these concepts, we gain a comprehensive understanding of printers and printing, encompassing local and network printing, printer pooling, and web printing. This knowledge enables organizations to effectively manage their printing infrastructure, enhance productivity, and leverage the benefits of modern printing technologies.

Exercise 5.6: Adding PDS role

This exercise outlines the procedure for adding a PDS role using Server Manager and PowerShell.

Adding PDS role using Server Manager

To begin the process of adding a PDS role in Windows Server 2025 using Server Manager, follow these steps:

1. Open **Server Manager** from the Start menu and click the **Add Roles and Features** link.
2. Click the **Next** button on the **Before you Begin** page of the Add Roles and Features Wizard.
3. Accept the default settings on the **Select Installation Type** page and click **Next.**
4. Accept the default settings on the **Select Destination Server** page and click **Next.**
5. Choose the **PDS** role, as in *Figure 5.13*, from the **Select Server roles** page list. When the **Add Features required for the PDS** window appears, click the **Add Features** button. Then, click the **Next** button to continue adding the PDS role.

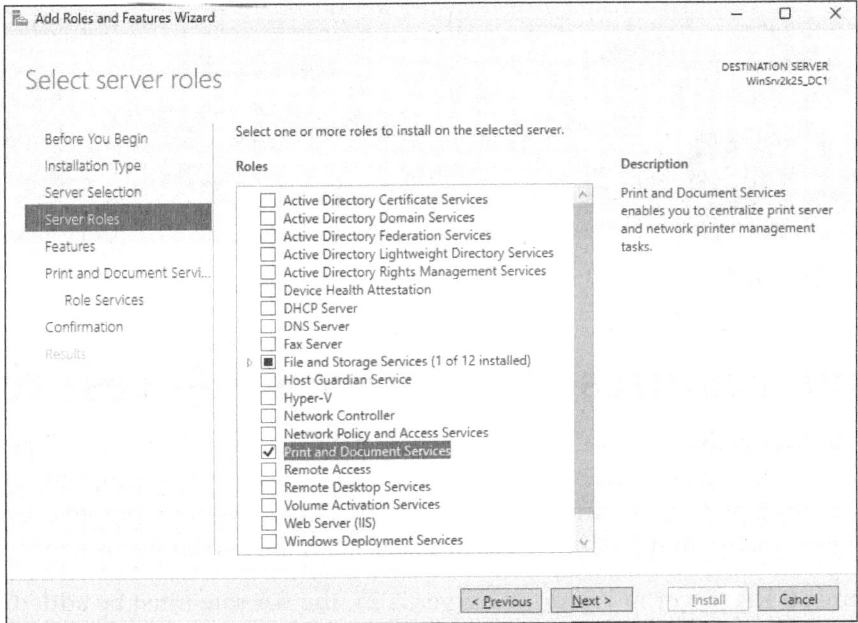

Figure 5.13: *Installing PDS role in Windows Server 2025 using Server Manager*

6. Accept the default settings on the **Select Features** page and click the **Next** button to proceed.

7. Click the **Next** button on the **Print and Document Services** page.
8. On the **Select role services** page, select the role services to install for the PDS role and click the **Next** button.
9. Review the options on the **Confirm installation selections** page and click the **Install** button.
10. The installation process for the PDS role will begin, as indicated by the progress bar shown in *Figure 5.13*. Once the installation is complete, click the **Close** button to exit the Add Roles and Features Wizard.

Adding PDS role using Windows PowerShell

To begin the process of adding a PDS role in Windows Server 2025 using Windows PowerShell, follow these steps:

1. Launch **Windows PowerShell** by right-clicking on the Start button.
2. Within the Windows PowerShell interface, input the provided cmdlet and then press *Enter*:

```
Install-WindowsFeature Print-Services -IncludeManagementTools
```

3. The installation of the PDS role will commence shortly, as depicted in *Figure 5.14*:

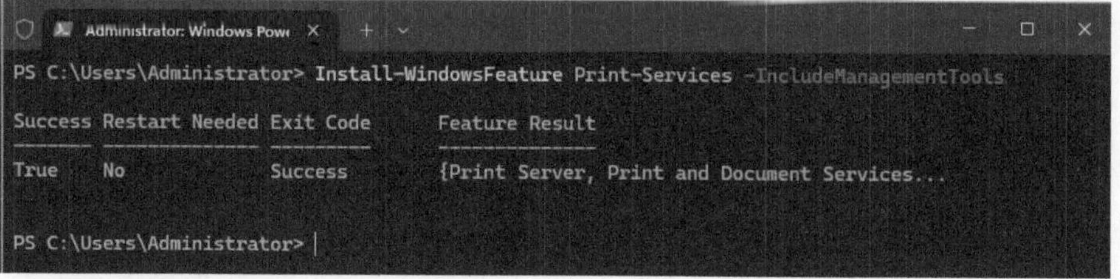

Figure 5.14: *Installing PDS role in Windows Server 2025 using Windows PowerShell*

Unique Features of the Remote Access role

The **Remote Access (RA)** role in Windows Server 2025 facilitates RA to corporate network resources. RA encompasses monitoring and controlling access to a computer or network from any location and at any time. This functionality empowers corporate users to work remotely while maintaining seamless connectivity with the corporate network.

To configure an RA server in Windows Server 2025, the RA role must be added. This role provides the necessary infrastructure and services to enable RA capabilities, including **DirectAccess**, **Routing and Remote Access Service (RRAS)**, and **Web Application Proxy**. By setting up the RA role, organizations can establish a robust and secure remote connectivity solution, empowering users to access network resources remotely while ensuring data confidentiality and integrity.

Deploying the RA role allows organizations to establish a **secure** and **reliable infrastructure** that enables authorized users to access resources within the corporate network remotely. This role enables remote workers to connect to file shares, databases, applications, and other essential resources, ensuring uninterrupted productivity and collaboration.

Moreover, the RA capabilities provided by the RA role go beyond simple connectivity. They include features such as **Virtual Private Network (VPN)** services, which enable secure and encrypted connections over public networks like the Internet. VPNs establish a protected tunnel between the remote user and the corporate network, ensuring the confidentiality and integrity of the data transmitted.

By leveraging the RA role, organizations can extend their network's reach beyond physical boundaries, empowering employees to work remotely while maintaining secure and efficient access to corporate resources. This flexibility promotes productivity, enables remote collaboration, and enhances business continuity by ensuring employees can perform their tasks from anywhere.

RA's network access technologies

In Windows Server 2025, the RA feature encompasses various network access technologies that enable remote connectivity. These technologies include:

- **DirectAccess:** Initially introduced in Windows Server 2008 R2, DirectAccess uses **IPsec** for secure communication between the DirectAccess client and server. It also encapsulates IPv6 traffic within IPv4, allowing access to the **corporate intranet** over the Internet without needing a traditional VPN. DirectAccess provides seamless and always-on connectivity for remote users.
- **Routing and Remote Access Service (RRAS):** RRAS is the successor to the **Remote Access Service (RAS)** introduced in *Windows NT* and has been available since *Windows 2000*. It combines various services to establish connections between remote locations through **VPNs and dial-up connections**, enabling communication between sub-networks.
- **Web Application Proxy:** As a reverse proxy in Windows Server 2025, the Web Application Proxy leverages **Active Directory Federation Services (AD FS)** for **user authentication**. It allows corporate users to securely access web applications hosted on the corporate intranet from an extranet environment. This enables controlled access to web resources while maintaining security and identity management.

By incorporating these technologies, Windows Server 2025 provides a robust and secure RA solution, empowering users to connect to corporate network resources from remote locations while ensuring data confidentiality and integrity.

Understanding Virtual Private Network

A VPN is a secure method for transmitting data over the Internet. As its name suggests, a VPN establishes a **virtual connection** between two computers, creating a **point-to-point** link between the **wide area network (WAN)** and the Internet. By using **tunneling protocols** and **encryption algorithms**, a VPN allows remote users to securely connect to a corporate network via the Internet. Typically, VPNs are deployed in two primary ways:

- **Remote Access VPN:** This facilitates the connection of **remote users**, such as **telecommuters**, with the server residing on their organization's private network. Through a RA VPN, authorized individuals can establish a secure and encrypted connection to access resources within the **corporate network**, regardless of their physical location.
- **Site-to-Site VPN:** This enables organizations to establish secure connections between two **separate networks** over the Internet. This VPN allows an organization's offices, branches, or locations to connect their respective networks securely, creating a unified and secure network environment.

To set up a VPN server in Windows Server 2025, a specific process must be followed. First, the RA role must be added to the server. Once this role is added, the next step is to include the necessary role services, such as DirectAccess and VPN (RAS). By configuring these role services, Windows Server 2025 can function as a VPN server, enabling secure RA and facilitating site-to-site connectivity.

By establishing a VPN server using Windows Server 2025, organizations can provide remote users with a secure and encrypted connection to access corporate resources. Additionally, site-to-site VPNs enhance connectivity and collaboration between multiple network locations, promoting seamless data transmission and communication.

Remote support and management

Remote Assistance and Remote Server Administration Tools (RSAT) are essential features in Windows Server 2025 that facilitate remote support and management capabilities.

- **Remote assistance:** This notable feature in Windows Server 2025 allows a trusted helper to access and control an **invitee's** desktop remotely, helping in troubleshooting computer-related issues. This functionality is commonly employed in **Help Desk** scenarios, where technical support is delivered remotely over the Internet. To enable the Remote Assistance feature on a Windows Server 2025, the Add Roles and Features Wizard must be utilized to configure the necessary settings.

- **Remote Server Administration Tools (RSAT):** Windows Server 2025 offers RSAT, which empowers system administrators to manage the roles and features of remote servers running Windows Server 2025. These tools can be accessed and operated in both GUI and CLI modes. It is worth noting that RSAT is not limited to Windows Server 2025 alone; it is also available for Windows 10 and 11 client computers. To enable Remote Server Administration Tools in Windows Server 2025, the Add Roles and Features Wizard can be employed to set up the required components.

By leveraging the Remote Assistance feature, organizations can streamline troubleshooting processes by allowing remote experts to address technical issues efficiently. Similarly, the Remote Server Administration Tools enable system administrators to manage and administer remote servers effectively, enhancing overall server management capabilities. These features contribute to the seamless operation and maintenance of Windows Server 2025-based environments.

Exercise 5.7: Adding Remote Access role

This exercise outlines the procedure for adding a RA role using Server Manager and PowerShell.

Adding Remote Access role using Server Manager

To begin the process of adding an RA role in Windows Server 2025 using Server Manager, follow these steps:

1. Open **Server Manager** from the Start menu and click the **Add Roles and Features** link.
2. Click the **Next** button on the **Before you begin** page of the Add Roles and Features Wizard.
3. Accept the default settings on the **Select Installation Type** page and click **Next**.
4. Accept the default settings on the **Select Destination Server** page and click **Next**.
5. Choose the **Remote Access** role (*Figure 5.15*) from the **Select Server Roles** page list. Then, click the **Next** button to continue adding the RA role.

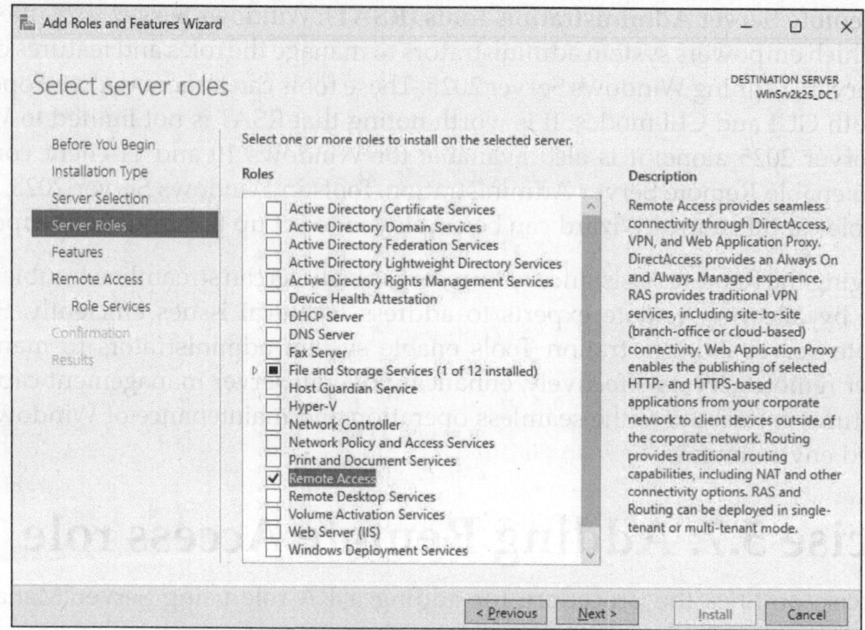

***Figure 5.15:** Installing Remote Access role in Windows Server 2025 using Server Manager*

6. Accept the default settings on the **Select Features** page and click the **Next** button to proceed.
7. On the **Remote Access** page, click the **Next** button.
8. On the **Select role services** page for the RA role, select the role services to install. When the **Add Features** required for the role services you are adding window appears, click the **Add Features** button. Then click the **Next** button.
9. Review the options on the **Confirm installation selections** page and click the **Install** button.
10. The installation process for the RA role will begin. Once the installation is complete, click the **Close** button to exit the Add Roles and Features Wizard.

Adding Remote Access role using Windows PowerShell

To begin the process of adding an RA role in Windows Server 2025 using Windows PowerShell, follow these steps:

1. Launch **Windows PowerShell** by right-clicking on the **Start** button.
2. Within the Windows PowerShell interface, input the provided cmdlet and then press *Enter*:

```
Install-WindowsFeature RemoteAccess
```

3. The installation of the RA role will commence shortly, as depicted in *Figure 5.16*:

```
PS C:\Users\Administrator> Install-WindowsFeature RemoteAccess

Success Restart Needed Exit Code      Feature Result
------- -------------- ---------      --------------
True    No             NoChangeNeeded {}

PS C:\Users\Administrator> |
```

***Figure 5.16**: Installing RA role in Windows Server 2025 using Windows PowerShell*

4. To install the **Routing** role services, input the provided cmdlet and then press *Enter*:

```
Install-WindowsFeature Routing -IncludeManagementTools
```

Need for a Remote Desktop Services role

Previously known as **Terminal Services (TS)** until the release of Windows Server 2008 R2, RDS acquired its new name and distinct identity. This crucial role empowers organizations to establish a robust and user-friendly **GUI** that enables RA to computers within their network, regardless of geographical location or network boundaries. Moreover, RDS goes beyond remote desktop access by offering the capability to deliver individual applications in a virtualized manner directly to users' desktops. This streamlined application delivery enhances productivity and efficiency while ensuring seamless user experiences.

By deploying an RDS server in Windows Server 2025, organizations can provide their users with a flexible and secure remote desktop infrastructure. Users gain the ability to access their workstations and applications from anywhere, enabling them to work remotely or collaborate effectively with distributed teams. The RDS role is a cornerstone in creating a dynamic and adaptive IT environment that caters to the evolving needs of modern organizations.

The first step in setting up an RDS server in Windows Server 2025 is adding the RDS role. This role brings a comprehensive suite of features and capabilities, including session-based virtualization, **virtual desktop infrastructure** (**VDI**), and remote application delivery. Administrators can then configure and manage these services to tailor the remote desktop experience to their organization's requirements.

With RDS in Windows Server 2025, organizations can embrace the advantages of remote accessibility, enhanced application delivery, and improved collaboration, ultimately driving productivity and enabling efficient workflows across their network.

Various RDS role services and features

With a focus on remote support and management, Windows Server 2025 offers various role services and features. These tools enable seamless RA, secure connections, and efficient administration, empowering organizations to enhance productivity and streamline their IT operations. Let us take a look at them:

- **RDS Licensing server:** The RDS Licensing server is crucial in managing **RDS Client Access Licenses (CALs)**, which users and computers require to access a **Remote Desktop Session Host (RDSH)** server. By default, the RDS Licensing server grants two concurrent connections at no cost. If additional RDS CALs are needed, they must be purchased. To establish an RDS Licensing server in a network using Windows Server 2025, the RDS role must be added to the server, followed by the Remote Desktop Licensing role services.

- **Remote Desktop Gateway (RDG) server:** Another significant component of the RDS role is the RDG server. This role service enables authorized users to connect to computers within an organization's network and over the Internet using a **Remote Desktop Connection (RDC)** client. To set up an RDG server in an organization's network with Windows Server 2025, the RDS role must be added to the server. Then, the RDG role services can be included.

- **Port utilization:** RDS utilizes **port 3389** for data transmission. However, this port is dedicated to accessing one computer at a time. So, what happens when attempting to access multiple computers simultaneously through RDS? **Sequential port numbers** starting with 3390 are assigned to the additional local area network computers. Furthermore, an IP socket is used when accessing multiple computers from a remote location. An IP socket comprises an IP address and a port number, which guide the application on where to deliver the data. The syntax for an IP socket is as follows: **`Public_IP_address:Port_number`**. For example, **`192.168.2.10:8080`** denotes accessing a computer with the IP address **`192.168.2.10`** through port number 8080.

Exercise 5.8: Adding Remote Desktop Services role

This exercise outlines the procedure for adding a RDS role using Server Manager and PowerShell.

Adding Remote Desktop Services role using Server Manager

To begin the process of adding a RDS role in Windows Server 2025 using Server Manager, follow these steps:

1. Open **Server Manager** from the Start menu and click the **Add Roles and Features** link.

2. Click the **Next** button on the **Before you begin** page of the Add Roles and Features Wizard.
3. Accept the default settings on the **Select Installation Type** page and click **Next**.
4. Accept the default settings on the **Select Destination Server** page and click **Next**.
5. Choose the **Remote Desktop Services** role, illustrated in *Figure 5.17*, from the **Select Server Roles** page list. Then, click the **Next** button to continue adding the role.

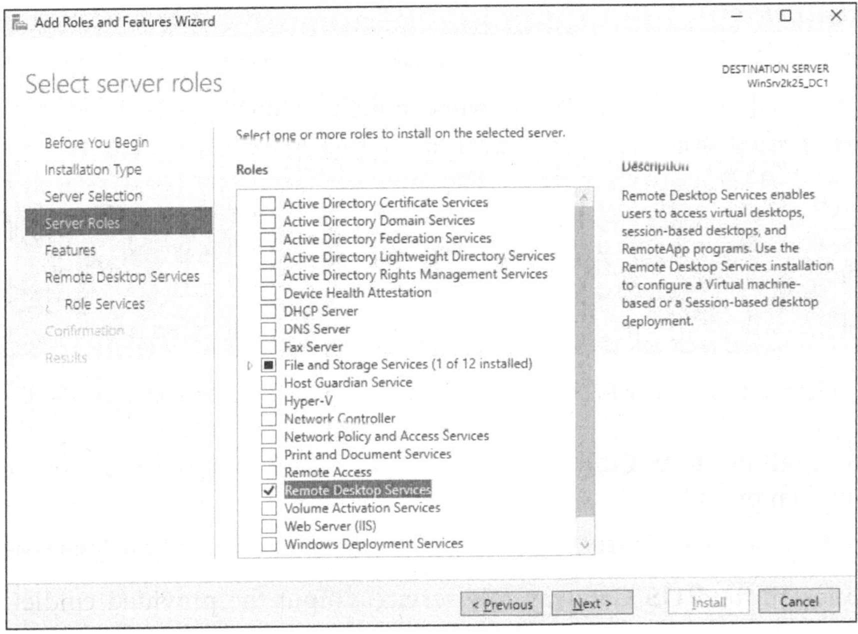

Figure 5.17: *Installing Remote Desktop Services role in Windows Server 2025 using Server Manager*

6. Accept the default settings on the **Select Features** page and click the **Next** button to proceed.
7. On the **Remote Desktop Services** page, click the **Next** button.
8. On the **Select role services** page for the RDS role, select the role services to install. When the Add Features required for the role services you are adding window appears, click the **Add Features** button. Then click the **Next** button.
9. Click the **Next** button on the **Network Policy and Access Services** page.
10. Review the options on the **Confirm installation selections** page and click the **Install** button.
11. The RDS role installation process will begin, as indicated by the progress bar shown in *Figure 5.17*. Once the installation is complete, click on the **Close** button to exit the Add Roles and Features Wizard.

Adding Remote Desktop Services role using Windows PowerShell

To begin the process of adding an RDS role in Windows Server 2025 using Windows PowerShell, follow these steps:

1. Launch **Windows PowerShell** by right-clicking on the **Start** button.
2. Within the Windows PowerShell interface, input the provided cmdlet and then press *Enter*:

```
Install-WindowsFeature Remote-Desktop-Services
```

3. The installation of the RDS role will commence shortly, as depicted in *Figure 5.18*:

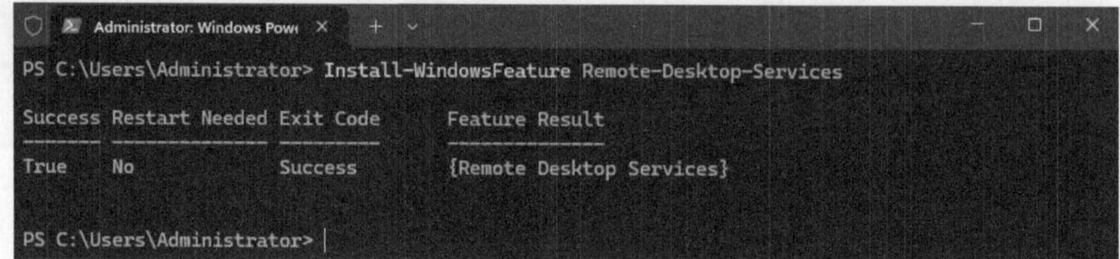

Figure 5.18: *Installing RDS role in Windows Server 2025 using Windows PowerShell*

4. To install the **RDS Connection Broker** role services, input the provided cmdlet and then press *Enter*:

```
Install-WindowsFeature RDS-Connection-Broker -IncludeManagementTools
```

5. To install the **RDS Gateway** role services, input the provided cmdlet and then press *Enter*:

```
Install-WindowsFeature RDS-Gateway -IncludeManagementTools
```

6. To install the **RDS Licensing** role services, input the provided cmdlet and then press *Enter*:

```
Install-WindowsFeature RDS-Licensing -IncludeManagementTools
```

Understanding Windows Server Update Services role

As the successor to **Software Update Services (SUS)**, WSUS empowers system administrators to efficiently manage the distribution of Microsoft's product updates across their organization's computer network. By leveraging WSUS, administrators can establish an infrastructure where updates, patches, and fixes are downloaded to a central server within the organization. This server then handles the approval and distribution of updates to the computers in the network.

WSUS provides administrators with comprehensive control over the update process. They can **selectively approve or decline updates**, schedule the installation of updates at specific times, and generate detailed reports to assess each computer's update status. With WSUS in place, there is no longer a need for the organization's computers to access Microsoft Updates directly, as WSUS is responsible for delivering the necessary updates.

In Windows Server 2025, WSUS is offered as a role that can be easily added to the server using the Server Manager tool. This allows organizations to seamlessly integrate WSUS into their server infrastructure, facilitating efficient and centralized management of Microsoft product updates.

However, it is important to note that Microsoft has announced the deprecation of WSUS in the near future. This means that while WSUS will continue to function and receive updates, Microsoft will no longer invest in new capabilities or accept new feature requests for WSUS. Organizations are encouraged to transition to modern cloud-based solutions such as *Windows Autopatch*, *Microsoft Intune* for client update management, and *Azure Update Manager* for server update management.

By staying informed about these changes, organizations can plan their transition to newer technologies and ensure continued efficient management of updates and patches.

WSUS deployment methods

WSUS plays a crucial role in **updating** Windows 10/11 computers within a corporate network. Organizations often deploy WSUS to reserve external traffic for business-critical services. By utilizing WSUS, end-user devices in the network receive updates directly from the WSUS server, which downloads the updates from the Microsoft Windows Update server. The following will explore these concepts in greater detail:

- **Several key decisions must be made to initiate the deployment of WSUS:** These include selecting the WSUS deployment scenario, determining the network topology, and understanding the system requirements. The number of client computers requiring updates drives hardware and database software requirements. Before adding the WSUS server role, it is essential to verify that the server meets the specified system requirements.

- **Fundamental WSUS deployment:** This involves a server within the corporate firewall, serving client computers on a private intranet. The WSUS server connects to Microsoft Updates for downloading updates, a process known as synchronization. During synchronization, WSUS identifies any newly available updates since the last synchronization. For the initial synchronization, all updates are made accessible for download. The WSUS server typically uses port 80 for HTTP protocol and port 443 for HTTPS protocol to communicate with Microsoft Updates. If a corporate firewall exists between the network and the Internet, these ports must be opened to enable direct communication with Microsoft Updates.

- **Multiple server deployment:** Alternatively, WSUS can be deployed with multiple servers synchronized within the organization's intranet. One server, the upstream server, is exposed to the internet and downloads updates from Microsoft Update. The remaining servers, called downstream servers, synchronize with the upstream server. Sometimes, servers may be distributed across geographically dispersed networks to ensure optimal connectivity to all client computers.

WSUS connection modes

WSUS servers offer two connection modes: **autonomous mode** and **replica mode**. It is advisable to deploy a WSUS solution that leverages both connection modes. Let us explore these modes further:

- **Autonomous mode:** Also known as **distributed administration**, this is the default installation option for WSUS. In this mode, an upstream WSUS server shares updates with downstream servers during synchronization. Downstream WSUS servers are managed independently and do not receive updated approval status or computer group information from the upstream server. With the distributed management model, each WSUS server administrator has control over selecting update languages, creating computer groups, assigning computers to groups, testing and approving updates, and ensuring the installation of the appropriate updates in the designated computer groups.

- **Replica mode:** Also called **centralized administration**, this mode involves an upstream WSUS server that shares updates, approval status, and computer groups with downstream servers. Replica servers inherit update approvals and are not administered separately from the upstream WSUS server. This mode provides a centralized administration approach and allows consistent update management across all replica servers.

By combining autonomous mode and replica mode in your WSUS deployment, you can benefit from the flexibility and distributed management capabilities of autonomous mode while maintaining centralized control and synchronization with replica mode.

In Windows Server 2025, WSUS is offered as a role that can be easily added to the server using the Server Manager tool. This allows organizations to seamlessly integrate WSUS into their server infrastructure, facilitating efficient and centralized management of Microsoft product updates.

Exercise 5.9: Adding Windows Server Update Services role

This exercise outlines the procedure for adding a WSUS role using Server Manager and PowerShell.

Adding Windows Server Update Services role using Server Manager

To begin the process of adding a RDS role in Windows Server 2025 using Server Manager, follow these steps:

1. Open **Server Manager** from the Start menu and click the **Add Roles and Features** link.
2. Click the **Next** button on the **Before you begin** page of the Add Roles and Features Wizard.
3. Accept the default settings on the **Select Installation Type** page and click **Next**.
4. Accept the default settings on the **Select Destination Server** page and click **Next**.
5. Choose the **Windows Server Update Services** role from the **Select Server roles** page list. When the Add Features required for the WSUS window appears, click the **Add Features** button. Then, click the **Next** button to continue adding the WSUS role.

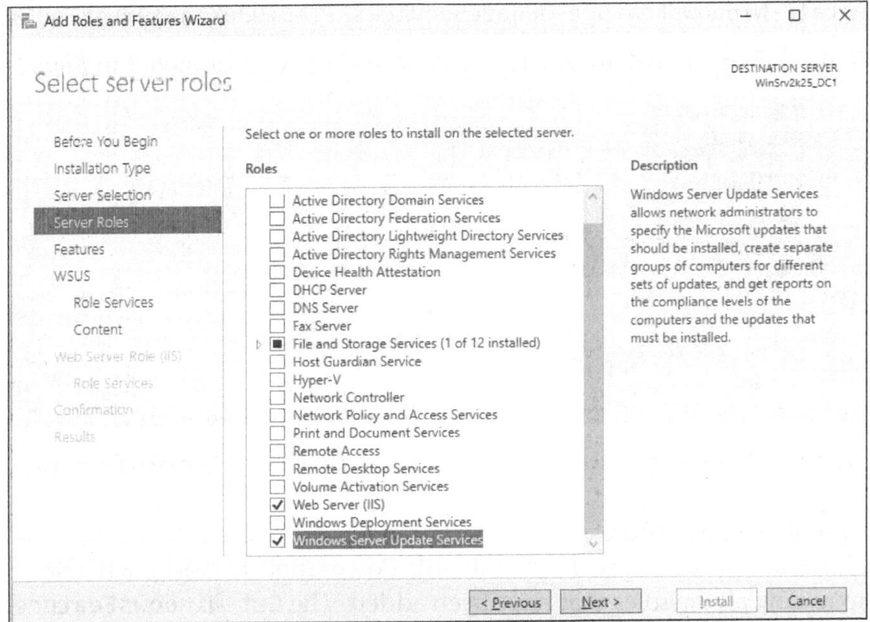

***Figure 5.19:** Installing WSUS role in Windows Server 2025 using Server Manager*

6. Accept the default settings on the **Select Features** page and click the **Next** button to proceed.
7. Click the **Next** button on the WSUS page.
8. Click the **Next** button on the WSUS page.

9. Select the **role services** to install on the **Select role services** page for the WSUS role. Then click the **Next** button.
10. Click the **Next** button to enter the local or remote paths on the c page.
11. Review the options on the **Confirm installation selections** page and click the **Install** button.
12. The installation of the WSUS role will begin. Once the installation is complete, click on the **Close** button to exit the Add Roles and Features Wizard.

Adding WSUS Role via PowerShell

To begin the process of adding a WSUS role in Windows Server 2025 using Windows PowerShell, follow these steps:

1. Launch **Windows PowerShell** by right-clicking on the **Start** button.
2. Within the Windows PowerShell interface, input the provided cmdlet and then press *Enter*:

```
Install-WindowsFeature UpdateServices -IncludeManagementTools
```

3. The WSUS role installation will commence shortly, as depicted in *Figure 5.20*:

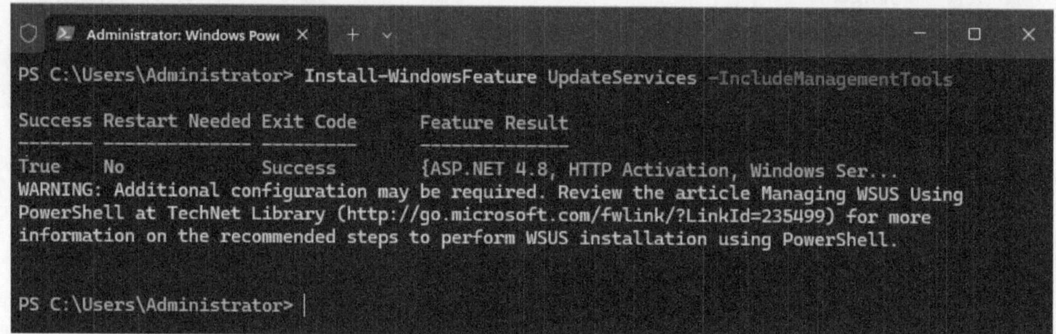

***Figure 5.20:** Installing WSUS role in Windows Server 2025 using Windows PowerShell*

Up to this point, we have successfully incorporated most of the roles offered by Windows Server 2025. The approach involved utilizing PowerShell to add each role. Now, it is essential to review all the roles that have been added. The **`Get-WindowsFeature`** cmdlet is particularly useful as it lists all the installed roles on the server. Additionally, if there are new roles that the system administrator wishes to add to the server, the **`Get-WindowsFeature`** cmdlet will provide the installation name (found in the **Name column**), which should be used when executing the cmdlet:

```
Install-WindowsFeature <name of the service>
```

Conclusion

In this chapter, you have explored the process of installing roles in Windows Server 2025 using the Add Roles and Features Wizard available in the Server Manager and PowerShell. You have received comprehensive guidance on the necessary steps and additional features required for each role to function correctly. The chapter covered roles such as AD DS, DHCP, Hyper-V, IIS, PDS, RDS, and WSUS. It also provided hands-on exercises for readers to follow.

Additionally, you have gained insights into the purpose of each role and how to configure them to meet your organization's needs. With this knowledge, you can efficiently install roles and customize your Windows Server 2025 environment to align with your organization's requirements.

In the next chapter, you will delve into exploring On-Premises Server Hotpatching with Azure Arc, a feature that enhances server management by allowing updates to be applied without requiring a reboot, thus minimizing downtime and ensuring continuous operation.

Questions

1. What is AD DS?
2. What are DNS zones?
3. Explain DORA in DHCP.
4. What is Hyper-V?
5. What is IIS?
6. Name the PDS role services.
7. List network access technologies of RA.
8. What is needed to set up RDS?
9. Which are WSUS connection modes?

Join our book's Discord space

Join the book's Discord Workspace for Latest updates, Offers, Tech happenings around the world, New Release and Sessions with the Authors:

https://discord.bpbonline.com

CHAPTER 6
Azure Arc On-Premises Hotpatching

Introduction

Welcome to this chapter on On-Premises Server Hotpatching with Azure Arc in Windows Server 2025. This chapter delves into the innovative capabilities of hotpatching, a method for applying updates to servers without requiring a reboot, enabled by Azure Arc, a powerful hybrid cloud solution from Microsoft. Using Azure Arc, you will learn how hotpatching can seamlessly integrate with on-premises servers. This chapter provides step-by-step instructions and practical examples to help you leverage Azure Arc to implement hotpatching solutions. You will gain insights into configuring Azure Arc for hotpatching, implementing hotpatching policies and schedules, and monitoring and managing hotpatching updates. The chapter also covers best practices for deploying and maintaining hotpatching, real-world use cases, and examples showcasing the benefits of hotpatching in on-premises server environments. By the end of this chapter, you will have a comprehensive understanding of how to enhance security and minimize downtime in your on-premises server environments using Azure Arc and hotpatching. Whether new to Azure Arc or looking to optimize your existing infrastructure, this chapter will equip you with the knowledge and tools to implement hotpatching in Windows Server 2025 effectively.

Structure

The chapter covers the following topics:

- Understanding hotpatching benefits
- Introduction to Azure Arc
- Exploring On-Premises Server Hotpatching with Azure Arc
- Exercise 6.1: Configuring Azure Arc
- Implementing hotpatching policies and schedules
- Monitoring and managing hotpatching updates
- Best practices for hotpatching
- Real-world use cases and examples

Objectives

The primary objective of this chapter is to provide comprehensive guidance on implementing On-Premises Server Hotpatching with Azure Arc in Windows Server 2025. This is achieved through step-by-step instructions and clear explanations on configuring Azure Arc for hotpatching, implementing hotpatching policies and schedules, and monitoring and managing hotpatching updates. Additionally, this chapter aims to help readers understand the benefits of hotpatching, best practices for deployment, and real-world use cases. By the end of this chapter, readers will have gained the necessary skills and knowledge to effectively implement hotpatching, enhance security and minimize downtime in their on-premises server environments.

Understanding hotpatching benefits

Hotpatching is a groundbreaking feature in server management. It allows critical updates and patches to be applied without requiring a system reboot. This functionality minimizes downtime, ensuring servers remain operational and highly reliable. In today's IT landscape, where uninterrupted service is paramount, hot patching offers a strategic advantage by eliminating the **disruptions** associated with update cycles.

With the release of Windows Server 2025, Microsoft has significantly enhanced hotpatching, increasing its flexibility and efficiency across diverse environments. Administrators can implement crucial real-time updates to preserve essential workloads' stability and prevent service interruptions. This capability is indispensable in demanding scenarios such as enterprise networks, data centers, and financial systems, where even brief downtime can result in significant productivity losses and economic implications.

Windows Server 2025 also extends hotpatching support to **virtualized and hybrid architectures**, enabling seamless integration across **on-premises** and **cloud-based infrastructures**. Additionally, the enhanced monitoring and management capabilities within the **Windows Admin Center** provide administrators with precise control over the patching process, ensuring security, compliance, and system health are maintained effortlessly.

Incorporating hotpatching enables Windows Server 2025 to optimize uptime, minimize operational risks, and achieve consistent service delivery. This innovation solidifies its role as a critical tool for IT professionals striving to maintain resilient and efficient infrastructure systems in an ever-evolving technological ecosystem.

Benefits of hotpatching with Windows Server 2025

As noted earlier, **hotpatching** is a transformative feature in Windows Server 2025, offering significant benefits that enhance server reliability and operational efficiency. Hotpatching helps organizations minimize service interruptions and maintain robust infrastructure performance by enabling updates without requiring a reboot. Key benefits include:

- **Minimized downtime:** Hotpatching eliminates the need for system restarts during updates, ensuring **uninterrupted server operation**. This is especially critical for high-availability environments where downtime can have severe consequences.
- **Enhanced security:** With the ability to deploy critical patches promptly, hotpatching **reduces the window of vulnerability**, strengthening system defenses against emerging threats.
- **Operational efficiency:** Avoiding disruptions during update cycles preserves server stability and performance, helping organizations maintain **smooth operations** during maintenance periods.
- **Flexible integration:** Windows Server 2025 enhances hotpatching by extending its capabilities across **on-premises**, **virtualized**, and **hybrid environments**. This flexibility ensures seamless adaptation to modern infrastructure needs.
- **Advanced management:** Administrators gain **precise control** over the patching process through the **Windows Admin Center**, which offers enhanced monitoring and management tools. These tools simplify compliance, improve system health oversight, and streamline the update experience.

Hotpatching with Windows Server 2025 is a cornerstone of modern IT infrastructure, providing organizations with the tools to ensure resilience, security, and efficiency. As IT environments grow increasingly complex, the ability to maintain continuous service availability while applying updates underscores the essential value of this innovative feature.

Hotpatching in Windows Server 2025 updates

Windows Server 2025 introduces significant advancements in hotpatching, revolutionizing how updates and patches are applied to critical systems. By minimizing downtime and reducing operational disruptions, hotpatching ensures that businesses reliant on high-availability environments—such as enterprise networks, cloud platforms, and large-scale data centers—can maintain optimal performance without compromising security or functionality.

Hotpatching eliminates the need for most system reboots when deploying patches, addressing one of the most challenging aspects of traditional update management. Here are the key requirements to effectively utilize this feature in Windows Server 2025:

- **Windows Server 2025 datacenter or standard edition:** Hotpatching is exclusive to these editions, offering enterprise-grade reliability and performance enhancements tailored for modern workloads.
- **Azure Arc integration:** Connectivity with Azure Arc is mandatory for managing and deploying hotpatches. Azure Arc enables centralized management across hybrid and multi-cloud environments, ensuring seamless patch deployment.
- **Active Software Assurance subscription:** An active Software Assurance subscription is a prerequisite to accessing hotpatching capabilities. This program provides organizations with tools and services to optimize their Microsoft environments.
- **Virtualization-Based Security (VBS):** VBS must be enabled and fully operational. It isolates sensitive parts of the operating system using hardware-assisted virtualization, bolstering the server's overall security posture.
- **Prerequisite security updates:** Before implementing hotpatching, ensure that all specified security updates have been applied. These updates lay the groundwork for enabling hotpatching functionality and maintaining compatibility with Windows Server 2025.

Windows Server 2025 hotpatching features

Windows Server 2025 brings several new and enhanced features to hotpatching, further improving its capabilities and making it an indispensable tool for maintaining server health and performance. These advancements ensure that hotpatching remains a critical component of modern IT infrastructure, providing seamless updates and minimizing disruptions:

- **Dynamic workload detection:** Windows Server 2025 intelligently identifies workloads and schedules updates during low-impact windows, reducing the risk of service interruptions.

- **Enhanced reporting and insights:** Administrators can leverage advanced analytics through the **Windows Admin Center** and Azure portal to monitor patch deployments and compliance.
- **Expanded virtualization support:** The feature now supports additional virtualization platforms integrated with Microsoft Hyper-V, ensuring broader compatibility across diverse IT environments.

Adhering to these requirements and utilizing the enhanced capabilities of hotpatching enables organizations to achieve a more secure, resilient, and efficient operational environment with Windows Server 2025. Ensuring all systems are prepared, and configurations are validated before implementing hotpatching maximizes its benefits.

Introduction to Azure Arc

As illustrated in *Figure 6.1*, **Azure Arc is** now an integrated feature of Windows Server 2025, extending the Azure platform's capabilities and enabling organizations to manage and deploy applications seamlessly across data centers, edge locations, and multi-cloud environments. With Azure Arc's integration, administrators gain a unified, hybrid cloud management solution directly into the Windows Server 2025 ecosystem.

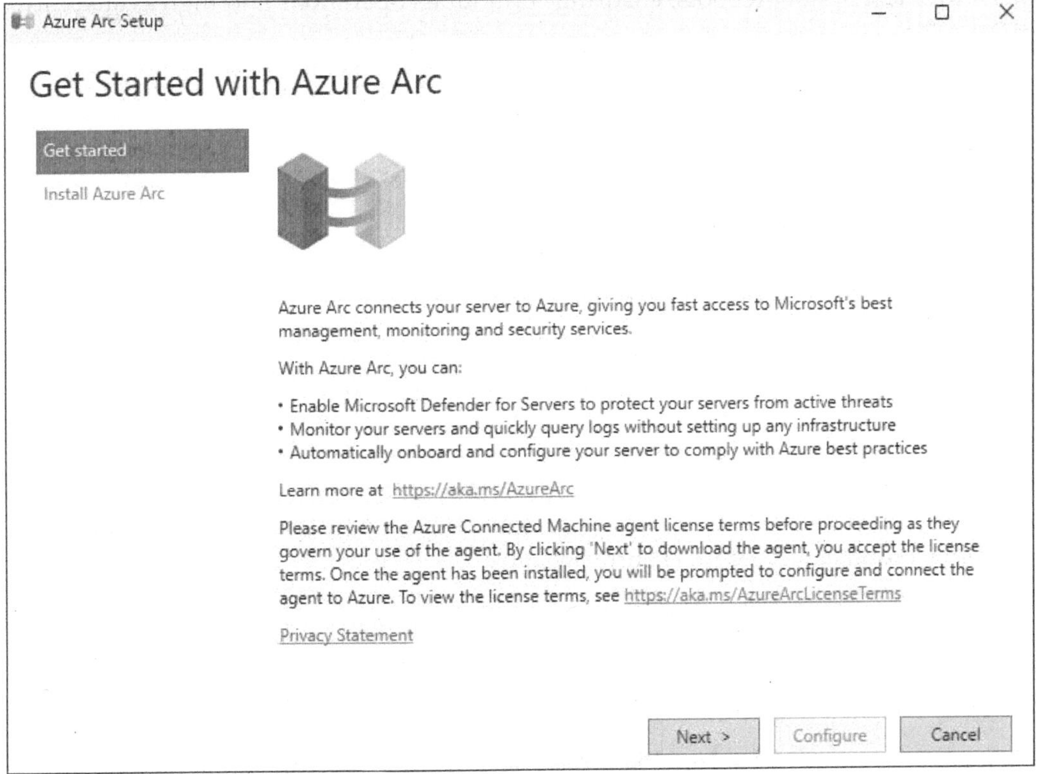

Figure 6.1. *Azure Arc integrated into Windows Server 2025*

This integration significantly enhances hotpatching, a critical feature in Windows Server 2025, by enabling efficient management of updates across both cloud-based and on-premises infrastructures. Azure Arc empowers IT professionals to govern on-premises, multi-cloud, and edge environments from a single control plane, streamlining management and reducing administrative complexity.

Leveraging Azure Arc's advanced management capabilities allows administrators to apply hotpatching consistently and securely without requiring server reboots. This ensures systems remain operational while benefiting from the latest security updates and patches, reducing the risk of vulnerabilities. Azure Arc simplifies the patching process by enabling the following:

- **Unified management:** Administrators can monitor and manage updates across diverse infrastructures, whether on-premises, in the cloud, or hybrid environments, all from a single pane of glass.
- **Efficient patch deployment:** Patches are created and deployed seamlessly, leveraging Azure Arc's built-in tools for tracking, scheduling, and verifying updates.
- **Minimized downtime:** Hotpatching, enhanced by Azure Arc, eliminates the need for most system reboots, ensuring continuous operations and high availability.
- **Enhanced reporting and analytics:** IT teams can verify successful patch applications and analyze system stability across their environments with integrated reporting features.

Growing role of hotpatching

In the evolving landscape of IT environments, hotpatching with Azure Arc has become an indispensable tool in modern server management strategies. This integration represents a cornerstone of Windows Server 2025's commitment to operational excellence and security by enabling organizations to maintain continuous operations, streamline updates, and enhance system security.

Azure Arc centralizes hybrid management and enhances the efficiency and security of patching workflows, as depicted in *Figure 6.2*. The integration ensures that updates are consistently applied to Windows Server 2025 instances regardless of deployment location, promoting a robust and secure IT infrastructure.

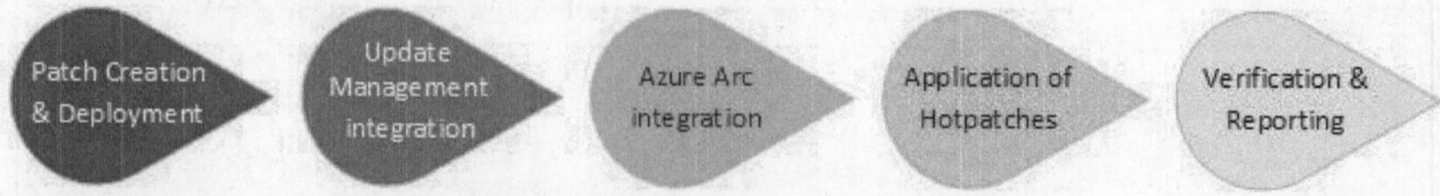

***Figure 6.2.** Hotpatching process overview*

Embedding Azure Arc as a core component makes Windows Server 2025 a comprehensive solution for managing hybrid and multi-cloud environments. It equips IT professionals with the tools to address today's dynamic challenges effectively.

Exploring On-Premises Server Hotpatching with Azure Arc

Windows Server 2025 introduces a robust integration of advanced **compatibility layers** and cutting-edge virtualization technologies, enabling enterprises to navigate the complexities of hybrid IT environments seamlessly. This approach is invaluable for organizations operating a mix of modern and legacy systems, ensuring diverse technologies coexist within a unified and efficient management framework.

Administrators can confidently deploy updates and new features in Windows Server 2025, supported by enhanced compatibility mechanisms designed to mitigate operational disruptions. The operating system demonstrates remarkable adaptability, catering to a broad spectrum of hardware configurations—from traditional on-premises servers to modern cloud-based architectures. This ensures optimal performance and reliability across diverse platforms, empowering organizations to sustain their technological edge.

Enhanced collaboration for unmatched compatibility

Microsoft's collaboration with leading hardware vendors and software developers has resulted in rigorous testing and certification processes. These initiatives ensure that hardware and software meet stringent performance, security, and reliability standards, further solidifying Windows Server 2025 as a robust enterprise choice.

Hybrid cloud capabilities with Azure Arc

The hybrid cloud support in Windows Server 2025 is a game-changer, blending on-premises infrastructures with the scalability and flexibility of cloud platforms like Microsoft Azure. This integration is now elevated through Azure Arc, which is embedded as a core component of Windows Server 2025. Azure Arc empowers businesses to extend Azure management capabilities to their on-premises servers, creating a cohesive management experience across hybrid and multi-cloud environments.

By leveraging Azure Arc, IT administrators can:

- **Seamlessly manage hybrid resources:** Use a single control plane to unify the management of on-premises and cloud-based servers, simplifying operations and improving efficiency.

- **Implement advanced hotpatching:** Deploy updates and patches across on-premises environments without disrupting operations, enhancing security and availability.

- **Scale with agility:** Utilize cloud scalability to address dynamic business demands while controlling critical on-premises resources.

Empowering IT operations

Windows Server 2025's hybrid capabilities, combined with Azure Arc integration, equip IT professionals with the tools to balance control, scalability, and flexibility. This hybrid approach meets the evolving demands of modern business environments, ensuring that organizations can harness the power of cloud technologies while preserving the stability and security of on-premises systems.

Windows Server 2025, with its advanced compatibility, rigorous certifications, and hybrid cloud capabilities powered by Azure Arc, delivers a powerful platform for enterprises aiming to stay agile and secure in a rapidly changing IT landscape.

Exercise 6.1: Configuring Azure Arc

This exercise will teach you how to **configure** Azure Arc in Windows Server 2025 to extend Azure's robust management capabilities to your on-premises servers. This process allows you to utilize cloud management features such as hotpatching and updates while ensuring smooth operation. Follow these steps:

1. Ensure you have an Active **Azure Subscription**.

2. Ensure your Windows Server 2025 machine meets Azure Arc's hardware and software requirements.

3. Ensure you have administrative access to the Windows Server 2025 machine to **install** and **configure** Azure Arc.

4. On your Windows Server 2025 machine, locate the Azure Arc icon in the system tray.

5. Right-click the **Azure Arc** system tray icon and select **Azure Arc Setup** to open the **Azure Arc Configuration** wizard.

6. The setup wizard will check for prerequisites and guide you through installing the **Azure Connected Machine Agent**, illustrated in *Figure 6.3*. This agent enables your server to communicate with Azure Arc. Once completed, click **Next** to proceed.

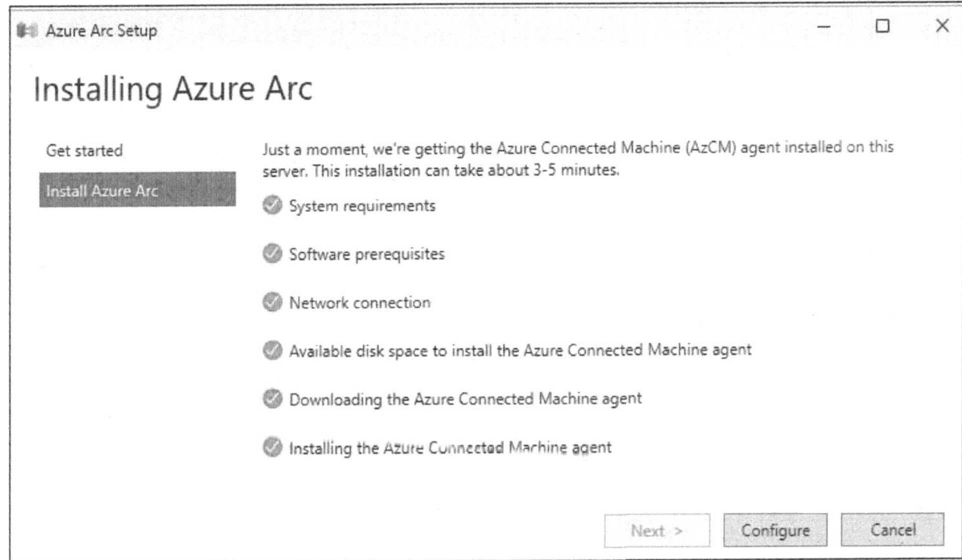

Figure 6.3. *Installing Azure Arc in Windows Server 2025*

7. Click **Configure**, then **Next** to continue with the configuration.
8. On the **sign in** to Azure page, select the **Azure cloud** you are using, sign in with your credentials, and generate the required authentication code. Click **Next** to proceed.
9. Choose the tenant, subscription, resource group, and Azure region on the **Resource Details** page. If you are using a **proxy**, configure the necessary settings. Once everything is configured, click **Next**.
10. If your organization has a license covered by Software Assurance, check the box labeled **I attest that I have a permit covered by Software Assurance**. Then, click **Next** to continue.
11. On the **Connecting your server** page, the wizard will prompt you to connect the server to **Azure Arc**. Click **Next** to initiate the connection process.
12. Once the server is connected, a **Connection and Configuration Successful** message will appear, as illustrated in *Figure 6.4*. This confirms that the server has been successfully configured and connected to **Azure Arc**.

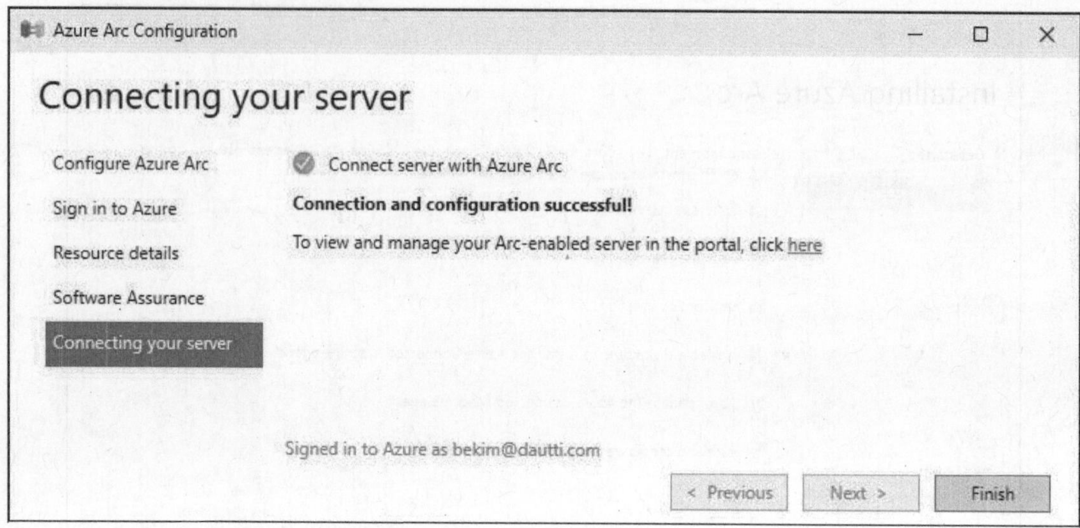

Figure 6.4. Successful configuration of Azure Arc and connection to Azure Portal

13. After completing the setup, go to **the Azure portal** and confirm that your server is listed as an **Azure Arc-enabled resource.**

14. As required for your environment, you can enable additional management features such as Hotpatching, Updates, and Logs (shown in *Figure 6.5*).

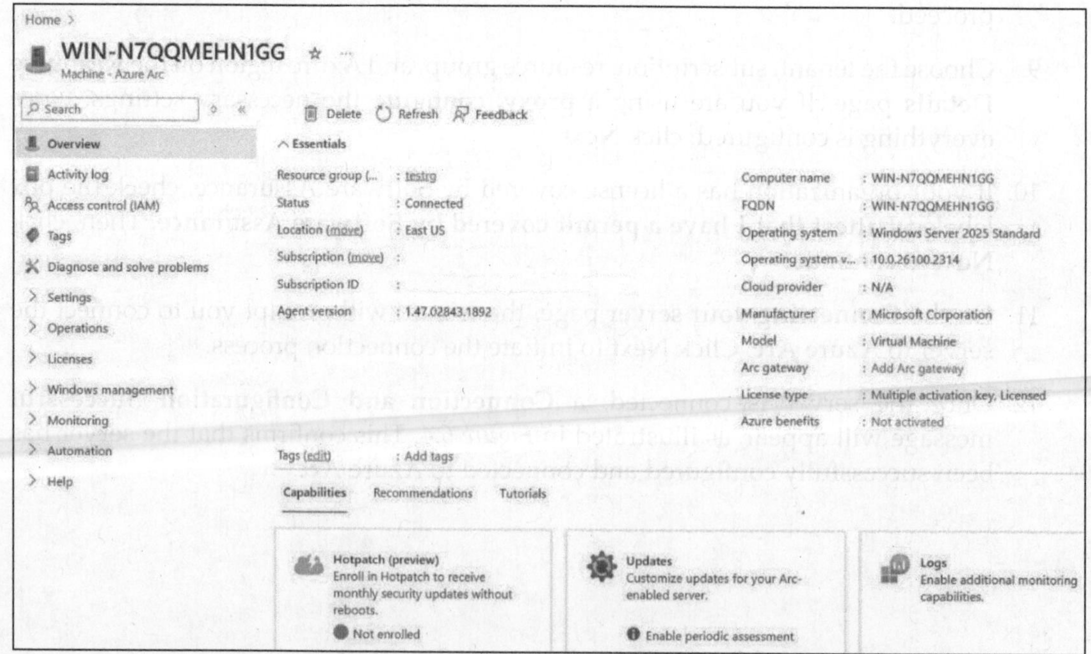

Figure 6.5. Verifying that the server is listed in Azure Arc and enabling features

Implementing hotpatching policies and schedules

In Windows Server 2025, implementing hotpatching policies and schedules is crucial for maintaining server security and performance without causing downtime. Enhanced capabilities integrated with Microsoft Azure Arc empower administrators to efficiently manage and deploy hotpatches across on-premises, hybrid, and cloud environments. By adopting a structured approach, organizations can ensure optimal results.

A successful hotpatching implementation begins with defining robust policies. These policies should specify:

- **Server eligibility:** Identify which servers or server groups require hotpatching, focusing on critical workloads and high-priority systems.
- **Update scope:** Outline the patches to be applied, including security updates and bug fixes, while excluding updates that can wait for standard maintenance cycles.
- **Compliance requirements:** Ensure adherence to organizational and regulatory standards.

Scheduling is equally crucial for minimizing disruption. Plan to patch during low-usage periods or pre-approved maintenance windows to reduce the impact on critical operations. For global deployments, stagger schedules to accommodate different time zones. Use Azure Arc analytics to identify the best patching windows based on workload trends.

Azure Arc serves as the backbone for managing hotpatching in Windows Server 2025. To leverage its capabilities:

- **Onboard servers:** Connect all relevant Windows Server 2025 instances, whether on-premises, hybrid, or cloud-hosted, to Azure Arc.
- **Install necessary agents:** Ensure the Azure Arc agent and required dependencies are installed and updated on all servers.
- **Validate compliance:** Use Azure Policy to ensure that servers meet the prerequisites for hotpatching.

Automation plays a pivotal role in streamlining hotpatching operations. With Azure Update Management, administrators can:

- Automate workflows for patch approval, deployment, and rollback.
- Configure automated patch approvals based on severity or compliance needs.
- Enable rollback mechanisms to address deployment failures, ensuring system stability.

Monitoring and verifying patch status are critical for a successful deployment. Utilize Azure Arc's monitoring tools to:

- Track the status of hotpatch deployments.
- Configure alerts for failed updates or servers requiring attention.
- Validate updates using tools such as **Windows Admin Center** and **Event Viewer**.

Lastly, regularly review and update your hotpatching policies. As threats evolve and environments change, adapt policies to address emerging vulnerabilities and improve performance. Ensure alignment with best practices and organizational objectives.

Integrating these practices allows administrators to leverage the advanced hotpatching features of Windows Server 2025 fully. This holistic approach guarantees a secure, compliant, resilient infrastructure while reducing downtime and administrative effort.

Note: Regularly updating your server inventory is essential for efficient lifecycle management in Windows Server 2025. Ensure your inventory includes server roles, configurations, and lifecycle stages to enable faster decisions on upgrades, decommissioning, and compliance audits. Utilize tools like Windows Admin Center and Azure Arc to automate asset tracking, enhancing accuracy and reducing manual effort. These tools streamline updates, centralize tracking, and integrate reporting capabilities for better oversight and planning. This practice ensures operational efficiency, compliance, and preparedness for evolving IT needs.

Monitoring and managing hotpatching updates

Effective **monitoring and managing** hotpatching updates in Windows Server 2025 are crucial for maintaining system security, ensuring compliance, and optimizing server performance. This dual approach ensures real-time oversight of patching processes and strategic coordination to minimize disruptions while maintaining operational efficiency. Let us take a look at them:

- **Comprehensive monitoring framework:** Monitoring is the foundation of effective hotpatching management. Tools such as **Azure Monitor** and **Microsoft System Center Operations Manager (SCOM)** provide real-time insights into the health and performance of servers. These tools allow IT teams to track key metrics such as patch deployment status, resource utilization, and system responsiveness. Alerts triggered by anomalies—such as failed patch installations or prolonged high **CPU usage**—enable proactive troubleshooting to avoid downtime or security vulnerabilities.

- **Policy-driven management of hotpatching:** Establish **clear and enforceable policies** that define criteria for hotpatching. These policies should include server classification, patch prioritization, and maintenance schedules. These policies can be centrally configured and enforced for environments managed via Azure Arc, ensuring consistency across on-premises and hybrid infrastructures.

- **Automation for streamlined operations:** Automation plays a key role in monitoring and managing hotpatching. Utilize the **automation** capabilities in Azure Arc to schedule, approve, deploy, and verify patches seamlessly. Automated workflows reduce human error and improve the reliability of patch applications while maintaining uniformity across diverse server environments.
- **Scheduling for minimal impact:** Effective management includes planning the timing of hotpatching to **minimize operational impact**. Schedule updates during designated maintenance windows or periods of low activity, ensuring critical services remain unaffected. Leveraging predictive analytics in Azure Monitor, IT teams can identify optimal patching windows based on historical workload patterns.
- **Real-time monitoring and visualization:** Visual dashboards in tools like **Windows Admin Center** offer a unified view of patching activities. These dashboards display the status of updates across servers, as shown in *Figure 6.6*, enabling administrators to quickly identify unpatched systems, verify successful deployments, and address issues in real-time.

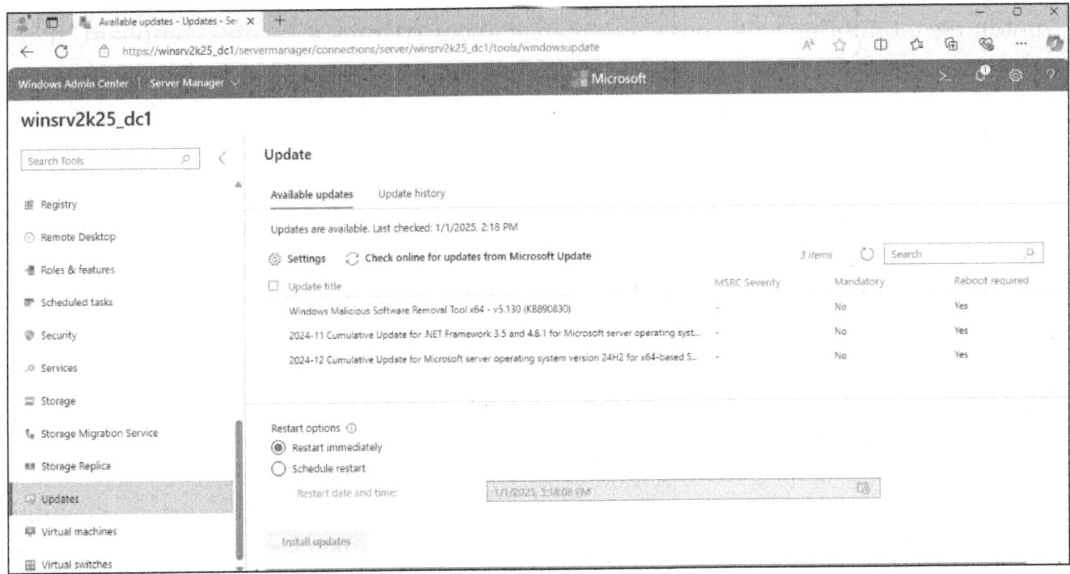

Figure 6.6. Windows Admin Center enables update monitoring

- **Advanced reporting for decision-making:** Detailed reports complement monitoring efforts by transforming collected data into **actionable insights**. Reporting capabilities in tools like **Azure Monitor** provide metrics on patching compliance, system performance, and resource usage. For instance, compliance reports help identify gaps in patching strategies, while performance reports may highlight trends necessitating system upgrades or resource reallocation.

- **Predictive analytics and preventative measures:** Incorporate predictive capabilities to anticipate potential failures or conflicts arising from hotpatching. Advanced analytics in **Azure Monitor** can flag early warning signs, such as disk utilization trends or temperature anomalies, enabling preemptive actions. This ensures smoother patching processes and enhances overall system resilience.
- **Ensuring compliance and audit readiness:** Monitoring and managing hotpatching are integral to regulatory compliance. Detailed logs and automated audit trails document every patching activity, meeting standards such as **Health Insurance Portability and Accountability Act (HIPAA)** or **General Data Protection Regulation (GDPR)**. These records simplify audits and ensure transparency in how updates are applied and managed.
- **Iterative improvements to hotpatching strategies:** Effective management goes beyond execution—it involves **continuous improvement**. Use performance analytics to refine hotpatching policies and schedules. For instance, recurring patterns of update delays might signal a need for additional bandwidth or revised patching workflows.

Combining monitoring with proactive management ensures a secure, compliant, high-performing server environment. These integrated practices optimize hotpatching processes to be efficient and responsive, enabling organizations to meet dynamic business demands while maintaining long-term infrastructure reliability.

Note: Consistently evaluate and adjust your monitoring thresholds and reporting parameters to align with changing business requirements and system performance. What is effective today might not meet future needs. Leveraging adaptive monitoring tools that analyze historical data can help predict potential issues and enhance the overall effectiveness of your monitoring approach.

Best practices for hotpatching

Effectively **managing hotpatching** implementations in Windows Server 2025 necessitates a structured approach grounded in best practices. These practices ensure system reliability while facilitating the seamless integration of live updates, which is crucial for maintaining high availability. For IT professionals managing complex environments, efficiently implementing hotpatching procedures helps mitigate risks and enhances the overall performance and security of the system. The following are key practices that ensure successful hotpatch deployment:

- **Conduct comprehensive pre-deployment testing:** Rigorous testing in a controlled environment is vital before deploying a hotpatch in a live production environment.

Simulating a replica of the live system using tools such as **Azure DevTest Labs** or virtualized environments to assess the impact on system performance and functionality is essential. For example, when deploying a hotpatch to critical applications, testing the patch under identical workloads can reveal performance degradation or conflicts with other services. This proactive testing ensures minimal disruption during live updates and allows for the early detection of potential issues before they affect production systems.

- **Implement robust logging and monitoring mechanisms:** Logging and monitoring are critical in identifying and diagnosing issues during the deployment of hotpatches. Tools like **Azure Monitor**, **Microsoft Sentinel**, and SCOM provide real-time insights into the health and performance of systems. Comprehensive logging captures important deployment events, enabling IT teams to track patch application steps, detect failures, and analyze performance metrics. By establishing a continuous monitoring process, IT professionals can ensure that the system remains operational and that any deviations are addressed promptly.
- **Ensure network readiness:** Hotpatching can significantly demand network resources, particularly during large-scale updates. Adequate network capacity is essential to prevent latency, packet loss, or deployment failures. Tools like **Azure Network Watcher**, depicted in *Figure 6.7*, allow IT professionals to assess network readiness by simulating traffic and evaluating how the network will handle the added load from hotpatching. Network optimizations, such as adjusting bandwidth allocation or configuring redundant pathways, should be part of the strategy. Additionally, implementing **rollback mechanisms** and **fallback procedures** ensures smooth recovery in case of network-related failures.

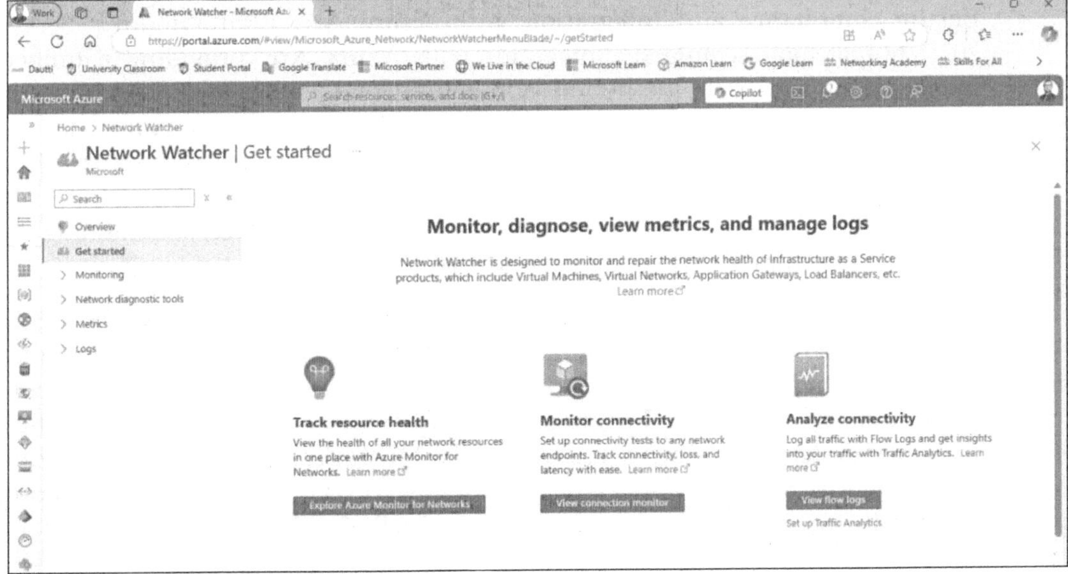

Figure 6.7: Azure Network Watcher enables network readiness

- **Maintain security throughout the process:** Security remains a top priority during hotpatching, as introducing vulnerabilities through faulty updates can jeopardize system integrity. Hotpatches must only be sourced from trusted vendors and thoroughly scanned for security issues using **Microsoft Defender for Endpoint**. Tools like **Azure Security Center** help verify the integrity of patches and monitor for any signs of malicious code or unauthorized modifications. Regular security audits throughout the patching process, as well as multi-layered security measures, help mitigate risks and maintain the system's security posture.
- **Foster collaboration and knowledge sharing:** Collaboration is essential for effective troubleshooting and continuous improvement. Platforms like **Microsoft Teams** and **SharePoint** offer collaboration spaces where IT teams can document findings, share troubleshooting steps, and exchange best practices. These platforms create a knowledge base that can be accessed across the organization, helping streamline the troubleshooting process and improve the overall efficiency of hotpatching operations. Encouraging team collaboration ensures efficient troubleshooting and that any recurring issues are resolved with better solutions.
- **Provide comprehensive user training and clear communication:** Clear communication and well-informed users are critical to the success of hotpatching efforts. IT professionals should conduct training sessions for technical staff and end users, ensuring everyone understands the purpose, process, and safety measures associated with hotpatches. Offering **workshops**, **online resources**, and **detailed documentation** can ease concerns and build trust in the hotpatching process. Organizations can minimize disruptions and encourage smooth deployments by preparing users for updates' potential impact and benefits.
- **Ensure compliance and integration with Azure Arc:** With Windows Server 2025, hotpatching seamlessly integrates with **Azure Arc**, providing a unified management approach for hybrid and multi-cloud environments. Azure Arc allows IT professionals to extend consistent hotpatching capabilities to on-premises servers, ensuring compliance across diverse infrastructure setups. This integration simplifies the patch management process, enabling administrators to oversee cloud and on-premises resources from a single interface, streamlining the deployment and monitoring of patches across hybrid environments.

Following these best practices ensures a resilient and efficient hotpatching process within Windows Server 2025 environments. By adopting a proactive approach that includes pre-deployment testing, detailed monitoring, network readiness, security validation, collaboration, and user education, IT professionals can confidently implement hotpatches, ensuring optimal system performance and reliability. Moreover, the integration of Azure Arc further enhances the ability to manage hybrid environments effectively, offering additional benefits for organizations seeking to optimize their infrastructure.

Real-world use cases and examples

As it is known now, hotpatching in Windows Server 2025 represents a groundbreaking advancement in system management, providing a mechanism for applying patches and updates without requiring server reboots. Therefore, this capability is critical for maintaining high availability and ensuring businesses experience minimal downtime during essential updates. The following are several real-world use cases and examples demonstrating how organizations can leverage hotpatching to keep secure, resilient, and efficient systems:

- **Critical application updates without disruption:** Downtime is not an option for organizations that rely on mission-critical applications, such as healthcare systems or financial platforms. Hotpatching enables the deployment of security updates or bug fixes on these systems without interrupting operations. For example, in a **hospital** environment using Windows Server 2025, updates to patient management systems can be deployed seamlessly across servers without taking down the application, ensuring continuous access to essential services for healthcare providers and patients. Integrating **Azure Arc** with Windows Server 2025, administrators can extend these capabilities to hybrid and multi-cloud environments, enabling updates to be applied across on-premises and cloud resources simultaneously. This ensures that all systems, regardless of their location, are updated without the need for downtime.

- **Patch management for e-commerce and web servers:** For **e-commerce** platforms or **high-traffic websites** hosted on Windows Server 2025, maintaining uptime during updates is crucial to ensuring customers can continue shopping and interacting with services without interruption. Hotpatching allows businesses to apply security patches or address vulnerabilities in real time without taking web servers offline. This ensures that any new security threats, such as zero-day exploits, can be mitigated promptly, all while keeping the website fully operational. Using **Microsoft Sentinel** and **Azure Monitor** to continuously track the performance of web servers during the hotpatching process ensures that any issues are detected immediately. Real-time visibility enables IT teams to respond proactively, minimizing the risk of outages or degraded performance.

- **Managing hybrid environments with seamless updates:** With many organizations embracing hybrid environments, ensuring consistency across on-premises and cloud infrastructure is more critical than ever. Hotpatching in Windows Server 2025 simplifies this challenge by allowing the deployment of updates across both environments without downtime. IT professionals can seamlessly manage Windows Server instances on-premises and Azure using **Azure Arc**. For example, a company with a mix of **on-premises** and **Azure-based workloads** can leverage Azure Arc to apply hotpatches to both sets of servers concurrently, eliminating the need for individual patching processes and reducing the administrative overhead associated with manual updates.

- **Enhancing business continuity in distributed systems:** In a distributed environment where servers are spread across different geographic locations, it cannot be easy to coordinate patching and updates without affecting system performance. Hotpatching and Windows Server 2025's integration with **Azure Site Recovery** enables IT teams to update distributed systems without causing disruptions. For example, a **global enterprise** with **data centers** in multiple regions can leverage hotpatching to ensure all servers remain secure while maintaining operational continuity. With advanced monitoring tools like SCOM and **Azure Network Watcher**, IT professionals can ensure that patches are applied smoothly and detect any network-related issues that may arise during the process. This proactive approach helps minimize the risk of service outages across regions.
- **Security Patching for High-Performance Computing (HPC) systems:** HPC environments often require continuous uptime to run critical simulations or process large datasets. Hotpatching in Windows Server 2025 allows these systems to remain operational while applying the latest security patches and performance improvements. This is particularly important in industries like **scientific research**, where interruptions can delay critical workflows and research timelines. Utilizing **Microsoft Defender for Endpoint**, administrators can ensure that hotpatches do not introduce security vulnerabilities into the HPC environment, maintaining the system's integrity while enhancing security. Additionally, **Azure Security Center** provides real-time monitoring of system health and patch integrity, further supporting the secure deployment of hotpatches.
- **Streamlining operations in virtualized environments:** Organizations with virtualized infrastructures, such as those utilizing **Hyper-V** in Windows Server 2025, benefit from hotpatching by minimizing the downtime of **virtual machines (VMs)**. Hotpatching can be applied to the underlying host systems without affecting the operation of VMs. This is particularly valuable in environments where multiple VMs run mission-critical applications, as it reduces the risk of performance degradation or service interruptions. Moreover, **Azure DevTest Labs** can create virtualized testing environments, allowing administrators to simulate the effects of hotpatching on VMs before applying updates in production. This ensures that potential issues are identified early in the process and mitigated before deployment.

Hotpatching in Windows Server 2025 is a powerful feature that enhances system uptime, reduces administrative burden, and strengthens security by allowing deployment updates without requiring server reboots. By leveraging technologies such as Azure Arc, Azure Security Center, and Microsoft Sentinel, organizations can ensure that hotpatching processes are efficient, secure, and seamlessly integrated into their hybrid and multi-cloud environments.

As organizations evolve and expand their IT infrastructure, embracing hotpatching as a key component of their patch management strategy will help ensure resilience, efficiency, and continuous service availability in today's fast-paced technological landscape.

Conclusion

In this chapter, you have learned about hotpatching with Azure Arc in Windows Server 2025, including its application across on-premises, hybrid, and cloud-based environments. You have comprehensively understood how hotpatching works to apply updates without requiring a reboot, thereby minimizing downtime and bolstering system reliability. Through practical examples, you have examined how Azure Arc can seamlessly integrate with on-premises servers, facilitating efficient management in hybrid environments. You have also learned the steps for configuring Azure Arc for hotpatching, implementing policies and schedules, and effectively monitoring and managing updates. Additionally, the chapter covered best practices and real-world use cases, illustrating the benefits of hotpatching for enhancing security and performance in various server setups. With this knowledge, you can implement hotpatching solutions in your Windows Server 2025 environments, ensuring heightened security and system uptime.

In the next chapter, you will explore the next-generation enhancements in Active Directory and SMB, focusing on the latest features and improvements in Windows Server 2025.

Questions

1. What is hotpatching in Windows Server 2025?
2. How does Azure Arc support hotpatching?
3. What are the benefits of hotpatching in on-premises environments?
4. How do you configure Azure Arc for hotpatching?
5. What are the best practices for implementing hotpatching?

Join our book's Discord space

Join the book's Discord Workspace for Latest updates, Offers, Tech happenings around the world, New Release and Sessions with the Authors:

https://discord.bpbonline.com

Conclusion

In this chapter, you have learned about hotpatching with Azure Arc in Windows Server 2025, including its application across on-premises, hybrid, and cloud-based environments. You have comprehensively understood how hotpatching works to apply updates without requiring a reboot, thereby minimizing downtime and bolstering system reliability. Through practical examples, you have examined how Azure Arc can seamlessly integrate with on-premises servers, facilitating efficient management in hybrid environments. You have also learned the steps for configuring Azure Arc for hotpatching, implementing policies and schedules, and effectively monitoring and managing updates. Additionally, the chapter covered best practices and real-world use cases, illustrating the benefits of hotpatching for enhancing security and performance in various server setups. With this knowledge, you can implement hotpatching solutions in your Windows Server 2025 environments, ensuring heightened security and system uptime.

In the next chapter, you will explore the next-generation enhancements in Active Directory and SMB, focusing on the latest features and improvements in Windows Server 2025.

Questions

1. What is hotpatching in Windows Server 2025?
2. How does Azure Arc support hotpatching?
3. What are the benefits of hotpatching in on-premises environments?
4. How do you configure Azure Arc for hotpatching?
5. What are the best practices for implementing hotpatching?

Join our book's Discord space

Join the book's Discord workspace for Latest updates, Offers, Tech happenings around the world, New Release and Sessions with the Authors:

https://discord.bpbonline.com

CHAPTER 7
Next-Generation Active Directory and SMB Enhancements

Introduction

This chapter explores the evolution of **Active Directory** (**AD**) and **Server Message Block** (**SMB**) protocols in Windows Server 2025. It covers cutting-edge enhancements and features in AD and SMB, emphasizing security, performance, and scalability improvements. You will discover the advancements in **Active Directory Domain Services** (**AD DS**) and the SMB protocol, with an in-depth exploration of new functionalities, fortified security measures, and optimized performance. Through practical examples and demonstrations, this chapter will guide you in leveraging these enhancements to streamline authentication, access control, and file sharing in your Windows Server 2025 environment. Whether you are upgrading your existing infrastructure or implementing new features, this chapter provides the insights you need to maximize the capabilities of AD and SMB in Windows Server 2025.

Structure

The chapter covers the following topics:

- Evolution of Active Directory
- New features in AD DS
- Improved Active Directory security

- Performance and scalability upgrades in Active Directory
- Exercise 7.1: Adding DNS Server role
- SMB protocol enhancements
- New features in the SMB protocol
- Enhanced SMB protocol security
- Enhancing SMB performance and scalability
- Exercise 7.2: Configuring and enabling SMB over QUIC

Objectives

The primary objective of this chapter is to provide an in-depth understanding of the evolution and advancements in AD and SMB protocols in Windows Server 2025. This chapter will guide you through detailed explanations and practical examples of the new features and enhancements in AD DS and the SMB protocol. By the end of this chapter, readers will have gained the knowledge and skills to implement and optimize AD and SMB in Windows Server 2025, focusing on enhanced security, improved performance, and scalability. You will be equipped to effectively manage authentication, access control, and file sharing in your organization's infrastructure, whether upgrading from a previous version or deploying new capabilities.

Evolution of Active Directory

Windows Server 2025 marks a pivotal evolution in AD DS, redefining its role to meet the demands of hybrid environments that integrate on-premises infrastructure with **cloud-based solutions**. These advancements reflect a natural progression in identity and access management technologies, enhancing scalability, security, and operational efficiency. The following are the evolutionary milestones in AD DS for Windows Server 2025:

- **Evolving integration with cloud services:** As hybrid environments become the standard, the evolution of AD DS ensures seamless connectivity with cloud platforms like **Microsoft Azure**. Windows Server 2025 introduces optimized synchronization processes, improving both speed and security. The enhanced **Microsoft Entra Connect**, illustrated in *Figure 7.1*, ensures reliable identity replication, allowing users consistent access to resources across on-premises and cloud environments. This evolution strengthens hybrid identity management while maintaining robust security protocols.

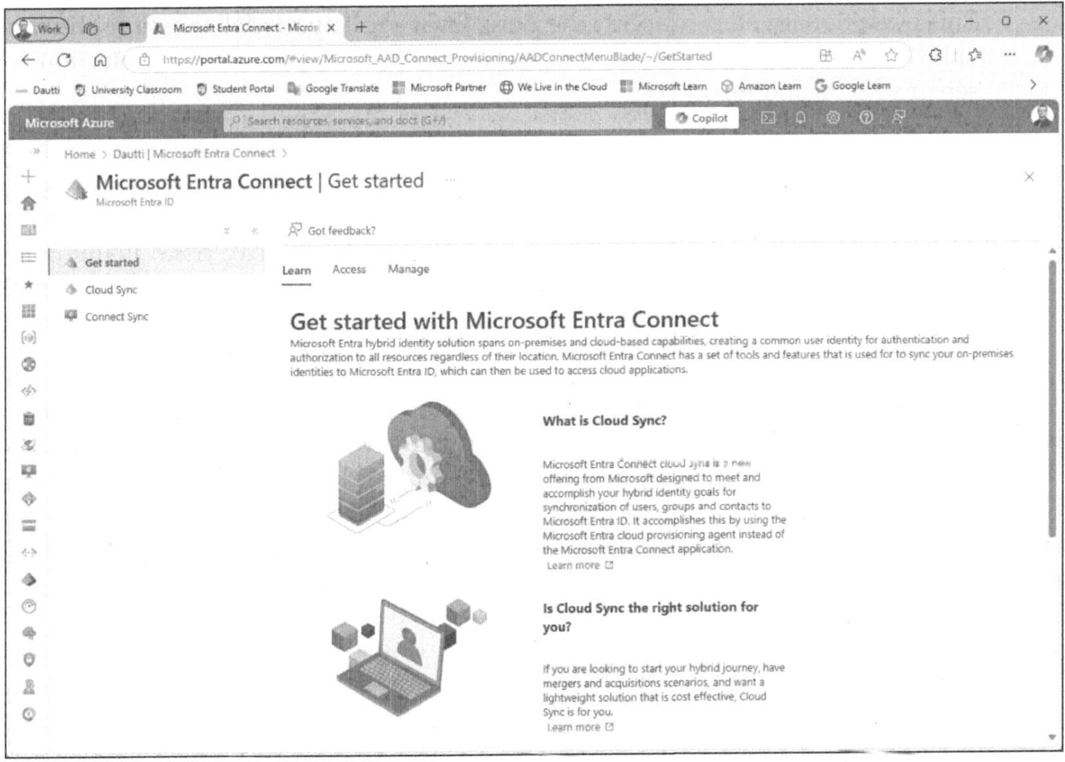

Figure 7.1: Microsoft Entra Connect on Azure

- **Hybrid identity models redefined:** The evolutionary enhancements in Windows Server 2025 extend AD DS capabilities into hybrid identity models. Organizations can now unify on-premises AD DS with **Microsoft Entra ID**, enabling advanced **Single Sign-On (SSO)** functionality. This evolution simplifies authentication workflows, allowing users to access cloud applications like Microsoft 365 and traditional on-premises resources with a single credential set. These refinements enhance user experience while adhering to stringent security standards.

- **Streamlined hybrid resource management:** The evolution of hybrid management tools in Windows Server 2025 brings unparalleled simplicity to managing hybrid environments. Tools like **Windows Admin Center** provide a unified interface for overseeing Azure-based services alongside on-premises resources by integrating cloud-native features directly into AD DS. This progression reduces complexity, enhances visibility, and ensures operational consistency, equipping IT teams with tools to manage hybrid infrastructures more effectively.

- **Expanded support for cloud-native applications:** Windows Server 2025 evolves AD DS to accommodate the growing reliance on modern cloud-native applications. By integrating with **Microsoft Entra ID**, organizations can implement conditional access policies tailored to specific scenarios, such as user location or device health.

This evolutionary step supports the **Zero Trust** security model, where continuous validation of access requests becomes the norm, ensuring robust protection for sensitive data and resources.

- **Granular control over hybrid identity management:** The evolution of identity and access governance in Windows Server 2025 gives administrators precise control across hybrid environments. **Enhanced monitoring** and **auditing tools** ensure organizations can swiftly detect and mitigate security risks, maintaining consistent compliance and governance across on-premises and cloud platforms. This advancement underscores AD DS's critical role in supporting hybrid operations securely and efficiently.

Windows Server 2025 exemplifies AD DS's evolutionary trajectory, adapting it to the demands of hybrid environments. By embracing seamless cloud integration, advanced identity models, and modern management tools, this release empowers organizations to streamline operations and enhance security without compromising flexibility. AD's continual evolution ensures its enduring relevance in modern IT landscapes, mainly as businesses rely on hybrid architectures to drive their success.

New features in AD DS

Windows Server 2025 introduces a range of groundbreaking new features to AD DS, enhancing its scalability, performance, and overall manageability. Among the most notable new features is the increased default Database Page Size, which significantly boosts the system's ability to handle large directories while minimizing fragmentation. This adjustment allows for more efficient processing and management of enterprise-level directories. Furthermore, updates to the **AD schema** ensure that AD remains fully compatible with modern Microsoft technologies and applications, allowing it to meet the increasingly complex needs of enterprises as they grow and evolve. Adding advanced object repair features also provides IT professionals with powerful tools to maintain the integrity of the **AD database**, ensuring reliable domain services and streamlined object management throughout the organization.

These new features in Windows Server 2025 include significant updates to AD DS, focusing on scalability, performance, functionality, and security. They are designed to meet the demands of modern IT environments, addressing everything from high-performance infrastructures to advanced security requirements. The following will explore these concepts in greater detail:

- **New domain and forest functional level (level 10):** One of the significant new features in Windows Server 2025 is introducing a **new domain** and **forest functional level**, referred to as **Level 10**, as illustrated in *Figure 7.2*. This new feature unlocks various functionalities and optimizations that benefit **AD DS** and **AD Lightweight Directory Services (AD LDS)**, providing more robust and scalable directory services across enterprise networks.

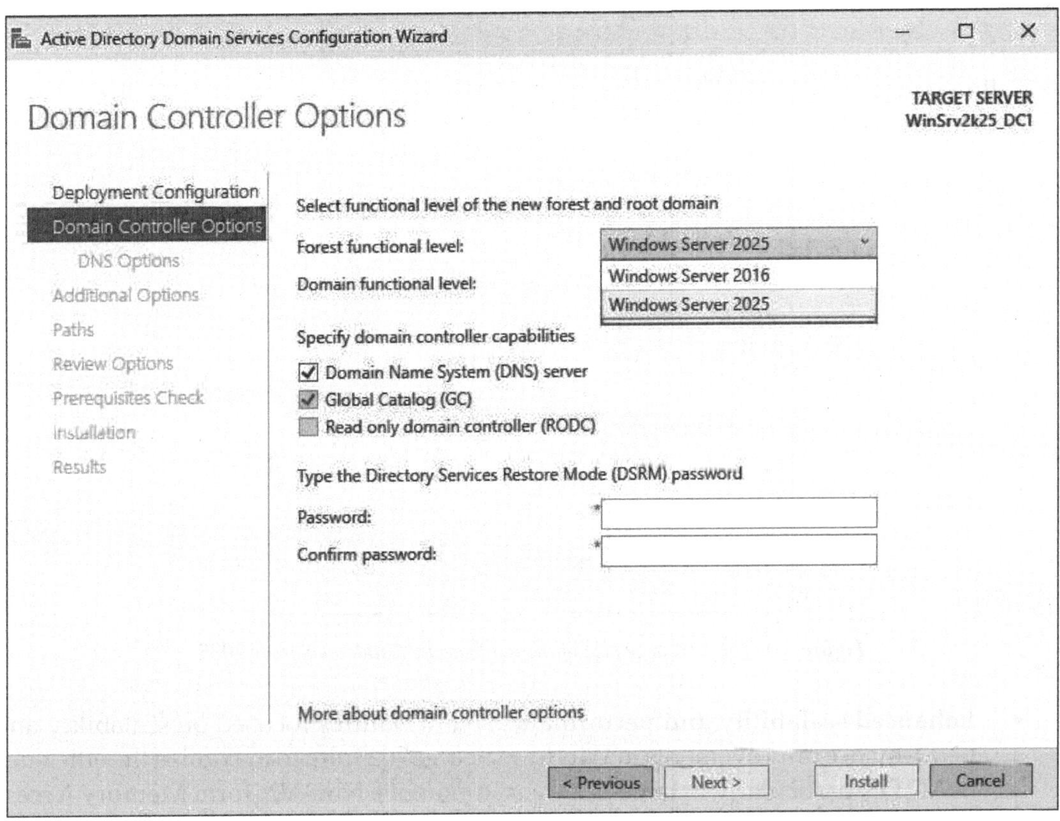

Figure 7.2: FFL and DFL in Windows Server 2025

- **Expanded database engine page size:** The database engine's page size has been expanded from **8K to 32K**, as shown in *Figure 7.3*, significantly increasing the capacity for storing large directory objects. This expansion supports up to **3,200 values** in multi-valued attributes, making it especially beneficial for environments with complex directory structures or extensive attribute usage. New domain controllers in Windows Server 2025 will default to the **32K page size**, while the **legacy 8K page** mode is still supported for compatibility in mixed environments. The upgrade to 32K is managed at the forest level, providing a controlled and gradual transition.

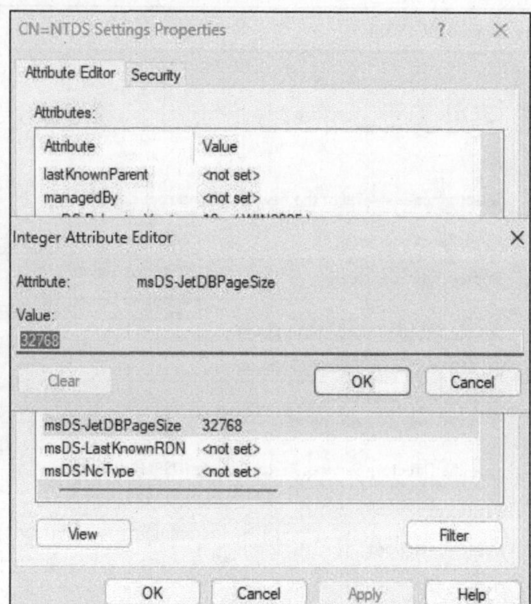

***Figure 7.3:** The 32K page size of the database in Windows Server 2025*

- **Enhanced scalability and performance:** New features focused on scalability and performance improvements in Windows Server 2025 aim to maximize the efficiency of AD DS, particularly in large-scale environments. **Non-Uniform Memory Access (NUMA)** support enables **AD DS** to utilize multiple processor groups efficiently, optimizing performance even in high-demand, multi-CPU systems. This new feature is crucial for organizations that rely on high-performance IT infrastructures.
- **New performance counters for monitoring:** Windows Server 2025 integrates new performance counters into performance monitor, offering administrators more detailed monitoring and analysis of *AD* **operations**. These new features track vital performance aspects, including **Local Security Authority (LSA)** lookups, **domain controller (DC)** locator efficiency, and **Lightweight Directory Access Protocol (LDAP)** client performance. Administrators are better equipped to identify bottlenecks and optimize directory services by providing these detailed insights.
- **Updated DC location algorithm:** The updated algorithm for controller discovery significantly improves the DC location process. By eliminating reliance on outdated techniques such as **Windows Internet Name Service (WINS)** and **Mailslots** for **Network Basic Input/Output System (NetBIOS)** name resolution, Windows Server 2025 introduces a more efficient and reliable method for locating DCs. This new feature reduces the chances of failure and improves the overall efficiency of network operations.
- **Enhanced security features:** Security is a central focus of Windows Server 2025, and AD DS has received several key new features to combat modern threats.

Kerberos authentication has been fortified with improved handling of the **RC4 algorithm**, while support for **Transport Layer Security (TLS) 1.3** has been added for **LDAP over TLS**. This enhances the encryption of directory communications and ensures secure data transmission between clients and DCs. These new features align with current best practices for securing directory services against evolving cyber threats.

- **Updated password change methodology:** The process for changing passwords has been updated to replace the older **Security Account Manager - Remote Protocol (SAM-RPC)** interface, which is being phased out in favor of more secure alternatives. This new feature also affects accounts within the **Protected Users** group and **local accounts** on domain-joined computers. The new feature ensures that password changes and authentication processes adhere to the highest security standards, reducing vulnerabilities associated with legacy protocols.

The new features introduced in Windows Server 2025 to AD DS significantly improve performance and security. These new features make AD DS a more robust and adaptable solution for modern enterprises that are modernizing their IT infrastructure. With enhanced scalability, security features, and performance optimization, Windows Server 2025 equips organizations to manage their network efficiently while safeguarding against emerging threats. Whether managing large-scale environments, integrating with Microsoft technologies, or enforcing cutting-edge security practices, Windows Server 2025 offers the tools to support modern enterprise IT operations.

Note: Ensure a full backup of the AD environment before implementing the new AD DS enhancements. This safeguard is necessary, as some updates introduce irreversible changes. A comprehensive backup allows restoration to the previous state if issues arise during the update process.

Improved Active Directory security

Windows Server 2025 introduces significant advancements to AD DS, focusing on improving scalability, performance, and manageability. Security continues to be a substantial enhancement area, with several features designed to strengthen authentication protocols and protect against increasingly sophisticated cyber threats. Key advancements include:

- **Kerberos authentication enhancements:** The Kerberos protocol, a cornerstone of AD DS, has been fortified with more robust **encryption algorithms**. These improvements help defend against vulnerabilities like **Pass-the-Ticket** and **golden ticket attacks**, commonly used in network lateral movement. By enforcing higher cryptographic standards, Windows Server 2025 reduces the risk of credential theft and unauthorized access.
- **Multi-Factor Authentication (MFA) integration:** Windows Server 2025 offers seamless and flexible integration of MFA capabilities into AD DS. Organizations

can implement **MFA** based on user role, resource sensitivity, or access location. This contextual approach ensures that **high-privilege resources** are safeguarded while regular users experience minimal friction. Support for biometrics and token-based authentication strengthens security and aligns with **Zero Trust** models, prioritizing continuous verification of identity and access.

- **Enhanced Group Policy Management:** AD's **Group Policy Management** has been improved to give administrators more control over security policies. A broader range of **predefined security templates** is now available, helping streamline the deployment of security configurations across AD DS environments. These enhancements enable faster detection and remediation of security threats, coupled with real-time monitoring and alerting features, further protecting the network from potential vulnerabilities.
- **Improved auditing and logging:** Windows Server 2025 includes more **granular auditing capabilities**, providing deeper insights into authentication patterns and enabling quicker detection of anomalies. Enhanced **event logging** allows security teams to track login attempts, access behaviors, and potential breaches more effectively, supporting compliance with security regulations and assisting in forensic investigations. These advancements ensure that organizations remain vigilant over their network and respond promptly to unauthorized access attempts.

These enhancements solidify AD DS in Windows Server 2025 as a critical enterprise security and IT management component. By improving authentication protocols, enhancing MFA capabilities, refining policy management, and providing greater visibility into security events, Windows Server 2025 empowers organizations to defend their infrastructures against emerging threats proactively. These innovations underscore the importance of AD in modern IT environments, particularly those adopting hybrid cloud architectures.

Note: Access free PowerShell scripts from Microsoft's Script Center: https://devblogs.microsoft.com/scripting/ and PowerShell Gallery: https://www.powershellgallery.com/. These repositories provide extensive collections of scripts, including those for AD and DNS, enabling IT professionals to automate and streamline complex administrative tasks.

Performance and scalability upgrades in Active Directory

Windows Server 2025 introduces a range of performance and scalability upgrades to AD DS, addressing the challenges organizations face managing large-scale and geographically distributed environments. These advancements enhance replication efficiency, minimize latency, and improve resource utilization, ensuring AD remains resilient and scalable even under demanding conditions.

- **Optimized replication algorithms for superior performance:** One of the most impactful enhancements in Windows Server 2025 is the implementation of advanced replication algorithms designed to accelerate synchronization between DCs. By leveraging **state-of-the-art compression techniques**, these algorithms reduce the volume of data transferred during replication, significantly conserving network bandwidth. These innovations ensure faster, more reliable replication processes, particularly for enterprises managing substantial AD databases or high change volumes.

- **Enhanced conflict resolution and incremental replication:** Addressing **replication integrity** is a core focus of Windows Server 2025. Improved conflict resolution mechanisms swiftly and accurately address discrepancies between DCs, preserving the consistency of directory data. Enhanced support for incremental replication allows only changes made since the previous synchronization to be transmitted, reducing the replication overhead and further optimizing performance in complex environments.

- **Advanced monitoring and diagnostics for scalability:** Recognizing the importance of visibility in maintaining performance, Windows Server 2025 introduces **enhanced monitoring** and **diagnostic capabilities** for replication health. These tools provide administrators with detailed logs, real-time performance metrics, and actionable insights into replication operations. This increased transparency enables proactive detection and resolution of potential issues, safeguarding the directory service's efficiency and scalability.

Delivering performance at scale

The enhancements in Windows Server 2025 enable AD to deliver unparalleled performance and scalability for global organizations. By reducing **replication latency, optimizing bandwidth utilization**, and **equipping administrators** with advanced monitoring tools, these upgrades establish a robust foundation for managing intricate IT infrastructures.

To fully leverage these performance upgrades, organizations should adopt a structured approach:

- Test **optimized replication features** in a non-production environment to ensure compatibility with existing services.

- Fine-tune **AD Sites and Services** settings to establish the most efficient replication topology.

- Configure monitoring tools to track **replication health** and **review logs** for discrepancies regularly.

- Implement a comprehensive **disaster recovery plan** to protect against unforeseen disruptions in distributed networks.

Note: Conduct thorough testing in a non-production setup to ensure optimal performance with Windows Server 2025's replication features in large-scale environments. Configure monitoring tools to track replication health, review logs for inconsistencies, and optimize AD Sites and Services for efficient topology. A solid disaster recovery plan is essential, particularly for geographically dispersed networks.

Exercise 7.1: Adding DNS Server role

This exercise will guide you through implementing the 32K Database Page Size in Windows Server 2025. This feature enhances AD performance, particularly in large-scale environments, by increasing database scalability and optimizing replication efficiency.

The steps to implement the 32K Database Page Size are as follows:

1. Right-click the **Start** button and select **Run**.
2. In the **Run** dialog box, type **`regedit`** and press *Enter* to open the **Registry Editor**.
3. In the Registry Editor, navigate to **`HKEY_LOCAL_MACHINE\SYSTEM\CurrentControlSet\Services\NTDS\Parameters`**
4. If the Database Page Size entry does not exist, right-click in the **right** pane, select **New | DWORD (32-bit) Value**, and name the new entry **Database Page Size**.
5. Right-click the **Database Page Size** entry, select **Modify**, and set the **Value Data** to **32768** (32K bytes).
6. Under **Base**, select **Decimal**, then click **OK**, as in *Figure 7.4*:

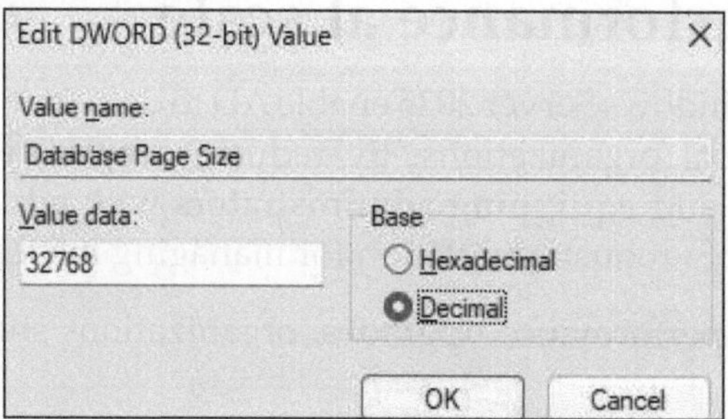

Figure 7.4: Setting the decimal value for the Database Page Size

7. Close the **Registry Editor** and **restart** the server for changes to take effect.
8. After the restart, right-click the **Start** button and select **Terminal (Admin)** to open **PowerShell** with administrative privileges.
9. In **PowerShell**, execute the following command to enable the **32K page size** feature:

```
$params = @{
        Identity = 'Database 32k pages feature'
```

```
Scope = 'ForestOrConfigurationSet'
Server = 'DAUTTI'  # Replace with your server name
Target = 'dautti.local'  # Replace with your domain
}
Enable-ADOptionalFeature @params
```

10. Type **Yes** or **Yes to All** to execute the command, as illustrated in *Figure 7.5:*

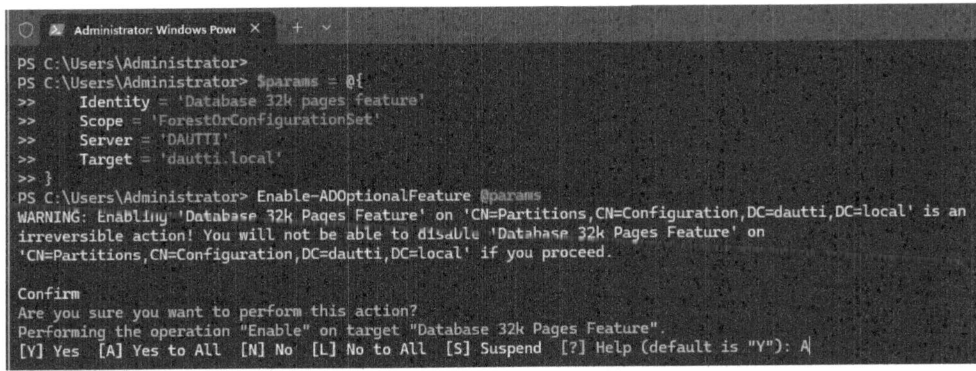

Figure 7.5: *Enabling the 32K page size for the database*

11. Open **Event Viewer** (search for it in the **Start** menu).
12. Navigate to **Applications and Services Logs | Directory Service**, as in *Figure 7.6*, and check the logs for events related to the AD database startup to confirm the **32K page size** is active.

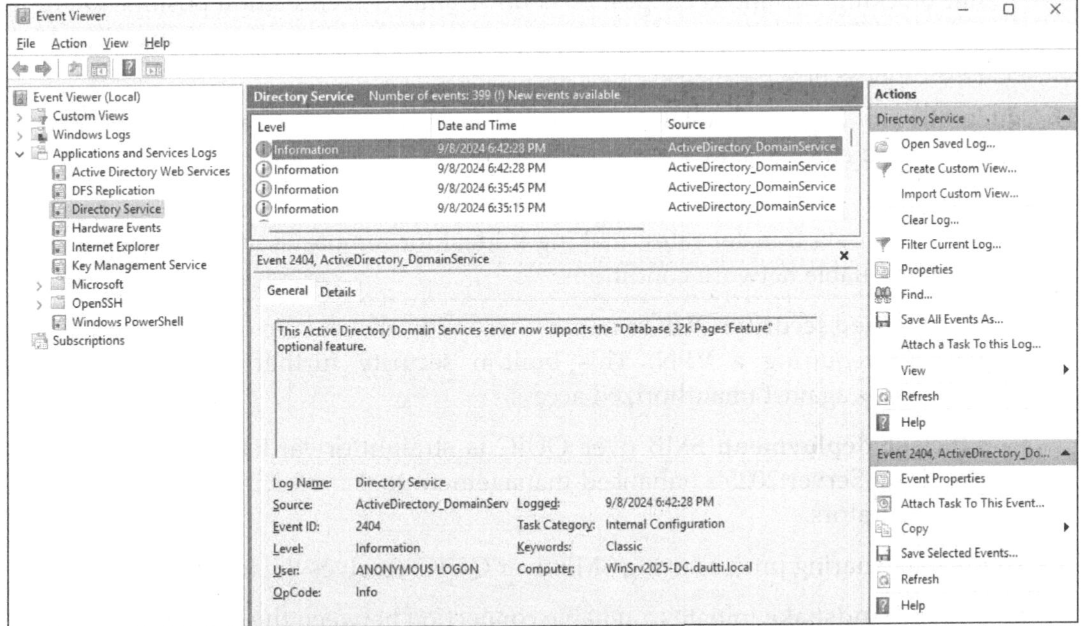

Figure 7.6: *Verifying that the 32K page size for the database has been set*

Following these steps, you will successfully implement the 32K Database Page Size in Windows Server 2025, optimizing AD performance and ensuring improved scalability for large-scale environments.

SMB protocol enhancements

Windows Server 2025 introduces a transformative advancement in network communication by integrating **SMB over QUIC**. By combining the versatile SMB protocol with the high-speed, low-latency **Quick UDP Internet Connections (QUIC)**, Microsoft offers a next-generation solution for secure and efficient data transfers. This enhancement caters to enterprises striving for robust, scalable, and secure digital infrastructures, delivering faster connections, improved reliability, and heightened security.

The key components of SMB over QUIC are as follows:

- **Server Message Block:** SMB is a cornerstone protocol in Microsoft environments, facilitating file, printer, and device sharing across networks. Over its iterations, **SMB** has evolved with significant upgrades in **encryption**, **signing**, and **cross-platform compatibility**, ensuring **secure and efficient communication**. These enhancements make it indispensable for enterprises to prioritize reliable and flexible data-sharing capabilities.

- **Quick UDP Internet Connections:** Initially developed by *Google*, **QUIC** operates at the transport layer and uses **UDP** instead of **TCP**, allowing faster connection establishment and reduced latency. Features like multiplexing without head-of-line blocking, advanced congestion control, and error correction position QUIC as a preferred protocol for real-time applications and web services demanding high performance and resilience.

The integration of SMB over QUIC blends the security and functionality of SMB with QUIC's speed and efficiency. Key advantages include:

- **Enhanced performance:** SMB over QUIC significantly reduces latency and improves data transfer rates, making it ideal for remote users and environments with unreliable network conditions.

- **Streamlined security:** QUIC's native encryption ensures secure data transmission without requiring a VPN. This built-in security further strengthens SMB's safeguards against unauthorized access.

- **Efficient deployment:** SMB over QUIC is straightforward to implement using Windows Server 2025's enhanced management tools, reducing complexity for IT administrators.

The secure data-sharing process using SMB over QUIC involves the following steps:

1. A **TCP handshake** initiates a reliable connection between the client and server.
2. A **TLS handshake** negotiates encryption protocols for secure communication.

3. Data is transmitted **over SMB using QUIC**, leveraging its low-latency and error-recovery features.

Figure 7.7 illustrates the reduced **round-trip times (RTTs)** achieved by QUIC compared to TCP with TLS 1.2 and TLS 1.3, demonstrating its efficiency for faster and more reliable file transfers.

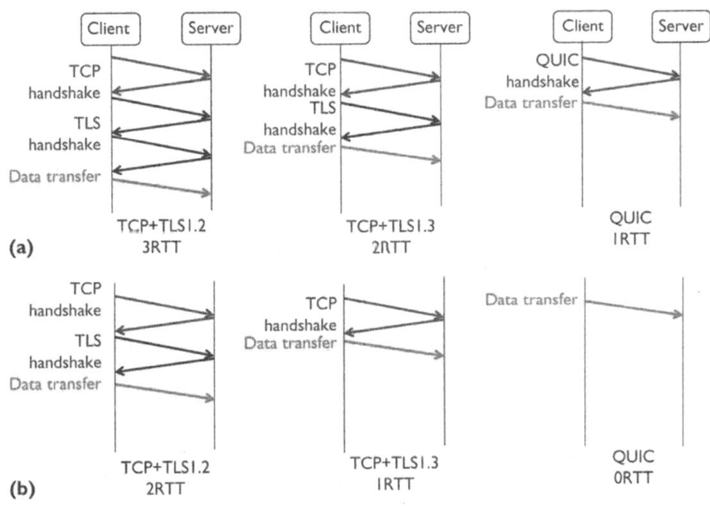

Figure 7.7: *QUIC vs TCP in reliable file transfer (source: Microsoft Tech Community)*

Administrators will appreciate the streamlined deployment and management of SMB over QUIC in Windows Server 2025. The transition is smooth with user-friendly interfaces and familiar tools, minimizing disruptions and downtime. This integration empowers IT teams to enhance network performance while maintaining stringent security protocols.

Integrating SMB over QUIC in Windows Server 2025 represents a significant step forward in modern networking. This powerful combination addresses the demands of evolving enterprise environments, enabling faster data transfers, greater resilience, and enhanced security. IT professionals can leverage these advancements to optimize operations, bolster productivity, and ensure robust network protection.

Note: To deploy SMB over QUIC effectively, ensure both the client and server environments support the QUIC protocol. Verify that the required firewall ports are correctly configured to allow QUIC traffic, as misconfigurations can critically affect connectivity and overall performance.

New features in the SMB protocol

The evolution of the SMB protocol has revolutionized enterprise networking, culminating in the integration of **SMB over QUIC** in Windows Server 2025. This advancement builds upon a rich history of protocol innovation, adapting to the needs of modern digital environments.

Initially developed by *IBM* in the mid-1980s to facilitate file and printer sharing across LANs, SMB has undergone continuous refinement. Early versions operated over NetBIOS frames and were integrated into Microsoft LAN Manager for OS/2 in the 1990s. By the mid-1990s, SMB was rebranded as the **Common Internet File System (CIFS)**, introducing features like symbolic and hard links, extensive file support, and experimental use of TCP.

In 2006, **SMB 2.0** emerged, marking a significant leap in performance by reducing protocol overhead and introducing pipelining and durable file handles. Subsequent updates, such as **SMB 2.1**, improved locking mechanisms, while **SMB 3.0** introduced critical enhancements like SMB Direct, Multichannel, Transparent failover, and AES-based encryption. By 2013, Microsoft **deprecated SMB 1.0** due to security and performance concerns, signaling a shift towards more secure and efficient versions. **SMB 3.1.1**, introduced in 2016, added cutting-edge features like **Advanced Encryption Standard (AES)-128 GCM (Galois/Counter Mode (GCM)** encryption and pre-authentication integrity using **Secure Hash Algorithm (SHM)-512**, setting new standards for secure data sharing.

Windows Server 2025 takes this evolution further with SMB over QUIC, a groundbreaking integration that leverages the strengths of both protocols. The following key features highlight the latest advancements in the SMB protocol:

- **Advanced encryption standards:** SMB now supports AES-128 GCM and AES-256 GCM encryption, ensuring secure data transfers with minimal performance overhead. These standards protect against modern cybersecurity threats, enhancing data integrity and confidentiality.
- **Pre-authentication integrity:** Introduced in SMB 3.1.1, pre-authentication integrity ensures that any tampering during the authentication phase is detected and mitigated. This feature uses SHA-512 hashing to validate the integrity of SMB connections, reinforcing security against **man-in-the-middle** attacks.
- **Multichannel and direct connections:** SMB fully leverages multi-channel capabilities, enabling multiple network connections for data transfers, improving throughput, and enhancing fault tolerance. Additionally, SMB Direct, which uses **Remote Direct Memory Access** (**RDMA**), facilitates low-latency, high-speed data transfers with minimal CPU utilization in high-performance computing environments.
- **Transparent failover:** Transparent failover ensures uninterrupted access to data during server maintenance or failures. This feature enables continuous availability of file shares in clustered environments, making it essential for business-critical applications requiring high availability.
- **Compression for faster transfers:** Native compression in SMB allows files to be compressed during transmission, reducing data sent over the network and accelerating file transfers, especially in wide-area or cloud-connected environments.

- **Enhanced large file support:** SMB now supports larger file sizes, making it ideal for industries dealing with massive datasets such as media production, scientific research, and data analytics.
- **Improved access control mechanisms:** Refined **access control lists (ACLs)** and auditing features provide IT administrators with granular control over file and resource permissions, simplifying compliance with regulatory standards and enhancing security.

As noted, among the new features of the SMB protocol, the integration of SMB over QUIC in Windows Server 2025 represents a significant milestone, offering enterprises unparalleled reliability, performance, and security in file sharing and network resource access. Building on a legacy of innovation, this latest iteration of SMB addresses the complex challenges of today's digital landscape while preparing organizations for future demands.

Note: Comprehending the evolution of both SMB and QUIC protocols is essential to ensure seamless backward compatibility. Before migrating to SMB over QUIC, it is crucial to evaluate and address the compatibility of legacy systems with the newer protocol. This will help mitigate potential disruptions in file-sharing operations and ensure uninterrupted network performance.

Enhanced SMB protocol security

As the digital landscape rapidly evolves, it becomes increasingly crucial for IT professionals to understand advanced encryption protocols and security strategies to protect sensitive organizational data. Windows Server 2025 introduces SMB over QUIC, adding an extra layer to meet modern security challenges by securing data during transmission. This section explores the security features and encryption protocols that form the backbone of SMB over QUIC, offering IT administrators a detailed understanding of the security mechanisms involved.

A robust encryption framework embedded in SMB over QUIC is at the heart of this evolution, ensuring that all transmitted data remains confidential and protected from tampering. These protocols, leveraging state-of-the-art cryptographic techniques, provide robust defense against evolving cyber threats, unauthorized access, and other vulnerabilities. As network conditions fluctuate, these encryption measures guarantee that the data is safe regardless of environmental challenges.

This section highlights the practical aspects of configuring security settings in Windows Server 2025 in addition to its encryption capabilities. Administrators will find step-by-step guidance for fine-tuning systems to meet rigorous data protection standards. A detailed analysis of best practices will provide IT professionals with the knowledge necessary to implement, maintain, and optimize secure networking environments. This proactive approach to security is indispensable for preventing data breaches and ensuring long-term network resilience.

Implementing robust security protocols becomes even more essential as organizations continue their digital transformation and expand their network infrastructures. A comprehensive understanding of the security features within SMB over QUIC allows IT professionals to maintain the confidentiality, integrity, and availability of organizational data, safeguarding a competitive advantage in today's increasingly interconnected world. Therefore, among the enhanced security features in SMB protocol in Windows Server 2025 are the following:

- **Public Key Infrastructure (PKI)** is a foundational framework that guarantees secure communication across digital networks through cryptography, authentication, and digital certificates. Within Windows Server 2025, PKI is critical in securing data exchanges and ensuring the integrity and confidentiality of data in transit. This subsection explores the core components of PKI, as illustrated in *Figure 7.8*, its functionalities, and its contribution to protecting network transactions.

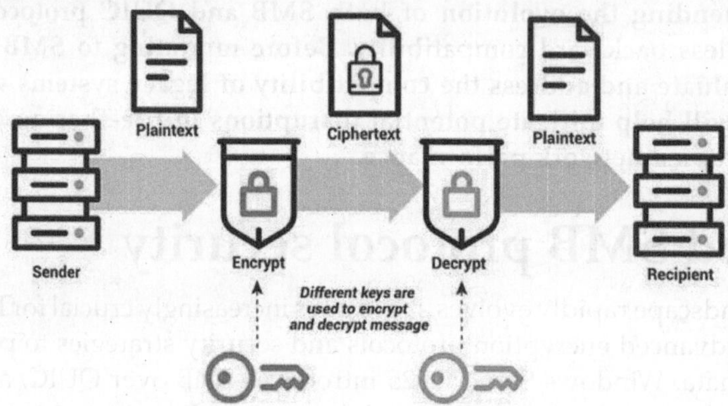

Figure 7.8: Asymmetric encryption in PKI leveraging private and public keys (source: Sectigo)

- **Advanced encryption protocols** in SMB over QUIC in Windows Server 2025 are designed to offer high security, ensuring that data remains confidential and intact as it moves across the network. One of the primary techniques at play is using advanced cryptographic protocols that facilitate end-to-end encryption for data packets. This ensures that unauthorized access and data manipulation are effectively prevented, providing IT administrators with confidence in the integrity of their network.

- A cornerstone of this security framework is incorporating **TLS 1.3** within QUIC. This protocol delivers cutting-edge cryptographic protection, ensuring all data transmitted over the network remains encrypted. TLS 1.3 utilizes forward secrecy and authenticated encryption—forward secrecy guarantees the security of past communications even if a session key is compromised, while authenticated encryption ensures that the data is encrypted and verified, preventing tampering or forgery during transmission.

- **Role-Based Access Control (RBAC)** is crucial in fortifying network security. RBAC is essential for restricting user and device permissions and minimizing the risk of unauthorized access. IT administrators must regularly review and update access control policies to stay ahead of evolving security threats. Tools like Group Policies and PowerShell scripts are invaluable in streamlining and automating the application of security settings across the network. These tools ensure consistency, reduce human error, and promote compliance, allowing IT professionals to focus on more strategic initiatives.
- **Continuous monitoring** is critical in maintaining a secure network environment. Windows Server 2025 provides comprehensive logging mechanisms that enable administrators to track and analyze SMB over QUIC traffic. This level of visibility is essential for detecting anomalies and identifying potential security incidents. Proper storage and regular review of logs ensure that network security is continuously assessed, providing administrators with the necessary insights to adapt to emerging threats and keep security measures up to date.

Comprehending and implementing the advanced security features in Windows Server 2025, including SMB over QUIC, IT professionals can significantly strengthen their network's defenses, safeguard sensitive data, and ensure compliance with industry standards. This comprehensive security approach helps organizations thrive in a rapidly changing digital world while maintaining robust protection against modern cyber threats.

Note: To fully leverage end-to-end encryption, ensure that TLS 1.3 is enabled when configuring encryption for SMB over QUIC in Windows Server 2025. Not using the recommended encryption standards can expose your environment to security vulnerabilities, jeopardizing the data's integrity and confidentiality.

Enhancing SMB performance and scalability

Maximizing the **performance and scalability** of SMB over QUIC is crucial for IT professionals aiming to enhance their network systems' efficiency, reliability, and growth potential. As organizations increasingly adopt SMB over QUIC in Windows Server 2025, it is essential to implement strategies that drive significant improvements in performance and scalability. This section examines key areas where SMB performance and scalability have been improved and provides actionable recommendations for enhancing them in your environment.

IT teams can substantially improve throughput, responsiveness, and overall network resilience by configuring network settings, selecting appropriate hardware, and engaging in continuous performance monitoring. These improvements enhance the user experience and bolster the network's ability to handle larger data transfers, reduce latency, and support smoother operations in evolving IT environments. Therefore, key improvements contributing to enhanced performance and scalability of SMB in Windows Server 2025 are as follows:

- **Network configuration for improved performance:** To achieve superior performance for SMB over QUIC in Windows Server 2025, IT professionals must take a comprehensive approach to network configuration. The first step is to ensure the network infrastructure can support high-speed data transfers. This involves upgrading network hardware, such as routers and switches, to meet current standards and ensuring network interfaces support gigabit or higher speeds. Additionally, configuring **Quality of Service (QoS)** settings is critical. QoS allows SMB over QUIC traffic to be prioritized above other network traffic, reducing latency and increasing responsiveness.

- **Hardware enhancements for scalability:** Hardware enhancements are essential to support improved scalability for SMB over QUIC. The first step involves upgrading network interfaces to support gigabit speeds or higher. Incorporating advanced **network interface cards (NICs)** with offloading capabilities, such as **TCP Offload Engine (TOE)**, can reduce CPU load by offloading specific tasks, thus increasing throughput. Moreover, deploying high-performance routers and switches, such as those supporting 100GbE, ensures that the infrastructure can scale to accommodate the growing data flows required by SMB over QUIC.

- **Performance tuning and continuous monitoring:** Ongoing adjustments and monitoring are essential for achieving continuous improvements in SMB over QUIC performance. Regularly reviewing and modifying TCP settings, including window sizes and congestion control mechanisms like **Explicit Congestion Notification (ECN)**, enhances data flow and minimizes latency. Optimally configured TCP window sizes impact the volume of data that can be transmitted before requiring acknowledgment, directly improving data transfer efficiency.

- **Continuous education and skill development:** Staying ahead of emerging technologies is vital for IT teams responsible for maintaining and improving SMB over QUIC in Windows Server 2025. As network management and server technologies evolve rapidly, ongoing training, participation in industry events, and certifications ensure IT professionals are well-equipped to implement new advancements and manage performance improvements. By investing in ongoing education, teams can proactively address future performance and scalability challenges as network demands grow.

Combining these performance and scalability improvements—network configurations, hardware enhancements, continuous performance tuning, and active monitoring—IT professionals can ensure that SMB over QUIC in Windows Server 2025 operates at its highest potential. Continuous skill development also enables IT teams to adapt to evolving network demands, providing the infrastructure remains robust, scalable, and capable of supporting modern workloads.

Note: Assess network performance regularly and refine TCP configurations, such as modifying buffer sizes and enabling ECN. Failing to track performance indicators can lead to unnoticed bottlenecks and reduced efficiency.

Exercise 7.2: Configuring and enabling SMB over QUIC

In this exercise, you will learn how to configure and enable SMB over QUIC in Windows Server 2025, an essential feature for secure and efficient file transfers in modern network environments. The process begins with preparing your server by ensuring all necessary updates are installed and the SMB and QUIC protocols are available and correctly configured. Next, you will install the required server roles and features using Windows Admin Center or PowerShell, such as the SMB service and QUIC support. Detailed instructions will guide you through configuring the server firewall to allow QUIC traffic and setting up certificates to secure the SMB over the QUIC connection.

To configure and enable SMB over QUIC in Windows Server 2025, follow these steps:

1. Launch the **Windows Admin Center**.
2. In **Windows Admin Center**, click **Settings** and **Register** to register with **Azure**, as shown in *Figure 7.9*:

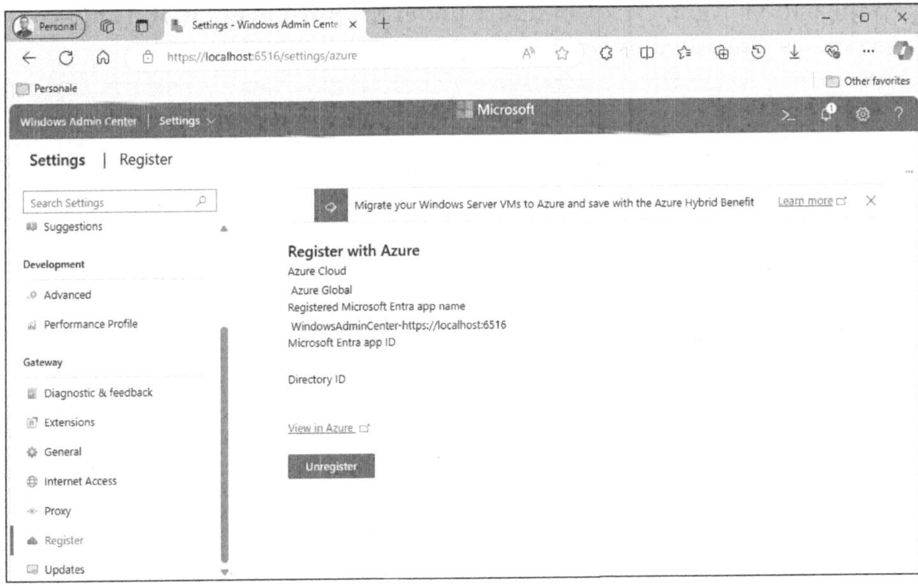

Figure 7.9: *Azure integration with Windows Admin Center*

3. In Windows Admin Center, click **+Add**, then **Add** under **Azure VMs**. Confirm that the server is **Windows Server 2025 Data Center—Azure Edition**.
4. Connect to the **Windows Server 2025** instance and **install a certificate** for secure communication.
5. Click **Sign in** under **Add an Azure VM**, enter the **required details**, and click **Add**, as depicted in *Figure 7.10*:

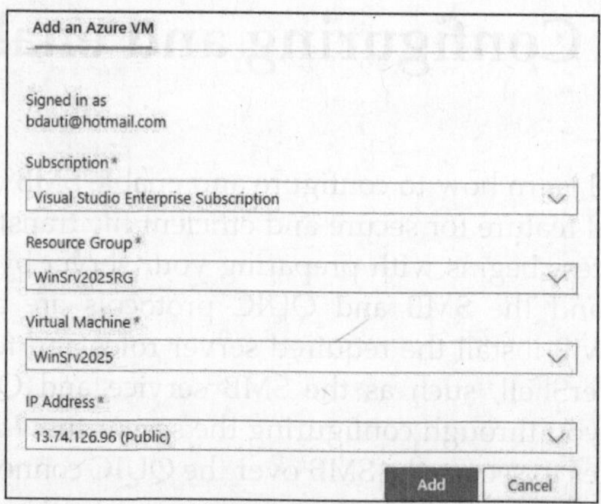

Figure 7.10: Adding an Azure VM in Windows Admin Center

6. In **Windows Admin Center**, select the **Windows Server 2025** instance, click **Settings**, and choose **File Shares (SMB Server)** under **General**.
7. At the bottom right, click **Configure** under the **SMB over QUIC is not configured** section, as illustrated in *Figure 7.11*:

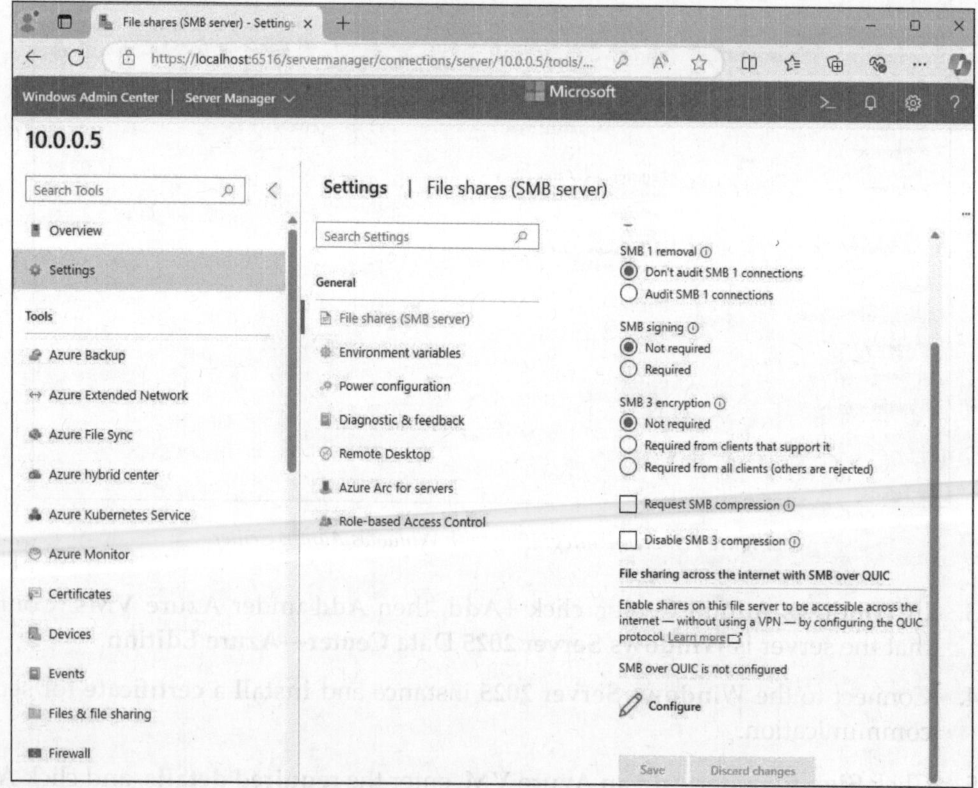

Figure 7.11: Configuring SMB over QUIC

8. In the **Configure file sharing across the Internet with SMB over QUIC** section, select the **TLS certificate**, specify the port (**default UDP 443**), and click **Enable**.

After completing the configuration, the service will be ready for use and marked as available. You may want to test the connection by ensuring that the file server is accessible over the Internet via the DNS record specified in the digital certificate.

Conclusion

In this chapter, you have explored the evolution and advancements of AD and SMB protocols in Windows Server 2025. You have gained a deep understanding of new features and improvements in AD DS, including security enhancements, performance optimizations, and scalability upgrades. Additionally, you have studied the SMB protocol, focusing on its security advancements and performance enhancements, particularly the integration of SMB over QUIC. The practical examples and configuration steps have equipped you with the knowledge to leverage these updates and streamline authentication, access control, and file sharing within your infrastructure. With this knowledge, you can confidently implement and optimize AD and SMB in your Windows Server 2025 environment.

In the next chapter, you will learn how to manage and configure services in Windows Server 2025 using the **graphical user interface** (**GUI**) and Windows PowerShell, further enhancing your ability to administer and customize your server infrastructure.

Questions

1. What is new in AD DS for Windows Server 2025?
2. How is AD security improved in Windows Server 2025?
3. How does SMB over QUIC improve file sharing?
4. What is the 32K Database Page Size?
5. How is SMB performance enhanced in Windows Server 2025?

Join our book's Discord space

Join the book's Discord Workspace for Latest updates, Offers, Tech happenings around the world, New Release and Sessions with the Authors:

https://discord.bpbonline.com

CHAPTER 8
Configuring Windows Server 2025 Services

Introduction

This chapter provides a comprehensive guide to configuring client/server network services in Windows Server 2025 using Windows PowerShell cmdlets. It enables readers to leverage PowerShell's enhanced efficiency and automation capabilities to perform critical administrative tasks. Topics covered include promoting a server to a **domain controller** (**DC**), managing DNS records, configuring a DHCP server, setting up **virtual machines** (**VMs**), establishing websites, configuring print servers, managing **Remote Desktop Services** (**RDS**) users, and implementing a **Windows Server Update Services** (**WSUS**) server. The chapter combines practical exercises with step-by-step instructions, guiding readers through the use of Server Manager and PowerShell cmdlets to manage these essential services. By mastering the techniques outlined, readers will acquire the knowledge and hands-on experience needed to proficiently configure and administer core network services in Windows Server 2025, benefiting from its latest technologies and improvements.

Structure

The chapter will cover the following topics:

- Promoting a server to a domain controller
- Exercise 8.1: Configuring domain controller

- Adding A Record in the DNS Manager
- Exercise 8.2: Configuring an A Record in the DNS server
- Configuring a DHCP server
- Exercise 8.3: Configuring a DHCP scope
- Configuring a virtual machine
- Exercise 8.4: Configuring a virtual machine
- Configuring a website
- Exercise 8.5: Configuring a website
- Configuring the print server
- Exercise 8.6: Configuring the print server
- Configuring Remote Desktop Users
- Exercise 8.7: Configuring Remote Desktop Users
- Configuring the WSUS server
- Exercise 8.8: Configuring the WSUS server

Objectives

This chapter equips readers with the knowledge and skills to configure and manage client/server network services in Windows Server 2025 using Windows PowerShell cmdlets. Readers will learn to efficiently set up and manage critical services, including DHCP, **Active Directory Domain Services** (**AD DS**), DNS, VMs, and web servers, to meet the demands of dynamic infrastructure environments. Additionally, the chapter covers configuring print servers, RDS users, and WSU to enhance operations and provide secure, centralized management. Through practical, step-by-step instructions and PowerShell automation, readers will gain hands-on experience and develop the expertise to effectively manage these essential network services in a modern and hybrid server environment.

Promoting a server to a domain controller

Promoting a server to a DC is critical in establishing a centralized authentication, authorization, and resource management framework in a Windows Server 2025 environment. By promoting a server to a **DC**, organizations gain the ability to manage user accounts, security policies, and access controls from a centralized location, ensuring a unified and secure network environment. This enables users to authenticate with single credentials, simplifying access management while enhancing overall security.

The DC hosts the **Active Directory (AD)** database, integral to managing user information, implementing group policies, and supporting directory-based services such as **DNS** and **LDAP**. Promoting multiple servers to **DCs** further enhances redundancy and fault tolerance, ensuring continuous availability of authentication and directory services. This redundancy supports scalability and allows the organization to efficiently manage growing network demands by distributing workloads across multiple controllers.

Additionally, **trust relationships** between domains can be configured to enable seamless collaboration and resource sharing across various parts of an organization. This capability ensures a robust, scalable, secure infrastructure for user authentication, centralized administration, and resource management.

Having previously installed AD DS in *Chapter 5, Installing Roles Using Server Manager and PowerShell*, we are now prepared to advance to the next phase: promoting the server to a DC. This pivotal step marks the transition toward fully leveraging AD's capabilities. Let us embark on this journey and explore the process of promoting the server to a DC, embracing the opportunities and efficiencies it provides.

Exercise 8.1: Configuring domain controller

This exercise provides a detailed walkthrough for configuring the DC in Windows Server 2025, leveraging both **Server Manager** and **Windows PowerShell**. It highlights the steps necessary to ensure proper configuration, taking advantage of the enhanced features and improved automation capabilities introduced in Windows Server 2025.

Configuring domain controller using Server Manager

Follow these steps to begin configuring the DC in Windows Server 2025 using **Server Manager**:

1. Open **Server Manager** from the **Start** menu.
2. Click the **Notifications** icon, then select **Promote this server to become a domain controller**, as shown in *Figure 8.1:*

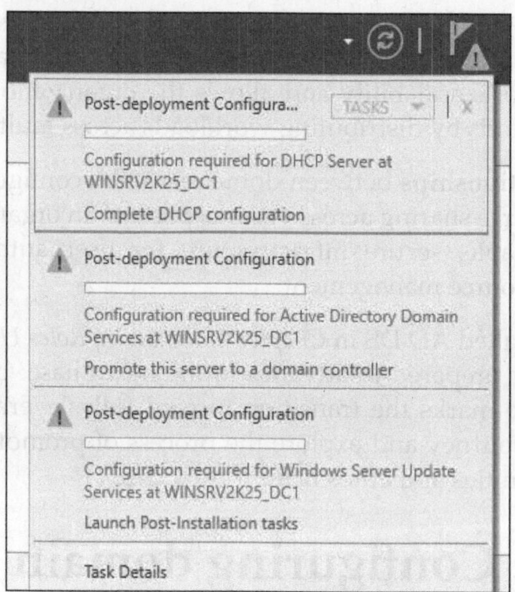

Figure 8.1: Promoting the server to a domain controller (DC) using Server Manager

3. On the **Deployment configuration** page, choose **Add a new forest**. Enter **`bpb.local`** as the **Root domain name**. Click the **Next** button to proceed.

4. On the **domain controller options** page, select the functional level for the new forest and root domain. Enter the **Directory Services Restore Mode (DSRM)** password. Click the **Next** button.

5. Accept the default settings on the **DNS options** page. Click the **Next** button to continue.

6. Accept the default settings on the **Additional Options** page. Click the **Next** button to continue.

7. On the **Paths** page, keep the default settings and click the **Next** button.

8. Review the settings on the **Review options** page, as shown in *Figure 8.2*, and click **Next**:

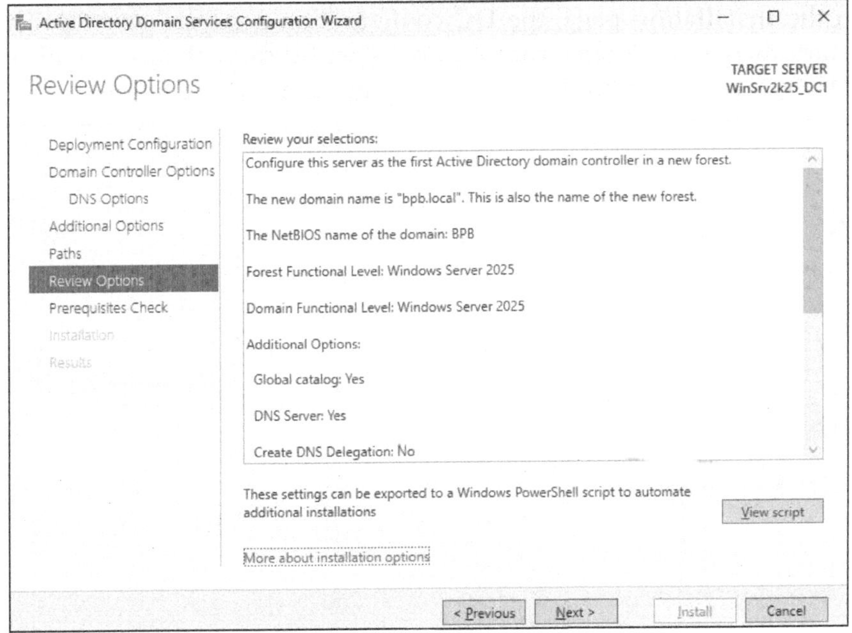

***Figure 8.2**: Reviewing the settings of configuring DC using Server Manager*

9. On the **Prerequisites check** page, validate the prerequisites. Then click the **Install** button, as shown in *Figure 8.3*, to proceed with the DC configuration. Take a look at the following figure:

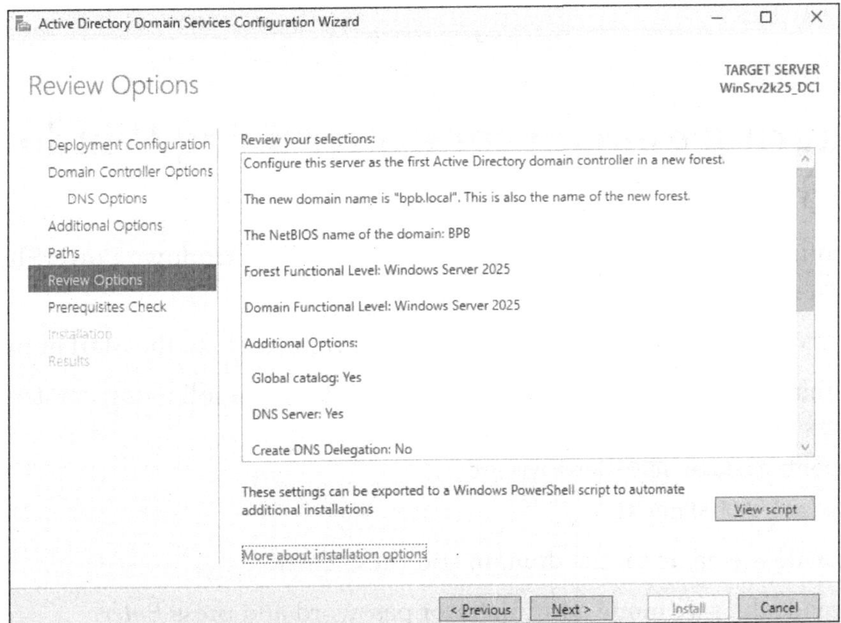

***Figure 8.3:** Validation of prerequisites using Server Manager*

10. On the **Installation** page, the **DC** configuration occurs, *Figure 8.4*. This process restarts the server automatically. Upon restart, the server boots up with an installed AD DS and a configured DC. Take a look at the following figure:

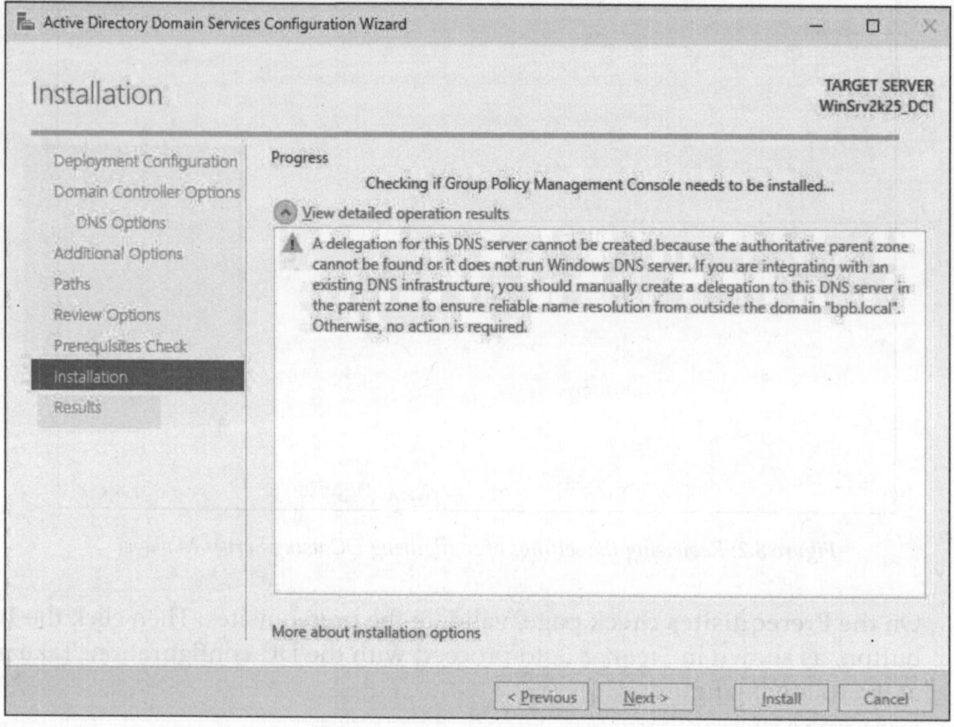

***Figure 8.4:** Installation of a DC*

Configuring domain controller using Windows PowerShell

To start configuring a DC in Windows Server 2025 using **Windows PowerShell**, follow these steps:

1. Launch **Windows PowerShell (Admin)** by right-clicking the **Start** button.
2. Within the **Windows PowerShel*l*** interface, type the following cmdlets and then press *Enter*:

```
Import-Module ADDSDeployment
Install-ADDSForest
```

3. Provide the name for the **domain** and press *Enter*.
4. Provide the **safe mode administrator** password and press *Enter*.
5. Confirm the **safe mode administrator** password and press *Enter*.

6. Type the letter **A** for **All**, and press *Enter*. The **DC** configuration occurs. This process restarts the server automatically. Upon restart, the server boots up with an installed AD DS and a configured **DC**, as shown in *Figure 8.5:*

```
Administrator: Windows Powe
PS C:\Users\Administrator> Import-Module ADDSDeployment
PS C:\Users\Administrator> Install-ADDSForest

cmdlet Install-ADDSForest at command pipeline position 1
Supply values for the following parameters:
DomainName: bpb.local
SafeModeAdministratorPassword: ********
Confirm SafeModeAdministratorPassword: ********

The target server will be configured as a domain controller and restarted when this
operation is complete.
Do you want to continue with this operation?
[Y] Yes  [A] Yes to All  [N] No  [L] No to All  [S] Suspend  [?] Help (default is "Y"): Y
```

Figure 8.5: *Configuring DC*

Adding A Record in the DNS Manager

The **Address Record** (**A Record**) plays a crucial role in the **Domain Name System (DNS)** of Windows Server 2025. It links a hostname or subdomain to its corresponding IPv4 address. **A Records** are essential because domain names like example.com are more straightforward for humans to understand and remember than numeric IP addresses like `192.168.0.1`. **A Record** enables devices and systems to find and connect to specific servers or resources across the network by mapping a domain name to its associated IP address. When a user enters a domain name or attempts to access a server, the DNS system resolves the domain name to the corresponding IP address. The **A Record** is integral to this resolution process, providing the necessary IP address to establish the connection.

Exercise 8.2: Configuring an A Record in the DNS server

This exercise demonstrates configuring an **A Record** in a DNS server using **DNS Manager** and **PowerShell** in Windows Server 2025.

Configuring an A Record using the DNS Manager

To begin the process of configuring an A Record in Windows Server 2025 using DNS Manager, follow these steps:

1. Open the **DNS Manager** console (*Figure 8.6*) by clicking the **Start** button and searching for **Windows Tools**. Then, double-click **DNS**.

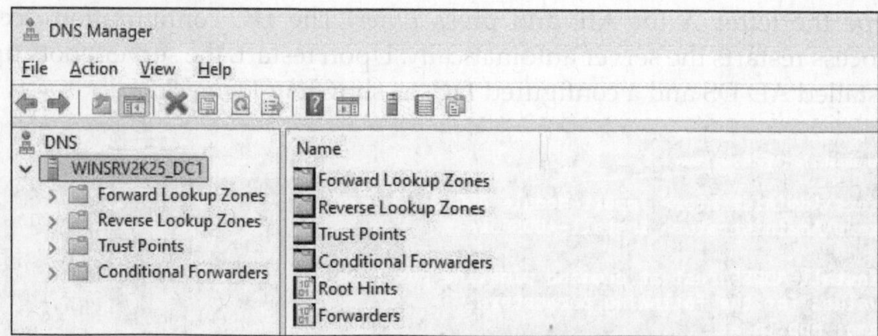

Figure 8.6 DNS Manager console in Windows Server 2025

2. Expand the **server** by selecting it from the tree on the console's left side.
3. Expand the **Forward Lookup Zone** by selecting it from the tree on the left side of the console.
4. Click **bpb.local**, then choose the **New Alias (CNAME)** option from the **Action** menu.
5. Enter a **Name** and **an IP address** for the new host, and then click **Add Host,** as shown in *Figure 8.7:*

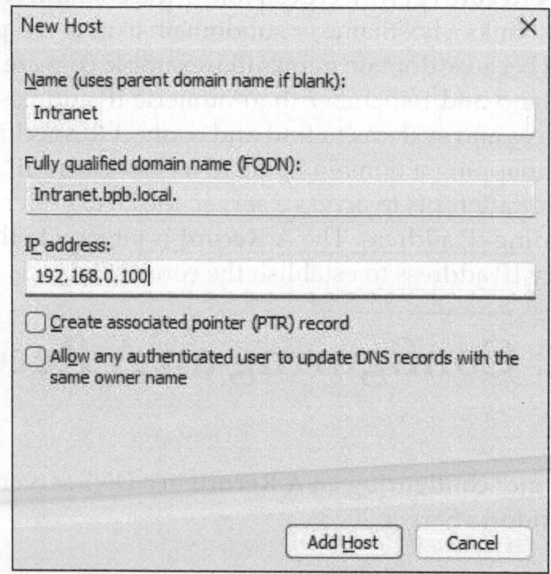

Figure 8.7: Adding an A Record of a new host

6. A dialog box states that the **host record has been created successfully**. Click **OK** and then click the **Done** button to close the **New Host** window. Also, you will notice that an **A Record** you added recently is listed in the right panel of the **DNS Manager** console.

Configuring an A Record using Windows PowerShell

To configure an **A Record** in Windows Server 2025 using **Windows PowerShell**, follow these steps:

1. Launch **Windows PowerShell (Admin)** by right-clicking the **Start** button.
2. Within the **Windows PowerShell** interface, type the following cmdlet and then press *Enter*:
   ```
   Add-
   DnsServerResourceRecordA -Name Extranet -IPv4Address 192.168.0.200
   -ZoneName bpb.local -ComputerName WinSrv2k25_DC1
   ```
3. The entered cmdlet will get executed, as shown in *Figure 8.8*:

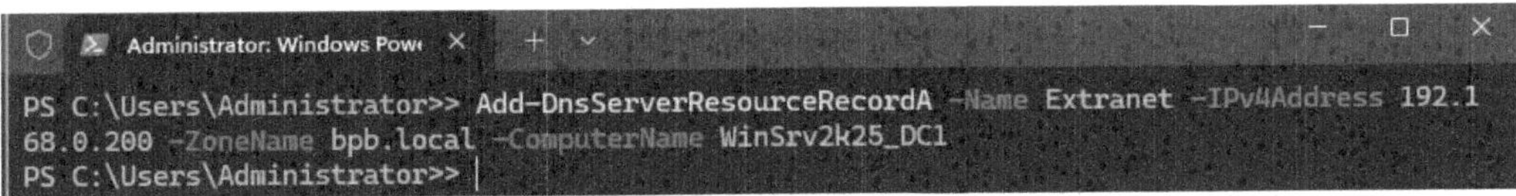

***Figure 8.8:** Configuring an A Record*

Configuring a DHCP server

Configuring a **DHCP server** in Windows Server 2025 offers several significant benefits, making it an essential tool for modern network management:

- **Automated IP address assignment:** DHCP automates the assignment of IP addresses to client devices, eliminating manual intervention. This reduces the administrative workload and minimizes the risk of address conflicts, ensuring smoother network operations.
- **Scalability and efficiency:** DHCP enables seamless network scaling by dynamically assigning IP addresses to new devices joining the network. Additionally, it distributes key network parameters, such as default gateways and DNS servers, ensuring consistent configuration across all devices. This streamlined approach simplifies troubleshooting and enhances operational efficiency.
- **IP address pool management:** With DHCP, administrators can allocate specific address ranges for different purposes or departments, improving resource efficiency and enabling network segmentation. This level of control also contributes to better network organization.
- **Cost and time savings:** DHCP reduces the time and effort required for manual configurations by automating IP address assignments. This allows IT professionals to focus on more strategic tasks, improving productivity and lowering

administrative costs.

- **Enhanced network security:** DHCP enhances security by configuring secure DNS server addresses and assigning specific IP addresses to trusted devices. This ensures better control over network access.

Configuring a DHCP server in Windows Server 2025 provides centralized IP address management, network scalability, consistent configuration, cost savings, and enhanced security, making it a critical component for effective and efficient network administration.

Exercise 8.3: Configuring a DHCP scope

This exercise details the steps for configuring a **DHCP scope** in Windows Server 2025 using the **DHCP console** and **PowerShell**.

Configuring a DHCP scope using a DHCP console

To start configuring a **DHCP scope** in Windows Server 2025 using the **DHCP console**, follow these steps:

1. Open **Server Manager** from the **Start** menu.
2. Click the **Notifications** icon, then select **Complete DHCP configuration**, as shown in *Figure 8.9:*

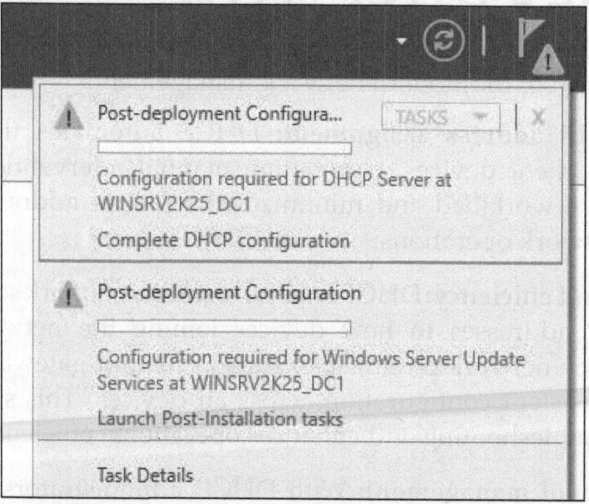

Figure 8.9: Completing DHCP configuration

3. Accept the default settings on the **Description** page and click Next.
4. On the **Authorization** page, specify the credentials to authorize **DHCP Server** and click the **Commit** button.

5. On the **Summary** page, illustrated in *Figure 8.10*, verify that **Creating security groups** and **Authorizing DHCP server** have **Done** status. Then click the **Close** button.

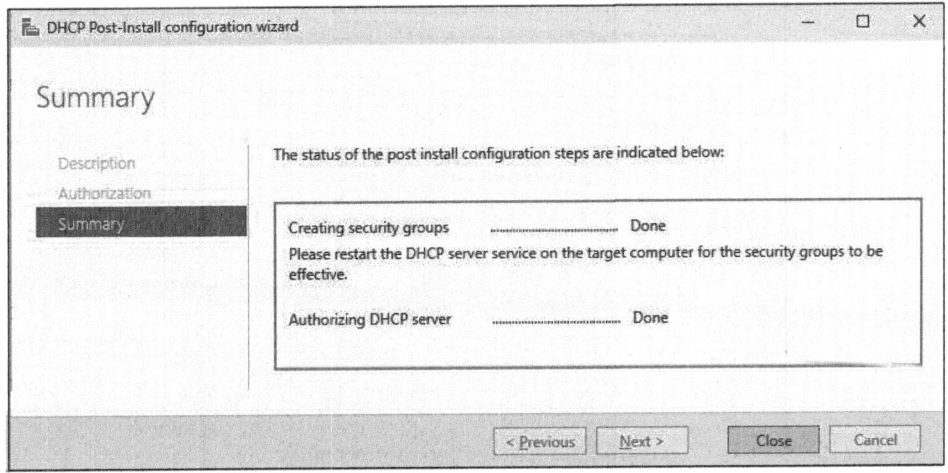

Figure 8.10: Authorizing DHCP Server

6. Open the **DHCP Manager** console by clicking the Start button and searching for **Windows Tools**. Then, double-click **DHCP**.

7. Expand the **DHCP server** from the tree on the left side of the window, as shown in *Figure 8.11*:

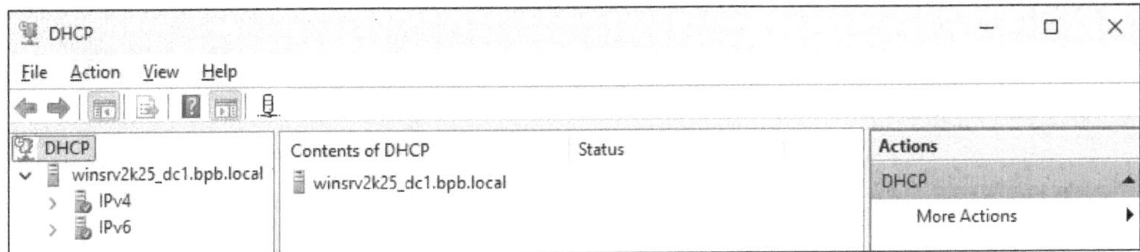

Figure 8.11: DHCP Manager console

8. Select the **IPv4 option**.

9. From the **More Actions** menu on the right side of the window, click on **New Scope**.

10. Click the **Next** button on the **Welcome to the New Scope Wizard**.

11. On the **Scope Name** page, provide the name and description for this scope, then click **Next**.

12. On the **IP address range** page, define the address range for the scope and specify the **Subnet mask**, as shown in *Figure 8.12*:

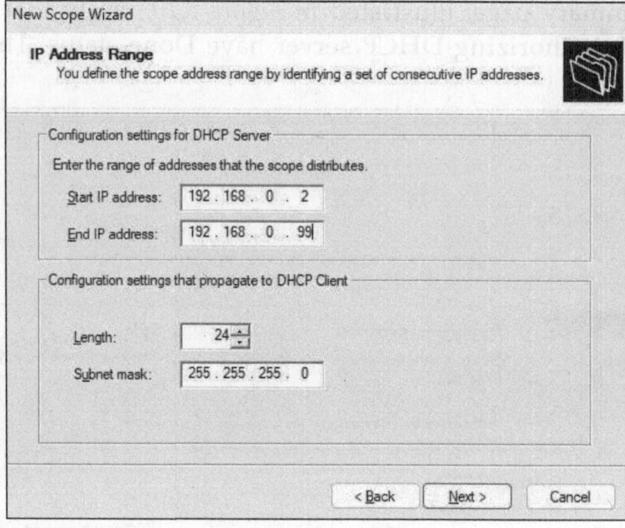

Figure 8.12: Setting the IP address range

13. On the **Add exclusions and delay** page, exclude **specific IP addresses** from the defined range if needed.
14. On the **Lease duration** page, specify the **lease duration** for the assigned IP addresses and click **Next.**
15. On the **Configure DHCP options** page, accept defaults and proceed by clicking **Next.**
16. On the **Router (default gateway)** page, as shown in *Figure 8.13*, add the **IP address** of your default gateway and click **Next.**

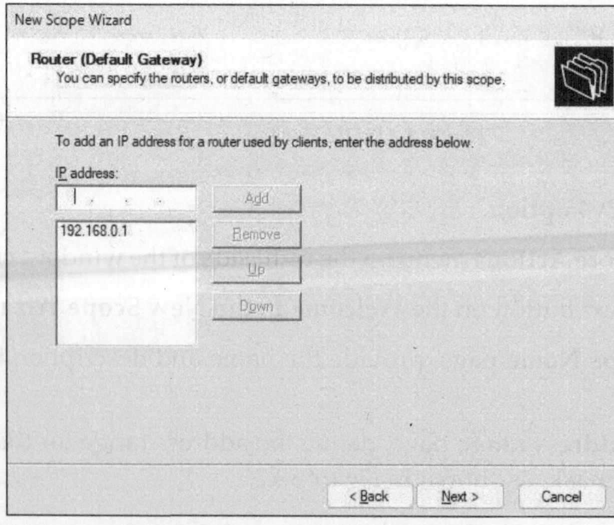

Figure 8.13: Setting the default gateway (DG)

17. On the **Domain name and DNS servers** page, specify your network's **parent domain and DNS server(s)** as shown in *Figure 8.14*:

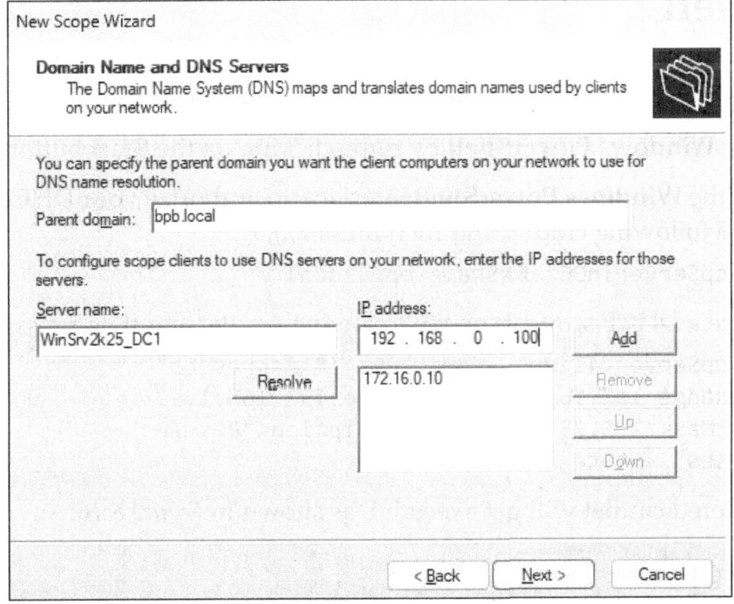

Figure 8.14: *Setting the domain name and DNS server*

18. On the **WINS servers** page, if applicable, enter the information for the **WINS** server on your network.
19. On the **Activate scope** page, confirm that you want to **activate this scope** now and click **Next**.
20. Click the **Finish** button to close the **Completing the New Scope Wizard**.
21. Your scope is now marked as ****Active**** in the **DHCP Manager**, as shown in *Figure 8.15:*

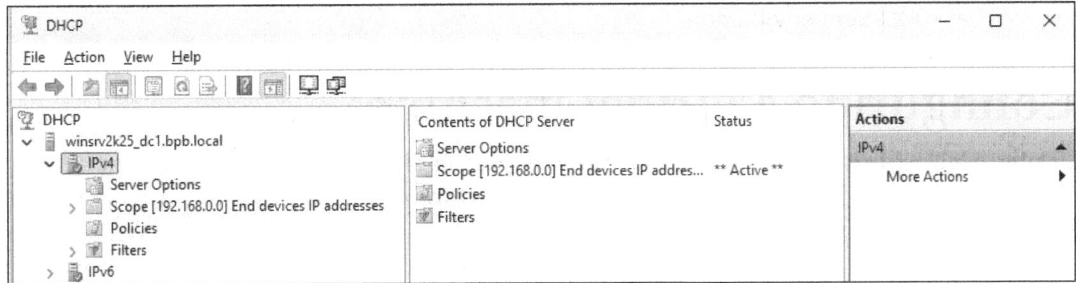

Figure 8.15: *An **Active** IPv4 scope*

Configuring a DHCP scope using Windows PowerShell

To configure a **DHCP scope** in Windows Server 2025 using **Windows PowerShell**, follow these steps:

1. Launch **Windows PowerShell** by right-clicking on the **Start** button.
2. Within the **Windows PowerShell** interface, to authorize your DHCP Server in AD, type the following cmdlet and then press *Enter*:
   ```
   Add-DhcpServerInDC -DNSName bpb.local
   ```
3. To create a DHCP scope, type the following cmdlet and then press *Enter*:
   ```
   Add-DhcpServerv4Scope -Name "PCs IP Addresses"
   -StartRange 192.168.1.2 -EndRange 192.168.1.99
   -SubnetMask 255.255.255.0 -Description "PCs IP
   Addresses" -State Active
   ```
4. The entered cmdlet will get executed, as shown in *Figure 8.16:*

```
PS C:\Users\Administrator>> Add-DhcpServerv4Scope -Name "PCs IP Addresses" -StartRange 192
.168.1.2 -EndRange 192.168.1.99 -SubnetMask 255.255.255.0 -Description "PCs IP Addresses"
-State Active
PS C:\Users\Administrator>>
```

***Figure 8.16:** Configuring an IPv4 scope*

5. To exclude a range within an IP scope, type the following cmdlet and then press *Enter*:
   ```
   Add-Dhcpserverv4ExclusionRange -ComputerName WinSrv2k25_DC1
   -ScopeId 192.168.1.0 -StartRange 192.168.1.70 -EndRange 192.168.1.80
   ```
6. To view the newly added scope, type the following cmdlet and then press *Enter*:
   ```
   Get-DHCPServerv4Scope
   ```

Configuring a virtual machine

Configuring VMs using **Hyper-V** in Windows Server 2025 offers a range of benefits that significantly enhance server management and performance. VMs provide strong isolation, allowing multiple operating systems and applications to run independently within their virtual environments. This isolation ensures that issues or reboots in one VM do not affect others, maintaining stability across the system.

Hyper-V allows for efficient allocation of resources such as CPU cores, memory, storage, and network bandwidth based on the specific needs of each **VM**. This resource management improves both performance and scalability. The key advantages of utilizing VMs in Windows Server 2025 are as follows:

- **Server consolidation:** Virtualization reduces the need for additional physical hardware, lowering data center power, space, and maintenance costs. Centralized management simplifies the maintenance of multiple VMs, while VMs also create secure and isolated environments for testing and development. Hyper-V's snapshot feature enables capturing the state of a VM, allowing for easy rollbacks to previous configurations.
- **High availability and disaster recovery:** Hyper-V provides built-in features such as replication and high availability, ensuring minimal downtime and robust disaster recovery solutions for mission-critical systems. This ensures continuous business operations even during unexpected events.
- **Scalability and flexibility:** VMs are highly adaptable to changing demands. Resources can be allocated dynamically, and VMs can be migrated seamlessly between hosts to optimize resource utilization. Windows Server 2025 enhances administrative tasks with powerful tools such as PowerShell integration and performance monitoring, making VM management more efficient and streamlined.

Configuring VMs with **Hyper-V** in Windows Server 2025 improves resource efficiency, strengthens security and isolation, simplifies management, and guarantees high availability and disaster recovery. This creates a robust IT infrastructure that can scale with your organization's needs.

Exercise 8.4: Configuring a virtual machine

This exercise outlines the steps for configuring a VM in Windows Server 2025 using **Hyper-V Manager** and **PowerShell**.

Configuring a virtual machine using Hyper-V Manager

To start configuring a VM in Windows Server 2025 with **Hyper-V Manager**, follow these steps:

1. Open the **Hyper-V Manager**, as depicted in *Figure 8.17*, by clicking the **Start** button and searching for **Windows Tools**. Then, double-click **Hyper-V Manager**.

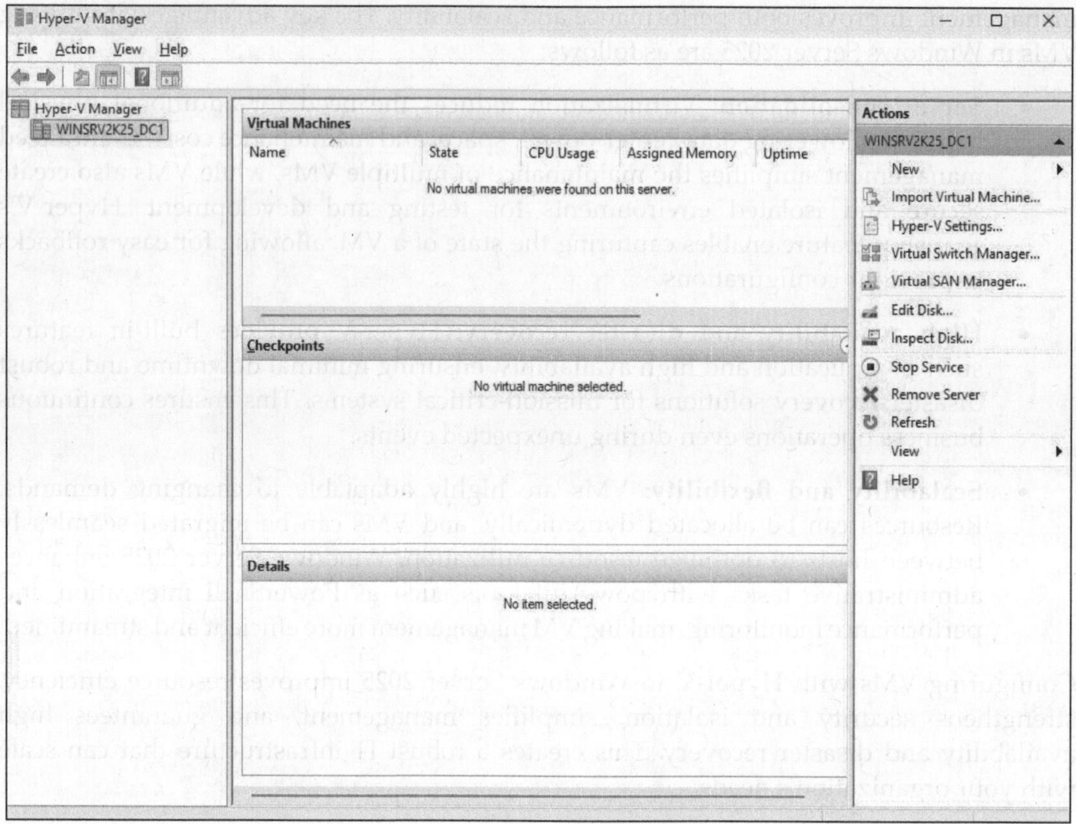

Figure 8.17: Hyper-V Manager console

2. On the left pane of the **Hyper-V Manager**, click on **Server**.

3. From the **Actions** menu on the right pane of **Hyper-V Manager**, select **New | Virtual Machine**.

4. A **New Virtual Machine Wizard** window will open, displaying preliminary information on the **Before You Begin** page. Click on **Next** to proceed.

5. On the **Specify the name and location** page, enter the **virtual machine's name** and location, then click **Next**.

6. On the **Specify Generation** page, choose the **generation** for the VM and click **Next**.

7. On the **Assign Memory** page, as shown in *Figure 8.18*, allocate **memory** for the VM and check the box labeled **Use Dynamic Memory**. Click the **Next** button to continue.

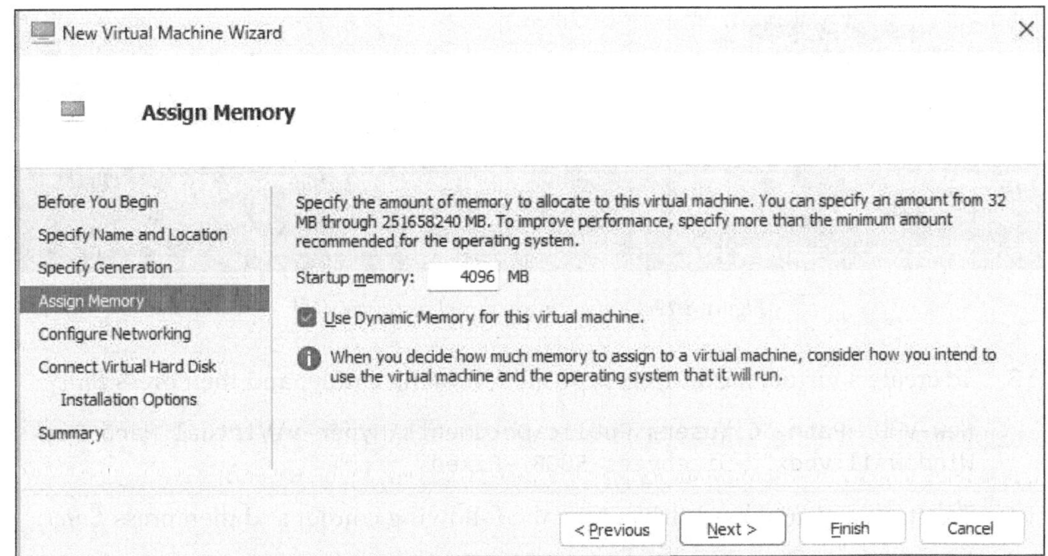

Figure 8.18: Assigning memory for the virtual machine (VM)

8. If no virtual switch is available on the **Configure network** page, accept the defaults, and click **Next**.

9. On the **Connect virtual hard disk** page, specify the **storage** configuration for the VM and click **Next** to proceed.

10. On the **Installation option** page, choose the **installation option** for the VM and click the **Next** button to continue.

11. On the **Summary** page, click **Finish** to create the VM and close the **New Virtual Machine Wizard**.

Configuring a virtual machine using Windows PowerShell

To start configuring a VM in Windows Server 2025 using **Windows PowerShell**, follow these steps:

1. Launch **Windows PowerShell** by right-clicking on the **Start** button.

2. Within the **Windows PowerShell** interface (as in *Figure 8.19*), to configure a VM, type the following cmdlet and then press *Enter*:

```
New-VM -VMName Windows11 -MemoryStartupBytes 4096MB
```

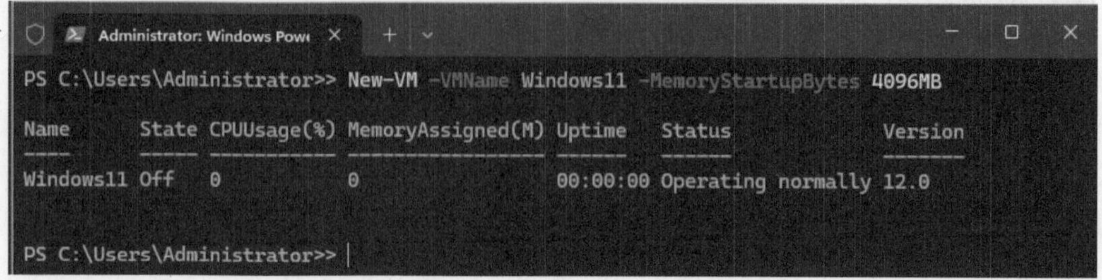

Figure 8.19: Configuring a virtual machine (VM)

3. To create a virtual hard drive, type the following cmdlet and then press *Enter*:

```
New-VHD -Path "C:\users\Public\Documents\Hyper-v\Virtual Hard Disks\
Windows11.vhdx" -Sizebytes 50GB -Fixed
```

4. To attach a virtual hard drive, type the following cmdlet and then press *Enter*:

```
Add-VMHardDiskDrive -VMName Windows11 -Path "C:\Users\
Public\Documents\Hyper-V\Virtual Hard Disks\Windows11.
vhdx" -ControllerType IDE -ControllerNumber 0 -ControllerLocation 1
```

5. To configure an internal virtual switch, as shown in *Figure 8.20*, type the following cmdlet and then press *Enter*:

```
New-VMSwitch -Name InternalSwitch -SwitchType Internal
```

6. To connect a network adapter to an internal virtual switch, as shown in *Figure 8.20*, type the following cmdlet and then press *Enter*:

```
Connect-VMNetworkAdapter -VMName Windows11 -VMNetworkAdaptername
"Network Adapter" -SwitchName "InternalSwitch"
```

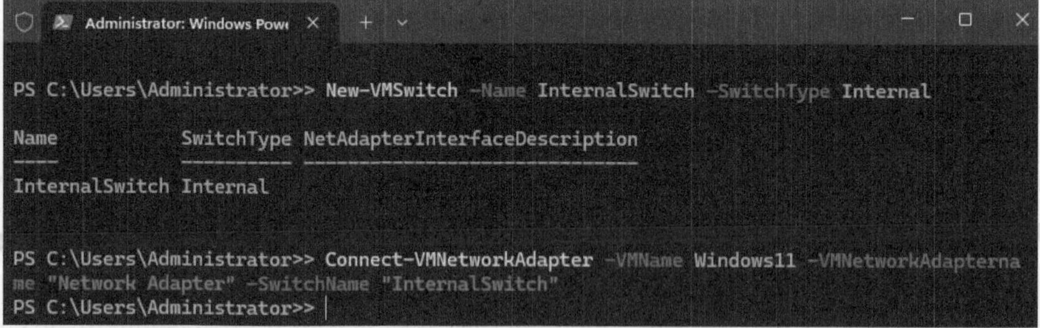

Figure 8.20: Configuring an internal virtual switch and connecting a network adapter

7. To specify a path to an ISO file, type the following cmdlet and then press *Enter*:

```
Set-VMDvdDrive -VMName Windows11 -ControllerNumber 1 -Path
"C:\ISO Images\Windows11.ISO"
```

Configuring a website

Configuring a website using **Internet Information Services (IIS)** in Windows Server 2025 offers numerous advantages, making it a trusted platform for hosting web applications. Key benefits include:

- **Reliability and performance:** IIS provides a stable and efficient hosting environment, ensuring consistent website performance and optimal resource utilization. Its extensive features enable tailored functionality and robust security configurations.
- **Seamless integration:** Fully integrated with the Windows Server ecosystem, IIS offers a familiar interface for administrators, simplifying website creation, configuration, and management. Its centralized management capabilities allow effortless handling of multiple sites from a single console.
- **Flexibility and adaptability:** IIS supports a broad range of web technologies and protocols, such as HTTP, HTTPS, and FTP, accommodating diverse application needs. Advanced features like load balancing, caching, and compression enhance website performance and responsiveness.
- **Enhanced security:** With built-in measures like SSL/TLS encryption, multiple authentication methods, and granular access controls, IIS ensures a secure hosting environment for protecting websites and sensitive data.

Using IIS in Windows Server 2025 delivers a robust, flexible, and secure platform, ideal for efficiently and reliably hosting modern web applications.

Exercise 8.5: Configuring a website

This exercise details configuring a **website** using **IIS Manager** and **PowerShell** in Windows Server 2025.

Configuring a website using IIS Manager

To initiate **website configuration** in Windows Server 2025 using **IIS Manager**, perform the following steps:

1. Open the **IIS Manager**, shown in *Figure 8.21*, by clicking the **Start** button and searching for **Windows Tools**. Then, double-click **Internet Information Services (IIS) Manager**.

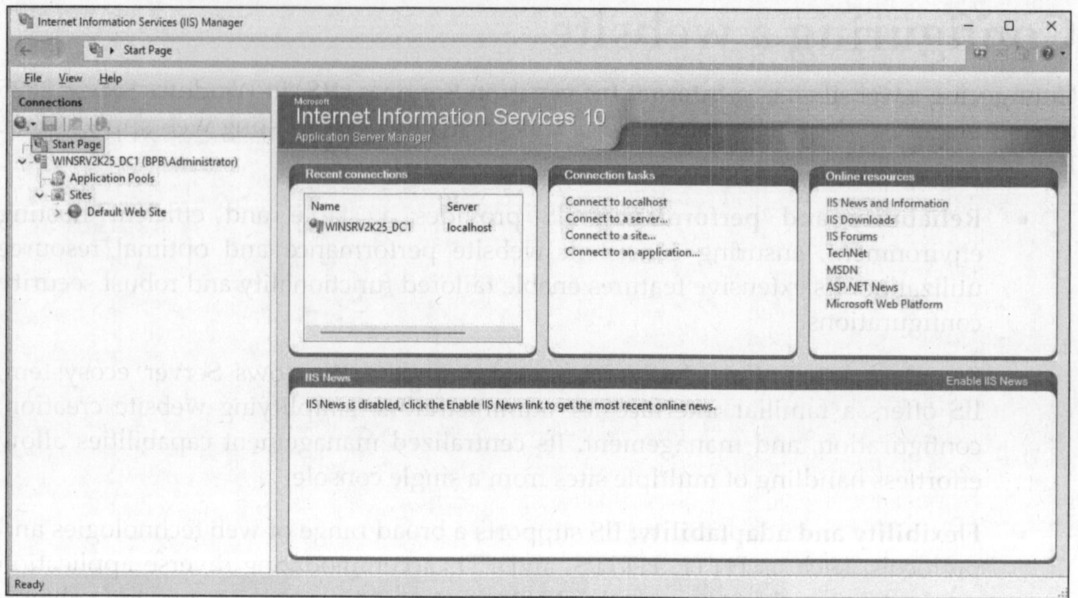

Figure 8.21: Internet Information Services (IIS) Manager console

2. Expand the **Webserver** from the tree on the left side of the **IIS Manager**.
3. Click on **Sites** on the left side of the console. From the **Actions** on the right pane of the **IIS Manager**, select **Add Website...**
4. When the **Add Website** window opens, enter the site's name and specify the **Content Directory** section's physical path.
5. In the **Binding** section (*Figure 8.22*), if *Port 80* is already in use, change it **to 8080**, as in Click **OK** to close the **Add Website** dialog box.

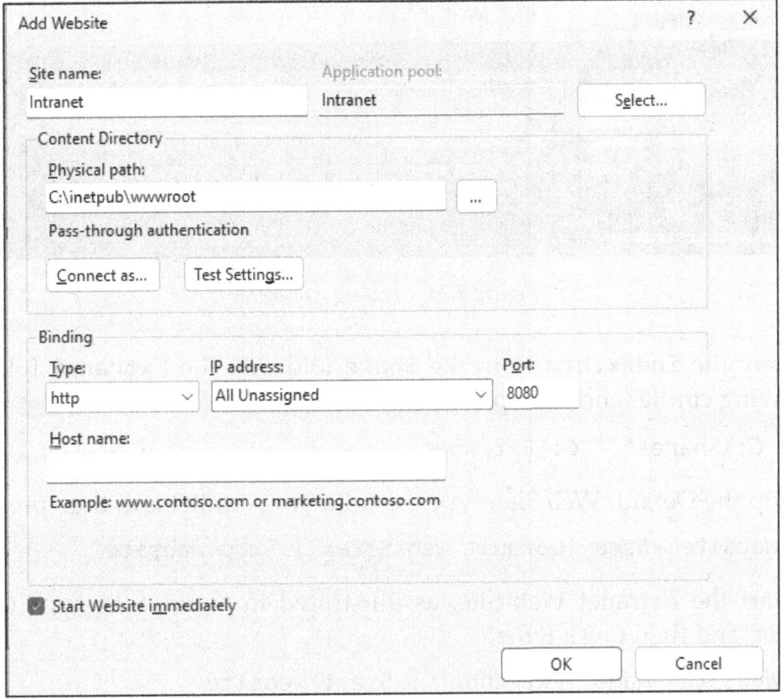

***Figure 8.22:** Configuring a website*

6. The recently added website will be listed in the middle pane of the **IIS Manager** console.

7. From the **Actions** on the right side of the **IIS Manager**, click **Browse *.8080 (HTTP)** to open the newly added website.

Configuring a website using Windows PowerShell

To initiate the configuration of a **website** in Windows Server 2025 using **Windows PowerShell**, follow these steps:

1. Launch **Windows PowerShell** by right-clicking on the **Start** button.

2. Within the **Windows PowerShell** interface, as illustrated in *Figure 8.23*, to create a website, type the following cmdlet and then press *Enter*:

```
New-Website -Name Extranet -PhysicalPath C:\Extranet
```

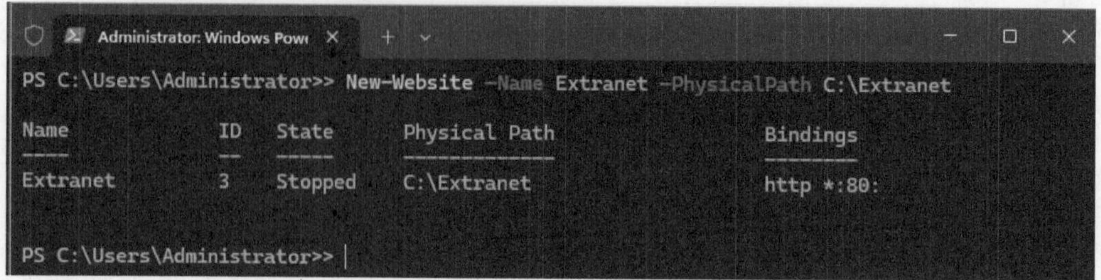

Figure 8.23: Creating a website

3. To copy the **index.htm** from the **Share** folder to the **Extranet** folder, type the following cmdlet and then press *Enter*:

```
Copy C:\Share\*.* C:\Extranet
```

4. To stop the Default Web Site, type the following cmdlet and then press *Enter*:

```
Get-Website -Name 'Default Web Site› | Stop-Website
```

5. To start the Extranet Web Site, as illustrated in *Figure 8.24*, type the following cmdlet, and then press *Enter*:

```
Get-Website -Name 'Extranet' | Start-Website
```

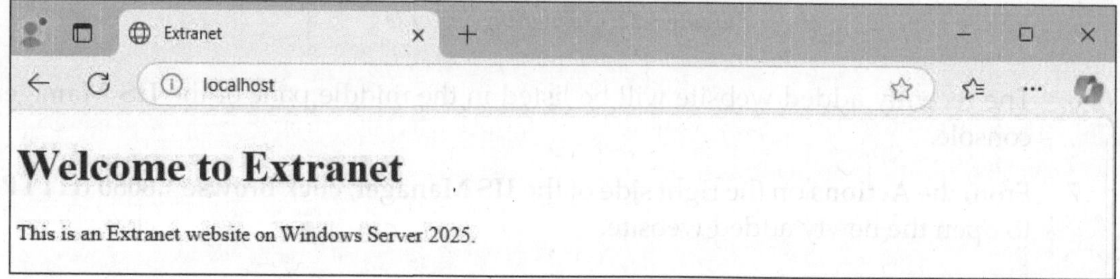

Figure 8.24: Browsing the new website

Note: To perform a test, we have generated a webpage named `index.htm` within a folder named Intranet on disk C. Once the website is started, browse it through a web browser, as illustrated in *Figure 8.24*.

Configuring the print server

Configuring a **print server** in Windows Server 2025 using the **Print Management** console is crucial for streamlined and centralized printer management across a network. This setup offers several advantages, including **centralized control** over printers, **simplified deployment**, **efficient driver distribution**, **enhanced sharing capabilities**, and **improved monitoring** and **management** of **print jobs**. Administrators can effortlessly add or remove printers, distribute drivers to client systems, monitor printer statuses, manage queues, prioritize print jobs, and optimize resource usage. By centralizing these tasks, print server configuration enhances productivity, reduces deployment complexity, and lowers operational costs, making it an invaluable component of modern IT infrastructure.

Exercise 8.6: Configuring the print server

This exercise provides a step-by-step guide for configuring a **print server** in Windows Server 2025 using the **Print Management** console and **PowerShell**.

Configuring print server using Print Management

To initiate the process of configuring a print server in Windows Server 2025 using the **Print Management** console, follow these steps:

1. Open **Print Management**, as in *Figure 8.25*, by clicking the **Start** button and searching for **Windows Tools**. Then, double-click **Print Management**.

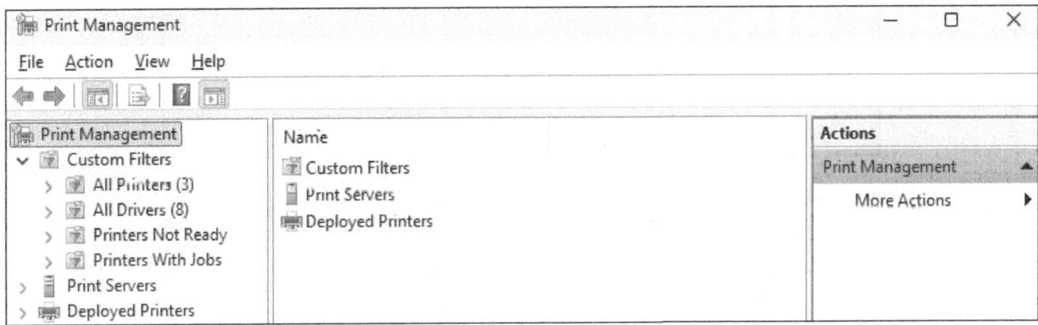

Figure 8.25: *Print Management console in Windows Server 2025*

2. Expand **Print Servers** from a tree structure pane, then expand the **server**. Right-click on **Printers** and select **Add Printer...**
3. The **Network Printer Installation Wizard** opens up to help you install a network printer.
4. On the **Printer installation** page, specify the **installation method** and click the **Next** button. Depending on the method chosen, you will search for a **network printer**, add an **IP address**, and use an **existing port** to add a **new printer** or **create a new port**. Click the Next button to proceed.
5. After completing the **printer installation**, observe the right pane of the **Print Management** console to find your newly added printer.
6. Select the **printer** and click on the **Action** menu. From the expanded menu, select **Manage Sharing...**
7. Ensure the **Share this printer** and **List in the directory** checkboxes are checked, as shown in *Figure 8.26:*

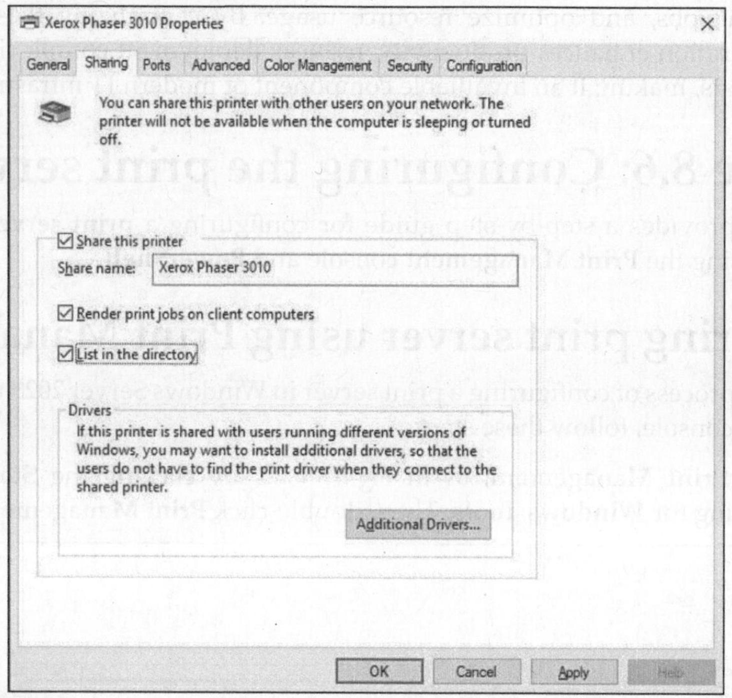

Figure 8.26: Sharing a printer in Windows Server 2025 using Print Management

8. Once the **sharing options** are maintained, click the **OK** button to close the dialog box.

Configuring print server using Windows PowerShell

To start configuring a **print server** in Windows Server 2025 using **Windows PowerShell**, follow these steps:

1. Launch **Windows PowerShell** by right-clicking on the **Start** button.
2. Within the **Windows PowerShell** interface, depicted in *Figure 8.27*, to install a printer, type the following cmdlet and then press *Enter*:

```
Add-Printer -Name Microsoft_Print -DriverName "Microsoft Print To PDF" -Port LPT1:
```

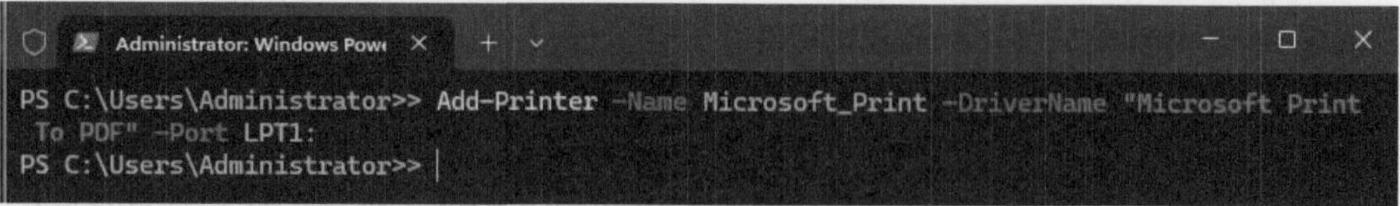

Figure 8.27: Installing a printer

3. To share the printer, type the following cmdlet and then press *Enter*:

```
Set-Printer -ComputerName WinSrv2k25_DC1 -Name Microsoft_
Print -Shared $True -ShareName MicrosoftPrint
```

Note: It is recommended that you install the driver before installing a printer. To do so, use the Add-PrinterDriver cmdlet.

Configuring Remote Desktop Users

Configuring **Remote Desktop Users** in Windows Server 2025 enables secure and efficient remote server access and streamlines management and administration tasks. This functionality offers numerous benefits, including allowing administrators to connect remotely from any location, promoting flexibility and convenience. **Remote Desktop** supports multiple simultaneous connections, fostering centralized management and collaboration among IT teams.

Remote Desktop minimizes downtime and enhances system availability by facilitating remote troubleshooting and maintenance. It also reduces the reliance on physical consoles, leading to potential cost savings in hardware and infrastructure. Advanced security features, such as access control and connection restrictions, ensure that only authorized individuals or groups gain access, strengthening the overall security posture.

Additionally, **Remote Desktop** supports business continuity by empowering administrators to manage servers during emergencies or when physical access is impractical. Configuring Remote Desktop Users in Windows Server 2025 delivers a robust, secure, and efficient approach to modern server management.

Exercise 8.7: Configuring Remote Desktop Users

This exercise outlines the steps to configure Remote Desktop Users in Windows Server 2025 using **Active Directory Users and Computers** (**ADUC**) and PowerShell.

Configuring Remote Desktop via Active Directory

To configure **Remote Desktop Users** in Windows Server 2025 using ADUC, follow these steps:

1. Open **Active Directory Users and Computers**, as in *Figure 8.28*, by clicking the **Start** button and searching for **Windows Tools**. Then, double-click **Active Directory Users and Computers.**

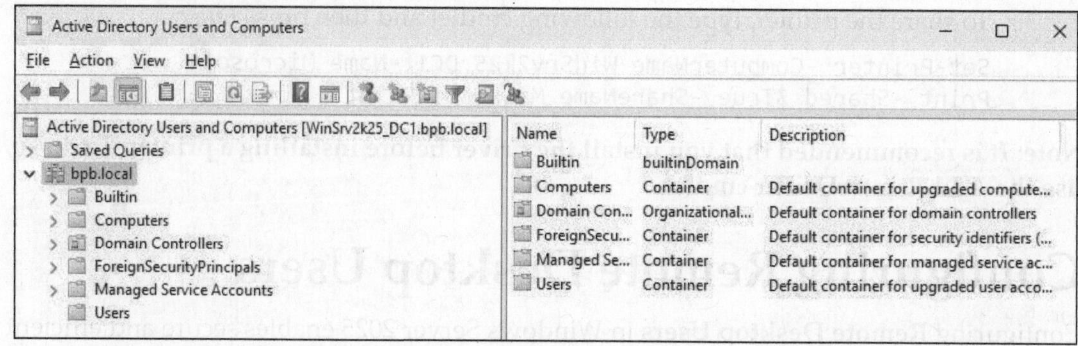

***Figure 8.28:** Active Directory Users and Computers (ADUC) console in Windows Server 2025*

2. Expand the **Server** on the left pane of the **Active Directory Users and Computers** console.
3. Click on **Users** in the tree view on the left pane of the **Active Directory Users and Computers** console.
4. Locate the **Test User** on the right pane of the **Active Directory Users and Computers** console and right-click it.
5. Select the **Add to a group...** option from the context menu.
6. On the **Select Groups** dialog box (*Figure 8.29*), enter the **Remote Desktop User** in the provided field and click the **Check Names** button to verify the group name. Click **OK** to close the dialog box.

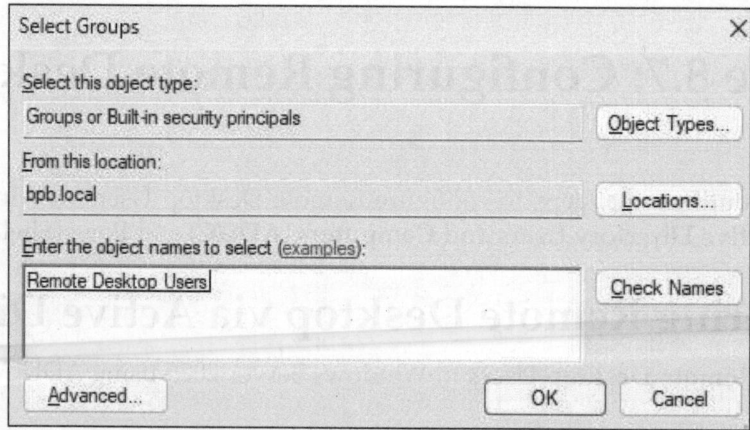

***Figure 8.29:** Adding a user to the Remote Desktop Users group*

7. Click **OK** to close the **Add to group operation was completed** dialog box.

Note: The Test User used for this practical demonstration has been pre-created beforehand.

Configuring Remote Desktop Users using Windows PowerShell

To begin configuring **Remote Desktop Users** in Windows Server 2025 using **Windows PowerShell**, follow these steps:

1. Launch **Windows PowerShell** by right-clicking on the **Start** button.
2. Within the **Windows PowerShell** interface, shown in *Figure 8.30*, to allow RDP connections on a server, type the following cmdlet and then press *Enter*:

```
Set-ItemProperty -Path 'HKLM:\SYSTEM\CurrentControlSet\Control\
Terminal Server' -Name fDenyTSConnections -Value 0
```

***Figure 8.30:** Allowing RDP connection on a server*

3. To configure Network Level Authentication, type the following cmdlet and then press *Enter*:

```
Set-ItemProperty -Path 'HKLM:\SYSTEM\CurrentControlSet\
Control\Terminal Server\WinStations\RDP-
Tcp' -Name UserAuthentication -Value 1
```

4. To allow the Remote Desktop firewall exception, type the following cmdlet and then press *Enter*:

```
Set-NetFirewallRule -DisplayGroup 'Remote Desktop' -Enabled True
```

5. To add a user to the Remote Desktop Users group, as shown in *Figure 8.31*, type the following cmdlet and then press *Enter*:

```
Net localgroup «Remote Desktop Users» testuser /add
```

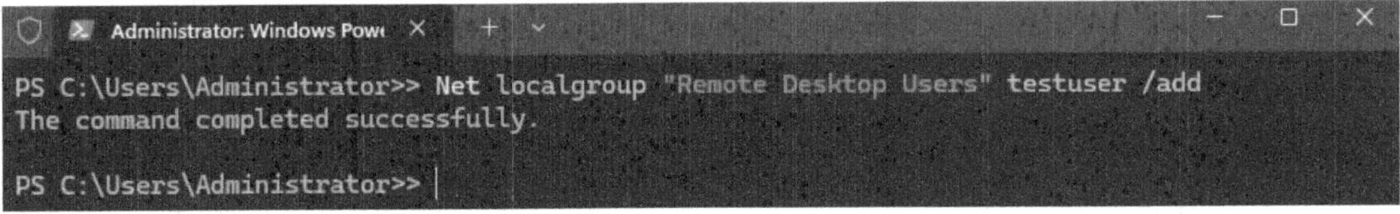

***Figure 8.31:** Adding a user to the Remote Desktop Users group*

Configuring the WSUS server

Configuring WSUS in Windows Server 2025 remains essential for centralized management of Windows updates within an on-premises network. WSUS enables administrators to deploy updates efficiently, ensuring consistency across systems. By downloading updates once from the **WSUS server** and distributing them internally, it helps optimize network bandwidth, preventing redundant downloads from the Internet.

In addition to streamlining update management, **WSUS** offers enhanced control, allowing administrators to test and approve updates for compatibility before deployment. This reduces the risk of system disruptions while ensuring all machines remain secure with the latest patches and fixes. WSUS also provides detailed reporting and monitoring features, offering valuable insights into the updated status of machines, and making it easier to track installations and resolve issues promptly.

Furthermore, WSUS allows for customization, enabling administrators to target specific updates and prioritize critical ones, improving the efficiency of update deployment and overall network management.

As mentioned in *Chapter 5*, Microsoft is planning to retire WSUS. Microsoft has provided further details, such as the upcoming deprecation of WSUS driver synchronization on April 18, 2025. While drivers will remain available through the Microsoft Update Catalog in on-premises environments, they will no longer be importable into WSUS. Administrators must explore alternative driver distribution methods, such as Device Driver Packages, to effectively manage drivers throughout the network.

Additionally, Windows Server 2025 enhances cloud-based management with Microsoft Endpoint Manager, offering seamless management of both on-premises and cloud-connected devices. Integration with Azure Arc enables hotpatching, allowing critical updates to be applied without requiring reboots and minimizing downtime. Azure Update Manager provides centralized control over updates, simplifying scheduling, deployment, and monitoring. This combined approach streamlines administrative workflows, improves device management consistency, and boosts flexibility across hybrid environments.

Exercise 8.8: Configuring the WSUS server

This exercise outlines the steps for configuring a **WSUS server** using **WSUS Manager** in Windows Server 2025. This tool allows administrators to manage and distribute updates efficiently across the network, improving control and security.

Configuring WSUS Server via WSUS Manager

To start configuring the **WSUS server** in Windows Server 2025 using **WSUS Manager**, follow these steps:

1. Open **Server Manager** from the **Start** menu.
2. Click the **Notifications** icon, then select **Launch Post-Installation tasks,** as shown in *Figure 8.32*:

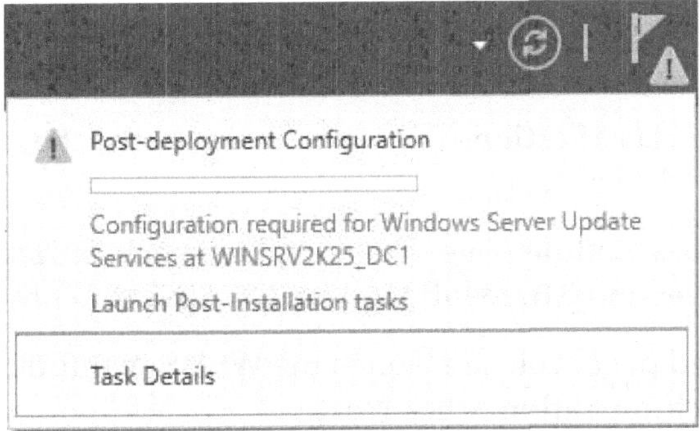

***Figure 8.32:** Finalizing WSUS post-installation tasks*

3. Open WSUS Manager by clicking the **Start** button, searching for Windows Tools, and double-clicking **Windows Server Update Services**.
4. The **Complete WSUS Installation** window will open shortly, as in *Figure 8.33*. Verify that the **Content directory path** is correct and click on **Run**. Keep the dialog box open during the **WSUS post-installation task**, although it may take a few minutes.

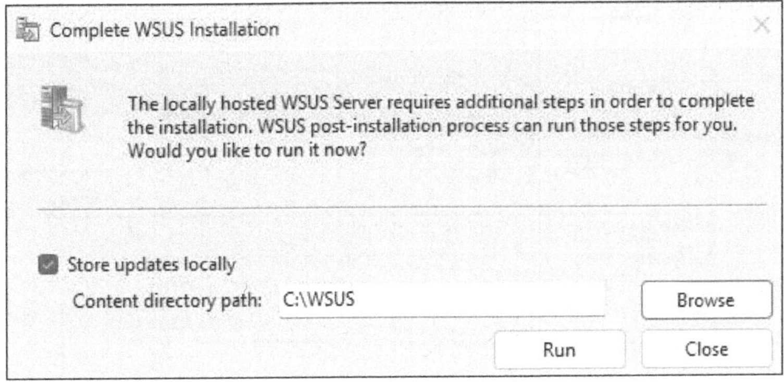

***Figure 8.33:** Running the WSUS post-installation task in Windows Server 2025*

5. Once the **WSUS post-installation task** is completed, click on **Close**.
6. The **WSUS Configuration Wizard** will open. Read the content on the **Before You Begin** page and click **Next**.
7. On the **Microsoft Update Improvement Program** page, you can optionally choose to join the Program and click **Next**.
8. On the **Choose upstream server** page, specify the **upstream server,** and click **Next**.
9. Enter the proxy server settings on the **Specify proxy server** page and click **Next** if applicable.
10. On the **Connect to Upstream server** page, click **Start Connection** and **Next**.

11. On the **Choose the Products** page, specify the **needed products** for updates and click **Next**.
12. On the **Choose classifications** page, you must choose the **update classification to synchronize** and click **Next**.
13. On the **Set sync schedule** page, configure the **synchronization schedule** between the **WSUS server** and **Microsoft Update**. Click **Next** to proceed.
14. On the **Finished** page, you can launch the **WSUS Administration** console or start the **initial synchronization**. Click **Next**.
15. Explore **additional topics** for fully configuring the **WSUS server** on the **What's Next** page.
16. After closing the **WSUS Configuration Wizard**, the **WSUS Manager** console will open, as shown in *Figure 8.34*:

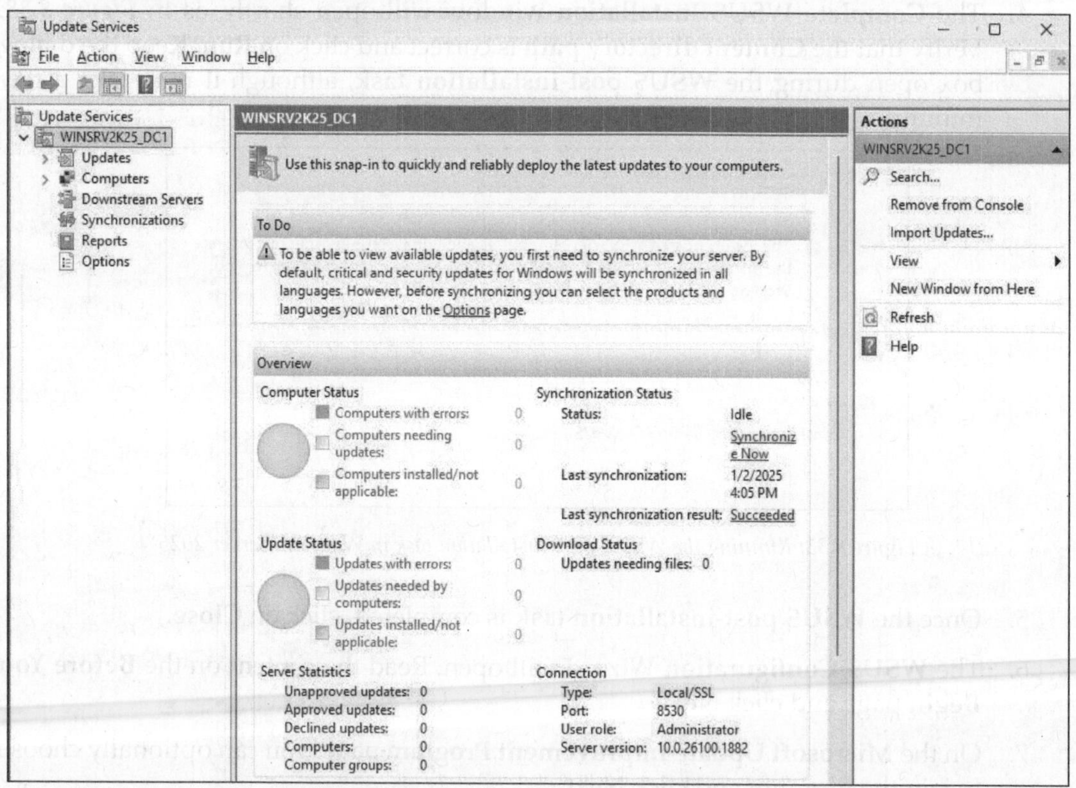

Figure 8.34: WSUS Manager in Windows Server 2025

Conclusion

This chapter presented a step-by-step guide for configuring client/server network services in Windows Server 2025 using Windows PowerShell cmdlets. By tapping into the robust capabilities of Windows PowerShell, you have explored effective ways to set up and manage key network services in Windows Server 2025. Topics covered include configuring a DC, managing DNS records, setting up an IPv4 scope for a DHCP server, deploying a VM, configuring a web server, setting up a print server, managing remote desktop users, and establishing a WSUS server. You have gained the expertise to configure and manage these critical network services in Windows Server 2025 through detailed instructions and cmdlets.

The next chapter will focus on enhancing storage performance with NVMe SSDs and optimizing **Storage Area Network** (**SAN**) integration in Windows Server 2025.

Questions

1. What is a domain controller (DC)?
2. What is an A Record?
3. What is an IPv4 scope?
4. What is a virtual machine (VM)?
5. What is a website?
6. What is a print server?
7. What is a remote desktop user?
8. What are WSUS benefits?

Join our book's Discord space

Join the book's Discord Workspace for Latest updates, Offers, Tech happenings around the world, New Release and Sessions with the Authors:

https://discord.bpbonline.com

CHAPTER 9
Enhancing Storage with NVMe SSDs and SAN

Introduction

This chapter explores how to improve storage performance in Windows Server 2025 using NVMe SSDs and better SAN integration. With NVMe SSDs offering faster data access, improved performance, and enhanced SAN capabilities providing scalable storage solutions, this chapter guides you through deploying and optimizing these technologies. You will learn to configure NVMe SSDs, tune performance, and implement SAN solutions in Windows Server 2025. Additionally, the chapter covers advanced topics like storage virtualization and **software-defined storage** (**SDS**), enabling you to build a high-performance, scalable storage environment. Step-by-step instructions and practical exercises are provided for configuring these technologies.

Structure

The chapter covers the following topics:

- Introduction to NVMe SSDs
- Understanding NVMe protocol
- Exercise 9.1: Deploying NVMe SSDs in Windows Server 2025
- Performance tuning for NVMe SSDs
- Real-world use cases of NVMe SSDs

- Exercise 9.2: Configuring SAN solutions on NVMe SSDs
- Exercise 9.3: SAN integration in Windows Server 2025
- Leveraging storage virtualization with SDS

Objectives

This chapter's primary objective is to guide readers in enhancing storage performance in Windows Server 2025. It provides step-by-step instructions on deploying and optimizing NVMe SSDs, integrating SAN solutions, and fine-tuning storage performance. The chapter also covers advanced topics like storage virtualization and SDS, offering practical insights for scalable, high-performance storage. By the end, readers will be equipped to implement modern storage solutions and maximize Windows Server 2025's storage capabilities.

Introduction to NVMe SSDs

Non-Volatile Memory Express (NVMe) SSDs, illustrated in *Figure 9.1*, have revolutionized modern storage solutions by delivering exceptional speed and efficiency, overcoming the inherent limitations of older protocols like **Serial Advanced Technology Attachment (SATA)** and **Serial Attached Small Computer System Interface (SAS)**.

Figure 9.1: *NVMe SSD drive*

The development of the NVMe specification has been a significant milestone in the evolution of storage technology. The NVM Express Work Group, later incorporated as NVM Express, Inc., has played a vital role in advancing NVMe standards. The following is a timeline highlighting the major milestones in the development of the NVMe specification and its related technologies:

Date	Event
March 1, 2011	Release of Version 1.0 of the NVM Express specification, developed cooperatively by member companies.
October 11, 2012	Release of Version 1.1 of the NVM Express specification.
November 3, 2014	Release of Version 1.2 of the NVM Express specification.
November 2015	Release of **NVM Express Management Interface** (**NVMe-MI**) specification, providing out-of-band management for NVMe components and systems.
2016 (Expected)	Version 1.3 of the NVM Express specification is expected to address the needs of mobile devices, including low power consumption and other features.

Table 9.1: *Milestone in NVMe development*

In the context of Windows Server 2025, NVMe SSDs unlock powerful storage capabilities, including advanced features like **Storage Spaces Direct (S2D)** and SDS. These tools leverage the speed and reliability of NVMe to deliver scalable, low-latency, high-throughput storage environments. Proper implementation, however, requires meticulous preparation, such as ensuring firmware and **BIOS compatibility**, updating drivers, and applying performance optimization techniques. Adjustments like tuning queue depths, enabling write caching, and optimizing file system configurations can maximize the benefits of **NVMe technology**.

Integrating *NVMe SSDs* can significantly enhance organizations' storage solutions' performance, scalability, and efficiency. As the backbone of modern IT infrastructures, NVMe represents the forefront of storage innovation, equipping enterprises with the tools needed to meet the demands of today's data-driven world.

NVMe storage benefits versus SAS and SATA

The evolution of storage technologies has significantly shifted from traditional **hard disk drives** (**HDDs**) to faster and more efficient solutions. During the era when HDDs were predominant, SATA and SAS served as effective interfaces for data transfer. These technologies were tailored for spinning disks, relying on the SCSI protocol for SAS and the ATA protocol for SATA to manage server connections via PCIe links. However, with the advent of NVMe storage, a new benchmark in performance and efficiency was established, outpacing SAS and SATA by leveraging modern **solid-state drive** (**SSD**) technology, depicted in *Figure 9.2:*

Figure 9.2: SATA SSD drive

The following are the key benefits of NVMe storage over SAS or SATA drives:

- **Superior performance:** NVMe uses a direct PCIe connection to interface SSDs with the server or **central processing unit (CPU)**, eliminating the bottlenecks associated with legacy protocols like SATA and SAS. This direct pathway allows NVMe drives to achieve significantly higher **input/output operations per second (IOPS)** and lower latency, making them the preferred storage solution for demanding applications such as gaming platforms, video editing workflows, and enterprise-scale data processing. By removing intermediaries and optimizing command structures, NVMe revolutionizes how data is accessed and stored, offering unmatched performance for high-demand environments.
- **Exceptional speed:** NVMe drives outpace SAS and SATA by leveraging streamlined command sets and optimized data paths. NVMe can handle up to 64,000 I/O queues, each capable of processing 64,000 commands simultaneously, allowing massive parallelism. This design ensures higher data transfer rates, reducing the time needed for intensive read/write operations, which is critical in real-time analytics and cloud environments.
- **Enhanced compatibility:** Unlike SAS and SATA, which are primarily tied to legacy systems, NVMe is designed for modern computing environments, ensuring compatibility across various platforms:
    - **Operating systems***:* Seamlessly integrates with all major systems, including Windows, Linux, and macOS.
    - **Devices***:* This category includes functions across various hardware, such as laptops, gaming consoles, smartphones, and enterprise servers.
    - **Emerging technologies***:* Supports advancements in AI, **machine learning (ML)**, and cloud computing, keeping pace with rapid innovation cycles.
    - Regular updates to NVMe specifications further extend its functionality, ensuring it remains a future-proof solution as technology evolves.
- **Unmatched bandwidth and scalability:** NVMe drives excel in bandwidth capabilities thanks to their PCIe connection:

- **Higher bandwidth**: PCIe links offer wider pathways for data transfer compared to the fixed bandwidths of SAS and SATA. With each new PCIe generation, the bandwidth doubles, continually improving performance.
- **Scalability with lanes**: NVMe connections can scale by increasing the number of PCIe lanes. For instance, a four-lane (x4) PCIe connection offers twice the bandwidth of a two-lane (x2) connection within the same generation, giving users the flexibility to customize performance according to their needs.

This **scalability** ensures that NVMe drives can adapt to varying workloads, from simple applications to highly complex enterprise tasks.

NVMe storage has set a new standard for speed, efficiency, and adaptability in the storage industry. Addressing the limitations of older interfaces like SAS and SATA, NVMe provides businesses and consumers with an innovative solution that meets the demands of modern computing environments. Whether for high-performance gaming, AI-driven analytics, or enterprise data centers, NVMe drives deliver unparalleled performance, compatibility, and scalability advantages, making them the cornerstone of next-generation storage solutions.

Understanding NVMe protocol

The **NVMe protocol** is a cutting-edge, high-performance storage interface designed to fully exploit the capabilities of SSDs, particularly in environments that demand rapid, low-latency data access. NVMe leverages the high-speed **Peripheral Component Interconnect Express** (**PCIe**) bus to connect SSD storage directly to servers or CPUs, significantly advancing older storage technologies like **SATA** and **SAS**. This protocol is tailored explicitly for **non-volatile memory** (**NVM**), such as **NAND flash**, and was developed to overcome the limitations of traditional HDDs, which used storage protocols like SATA and SAS optimized for spinning disks.

Unlike legacy storage protocols, NVMe is engineered to provide high performance and parallelism to modern SSDs. One of its most critical enhancements is supporting deep queues, allowing more commands to be processed simultaneously. SAS and SATA protocols are limited in their capacity to handle multiple operations: SAS supports up to 256 commands in a single queue, and SATA supports up to 32 commands per queue. In contrast, the NVMe protocol can handle up to **64,000 commands** per queue and supports up to **64,000 queues**. This vast increase in throughput and efficiency enables NVMe to manage the demands of multi-threaded and highly parallel workloads in enterprise environments.

In addition to its **high queue depth**, the NVMe protocol is designed to optimize data paths and minimize latency. Traditional storage protocols consume significant CPU cycles to process I/O operations, creating bottlenecks that slow down system performance. NVMe reduces this overhead by allowing **data transfer** to occur more directly between the

SSD and the CPU, bypassing many of the inefficiencies found in previous protocols. The result is faster data access with lower latency, essential for high-performance computing tasks like big data analytics, virtualization, and real-time data processing. In that line of discussion, *Figure 9.3* shows data flow in an **NVMe over Fabrics (NVMe-oF) architecture**, where an application server and storage target transfer data via **direct memory access (DMA)** through adapters and a fabric network. The server connects to an adapter, which interfaces with the *NVMe-oF fabric*, while another adapter links to the storage target, enabling high-speed data transfer.

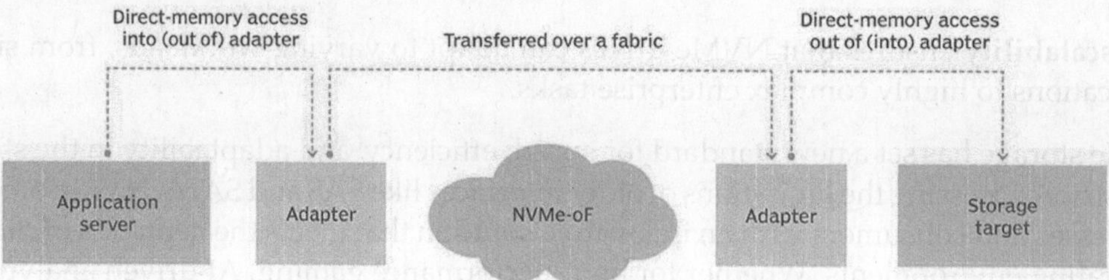

***Figure 9.3:** NVMe over Fabrics (NVMe-oF) architecture*

The core strength of NVMe lies in its ability to leverage the **PCIe interface**, which provides much higher data transfer speeds than older interfaces. While SAS and SATA were initially designed for mechanical drives, PCIe was designed for faster, more scalable data transfer between the CPU and various system components, including storage. NVMe's data transfer capabilities increase with each new PCIe generation, enabling the technology to scale with future hardware developments. This starkly contrasts SAS and SATA, which have fixed data transfer limits and are constrained by older hardware designs' physical and protocol limitations.

Another critical aspect of NVMe is its impact on **power efficiency**. By minimizing the overhead of I/O processing, NVMe-based drives can provide more excellent performance per watt than legacy storage technologies. This efficiency is critical for modern data centers, prioritizing energy savings and sustainability while maintaining high performance. NVMe's low-power design and ability to scale with each new PCIe generation make it a compelling option for high-performance applications and energy-conscious environments.

The NVMe protocol also significantly improves **scalability**. Its design allows for interrupt steering and **Message Signaled Interrupts Extensions (MSI-X)**, further preventing CPU bottlenecking. This architecture enables the protocol to scale efficiently across large systems, making it suitable for everything from mobile devices and laptops to high-demand data centers and enterprise computing environments. As systems become complex, NVMe ensures that performance does not degrade, providing a stable and efficient storage interface for increasingly demanding workloads.

NVMe protocol is purpose-built to take advantage of the unique characteristics of modern SSDs, such as speed, efficiency, and low latency. Its architecture—focused on parallelism, scalability, and minimal overhead—allows it to outperform traditional storage technologies, making it an essential component of today's IT infrastructures. Whether for applications requiring rapid data access, high throughput, or energy efficiency, NVMe offers a clear path to optimizing storage performance and meeting the ever-increasing demands of modern enterprise environments.

Exercise 9.1: Deploying Windows Server 2025 on NVMe SSDs

Windows Server 2025 introduces advanced NVMe optimization, significantly enhancing system performance with higher IOPS and reduced CPU utilization. These advancements position NVMe technology as a critical component of modern server infrastructures, meeting the increasing demand for superior performance, scalability, and reliability.

According to Microsoft's performance benchmarks, Windows Server 2025 achieves up to 60% higher storage IOPS than Windows Server 2022 on identical hardware configurations. To leverage these performance gains, specific hardware and software requirements must be met. Thorough preparation and consideration of key deployment factors are vital to ensure seamless and efficient integration of NVMe storage.

This exercise will guide you through deploying NVMe storage in a Windows Server 2025 environment, focusing on the prerequisite verifications and steps necessary to achieve optimal performance and reliability.

Prerequisites verification

This subsection focuses on verifying the necessary hardware and software components, ensuring the environment is fully prepared for deployment. Deploying Windows Server 2025 on NVMe SSDs is critical in modernizing server infrastructure, offering exceptional performance, reliability, and scalability. By utilizing NVMe SSDs, organizations can significantly improve storage speeds and reduce latency, which is vital for meeting the demands of today's high-performance workloads. To ensure a smooth deployment and achieve optimal performance, follow these steps:

1. **Validate motherboard compatibility:** The server's motherboard must support NVMe drives, typically through PCIe slots or dedicated interfaces such as NVMe M.2 or U.2 connectors. Ensuring compatibility at this foundational level is a critical first step in deploying NVMe storage. Without the appropriate interfaces, the benefits of NVMe cannot be fully realized.

2. **Use high-performance processors:** Modern multi-core processors, such as Intel Xeon or AMD EPYC, are essential for unlocking NVMe's high-throughput, low-latency capabilities. These processors are designed to handle the data-intensive operations required by NVMe-based storage solutions, ensuring seamless performance under heavy workloads.

3. **Select NVMe SSDs based on workload requirements:** Choose NVMe SSDs that align with the intended use case of the server. For example:
   a. **Primary storage**: High-capacity SSDs designed for large datasets.
   b. **Caching**: High-speed SSDs to optimize frequently accessed data.
   c. **Data-intensive workloads**: SSDs with exceptional endurance and performance metrics.

   Consider factors such as endurance, speed, and capacity to ensure the selected SSDs meet the organization's operational demands.
4. **Install updated NVMe drivers:** Drivers are the critical interface between hardware and the operating system. Using the latest NVMe drivers from the SSD manufacturer or server vendor ensures compatibility and optimal performance. Updated drivers often include fixes for potential bottlenecks and enhancements for new features.
5. **Update firmware and BIOS/UEFI:** To enable full NVMe functionality, verify that the server's firmware supports NVMe drives. Sometimes, a BIOS or UEFI firmware update may be required to activate NVMe boot capabilities and ensure proper integration. Always consult the server manufacturer's documentation for guidance on updating firmware to avoid misconfiguration.
6. **Leverage native support in Windows Server 2025:** Windows Server 2025 includes native support for NVMe storage, designed to handle modern workloads with enhanced scalability and reduced latency. Ensure the operating system is fully updated with all relevant patches and that NVMe drivers are correctly configured to leverage these features.

NVMe SSDs can dramatically transform storage performance in Windows Server 2025 environments when deployed correctly. Organizations can achieve a robust and high-performing storage solution by addressing hardware compatibility, driver updates, firmware configurations, and operating system readiness. Proper planning and execution enhance efficiency and provide the scalability needed to meet the evolving demands of data-driven operations.

This comprehensive approach enables businesses to harness the full capabilities of NVMe technology, ensuring that their server environments remain at the forefront of performance and reliability.

Deployment steps

This subsection focuses on validating the required hardware and software components, ensuring the environment is adequately prepared for deployment. Deploying Windows Server 2025 on NVMe SSDs is key to modernizing server infrastructure, providing superior performance, reliability, and scalability. By leveraging NVMe SSDs, organizations can significantly improve storage speed and reduce latency, which is critical for handling today's demanding workloads. To achieve a seamless installation and optimal performance, follow these steps:

1. **Power on** the server and verify that all **hardware components**, including the NVMe SSD, function correctly.
2. press the designated key (e.g., DEL, F2, or ESC) to enter the BIOS/UEFI interface during the server's startup.
3. **Check** the server or motherboard manufacturer's website for the **latest firmware updates**. **Apply the updates** to ensure compatibility and optimize performance with NVMe SSDs.
4. Navigate to the **storage settings** in BIOS/UEFI and enable any NVMe-related options, such as **Advanced Host Controller Interface (AHCI)** or **Redundant Array of Independent Disks (RAID) mode**, depending on your configuration.
5. Use tools like **Rufus** or the **Microsoft Media Creation Tool** to create a **bootable USB drive** with *Windows Server 2025* installation files.
6. **Connect** the bootable USB to the server, **restart it**, and **configure the boot sequence** in BIOS/UEFI to prioritize the USB drive.
7. **Follow** the on-screen instructions to **initiate** the Windows Server 2025 installation process.
8. **Choose** the NVMe SSD as the target installation drive. If the installation does not detect the drive, **load the necessary drivers** provided by the NVMe SSD manufacturer.
9. **Proceed** with the remaining steps, such as setting the **administrator's password**, depicted in *Figure 9.4*, and **configuring initial** system settings.

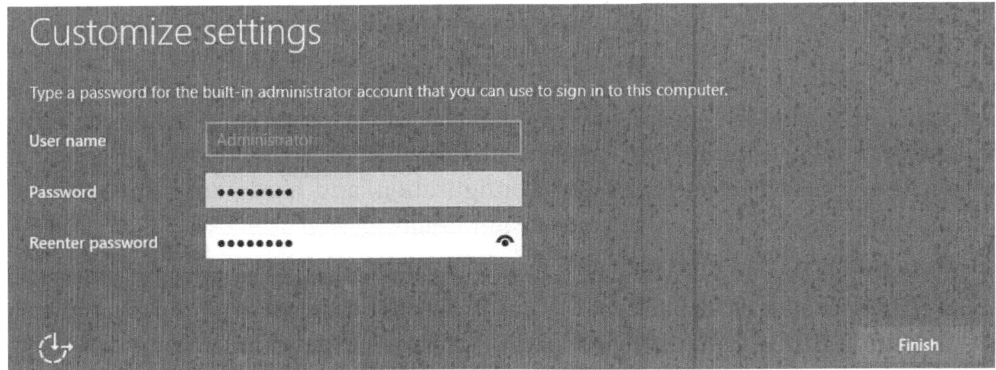

***Figure 9.4:** Setting administrator's password*

10. **After installation**, use **Windows Update** or manufacturer-provided tools to install missing drivers, firmware updates, and system patches.

11. Use **Server Manager** or **PowerShell** to configure **roles and features** according to the server's intended workload.

12. **Enable write caching, adjust power management** settings, and **fine-tune storage** configurations to maximize the performance of the NVMe SSD.

13. **Utilize** tools like **Event Viewer, Performance Monitor**, or third-party utilities to monitor the health and performance of the NVMe SSD regularly.

When deploying Windows Server 2025 on NVMe SSDs, it is essential to go beyond the basic installation steps to ensure optimal performance, reliability, and data integrity. Addressing these considerations beforehand can help mitigate potential issues during or after deployment. Proper preparation and ongoing maintenance are key to maximizing the value of NVMe SSDs in a server environment. The following are critical factors to keep in mind:

- **Backup data:** Before installing, ensure any critical data on the NVMe SSD is backed up, as the installation process will format the drive.
- **Partitioning:** Partitions are created for better organization and performance during installation.
- **Firmware updates:** Periodically check for NVMe firmware updates to maintain reliability and performance.

Following these steps and considerations, you can effectively deploy Windows Server 2025 on NVMe SSD-equipped servers, unlocking the full potential of this innovative storage technology. Proper planning and adherence to these guidelines will give your infrastructure exceptional performance, reliability, and scalability, making it ready to handle the most demanding applications and workloads.

Performance tuning for NVMe SSDs

NVMe SSDs have revolutionized server storage with their exceptional read and write speeds, impressive bandwidth, and superior IOPS. These capabilities make them indispensable for modern server environments where performance and reliability are critical. However, to fully harness the potential of NVMe SSDs, careful attention must be paid to specification selection, system configuration, and hardware compatibility. The following will explore these concepts in greater detail:

1. When selecting an NVMe SSD, it is essential to evaluate **key specifications** such as **read/write speeds, capacity**, and **bandwidth**. These metrics should align with the specific demands of your workload to ensure optimal performance under typical operating conditions. Equally important is assessing the compatibility of your server's hardware and software. Whether your infrastructure uses M.2, U.2, or PCIe slots, confirming support for the desired NVMe connection type is vital. The software ecosystem must also be optimized for NVMe; without proper drivers and settings, even the fastest SSDs may not deliver their full potential.

2. The **configuration process** often begins in the server's **BIOS** or **UEFI settings,** where NVMe-specific features, such as advanced PCIe modes, can be enabled. Misconfigurations in these settings, such as improper bandwidth sharing between SATA and NVMe ports, can significantly hinder performance. For instance, shared bandwidth in M.2 ports can lead to bottlenecks, but proper adjustments can unlock the true capabilities of NVMe drives. Keeping the BIOS/UEFI firmware up to date is equally important, as updates frequently address compatibility and performance issues.

3. NVMe SSDs leverage the **PCIe interface** to achieve their impressive **speeds,** bypassing the limitations of legacy interfaces like SATA. This architecture enables direct communication with the CPU, reducing latency and enhancing throughput. Most NVMe SSDs use NAND flash storage, a high-speed semiconductor medium. However, NAND technology presents challenges like limited endurance and asymmetrical read/write performance. To mitigate these, NVMe SSDs employ a **Flash Translation Layer (FTL),** standardizing the interaction between the drive and applications, ensuring compatibility and durability. *Figure 9.5,* illustrates the architecture of an NVMe SSD, showing the interaction between the Host CPU and the NVMe SSD via a PCIe Bus. It highlights internal components like the firmware section, which includes the GC Manager, Meta Manager, FTL Core, and NVMe Manager, and the Flash Channel Controller section, which interfaces with the NAND flash memory. This diagram provides a clear overview of the SSD's internal components and data flow, crucial for understanding its performance and functionality.

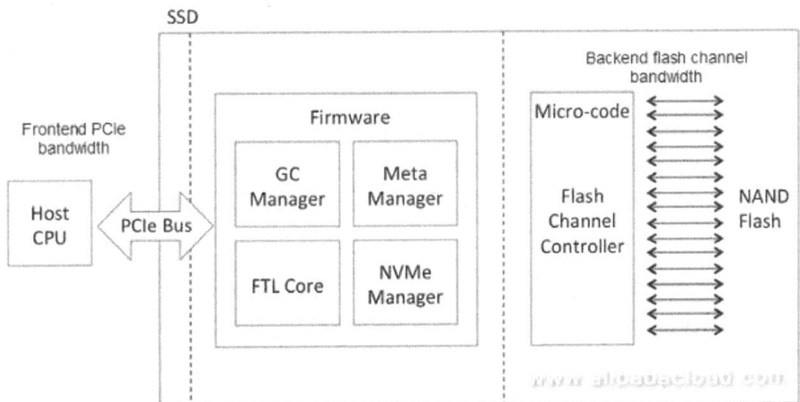

Figure 9.5: *Interaction between CPU and NVMe SSD (source: Alibaba Cloud)*

4. Advances in NAND flash technology have further transformed the NVMe landscape. While most NVMe drives utilize **Triple-Level Cell (TLC) NAND** to balance performance and durability, the emergence of **Quad-Level Cell (QLC) NAND** has significantly increased storage density. This innovation allows SSDs to achieve capacities of up to **128 TB,** far exceeding the limits of traditional hard

drives. Despite these advancements, selecting the right NAND type for your server environment is critical. TLC NAND is often preferred for performance-intensive applications, whereas QLC NAND offers cost-effective solutions for less demanding workloads.

5. Optimal use of NVMe SSDs also requires **proactive management and monitoring**. Regularly updating drivers and firmware ensures that the drives operate at peak efficiency and benefit from the latest performance enhancements. Tools like **Event Viewer** and **Self-Monitoring, Analysis, and Reporting Technology (SMART)** monitoring utilities can help track performance metrics and detect potential issues early. Maintaining adequate cooling is another essential consideration, especially for high-performance **PCIe Gen 4** or **Gen 5 NVMe** drives, which can generate significant heat. Proper airflow and, where necessary, heatsinks can prevent thermal throttling and maintain consistent performance.

NVMe SSDs offer unparalleled speed, efficiency, and scalability, but realizing these benefits demands a holistic selection, configuration, and management approach. By prioritizing compatibility, leveraging advances in NAND technology, and ensuring optimal system settings, organizations can unlock the full potential of NVMe storage. These considerations enable the creation of high-performance, reliable storage systems tailored to the needs of modern workloads, paving the way for efficient and future-ready server infrastructures.

Real-world use cases of NVMe SSDs

In the rapidly evolving landscape of modern computing, **data centers** have become the nerve centers of countless businesses, managing everything from website hosting and cloud services to real-time data analytics. The backbone of these operations is the storage infrastructure. As demands for speed, reliability, and efficiency grow, traditional storage solutions like HDDs and earlier-generation SSDs often fail to keep pace. NVMe SSDs have emerged as a revolutionary technology that addresses these challenges, transforming data center operations and redefining industry benchmarks. Let us take a look at some use cases:

- The journey from traditional storage to NVMe SSDs begins with **performance**. The limitations of HDDs and SATA-based SSDs are well-known: HDDs rely on mechanical components that slow down data retrieval. SATA-based SSDs are constrained by interface bandwidth, typically capping at 600 MB/s. NVMe SSDs eliminate these bottlenecks by leveraging the PCIe interface, delivering transfer speeds in gigabytes per second. This unprecedented speed enables near-instantaneous data access, a critical feature for applications requiring high throughput and responsiveness, such as real-time analytics and cloud-based services.
- **Latency**, the delay between a data request and its fulfillment, is another area where NVMe SSDs excel. HDDs inherently suffer from high latency due to their

mechanical nature, and while traditional SSDs improve on this, they still face protocol-induced delays. NVMe technology is engineered to minimize latency, employing a streamlined communication protocol that allows the CPU and storage to interact directly and efficiently. This architecture supports parallel data processing, enabling NVMe SSDs to easily handle high-demand workloads like virtualization, artificial intelligence, and ML.

- As businesses grow, so do their data storage and processing needs. **Scalability** becomes a critical consideration in maintaining operational efficiency. Traditional storage systems often struggle to scale effectively, leading to performance degradation as data demands increase. NVMe SSDs, on the other hand, are designed for scalability and can support numerous concurrent data streams without compromising speed or reliability. This makes them indispensable for enterprises anticipating growth or operating in dynamic environments requiring constant adaptability.
- **Energy efficiency** is another key factor driving the adoption of NVMe SSDs. Data centers are among the largest consumers of power, and traditional HDDs, with their mechanical components, consume significant amounts of energy. Even older SSDs require more power than modern solutions. NVMe SSDs address this issue by offering superior performance at a lower power cost. This reduces operational expenses and supports sustainability initiatives, helping organizations minimize their environmental impact while staying competitive.
- **Reliability** is paramount in data centers, where downtime or data loss can lead to significant financial and reputational harm. NVMe SSDs incorporate advanced error correction, wear-leveling technologies, and robust hardware designs to ensure data integrity and longevity. These features give businesses the peace of mind that their critical operations will remain uninterrupted and their data secure.

Looking to the future, NVMe SSDs are **well-positioned** to meet the challenges of emerging technologies. With the ongoing development of PCIe 4.0 and PCIe 5.0 standards, NVMe SSDs are set to deliver even faster transfer speeds and lower latencies. These advancements will support high-performance applications such as **big data analytics, artificial intelligence**, and **ML**, ensuring businesses remain agile and ready to adapt to the ever-evolving technological landscape.

NVMe SSDs' applications are **vast and transformative**. In cloud computing, they provide the high-speed, low-latency storage required to deliver seamless virtual machine experiences and SaaS platform performance. NVMe SSDs enable real-time analytics by processing vast datasets at unprecedented speeds for industries like healthcare, finance, and retail. **Content delivery networks (CDNs)** leverage NVMe SSDs to distribute multimedia content globally, enhancing user experiences for streaming platforms, gaming services, and social media.

AI and ML workloads particularly benefit from NVMe SSDs' **superior performance**. Training complex models on massive datasets demands rapid read/write speeds and minimal latency, which NVMe SSDs deliver. This reduces training times and improves model accuracy, empowering innovations across sectors like automation, predictive analytics, and natural language processing. Virtualization environments, too, thrive with NVMe SSDs, as they support higher densities of virtual machines per server while maintaining optimal performance, reducing costs, and increasing scalability.

NVMe SSDs are not merely an upgrade over traditional storage solutions—they represent a change in basic assumptions in data storage technology. By offering unmatched speed, reliability, and scalability, NVMe SSDs enable businesses to tackle the challenges of today's data-driven world while preparing for tomorrow's demands. As data centers evolve, NVMe SSDs will remain at the forefront of innovation, driving operational excellence and ensuring competitiveness in an era defined by high-speed computing and real-time decision-making.

Exercise 9.2: Configuring SAN solutions on NVMe SSDs

A **storage area network** (SAN), depicted in *Figure 9.6,* is a high-performance, dedicated network that connects servers to centralized storage resources like SSD arrays, tape libraries, or optical storage systems. Its primary objective is to optimize data accessibility, availability, and performance, which are critical for managing enterprise workloads effectively. When SANs incorporate modern SSDs, particularly NVMe drives, they deliver exceptional speed and reliability, making them ideal for demanding applications.

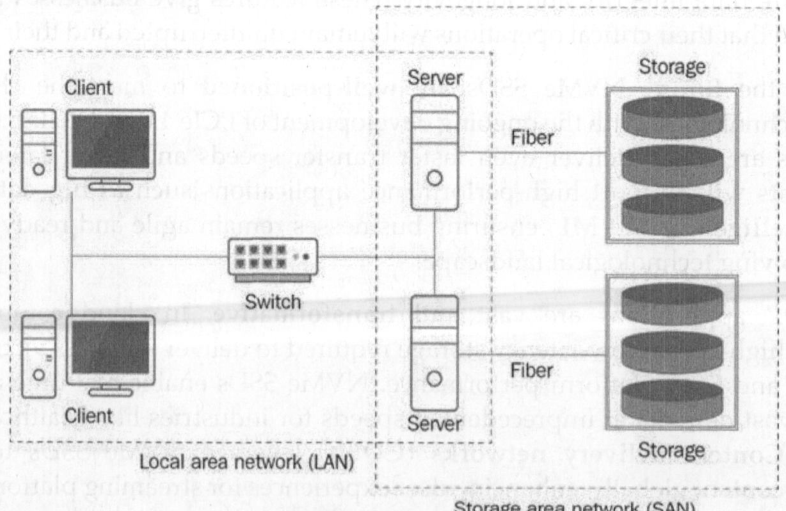

Figure 9.6: *SAN topology*

In this exercise, you will design and configure a SAN solution using NVMe SSDs, applying universal principles that can be adapted to any vendor's platform. The tasks will guide you through the essential steps, from assessing storage requirements to implementing and testing your SAN solution. Upon completion, you will comprehensively understand SAN architecture and how to integrate NVMe technology to achieve optimal performance and scalability. The following will explore these concepts in greater detail:

1. SAN operates using **transport protocols** like **Fibre Channel** (**FC**), iSCSI, or **NVMe-over-Fabrics** (**NVMe-oF**). These protocols ensure efficient communication between storage arrays and connected hosts through switches, providing a scalable infrastructure. To ensure redundancy and avoid single points of failure, a SAN is often configured with **high availability (HA)** in mind, utilizing dual fabrics or multi-network setups. This design protects against hardware failures or network disruptions, ensuring uninterrupted access to data. While single-node or single-network configurations are more straightforward, they lack redundancy and are generally unsuitable for production environments. *Figure 9.7*, illustrates three configurations for standalone servers and how each setup connects Windows Server 2025 to storage resources, highlighting the use of local drives, network-based file shares, and block-level storage over iSCSI, FC, or NVMe protocols. This comparison helps visualize the various storage options and their connectivity methods.

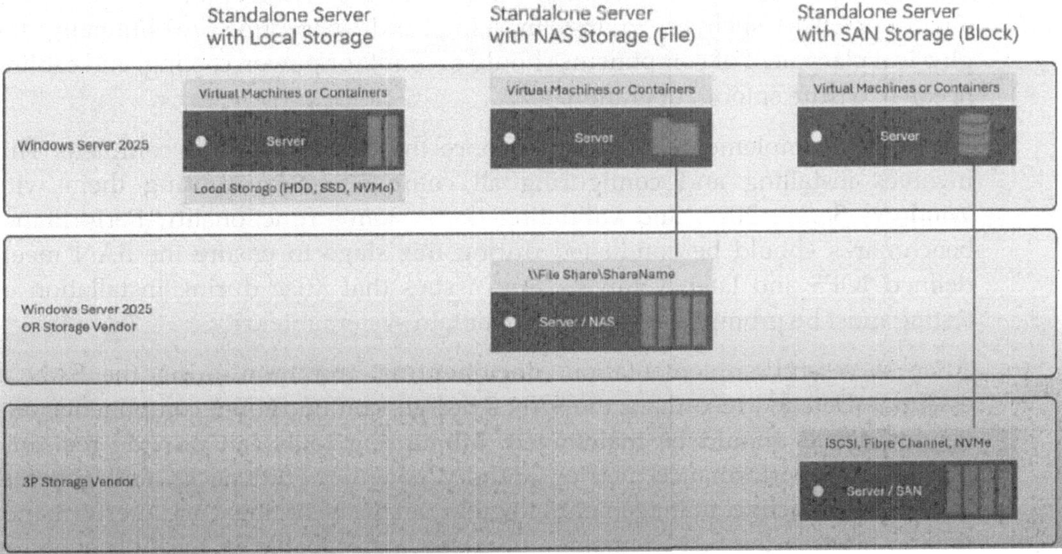

Figure 9.7: *Windows Server 2025 on three storage configurations (source: Virtualization How To)*

2. Designing a SAN solution begins with assessing **storage requirements**. This involves analyzing current and anticipated data storage needs, evaluating performance metrics like IOPS, determining availability expectations, and planning backup, recovery, and security measures. Additionally, it is essential to identify

which servers and applications will utilize the SAN and assess the available network bandwidth. With this information, the architecture and components of the SAN can be selected to meet both technical and budgetary constraints.

3. Choosing the appropriate SAN architecture is a critical step:
    a. FC offers low-latency, high-throughput communication, making it suitable for performance-critical workloads.
    b. **iSCSI** provides a cost-effective alternative by leveraging existing Ethernet infrastructure. Hybrid solutions that combine the strengths of multiple protocols can also be considered.
    c. SSD-based storage arrays, especially those leveraging **NVMe technology**, are highly recommended for superior performance. Complementary components, such as switches, controllers, cables, connectors, and management software, must also be chosen to align with the desired architecture.
4. The physical and logical layout of the SAN plays a significant role in its **efficiency**. Establishing a **topology** that balances performance, availability, and security is crucial. Connections between servers, switches, and storage devices should be optimized for minimal latency and maximum throughput. Key considerations include implementing redundancy, load balancing, failover mechanisms, and secure practices such as zoning, masking, and encryption. Additionally, the physical placement of components should account for power, cooling, and cabling needs to ensure smooth operation.
5. SAN can be implemented and tested once the design phase is complete. This involves installing and configuring all components, **integrating** them with Windows Server 2025, and validating the system's functionality. Performance benchmarks should be conducted during this stage to ensure the SAN meets defined IOPS and latency targets. Any issues that arise during installation or testing must be promptly resolved to maintain system integrity.
6. After successful implementation, **documenting** and **monitoring** the SAN is essential. Detailed records of the SAN's design, configuration, components, and vendor details should be maintained. Monitoring tools can provide real-time insights into performance metrics, identify potential bottlenecks, and generate alerts for proactive management. Regular analysis of logs and performance reports ensures the SAN remains optimized and capable of meeting evolving organizational demands.

Incorporating SSDs, particularly NVMe drives, into a well-designed SAN solution provides organizations with a robust, scalable infrastructure that supports the high-performance demands of modern IT environments. SAN solutions become a cornerstone for reliable and efficient data storage by following the best design, implementation, and management practices.

Exercise 9.3: SAN integration in Windows Server 2025

Integrating a **SAN** with Windows Server 2025 is crucial for organizations aiming to modernize their storage infrastructure. SANs provide **high-speed, dedicated storage connectivity**, significantly enhancing **performance**, **scalability**, and **reliability**. With Windows Server 2025, new features and improvements simplify SAN integration, making it an excellent choice for contemporary data centers. Follow these detailed steps to ensure a seamless integration process:

1. **Verify hardware compatibility:** Confirm that your server hardware is compatible with SAN technologies such as FC or **Internet Small Computer Systems Interface (iSCSI)**. Ensure your system supports the required adapters, including **host bus adapters (HBAs)** or **network interface cards (NICs)**.

2. **Prepare and connect SAN components:** Set up all SAN components, including storage arrays, switches, and HBAs. Establish physical connections between these components and verify that cabling and port configurations adhere to recommended optimal performance and reliability guidelines.

3. **Update drivers and firmware:** Install the latest drivers for all SAN-related components, such as HBAs, storage controllers, and network adapters. Regularly update firmware on storage arrays and other SAN devices to maintain compatibility and stability.

4. **Configure network settings for SAN access:**

    a. **For iSCSI SANs***:* Assign appropriate IP addresses, subnet masks, and gateways to the NICs used for SAN traffic. Use dedicated network interfaces or VLANs to isolate SAN traffic from regular traffic.

    b. **For fiber channel SANs***:* Set up zoning on your SAN switches to restrict device communication to authorized servers and storage targets.

5. **Enable and Configure Multipath I/O (MPIO):** Install and enable MPIO on your Windows Server 2025. This feature ensures redundancy and load balancing by utilizing multiple SAN paths. Use the MPIO control panel to identify and configure preferred paths for optimal performance and fault tolerance.

6. **Create and assign logical unit numbers (LUNs):** On the SAN storage array, create LUNs that match your storage needs regarding size, performance, and redundancy. Depending on the SAN protocol, assign these LUNs to the server using **World Wide Names (WWNs)** or **iSCSI Qualified Names (IQNs)**.

7. **Initialize and format LUNs:** Once the LUNs are visible to Windows Server 2025, initialize them using the Disk Management tool or Windows Admin Center. Based on your storage use case, partition and format the LUNs with a suitable file system, such as NTFS or ReFS.
8. **Leverage Storage Spaces for advanced management:** Use Storage Spaces in Windows Server 2025 to organize your SAN storage into pools and create virtual disks. This feature enables advanced storage capabilities like thin provisioning, deduplication, and tiered storage, optimizing storage efficiency and cost-effectiveness.
9. **Monitor and maintain the SAN environment:** Regularly monitor the performance and health of your SAN using tools provided by your SAN vendor and Windows Server 2025. Utilize event logs and performance counters to identify potential issues. Schedule routine maintenance tasks, such as updating firmware and replacing aging hardware, to prevent disruptions.
10. **Implement backup and recovery practices:** Integrate your SAN with the server's backup strategy to safeguard critical data. Use features like **Volume Shadow Copy Service (VSS)** and Windows Server Backup to create reliable recovery points for your SAN volumes.

Following these steps, organizations can integrate SAN solutions with Windows Server 2025. The result is a robust, high-performance storage environment capable of supporting the demands of modern data centers, ensuring operational efficiency and business continuity.

Leveraging storage virtualization with SDS

In the ever-evolving landscape of modern IT infrastructure, SDS, also known as **storage virtualization**, emerges as a transformative solution designed to meet the dynamic needs of organizations embracing digital transformation. SDS decouples the control and management of storage from the physical hardware, providing a more adaptable, scalable, and cost-efficient approach compared to traditional storage systems. According to the **Storage Networking Industry Association (SNIA)**, **storage virtualization applies virtualization techniques to storage systems, aggregating storage functions and simplifying complexity**. This abstraction enhances storage management capabilities, offering businesses greater agility, especially in multi-cloud environments. *Figure 9.8* illustrates the configuration of a virtual NVMe drive, which uses a large pool of HDDs in a fault-tolerant RAID setup to create a single large-capacity volume. A small-capacity NVMe drive acts as a write-back cache for the RAID volume, improving write performance. This hybrid block device is then exported across a network, allowing a host to access it as if it were a locally attached NVMe drive.

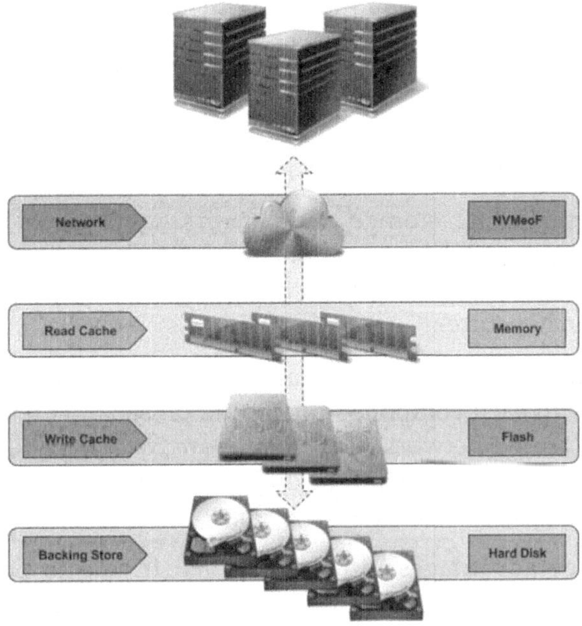

Figure 9.8: *Virtual NVMe drive configuration (source: Admin Magazine)*

At its core, SDS is a software-driven model that separates the management of storage from the physical infrastructure on which it resides. By using **commodity hardware**, organizations can bypass the expensive proprietary storage systems typically used in traditional setups. This approach leverages virtualization technologies that abstract and pool physical storage resources, allowing for their dynamic allocation across the organization. The key benefit is flexibility:

- Organizations can easily scale their storage needs without the constraints of proprietary hardware limitations.
- New hardware can be integrated into the system swiftly, detected, and added to the virtual storage pool seamlessly—without affecting ongoing operations.

This makes it possible to create highly customized storage architectures tailored to specific performance, capacity, and scalability requirements.

While the terms **SDS** and **storage virtualization** are often used interchangeably, it is important to distinguish the two. **Storage virtualization** refers specifically to the process of pooling multiple local or remote storage devices into a unified logical volume, enabling more efficient management and usage of storage. In contrast, **SDS** is a broader concept that may or may not include storage pooling, allowing for flexible implementation based on organizational needs. Unlike other cloud models such as **Software-as-a-Service (SaaS)** or **Infrastructure-as-a-Service (IaaS)**, SDS is typically deployed and managed on-premises by the organization itself. While traditional solutions like NAS or SAN often rely heavily on network infrastructure, SDS offers the flexibility to operate without dependency on specific network interconnects, though these technologies can still be incorporated when necessary.

Within the realm of SDS, two popular architecture models are **Hyperconverged Infrastructure (HCI)** and **Converged Infrastructure (CI)**:

- HCI merges computing, storage, and networking resources into a single, unified, virtualized platform. This integration simplifies system management and boosts scalability, though it often comes with a higher price tag due to its flexibility and streamlined architecture.

- On the other hand, CI combines computing, storage, and networking in a single system, but with each component operating on separate hardware that connects through a dedicated network. CI can be more cost-effective than HCI, though it tends to offer less scalability and flexibility. The choice between HCI and CI often hinges on the organization's specific needs for scalability, flexibility, and budget.

SDS offers several **key advantages** to organizations striving to optimize their storage environments:

- One of the standout benefits is the ability to utilize commodity hardware, eliminating the need for costly proprietary storage systems.

- Additionally, SDS scales efficiently both horizontally and vertically, allowing organizations to quickly adapt to increasing storage demands.
- Furthermore, SDS improves administrative efficiency by centralizing management, enabling the automation of many tasks through APIs.

- By enabling data replication across multiple locations, organizations can ensure critical data remains accessible even in the event of hardware failure or other disruptions.

- Additionally, SDS supports a range of storage types, including block, object, and file storage, within a single infrastructure, further enhancing the versatility of the storage solution.

However, implementing SDS is not without its challenges:

- The main hurdle for many organizations lies in the transition from hardware-based storage systems to a fully software-driven management approach.

- The reliance on software for storage management introduces complexity, particularly when it comes to maintaining a reliable and secure software environment.

- Moreover, since storage resources are abstracted away from physical hardware, additional security measures may be necessary to ensure data protection and mitigate risks associated with this level of abstraction.

SDS marks a significant shift in how organizations manage their storage infrastructure. By decoupling storage from hardware, SDS offers businesses a flexible, scalable, and cost-efficient solution to meet the demands of modern IT environments. While there are challenges in terms of software dependency and the need for skilled expertise, the benefits of SDS, such as improved scalability, cost reduction, and enhanced data resilience—make it an attractive option for organizations aiming to future-proof their storage solutions and stay competitive in an increasingly digital, cloud-driven world.

Conclusion

In this chapter, you have learned about improving storage performance in Windows Server 2025 using NVMe SSDs and better SAN integration. You have gained comprehensive guidance on configuring NVMe SSDs, tuning their performance, and implementing SAN solutions to enhance data access and scalability. The chapter covered topics such as the introduction to NVMe SSDs, understanding the NVMe protocol, deploying NVMe SSDs in Windows Server 2025, performance tuning, real-world use cases, configuring SAN solutions on NVMe SSDs, SAN integration, and leveraging storage virtualization with SDS. Additionally, you have learned about advanced storage technologies and how to build a high-performance, scalable storage environment using Server Manager and PowerShell. With this knowledge, you can efficiently deploy and optimize modern storage solutions to maximize Windows Server 2025's storage capabilities.

In the next chapter, you will learn about performing robust in-place upgrades for streamlined version updates.

Questions

1. What is the NVMe protocol?
2. How do you deploy NVMe SSDs in Windows Server 2025?
3. How do you tune performance for NVMe SSDs?
4. What is SAN integration in Windows Server 2025?
5. What is Software-Defined Storage (SDS)?

Join our book's Discord space

Join the book's Discord Workspace for Latest updates, Offers, Tech happenings around the world, New Release and Sessions with the Authors:

https://discord.bpbonline.com

CHAPTER 10
In-Place Upgrades for Version Updates

Introduction

This chapter explores how to perform in-place upgrades in Windows Server 2025. In-place upgrades offer numerous benefits, including maintaining existing configurations and minimizing downtime. This chapter guides you through the entire process, from understanding the benefits and prerequisites to planning and executing the upgrade. You will learn how to prepare your environment, validate compatibility, and resolve issues that may arise during the upgrade. Additionally, the chapter covers managing dependencies, mitigating risks, and ensuring data integrity. Advanced topics such as fine-tuning and optimizing the upgraded environment are also discussed. Real-world case studies provide practical insights and examples of successful in-place upgrades. Step-by-step instructions and best practices are provided to help you achieve a seamless upgrade experience.

Structure

The chapter will cover the following topics:

- Understanding in-place upgrades
- Planning for an in-place upgrade
- Preparing the environment
- Exercise 10.1: Executing the upgrade

- Validating compatibility and resolving issues
- Managing dependencies and integrations
- Mitigating risks and ensuring data integrity
- Monitoring and verifying success
- Fine-tuning and optimizing
- Real-world use cases

Objectives

This chapter's primary objective is to guide readers in performing robust in-place upgrades for streamlined version updates in Windows Server 2025. It provides step-by-step instructions on understanding the benefits and prerequisites, planning and executing the upgrade, and preparing the environment. The chapter also covers advanced topics like validating compatibility, resolving issues, managing dependencies, mitigating risks, and ensuring data integrity. Additionally, it offers practical insights into fine-tuning and optimizing the upgraded environment. By the end, readers will be equipped to implement successful in-place upgrades and maximize the efficiency and performance of their Windows Server 2025 environments.

Understanding in-place upgrades

An **in-place upgrade** allows you to transition the server's **operating system** (**OS**) to a newer version without reinstalling the OS or reconfiguring your existing settings and data. This approach is particularly valuable when **minimizing downtime** and **maintaining compatibilit**y with installed applications, which are key priorities. An in-place upgrade involves updating the OS on the same physical hardware and preserving your files, settings, and configurations. Upon successful completion, the server will run Windows Server 2025 with its latest features, enhanced performance, and improved security.

Microsoft emphasizes upgrading to the latest Windows Server version to take advantage of **new functionalities** and **robust security enhancements**. Beginning with Windows Server 2025, upgrades can span up to four versions in a single step. For instance, you can upgrade directly from Windows Server 2012 R2 to Windows Server 2025. In contrast, earlier versions of Windows Server, such as 2022, allow upgrades of up to **two versions** simultaneously, enabling transitions like moving from Windows Server 2016 to 2019 or 2022. Upgrades can only proceed one version at a time for those using the Cluster OS Rolling Upgrade feature. Additionally, upgrades are possible from **evaluation editions** to **retail editions** and from older **retail** or **volume-licensed editions** to **newer versions**. This versatility accommodates a variety of deployment scenarios.

The following table illustrates the supported in-place upgrade paths based on your current Windows Server version. This table highlights the compatibility of in-place upgrades between different Windows Server versions, enabling better planning and preparation for your migration path:

Upgrade from	Windows Server 2012 R2	Windows Server 2016	Windows Server 2019	Windows Server 2022	Windows Server 2025
Windows Server 2012	**Yes**	**Yes**	Not Supported	Not Supported	Not Supported
Windows Server 2012 R2	Not Supported	**Yes**	**Yes**	Not Supported	**Yes**
Windows Server 2016	Not Supported	Not Supported	**Yes**	**Yes**	**Yes**
Windows Server 2019	Not Supported	Not Supported	Not Supported	**Yes**	**Yes**
Windows Server 2022	Not Supported	Not Supported	Not Supported	Not Supported	**Yes**
Windows Server 2025	Not Supported	Not Supported	Not Supported	Not Supported	**Yes**

Table 10.1: *Windows Server supported in-place upgrade paths*

While an in-place upgrade offers clear benefits, it also has potential drawbacks. On the positive side:

- It preserves existing configurations, applications, and files, reducing the need for reinstallation and minimizing downtime.
- It simplifies the upgrade process and mitigates the risks associated with complex data migrations.

However, challenges include the possibility of:

- Compatibility issues with specific applications or drivers after the upgrade, difficulties in troubleshooting configuration problems.
- Limited flexibility in changing the system architecture or transitioning to a different license type.

To ensure a smooth upgrade process, specific prerequisites must be met:

- You need to select the **appropriate version** of Windows Server for the upgrade and verify that you have a **valid product key** and **activation method**.
- The required **setup media** can be obtained from OEM, Retail, Visual Studio Subscriptions, and the **Volume Licensing Service Center (VLSC)** or created using Rufus or the Windows Media Creation Tool.

- Preparing a backup location, such as a USB drive or network share, is essential to secure critical files.
- Additionally, **it is crucial to review the compatibility of Windows Server roles, features, Microsoft server applications, and third-party software**.
- Confirm that your hardware **meets or exceeds the requirements** for Windows Server 2025 and that the server is not running in an Azure environment, as in-place upgrades are not supported there.
- Lastly, a **full backup** is an indispensable step to safeguard your data.

Carefully addressing these considerations and prerequisites, you can successfully upgrade to Windows Server 2025, ensuring your server benefits from the latest advancements while retaining the stability and functionality of your existing environment.

Note: Microsoft provides an optional in-place upgrade feature through Windows Update, known as a feature update. This feature update is available for Windows Server 2019 and Windows Server 2022 devices.

Planning for an in-place upgrade

When **planning an in-place upgrade**, it is essential to address two key considerations: hardware and software.

- On the hardware side, it is crucial to assess the **server's lifespan**, which typically averages 10 years, and the **hard drive's longevity**, which is approximately five years. Peripheral systems, such as desktops, laptops, tablets, phones, and printers, often have shorter lifecycles and may be replaced multiple times within the server's operational span. This disparity can lead to performance issues and compatibility challenges that must be factored into your upgrade strategy.
- On the software side, Microsoft's fixed lifecycle policy governs major Windows Server releases, offering 10 years of support—5 years of **Mainstream Support** and 5 years of **Extended Support**. This policy ensures access to updates and security patches, making it vital to align your upgrade plans with these lifecycle timelines.

Additionally, verifying that your hardware and hypervisor meet the minimum requirements for Windows Server 2025 is essential to avoid resource limitations and ensure compatibility with the target OS.

Beyond hardware and software readiness, several specific elements warrant attention:

- **Roles and features**, such as **Active Directory Domain Services (AD DS)**, DNS Server, and DHCP Server, should be evaluated for compatibility with Windows Server 2025. Ensure all currently enabled roles and features are supported and address any dependencies beforehand.

- Similarly, **Microsoft applications** like Exchange Server, SQL Server, and Teams have distinct OS requirements and upgrade paths that must be reviewed carefully.
- Additionally, **third-party applications**, including antivirus solutions, backup and replication software, and business-critical tools like print management systems or building access control software, must be assessed for compatibility and updated as necessary.

Most on-premises servers today are virtualized, making **testing and validation** a vital step in the process. Cloning the target server, isolating it in a sandbox environment, and performing the upgrade there first allows for functional testing of the upgraded server OS, installed roles, and applications. This approach minimizes risks and ensures issues are identified and resolved before the live upgrade.

A reliable and thoroughly **tested backup strategy** is also indispensable. Ensure backups are current and not only for the server undergoing the upgrade but also for any dependent systems. These backups safeguard data integrity and provide a fallback in case of unforeseen complications.

Ultimately, the success of an in-place upgrade lies in meticulous preparation. While the upgrade process may seem straightforward, dedicating ample time to planning, testing, and validating ensures a seamless transition to Windows Server 2025, minimizing disruptions and maximizing reliability.

Preparing the environment

Before upgrading to Windows Server 2025, it is crucial to meticulously prepare your environment to ensure a smooth transition and minimize potential issues:

- Review your server infrastructure thoroughly, focusing on hardware and software compatibility. Verify that all hardware components and installed applications, including the OS, support Windows Server 2025. Pay close attention to application compatibility, and determine whether each application is compatible with the new OS and if updates are required for optimal functionality.
- Ensure that the current Windows Server version (from Windows Server 2012 R2 to Windows Server 2022) is **fully updated**, including your hardware's latest patches, drivers, and firmware updates. While meeting the minimum hardware requirements for Windows Server 2025 is essential, aim to satisfy the recommended specifications for enhanced performance and reliability, especially since this is likely a production server.
- Although the upgrade process typically retains data, settings, and installed applications, creating a **complete server backup** is a best practice. A reliable backup safeguards against unexpected issues and provides a recovery option.

- Next, download the Windows Server 2025 **ISO file** from the Microsoft VLSC or the Microsoft Evaluation Center for trial purposes. Ensure the ISO file matches your server's current configuration (e.g., Standard or Datacenter edition). Insert the installation DVD or connect a bootable USB drive to the physical server. For virtual machines, mount the ISO file using the hypervisor's virtual media manager.
- Finally, navigate to the installation media, whether a DVD, USB drive, or mounted ISO—and double-click on **`setup.exe`** to initiate the upgrade process. These preparation steps set the foundation for a successful upgrade to Windows Server 2025.

Exercise 10.1: Executing the upgrade

This exercise teaches you how to upgrade a server from Windows Server 2022 to Windows Server 2025. Upgrading your server ensures you can use the new version's latest features, performance enhancements, and security updates. Completing this exercise, you will gain hands-on experience with essential upgrade procedures crucial for maintaining a modern and secure server environment. Therefore, follow these steps to perform the upgrade:

1. On a server with Windows Server 2022, insert the Windows Server 2025 **installation disc** or connect a **bootable USB flash drive** and run the **setup file**.
2. The **Install Windows Server** window will appear. Click **Next** to proceed, as in *Figure 10.1*).

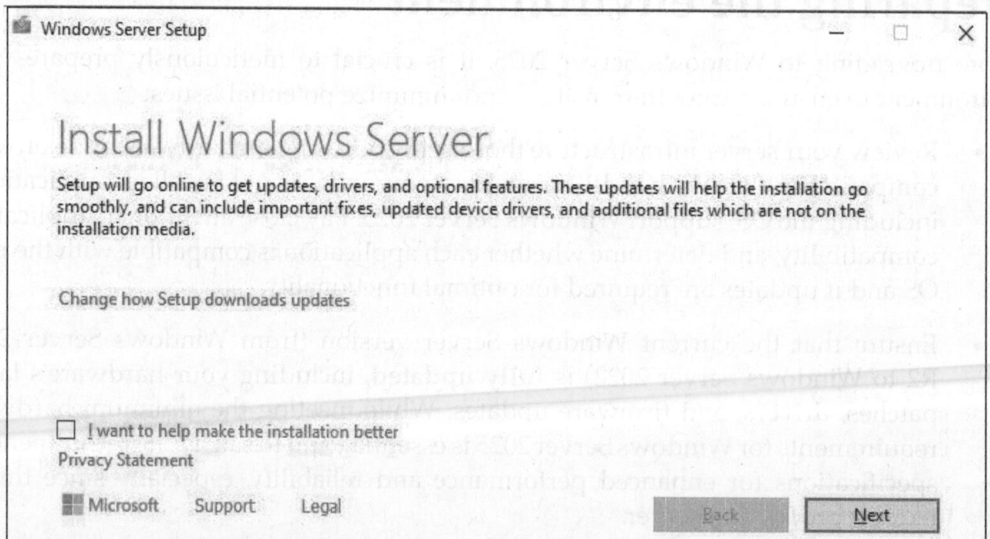

***Figure 10.1:** Beginning the in-place upgrade in Windows Server 2022*

3. Select the Windows Server 2025 **edition** you wish to install and click **Next** (Figure *10.2*).

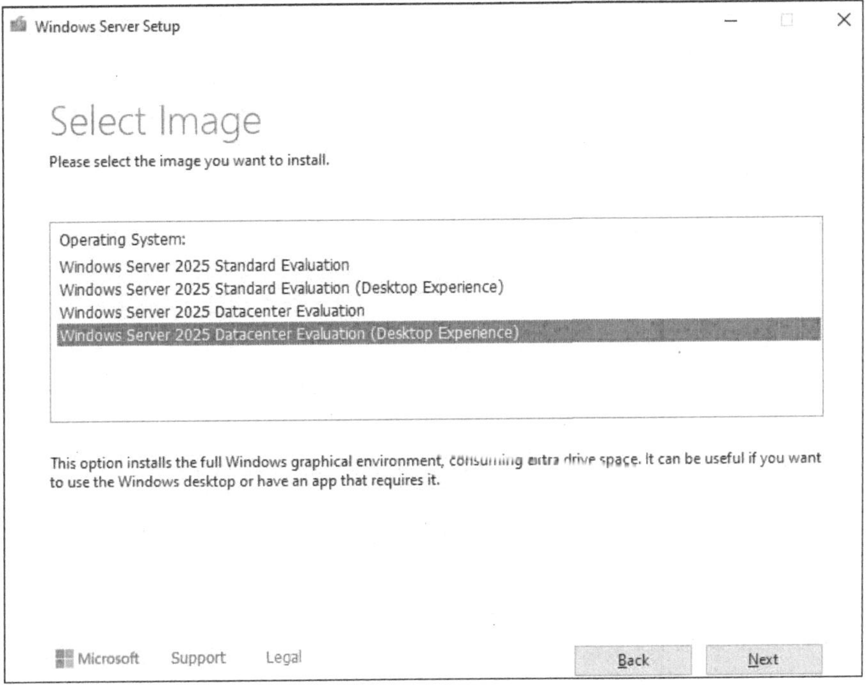

Figure 10.2: *Selecting the desired Windows Server 2025 edition to install*

4. Accept the **license terms** by clicking the **Accept** button in the **Applicable Notices and License Terms** section.
5. Choose **what to keep**, then click **Next** to continue.
6. After the **updates** are **downloaded** and the **setup verifies** sufficient disk space on the server, click the **Install** button to initiate the upgrade, depicted in *Figure 10.3*).

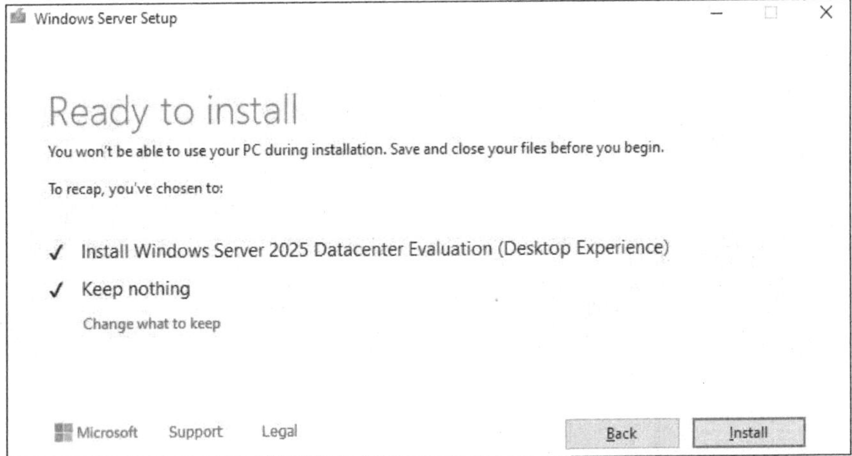

Figure 10.3: *Ready to run the in-place upgrade*

7. The **in-place upgrade** process will **begin**. You can *relax* or attend to other **tasks** while the upgrade is completed.

8. After several **restarts**, the upgrade from Windows Server 2022 to Windows Server 2025 will be **completed**, as illustrated in *Figure 10.4*:

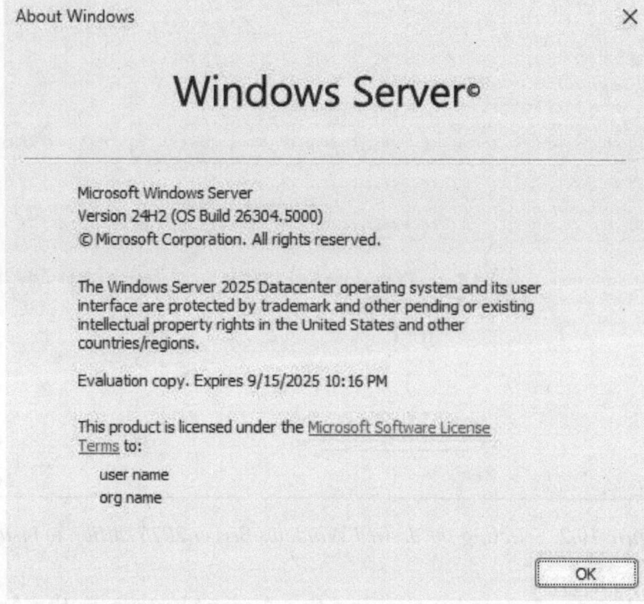

***Figure 10.4:** About Windows confirming the in-place upgrade*

9. You can execute the following **command** in **PowerShell** to verify that the **version and edition** depicted in *Figure 10.5* match the media and values selected during setup.

```
Get-ComputerInfo -Property WindowsProductName
```

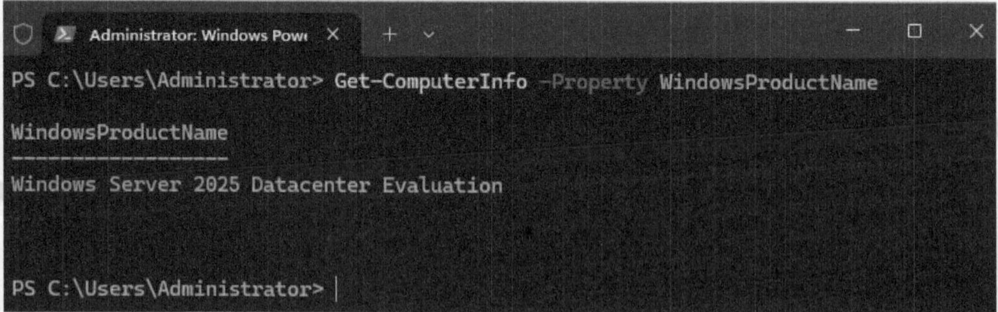

***Figure 10.5:** Confirming the in-place upgrade with PowerShell*

Once the **in-place upgrade** is **complete**, reviewing the server's performance and validating that all roles, features, and applications are functioning as expected is recommended.

Validating compatibility and resolving issues

After **successfully upgrading** to Windows Server 2025, validating the system's compatibility and addressing any issues is essential. Begin by **thoroughly testing** the system to ensure that all roles, features, and applications, such as **Active Directory** (**AD**), **Domain Name System** (**DNS**), and other critical services, function correctly. Revisit the configurations of these services, as some settings may require **fine-tuning** to adapt to the new OS environment.

Once the system has been tested and confirmed to **operate as expected**, activate the OS. Ensure you purchase a valid license for your Windows Server 2025 edition (e.g., Standard or Datacenter) and activate the server using the appropriate method, such as a product key or volume licensing, as shown in *Figure 10.6*:

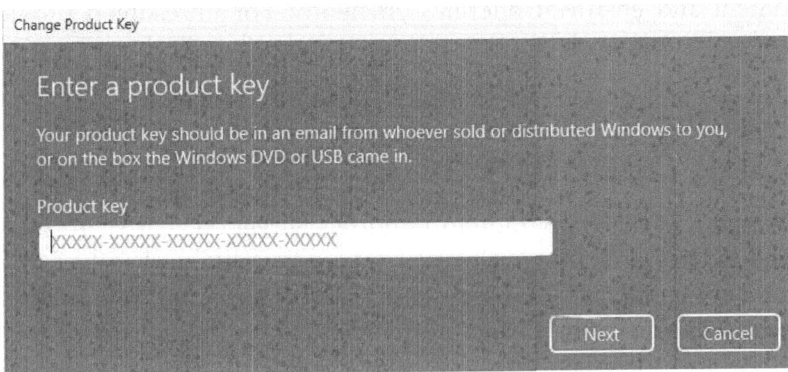

Figure 10.6: *Activating Windows Server 2025*

Despite careful planning, specific issues may arise after an in-place upgrade. Following are common post-upgrade issues and their potential resolutions:

- **Service failures or misconfigurations:** Some services, such as DNS, DHCP, or AD DS, may fail to start due to dependency or configuration issues. Review the service logs and reapply configurations if necessary. Ensure that any third-party applications integrated with these services are also compatible.
- **Driver incompatibilities:** Hardware devices might experience issues if their drivers are outdated or incompatible. Check the manufacturer's website for updated drivers and firmware and apply them accordingly.
- **Application failures:** Some third-party or custom-built applications might malfunction after the upgrade. Verify application compatibility with Windows Server 2025 and update or patch them as needed.
- **Security settings**: After an upgrade, certain security configurations, such as group policies or firewall rules, may reset or behave differently. Audit these settings and align them with your organization's security policies.

- **Disk space issues:** If the upgrade leaves insufficient disk space, it may hinder system performance. To resolve storage constraints, clean up temporary files or extend the partition.
- **Backup or replication failures:** Post-upgrade, backup, or replication software may encounter compatibility problems. Test your backup and disaster recovery solutions to ensure they work as expected. Update or replace any software that fails compatibility checks.
- **Event Viewer warnings and errors:** Regularly monitor the Event Viewer for any warnings or errors. These logs provide critical insights into underlying issues that need to be addressed.

Addressing these potential issues proactively can stabilize your Windows Server 2025 environment and ensure it operates efficiently. For unresolved problems, consult Microsoft's official support documentation or engage their technical support team for guidance.

Managing dependencies and integrations

After completing an in-place upgrade to Windows Server 2025, it is crucial to effectively **manage dependencies** and **integrations** to ensure a stable and fully functional server environment. This involves verifying **core server services**, **reviewing application compatibility**, **updating scripts**, and **addressing potential performance issues**. The following will explore these concepts in greater detail:

- Start by **validating** those essential services like AD, DNS, and DHCP are operating correctly in the new OS environment. Carefully review their configurations to ensure alignment with the updated system. Perform connectivity and functional tests to confirm that these critical roles remain operational without errors.
- Next, assess the **compatibility** of third-party applications and integrations. Identify any software tools, such as antivirus programs, backup and replication solutions, and other business-critical applications, that interact with the server. Check for **vendor updates or patches** to ensure full compatibility with Windows Server 2025. Resolve any incompatibility issues promptly by applying patches or replacing outdated tools.
- Automation tools, such as **PowerShell scripts**, **batch files**, and **scheduled tasks**, should also be **reviewed and tested**. The upgrade may introduce changes that affect their functionality. Verify their compatibility and make necessary adjustments to ensure they perform as intended in the upgraded environment.
- Monitoring the server's performance is equally important. Use tools such as the **Event Viewer**, illustrated in *Figure 10.7*, to examine logs for warnings, errors, or anomalies that could indicate underlying issues. Please pay attention to any new

or recurring errors and resolve them proactively. Additionally, update all drivers and firmware to their latest versions to address potential hardware compatibility issues and enhance stability.

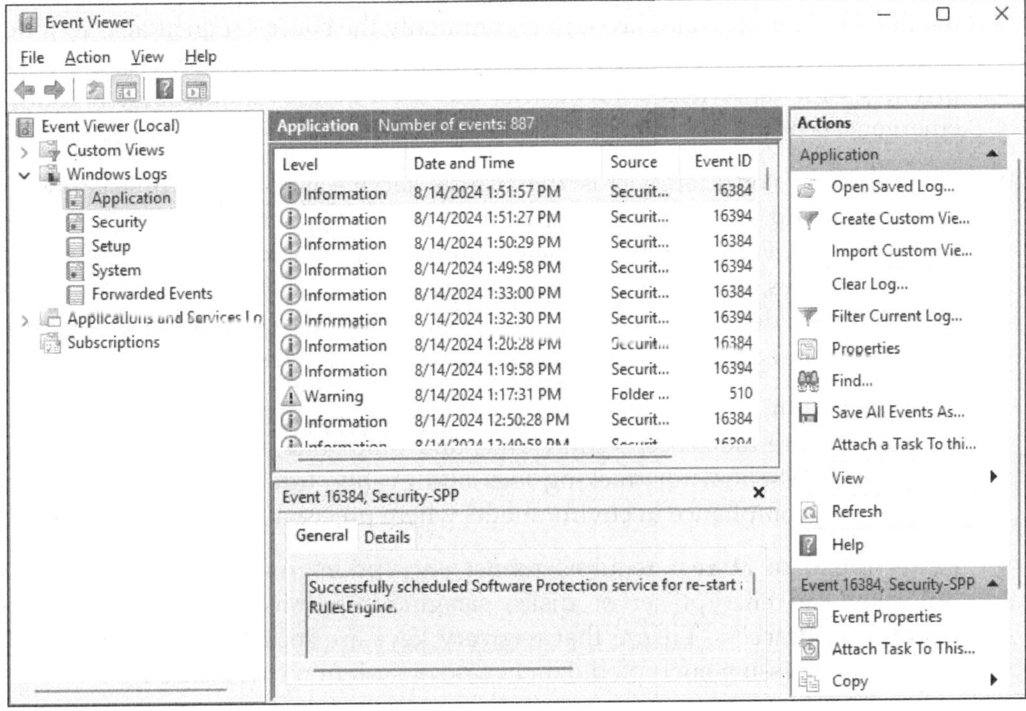

Figure 10.7: *Examine logs with Event Viewer*

- Finally, **document** all changes made during the upgrade process. This includes **updates to service configurations**, **application settings**, **scripts**, and any other **modifications** performed to adapt to Windows Server 2025. Such documentation is invaluable for future reference, troubleshooting, and consistency across similar upgrades.

By carefully managing dependencies and integrations after the upgrade, you can achieve a smooth transition to Windows Server 2025 while maintaining the reliability, performance, and security of your server environment.

Mitigating risks and ensuring data integrity

After **upgrading** to Windows Server 2025, a thorough **post-upgrade review** and **configuration process** is essential to mitigate risks and ensure data integrity:

- The first and most critical step is **updating the OS** to the latest version. If the installation was completed using outdated media, applying all updates and patches immediately is vital. These updates address vulnerabilities and enhance performance, making them indispensable for maintaining a secure and stable server environment.

- Securing **administrative access** is equally important. In domain environments, the default Administrator account is commonly the source of an attack. To reduce exposure, create a dedicated user account with appropriate administrative privileges for daily tasks and restrict the use of the Administrator account to emergencies or initial setups.
- Another vital consideration is the use of **service accounts**. Applications and services should not rely on regular user accounts, as this practice introduces multiple risks. For example, changes to a user's password or account status can disrupt services, and compromised user accounts can lead to security breaches. Instead, create dedicated accounts for each service with clear descriptions, strong passwords, and minimal permissions required for operation.
- **Time synchronization** is crucial in maintaining server reliability and accurate logging. Ensure the server's time, date, and time zone are configured correctly. This step is essential for tracking logs and events, troubleshooting issues, and maintaining compliance in environments where precise timekeeping is critical.
- **Protecting data at rest** requires robust encryption. As shown in *Figure 10.8*, BitLocker can encrypt server disks, safeguarding sensitive information from unauthorized access. Ensure that recovery keys are securely stored, as they are critical for accessing encrypted data in case of system recovery needs.

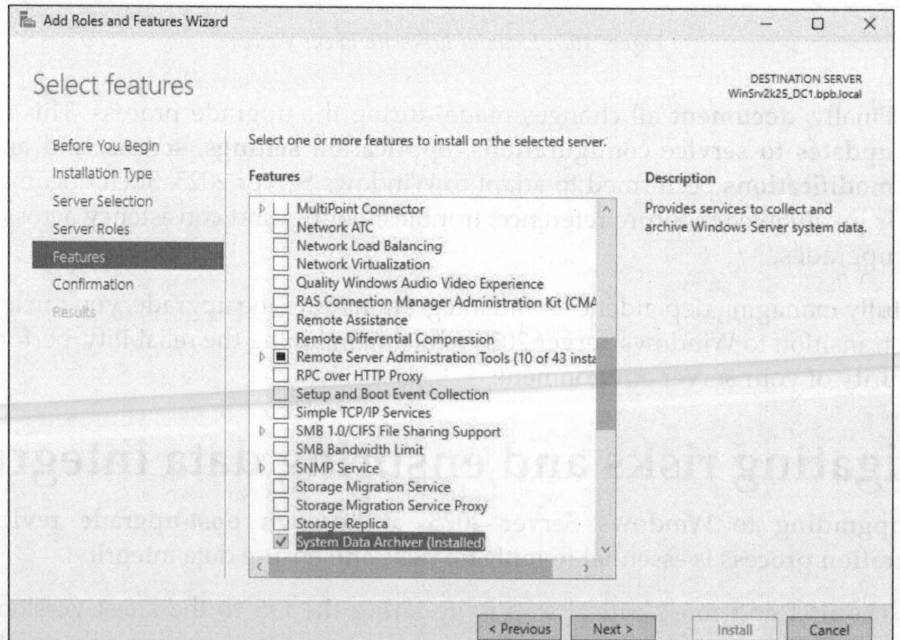

Figure 10.8: *BitLocker is a feature that needs to be installed in Windows Server 2025*

- **Data in transit** must also be secured. Windows Server 2025 introduces support for **TLS 1.3**, depicted in *Figure 10.9*, providing enhanced encryption for network communications. Configure secure protocols such as **HTTPS**, **SSH**, and other encryption protocols for all data transmissions. Implement these protocols for web applications, remote management, and other communication-dependent services.

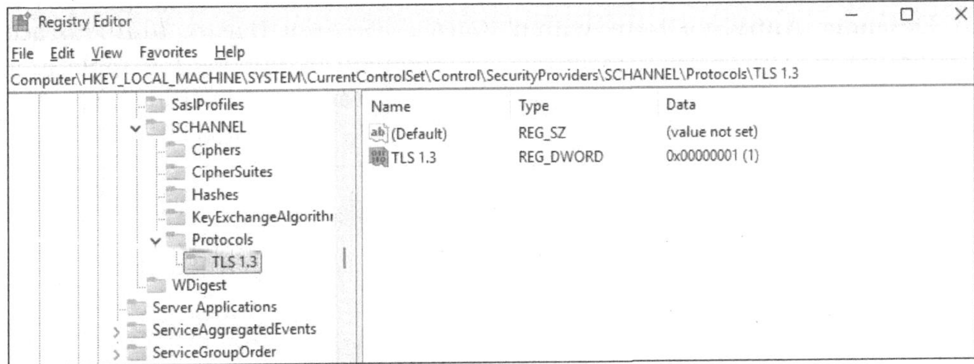

***Figure 10.9:** Enabling TLS 1.3 in Windows Registry*

- **Firewall hardening** is another key element of risk mitigation. The firewall should always remain active, with configurations tailored to the server's specific roles. Apply the principle of least privilege by opening only the necessary ports and allowing only the required network traffic. An improperly configured or disabled firewall can expose your system to significant vulnerabilities.

- For file servers, consider the Windows Server 2025 advanced security features of **SMB over QUIC**, which provides secure file-sharing capabilities. Define access permissions at the user or group level with the minimum privileges required. As SMB1 has been officially retired, organizations relying on it should explore modern alternatives to enhance security and functionality.

- **Regular monitoring** of server logs is indispensable for **maintaining operational security**. **Proactively reviewing logs** helps detect potential breaches or problems early and provides insights into past events, making diagnosing and resolving issues easier. Use tools like the **Event Viewer** to monitor system activities effectively.

- **Remote access configurations** require careful attention. Directly exposing **Remote Desktop Protocol** (**RDP**) to the internet is a high-risk practice. Instead, deploy a **VPN** as the primary method of accessing your server. A dedicated VPN appliance provides enhanced protection and ensures secure remote connections.

- **Minimizing installed roles** and **software** further reduces the server's attack surface. Install only the roles and applications necessary for the server's purpose and avoid treating the server as a **workstation**. Non-essential software and office tools should not be installed. A **Server Core** installation is recommended wherever possible for its reduced resource footprint and smaller attack surface.

- **Disabling unnecessary services** is another practical measure. For example, the **Print Spooler** service is often superfluous for servers that do not function as print servers. Turning off such services reduces potential vulnerabilities and improves server performance.
- An **antivirus solution** is a critical additional layer of security. Configure **Microsoft Defender Antivirus** from within *Windows Security* (*Figure 10.10*) to account for specific server roles, including any required exceptions for applications or databases. Perform regular scans and ensure that all security settings are optimized for maximum protection.

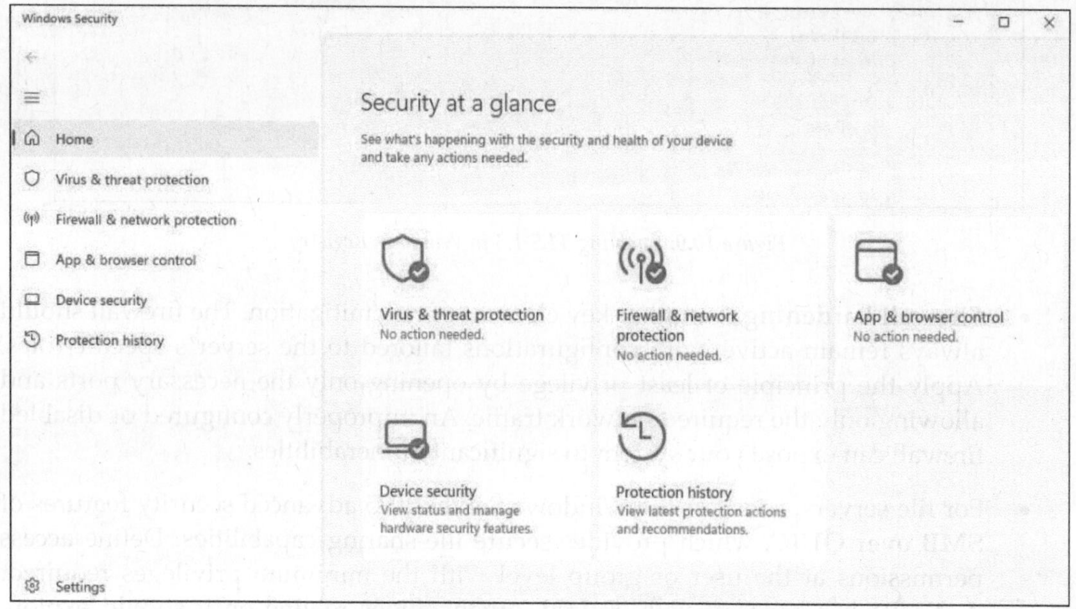

Figure 10.10: Windows Security in Windows Server 2025

- Finally, establish a **robust** and **reliable backup system**. Backups should be among the first considerations during server deployment. Use appropriate backup tools for smaller environments, such as Windows Backup, or implement advanced Azure Backup solutions for more extensive infrastructures. Remember that snapshots and RAID configurations are not substitutes for proper backups. Test backup and restore processes regularly to ensure data recovery readiness.

Following these best practices, you can significantly reduce risks, secure your environment, and ensure data integrity for your Windows Server 2025 infrastructure.

Note: Since BitLocker is not installed by default, you can use Server Manager to add it from the available features in Windows Server 2025. To enable the latest secure communication protocols, add TLS 1.3 as a DWORD (32-bit) value in the Windows Registry.

Monitoring and verifying success

After completing the upgrade to Windows Server 2025, it is essential to establish a **consistent monitoring** and **verification process** to ensure the system operates smoothly and remains stable. By proactively monitoring **key performance indicators** and **system health**, administrators can detect potential issues early, preventing downtime and minimizing disruptions to the organization's operations. The following will explore these concepts in greater detail:

- To begin, leverage **performance counters** in **Performance Monitor**, as shown in *Figure 10.11*, to monitor the server's overall health. These counters track critical system metrics such as *CPU* **usage**, **memory consumption**, **disk I/O**, and **network performance**, helping identify resource bottlenecks that could impact the server's efficiency. By closely monitoring these metrics, administrators can ensure that the server is running optimally and address any issues before they escalate.

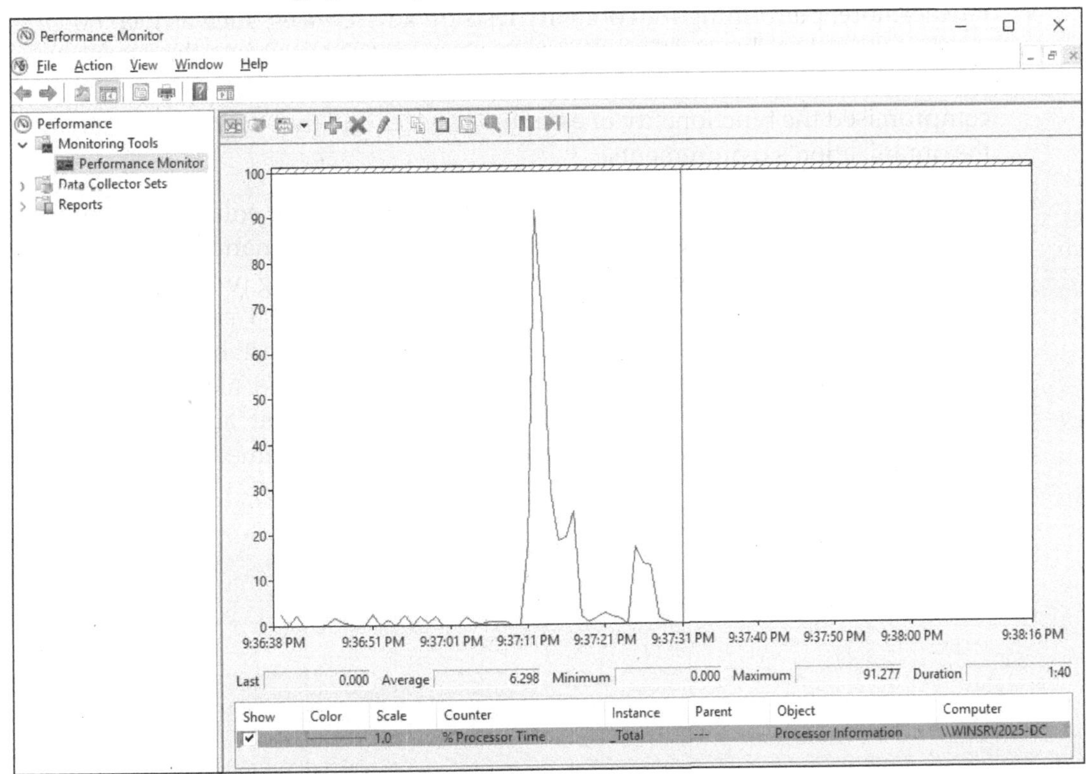

Figure 10.11: *Using Performance Monitor to monitor server's health*

- Additionally, for servers running within an *AD* environment, monitoring AD DS **search performance** and **identity lookups** is essential. These checks ensure that user authentication requests are processed without delays and that there are no connectivity issues or replication failures within the AD infrastructure. Regular verification of AD DS functionality helps maintain the integrity of the domain and ensures smooth user access.

- If the server is **hosting file-sharing services**, conducting regular **Server Message Block (SMB) audits** is necessary. SMB auditing allows administrators to monitor file access and modifications, providing a detailed view of who is accessing shared resources. With *SMB over QUIC* being supported in Windows Server 2025, these audits also help ensure that data in transit is secure, meeting organizational and regulatory requirements for data protection.
- An essential component of the verification process is **reviewing logs** regularly through tools like **Event Viewer** or other centralized logging systems. By analyzing log entries, administrators can identify errors, warnings, or unexpected behaviors, allowing for a timely investigation and resolution of potential issues.
- Furthermore, performing functionality tests on key services, such as web hosting, databases, and authentication processes, is essential to ensure they operate as expected after the upgrade. These tests help confirm that the upgrade has not compromised the functionality of essential services and that they continue to meet the organization's requirements.
- Establishing performance baselines is recommended to enhance monitoring efforts. By setting baseline values for typical system performance, administrators can more easily spot anomalies that may indicate underlying problems. Windows Server 2025 native tools such as *Performance Monitor*, *Event Viewer*, and *Windows Admin Center*, depicted in *Figure 10.12*, can be leveraged to establish performance baselines, monitor system health, and configure automated alerts. Configuring computerized alerts based on these baselines ensures that administrators are notified immediately of any deviations, allowing for swift remediation.

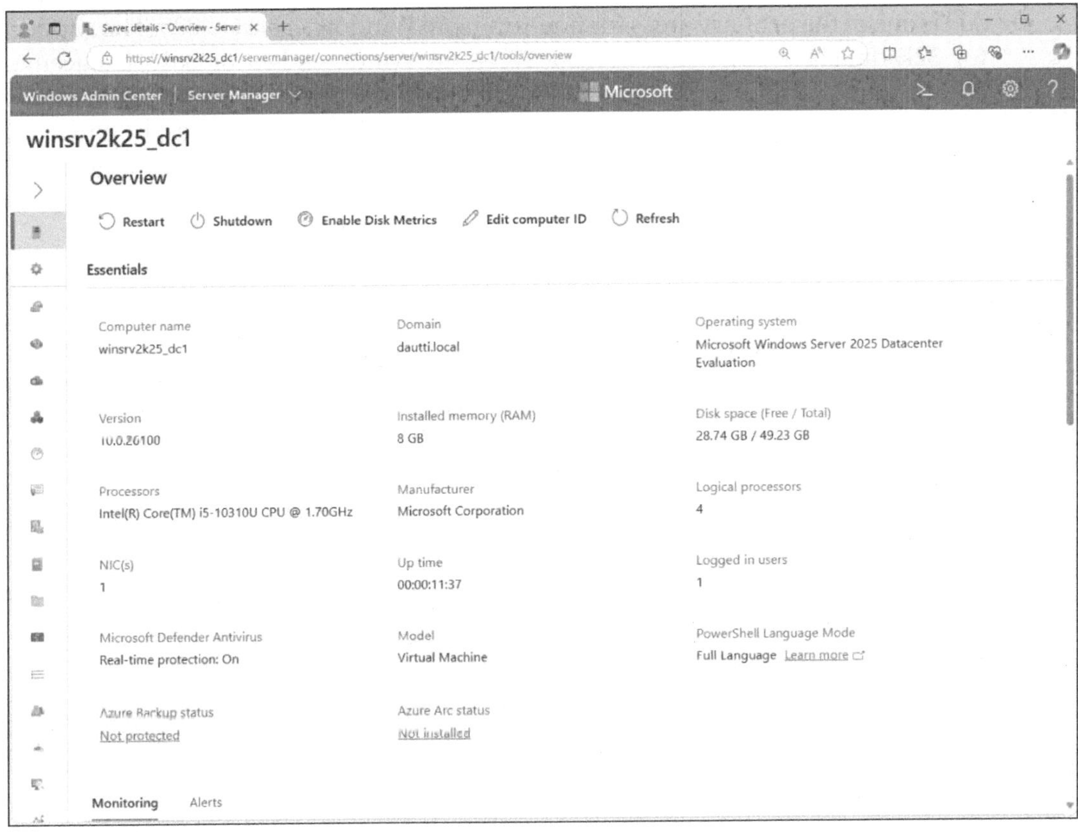

Figure 10.12: Using Windows Admin Center to administer Windows Server 2025

By incorporating these monitoring practices and regularly validating the system's health, administrators can ensure that the upgrade to Windows Server 2025 has been successful. Proactive monitoring and verification not only help maintain the server's stability but also safeguard business-critical services, providing a foundation for smooth and uninterrupted operations moving forward.

Fine-tuning and optimizing

After all the post-in-place upgrade considerations discussed so far, optimizing the performance of Windows Server 2025 involves a **comprehensive approach** to fine-tuning both hardware and software components to achieve the most efficient operation possible. **Fine-tuning** improves response times, maximizes resource usage, ensures system reliability, and contributes to a smoother user experience. By leveraging **built-in features** and **adjusting configurations**, administrators can unlock the full potential of the server environment. The following are some key areas where fine-tuning can significantly impact performance:

- AD is one of the primary areas for fine-tuning in Windows Server 2025. The support for 32k database page sizes (*Figure 10.13*) in Windows Server 2025 Datacenter allows administrators to adjust settings related to object size and multivalued attributes. Fine-tuning AD in this way enhances scalability, improves the efficiency of database searches, and optimizes replication performance. With larger page sizes, AD performance becomes more efficient, especially in larger environments that require managing many users and complex attributes.

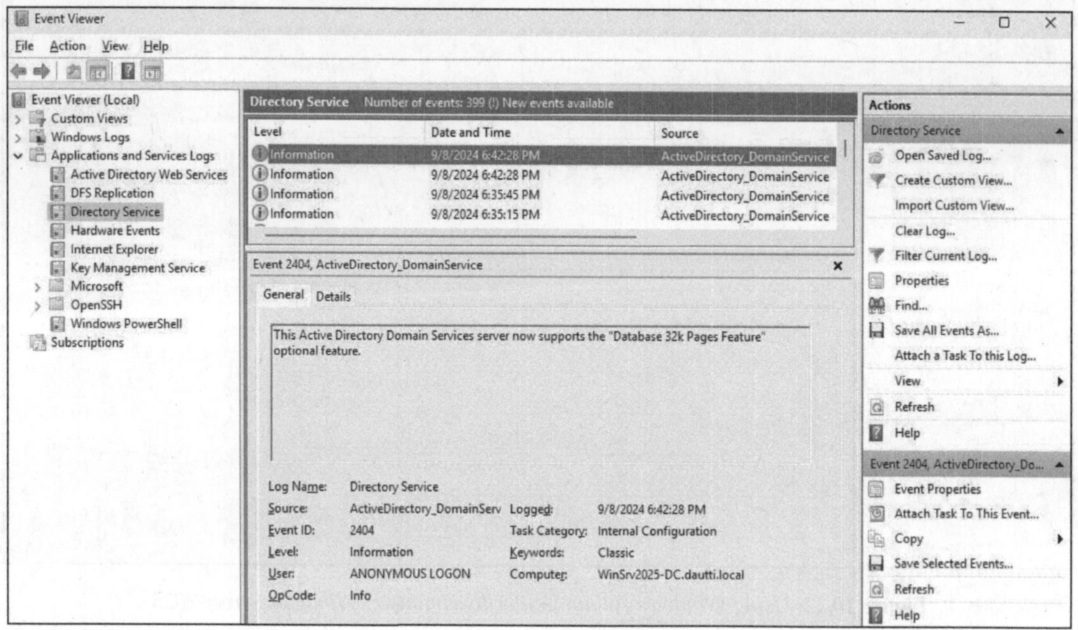

Figure 10.13: *Leveraging 32k database page size*

- Another key optimization area lies in **Azure Arc integration**. This feature enhances hybrid cloud management by providing centralized control over on-premises, multi-cloud, and edge environments. Fine-tuning the Azure Arc integration involves adjusting the synchronization and management settings, ensuring that resources across all environments are efficiently monitored and managed from a single interface. Optimizing Azure Arc integration reduces routine administrative overhead, allowing IT teams to focus on higher-priority tasks and business needs while simplifying overall management.
- In terms network file sharing, **SMB over QUIC** is a valuable performance-enhancing feature. By enabling fine-tuning SMB settings, administrators can significantly enhance file-sharing performance, especially over remote connections. Adjusting SMB compression settings optimizes bandwidth usage and reduces the latency of file transfers. Enabling and configuring SMB over QUIC for secure, high-speed connections ensures smooth operations even in geographically dispersed environments. The added compression support further improves performance by

reducing data size during transmission, making file sharing more efficient across the network.

- Another optimization aspect in Windows Server 2025 is **Virtualization-Based Security (VBS)** and **VBS enclaves**. By fine-tuning **virtualized security settings**, administrators can isolate critical application components from potentially compromised systems, ensuring that application data remains secure even if the underlying OS is breached. Fine-tuning the hardware and software configurations to support VBS enclaves can reduce the performance overhead of virtualized environments while enhancing security.
- For systems that rely on local accounts, the **Windows Local Administrator Password Solution (LAPS)** offers an effective way to fine-tune password management for local accounts. By automating the management and rotation of local administrator passwords, LAPS helps enhance security without creating manual intervention. Fine-tuning LAPS settings can prevent unauthorized access by ensuring the passwords remain secure and compliant with organizational policies. This feature also extends to securing the **Directory Services Restore Mode (DSRM)** account on domain controllers, making it an essential tool for improving overall server security.
- In storage performance, Windows Server 2025 supports **NVMe over Fabrics (NVMe-oF)**, which enables high-performance storage across multiple servers. Fine-tuning the NVMe-oF configuration allows organizations to use low-latency, high-throughput storage without adding additional hardware or physical resources. By adjusting network settings and optimizing NVMe-oF protocols, administrators can ensure that storage resources are fully utilized, improving overall server efficiency and reducing bottlenecks in data access.
- Last but not least, command-line tools such as `DTrace` and the `Winget` package manager, illustrated in *Figure 10.14*, provide powerful means to fine-tune system performance through scripting and automation. Fine-tuning these tools can significantly improve productivity by automating troubleshooting, performing diagnostics, and application management. The Winget package manager streamlines software deployment, while DTrace enables in-depth performance monitoring, allowing IT professionals to identify and address performance issues quickly.

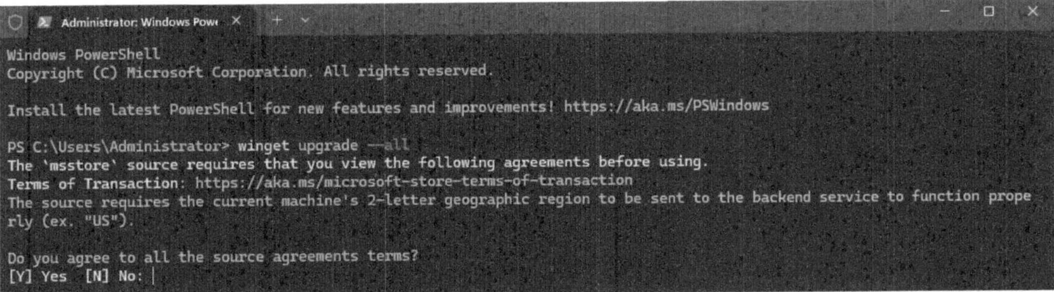

Figure 10.14: *Using Winget to streamline software deployment*

Focusing on these areas for fine-tuning, Windows Server 2025 allows administrators to optimize performance, improve security, and maintain a high level of system reliability. Whether adjusting AD configurations, optimizing network file sharing, or refining virtualized security, these optimizations enable IT professionals to manage their server infrastructure more efficiently, delivering superior performance with minimal resource overhead. Fine-tuning the server environment in these ways ensures that Windows Server 2025 operates at peak performance, providing a seamless and scalable solution for businesses of all sizes.

Real-world use cases

Windows Server 2025 offers a **robust platform** designed to tackle complex business challenges. It features innovative capabilities that can be fine-tuned to enhance performance and optimize workflows. Its advanced features make it a cornerstone for enterprises aiming to achieve **efficiency**, **scalability**, and **reliability**. Here are some potential real-world applications of Windows Server 2025, highlighting how its features can be leveraged to meet specific organizational needs:

- In large-scale manufacturing environments, where production processes require precise coordination, Windows Server 2025 can serve as the **backbone for Industrial IoT (IIoT) systems**. Manufacturers can streamline data collection and analysis from machinery and sensors by optimizing their integration with edge devices and leveraging support for hybrid cloud solutions. This enables real-time monitoring, predictive maintenance, and improved operational efficiency. The server's network performance and resource allocation ensure minimal latency and support the high-volume data processing required in industrial settings.

- For organizations **managing smart cities**, Windows Server 2025 provides a powerful solution for handling the vast amounts of data generated by interconnected systems such as traffic management, energy grids, and public services. Its support for advanced storage solutions, like NVMe over Fabrics, allows for efficiently handling high-speed data transactions. At the same time, virtualization capabilities enable the deployment of isolated workloads for different city functions. By optimizing server performance, cities can ensure seamless integration between systems and respond effectively to dynamic urban challenges.

- Educational institutions **transitioning to hybrid or fully remote learning** can benefit significantly from Windows Server 2025. Schools and universities can deploy optimized virtualized environments to provide students and staff with secure access to learning management systems and shared resources. Features such as SMB over QUIC facilitate fast and secure file access, even for users in remote locations. Leveraging this feature of Windows Server 2025 ensures the smooth delivery of online lectures, resource sharing, and collaborative projects, enhancing the overall learning experience.

- In healthcare, where system reliability and security are paramount, Windows Server 2025 offers enhanced tools for **managing electronic health records (EHR)** and supporting **telemedicine applications**. By optimizing performance settings and leveraging security features like **VBS enclaves**, healthcare providers can protect sensitive patient data while maintaining high availability for critical applications. This enables seamless patient care and supports advanced diagnostics powered by machine learning and AI integrations.

- In software development and testing, Windows Server 2025 is an ideal platform for **DevOps practices**. Its improved support for **containerized applications** and **orchestration tools** allows development teams to efficiently build, test, and deploy software in isolated environments. Resource allocation and performance monitoring tools ensure developers can iterate quickly without compromising system stability. This streamlined approach reduces deployment times and enhances collaboration between development and operations teams.

By tailoring Windows Server 2025 to these diverse real-world scenarios, organizations can unlock their full potential and ensure that their IT infrastructure is capable and optimized to meet their unique demands.

Conclusion

In this chapter, you have explored the essential processes for performing robust in-place upgrades in Windows Server 2025. You gained comprehensive guidance on understanding the benefits and prerequisites of in-place upgrades, planning and preparing your environment, and executing the upgrade while maintaining existing configurations. The chapter also covered advanced topics such as validating compatibility, resolving potential issues, managing dependencies and integrations, mitigating risks, and ensuring data integrity throughout the upgrade process. Additionally, you learned how to monitor and verify the success of the upgrade, fine-tune and optimize the upgraded environment, and apply best practices for achieving a seamless transition. Real-world use cases illustrated practical applications and demonstrated how organizations can leverage in-place upgrades to maintain high availability and performance.

With the knowledge acquired, you can perform efficient and streamlined version updates, ensuring your Windows Server 2025 environments remain secure, stable, and optimized for performance. In the next chapter, you will delve deeper into tuning Windows Server 2025 for peak performance, learning techniques to maximize efficiency and reliability across various workloads.

Questions

1. What is an in-place upgrade?
2. How do you prepare for an in-place upgrade?
3. How do you validate compatibility before an upgrade?
4. How do you mitigate risks during an in-place upgrade?
5. How do you optimize performance after an upgrade?

Join our book's Discord space

Join the book's Discord Workspace for Latest updates, Offers, Tech happenings around the world, New Release and Sessions with the Authors:

https://discord.bpbonline.com

CHAPTER 11
Tuning Windows Server 2025 for Peak Performance

Introduction

This chapter offers in-depth guidance on optimizing the performance of Windows Server 2025. To achieve this, system administrators must first develop a solid understanding of server hardware components and their roles within a network infrastructure. This foundational knowledge allows administrators to make well-informed decisions when selecting and configuring server hardware, ensuring peak performance. The chapter then explores Performance Monitoring, a critical task for sustaining high efficiency and addressing potential issues promptly. The Windows Admin Center, a powerful tool for centralized management, is introduced as a key resource for monitoring server performance.

Additionally, performance management tools such as Performance Monitor, Resource Monitor, and Task Manager are explained to help administrators track and analyze server performance metrics effectively. The chapter also highlights the significance of logs and alerts, which are crucial for diagnosing and resolving issues quickly. Through proper log collection and alert configuration, administrators can stay ahead of potential problems. By following the best practices and methodologies outlined in this chapter, readers will be equipped to ensure their Windows Server 2025 environments operate at maximum efficiency while maintaining effective monitoring and troubleshooting practices.

Structure

The chapter covers the following topics:

- Server hardware components and performance
- Understanding Performance Monitoring tools and methodologies
- Exercise 11.1: Configuring Data Collector sets for monitoring
- Best practices for server hardware setup
- Windows Admin Center for centralized management
- Exercise 11.2: Installing Windows Admin Center
- Exercise 11.3: Connecting to a server from Windows Admin Center
- Importance of logs and alerts in monitoring
- Exercise 11.4: Enabling performance logs and alerts service
- Exercise 11.5: Exploring the PerfLogs folder
- Exercise 11.6: Creating and configuring performance data logs
- Exercise 11.7: Performance counter alert configuration

Objectives

The primary objective of this chapter is to equip system administrators with the knowledge and skills necessary to optimize the performance of Windows Server 2025. It focuses on key areas such as understanding the role of server hardware components and making informed decisions when selecting and configuring hardware for maximum performance. The chapter also delves into the use of powerful tools like Windows Admin Center and Performance Monitor to track and assess server performance metrics efficiently. Additionally, it highlights the critical role that logs and alerts play in maintaining system health, guiding administrators through the process of configuring them for real-time issue detection and resolution. By adhering to the best practices and techniques outlined, readers will be able to ensure their Windows Server 2025 environments consistently operate at peak efficiency, with robust monitoring and management capabilities in place.

Server hardware components and performance

Understanding server hardware components is fundamental to ensuring optimal server performance. While a server may appear similar to a standard computer, its internal components are specifically designed to handle the unique demands of a network environment. These components, often referred to as hardware elements, directly influence the server's ability to manage tasks effectively. Although a server's primary function is not necessarily to perform data processing, its role as a provider of network services and a responder to user requests for these services is heavily dependent on the hardware it utilizes.

As highlighted in *Chapter 5*, where we discussed using the Server Manager and Windows PowerShell to add roles in Windows Server 2025, the server's capacity to deliver these services efficiently is directly tied to the quality and configuration of its hardware. Critical components such as the processor (CPU), memory (RAM), storage drives, and **network interface cards** (**NICs**) each play a vital role in determining the server's overall performance. Understanding how these components interact and contribute to server operations enables system administrators to make informed decisions when selecting and upgrading hardware, ensuring the server is well-equipped to handle its workload. Now, let us look further into the specific roles these components play in maintaining and enhancing server performance.

Processor

When selecting a suitable **processor**, as depicted in *Figure 11.1*, for a server, speed is certainly an important factor, typically measured in **Hertz** (**Hz**) and often reaching **Gigahertz** (**GHz**) in modern processors. However, speed alone does not determine a processor's efficiency. Other critical elements must be taken into account to ensure optimal server performance. One such element is the cache, which acts as the processor's memory. The larger the cache, the more data the processor can retrieve and process directly from memory, reducing the need to fetch data from slower storage. Modern processors feature multiple cache levels, L1, L2, and L3, each contributing to performance in different ways, with speed varying based on cache size and proximity to the processor core.

Figure 11.1: *Intel's Xeon processor powers modern servers*

Speaking of cores, modern processors often come equipped with multiple cores, sometimes dozens, which significantly enhance the ability to handle multiple tasks simultaneously (multithreading). The more cores a processor has, the more efficiently it can manage concurrent processes, which is particularly important for server environments with high user demands. Another vital factor is the processor's word size, referring to its internal architecture, either 32-bit or 64-bit, where 64-bit processors can handle more data and larger memory spaces than their 32-bit counterparts, resulting in improved performance.

Additionally, the processor's registers, which are high-speed memory locations, play a key role in executing instructions quickly. They are considered the fastest memory in the system. Lastly, virtualization technology has become a crucial feature in modern servers, enabling multiple operating systems to share a processor's resources simultaneously. This capability allows for more efficient resource allocation and is especially valuable in environments running virtual machines. When choosing a processor for server needs, considering these factors, speed, cache size, core count, word size, registers, and virtualization support, ensures the server can handle its workload effectively and scale as demands grow.

Memory

Memory plays a crucial role in a server's overall performance, as it serves as the system's primary storage, allowing the processor to access data that is actively being used quickly. There are two main types of memory in a server: **Random access memory (RAM)** and **read-only memory (ROM)**. RAM is volatile, meaning that it only retains data while the server is powered on. It is used as the server's working memory, where the operating system, applications, and active processes are loaded for quick access by the processor. In contrast, ROM is non-volatile and is responsible for crucial hardware initialization tasks, such as running the **Power-On Self-Test (POST)** during boot-up.

Servers generally employ specialized types of memory, such as **error-correcting code (ECC)** memory, which is designed to detect and correct memory errors, ensuring data integrity and system stability. As shown in *Figure 11.2*, ECC memory modules typically have one additional chip compared to standard PC RAM, which allows them to correct single-bit errors automatically. This feature is critical in server environments where data accuracy and uptime are essential.

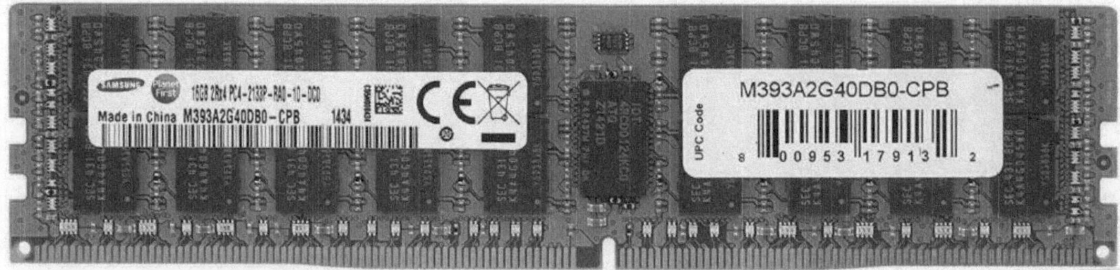

Figure 11.2: ECC RAM is standard for servers

In addition to ECC memory, advanced types of RAM, such as **Single Device Data Correction (SDDC)** and **Double Device Data Correction (DDDC)**, are used in high-end servers to provide even greater levels of error correction. These types of RAM are designed to handle more complex error scenarios, making them particularly valuable in mission-critical systems. However, server-grade RAM is often more expensive than standard PC memory due to these advanced features. Therefore, understanding the specific requirements and characteristics of a server's primary storage is essential for selecting the most appropriate RAM balancing performance, reliability, and cost. By investing in the correct memory, system administrators can ensure that their servers run efficiently, even under heavy workloads.

Disk

Servers play a pivotal role in modern information systems, and their ability to remain operational at all times is crucial to maintaining data and service availability. To achieve this, servers rely on robust storage solutions like **direct-attached storage (DAS)**, which consists of a group of **disks**, as illustrated in *Figure 11.3*, directly connected to the server. This setup allows for quick data access and supports continuous uptime by ensuring that stored information is readily available to users and applications. One key feature of DAS in servers is the inclusion of hot-swappable technology, which allows damaged or failing disks to be replaced without requiring the server to go offline. This capability helps minimize downtime and keeps critical services running smoothly, even during hardware maintenance or failure.

Additionally, high-performing servers often incorporate redundant disk configurations such as **Redundant Array of Independent Disks (RAID)**. This further ensures data integrity and fault tolerance by distributing data across multiple disks. Together, these features enable servers to deliver the high availability and reliability required in modern IT infrastructures, ensuring that services remain accessible and data remains protected at all times.

Figure 11.3: *SAS Disks are used in modern servers*

Network interface

A **network interface**, as shown in *Figure 11.4*, acts as the crucial link between a computer and its network, facilitating communication either physically or virtually, as is the case with virtual machines using software-defined interfaces. Servers often come equipped with multiple network interfaces, and expanding this capacity through the addition of NICs offers several key advantages. For example, having multiple NICs allows for **NIC teaming,** a technique that combines bandwidth from various network connections, thereby boosting overall data throughput and improving server performance. Furthermore, **network load balancing (NLB)** plays a vital role in spreading network traffic across multiple servers, ensuring better performance under heavy loads and improving fault tolerance. Another practical advantage of additional NICs is the ability to separate different types of network traffic, such as isolating internal (intranet) communications from external (internet) traffic, which enhances both security and performance. By leveraging these benefits, system administrators can significantly improve a server's network efficiency, security, and reliability, ensuring it can handle the demands of modern IT environments effectively.

Figure 11.4: *A server's NIC with dual network interfaces*

Server's miscellaneous hardware

Servers play a pivotal role in contemporary computing, relying on a diverse array of components to operate effectively. One critical aspect is the **processor**; the distinction between 32-bit and 64-bit architectures is particularly notable. While 32-bit processors are increasingly viewed as outdated, 64-bit processors are the standard in modern systems, offering enhanced speed and performance. Specifically, 32-bit processors can address up to 4 GB of RAM (2^{32}), whereas 64-bit processors can access significantly more significant amounts, up to 16 exabytes (2^{64}), enabling more efficient processing of extensive datasets.

Removable drives are another vital component that provides external and portable storage solutions. These drives, which include CDs, DVDs, USB flash drives, and external backup drives, can easily connect and disconnect from servers via USB and IEEE 1394 ports, facilitating data transfer and backup.

In terms of graphics capabilities, most servers do not require high-end **graphics cards**; however, the need can vary based on specific applications. For instance, servers dedicated to graphic-intensive tasks like video processing or 3D rendering may necessitate advanced graphics cards to handle the demands of software like AutoCAD.

Given that servers generate considerable heat—primarily from their processors and hard drives, effective cooling solutions are essential to maintain optimal operating temperatures. This includes using processor **coolers and case fans** that expel hot air from the server chassis. Additionally, air conditioning systems are critical in server rooms and data centers to regulate the overall climate.

Power supplies are equally important, as they convert **Alternating Current** (**AC**) to **Direct Current** (**DC**), delivering power to the motherboard and other peripherals. To enhance reliability, servers often feature redundant power supplies, which mitigate the risk of a single point of failure. These redundant systems typically include two or more **Power Supply Units (PSUs)** that can be hot-swapped, allowing for maintenance without interrupting server operation.

Lastly, servers are equipped with various **physical ports** that serve as communication interfaces for connecting cables and peripherals. These ports encompass AC power connectors, Ethernet ports for network connectivity, PCIe slots for expansion cards, USB ports for peripheral connections, HD-15 video connectors for display outputs, management ports for server administration, and legacy ports such as serial, parallel, and PS/2 ports for backward compatibility with older devices. This diverse range of hardware ensures that servers can meet a variety of operational demands in today's dynamic IT environments.

Note: ServeTheHome (https://www.servethehome.com/) is a valuable online platform that offers insights and resources for IT professionals focusing on servers, storage solutions, networking, and high-performance workstation hardware. Additionally, the site showcases a range of outstanding open-source projects.

Understanding Performance Monitoring tools and methodologies

Performance Monitoring is a critical aspect of effective server maintenance that should not be underestimated. The adage **prevention is better than cure** encapsulates the essence of early detection; promptly identifying server issues is essential to avoiding potentially costly disruptions to operations and resources. A successful Performance Monitoring strategy requires a well-defined approach and the appropriate tools. This includes establishing clear metrics to gauge performance, which relies on baseline data to evaluate current server performance, identify when upgrades are necessary, and measure the success of implemented enhancements. Without a structured plan, the insights derived from Performance Monitoring may rest on unfounded assumptions, potentially leading to poor business decisions.

To mitigate such risks, a comprehensive Performance Monitoring methodology should be implemented. This involves conducting thorough research and designing a questionnaire that addresses key aspects, such as the server's intended function, the services it offers, the specific components that need monitoring, performance metrics for those components, and the analytical tools required for data collection and system assessment. By adopting this structured approach, organizations can ensure that their Performance Monitoring efforts are grounded in empirical data rather than mere speculation, ultimately enabling informed decision-making regarding their server systems. For example, a company might track CPU usage, memory performance, and disk activity over time to pinpoint inefficiencies, leading to targeted upgrades that optimize server performance and enhance overall productivity.

Overview of Performance Monitoring procedures

An effective **Performance Monitoring methodology** is vital for establishing well-organized procedures in the realm of server Performance Monitoring. To achieve optimal server efficiency, it is crucial to adhere to several specific guidelines:

- First, comprehensive **documentation** of the server's hardware, software, and configuration is essential, as it provides a clear reference for future assessments and troubleshooting.
- Second, establishing a **performance baseline** enables the setting of measurable standards against which current performance can be evaluated.
- As technology advances, it is equally important to **upgrade** the server's hardware and software to remain competitive and efficient.
- Following any upgrades or changes, conducting a **baseline check** is necessary to compare new performance metrics against previous data. This comparison helps identify any bottlenecks that may hinder server efficiency, allowing for timely intervention and resolution.
- Finally, implementing **targeted strategies** to fine-tune the server's performance will help ensure it operates at its best.

By following these guidelines, organizations can create structured procedures for effectively monitoring and maintaining server performance, ultimately leading to improved reliability and user satisfaction. For instance, regularly assessing CPU usage and memory allocation after upgrades can reveal any new performance issues, enabling administrators to make informed adjustments to enhance server functionality.

Importance of server baselines

Regular monitoring of server performance is crucial for maintaining optimal functionality, and as a system administrator, it is important to pose essential questions to enhance the effectiveness of this process. Key inquiries might include how to determine when servers are nearing capacity and whether benchmarks exist to assess their performance. Establishing a *server baseline* is a fundamental step in this process; it serves as a comprehensive report detailing the performance of various server components under typical operating conditions. This includes metrics such as:

- Processor and memory utilization
- Disk read-and-write operations
- Network connection utilization

However, it is important to understand that **Performance Monitoring** extends beyond merely observing hardware components. Different networks may necessitate the monitoring of additional parameters tailored to their specific operational needs. Therefore, creating a **baseline** is critical for gaining insight into a server's expected performance levels. This allows for accurate comparisons that can help identify potential issues early on. For instance, if a server's disk read speeds significantly deviate from the established baseline, it could indicate an underlying problem that requires immediate attention. Overall, the establishment of a **robust baseline** not only facilitates effective Performance Monitoring but also aids in proactive maintenance and optimization of server resources.

Note: The TechRepublic article (https://www.techrepublic.com/article/pro-tip-using-server-manager-to-baseline-your-windows-hardware/) offers a professional tip on utilizing the Server Manager tool in Windows to create a server baseline, which represents a snapshot of a server's performance during typical workload conditions. Furthermore, the article outlines the process for establishing this baseline and discusses how to analyze the performance data to pinpoint potential issues and enhance the server's overall performance.

Understanding Performance Monitor

Performance Monitor is an indispensable utility for server administrators, offering in-depth insights into server performance and operational efficiency. By continuously tracking various performance metrics, administrators can proactively identify and address potential issues or bottlenecks that could compromise the server's functionality or availability. This tool visualizes real-time performance data, enabling administrators to monitor server operations live or analyze historical data through log files.

The information collected by Performance Monitor is presented in diverse formats, including line graphs, histograms, and detailed reports, which provide a comprehensive view of the server's health and performance trends over time. Such visualizations help administrators quickly grasp performance fluctuations and pinpoint areas requiring attention, facilitating timely interventions.

Additionally, Performance Monitor allows for the customization of data collection to focus on specific metrics relevant to the server's role, such as CPU usage, memory allocation, disk read / write speeds, and network throughput. This tailored approach not only enhances the monitoring process but also ensures that critical performance indicators are continuously assessed.

To access Performance Monitor in Windows Server 2025, follow these straightforward steps:

1. Open the Run dialog box by pressing the *Windows key + R* on your keyboard.
2. Type in **`perfmon.exe`** in the Run dialog box and hit *Enter*.

3. The Performance Monitor tool, shown in *Figure 11.5*, will quickly open and display the server's current performance data in real-time.

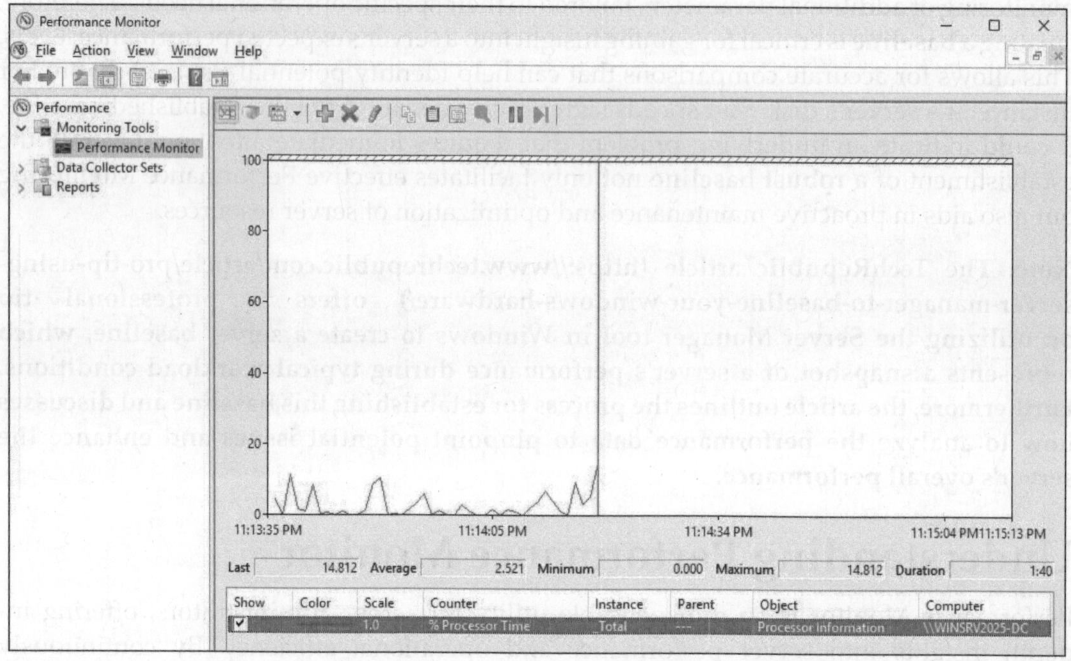

Figure 11.5: Performance Monitor in Windows Server 2025

In Performance Monitor, administrators can collect detailed data on server hardware performance through the use of counters and instances associated with selected objects. **Counters** track various performance metrics related to the operating system, applications, services, or drivers, providing valuable insights into their functionality. Each object, which represents a specific component or process within the server environment, contains multiple counters that measure different aspects of performance. Additionally, these objects can have multiple **instances**, each representing a distinct copy of a particular object type. This capability allows administrators to monitor individual processes or services, making it easier to pinpoint specific performance bottlenecks. Once these bottlenecks are identified, administrators can take appropriate actions—such as optimizing resource allocation, adjusting configurations, or upgrading hardware—to fine-tune server performance and prevent further degradation, ensuring that the server continues to operate efficiently under varying workloads.

Exercise 11.1: Configuring Data Collector Sets for monitoring

This exercise focuses on configuring a Data Collector Set within the Performance Monitor of Windows Server 2025. To complete this task, please follow the outlined steps:

1. Open Performance Monitor and expand Monitoring Tools.
2. Select Performance Monitor and right-click to select **New | Data Collector Set**.
3. Name your **Data Collector Set** and click **Next**.
4. Please specify the location to save it by clicking **Browse** and **Next**.
5. Set the user in Run and select either Start this data collector set now or Save and Close.
6. Click **Finish**.
7. Right-click **Graph** and select **Add Counters...**
8. Choose counters from the **Available Counters** section and click the **Add** button to add them to the **Added Counters** section.
9. Repeat *Step 8* to add more counters. Refer to *Figure 7.6*.
10. Click **OK** to close the window.

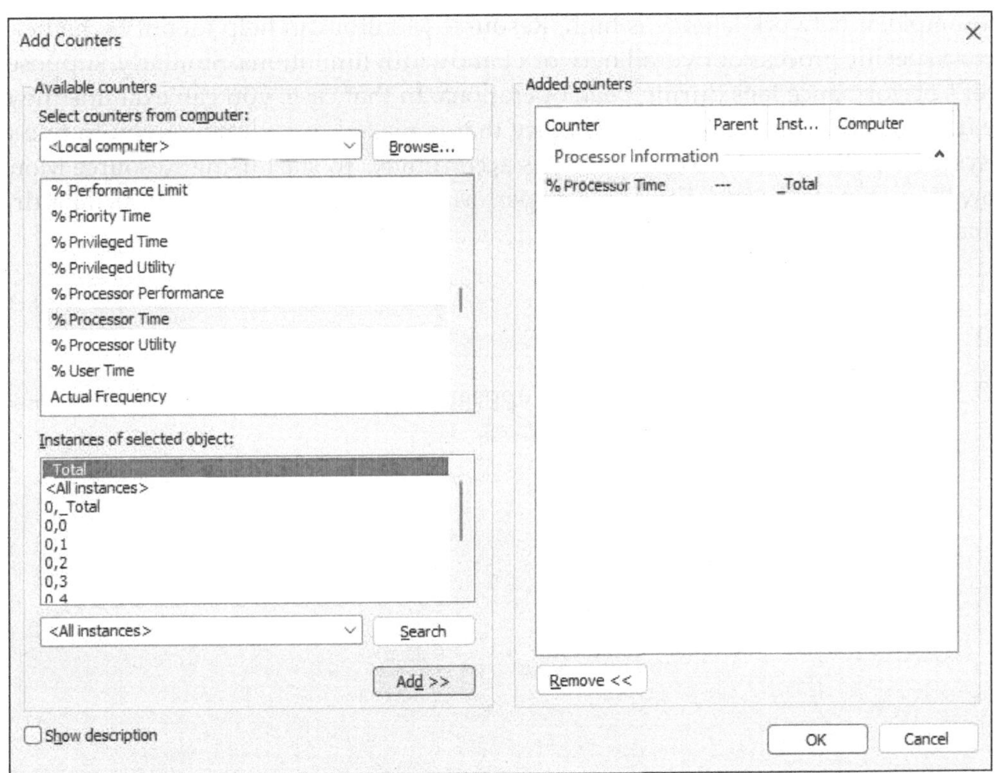

Figure 11.6: Adding Counters in Performance Monitor of Windows Server 2025

Resource monitor explained

Resource Monitor, as shown in *Figure 11.7*, a key diagnostic tool in Windows Server 2025, offers server administrators a detailed, real-time view of the system's resource usage. It enables you to monitor hardware components like the CPU, memory, disk, and network, as well as software processes that impact overall server performance. This granular monitoring helps identify the root cause of slowdowns—whether it's excessive CPU usage by a specific application, memory bottlenecks due to heavy processes, or disk I/O limitations from high read/write operations.

Resource Monitor allows administrators to track live data and historical trends, making it easier to spot patterns that may indicate more significant performance issues, such as memory leaks, inefficient network utilization, or disk saturation. By analyzing this data, you can determine which components are consuming disproportionate amounts of system resources and take appropriate action, such as reallocating tasks, optimizing configurations, or upgrading hardware where necessary.

For example, if network latency is high, Resource Monitor can help identify whether it is due to a specific process or overall network bandwidth limitations. Similarly, suppose the server's performance lags during peak operations. In that case, you can examine the real-time data to see if it is the CPU or memory that is maxed out, allowing you to fine-tune the system or allocate additional resources accordingly. To start using Resource Monitor, follow these steps to diagnose and resolve performance issues in a methodical, data-driven manner:

1. Press the *Windows key* + *R*.
2. Enter **`resmon.exe`** and press *Enter*.
3. Shortly, the Resource Monitor will appear, allowing you to view real-time usage of both hardware and software resources.

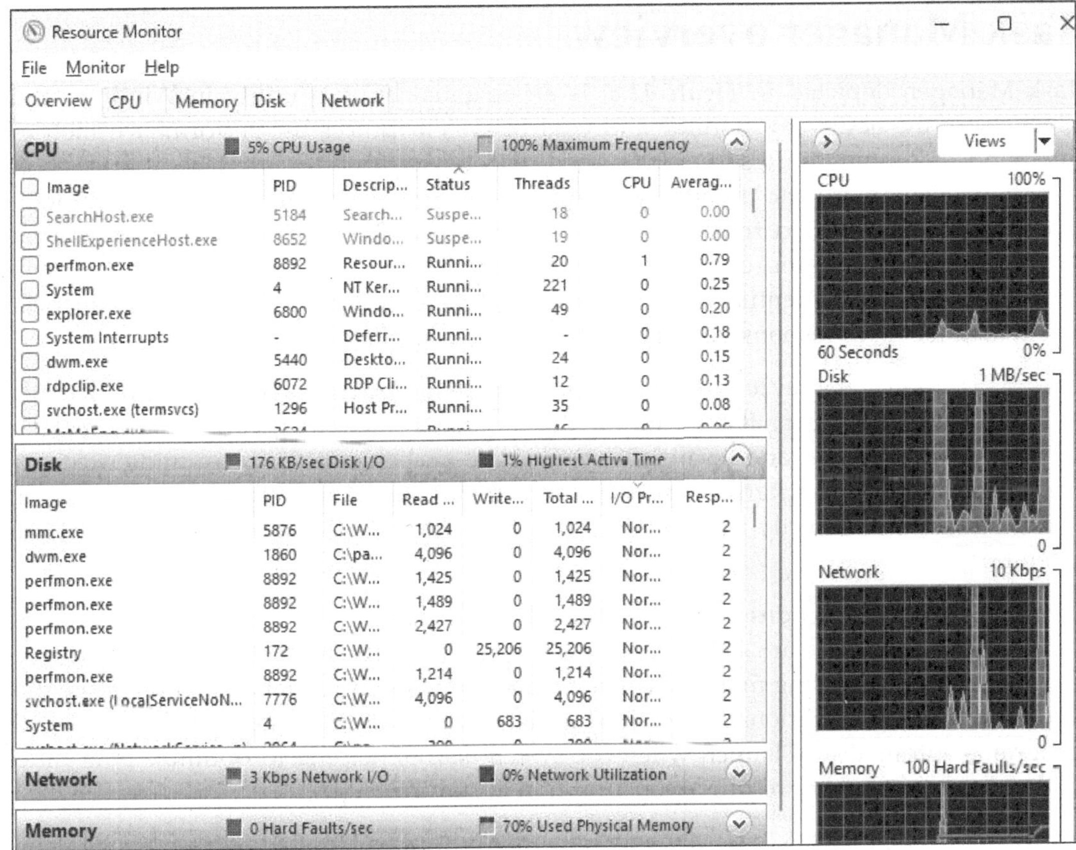

***Figure 11.7:** Resource Monitor in Windows Server 2025*

The **Overview** tab in Resource Monitor provides a quick snapshot of your system's resource usage, offering a high-level view of key performance metrics such as CPU, memory, disk, and network activity. This gives administrators a fast way to assess the general health of the server. However, for more detailed insights, Resource Monitor includes separate tabs for each resource category, allowing you to dive deeper into the specific processes and services consuming resources. For example, in the CPU tab, you can identify which processes are using the most processing power. In contrast, the **Memory** tab shows how system memory is being allocated across different tasks. The **Disk** and **Network** tabs reveal detailed read/write activity and network traffic, respectively. By analyzing this data, administrators can efficiently diagnose performance bottlenecks, such as an overburdened CPU, memory leaks, or network congestion, and take targeted action to resolve them. Resource Monitor is a powerful tool for not only troubleshooting performance issues but also fine-tuning system configurations to optimize the server for better overall performance. This can be especially useful when managing large-scale environments where resource allocation directly impacts operational efficiency.

Task Manager overview

Task Manager, depicted in *Figure 11.8*, is an essential built-in utility in Windows that gives users the ability to monitor and control system processes, performance metrics, and services running on a server. Designed with a user-friendly interface, it offers both a high-level summary and detailed graphical views, making it easy for administrators to understand the server's current performance at a glance. Through Task Manager, you can monitor key system resources like CPU, memory, disk, and network usage in real-time, which helps quickly identify bottlenecks or performance issues. This tool is beneficial when diagnosing unresponsive or resource-intensive applications.

One of Task Manager's key features is its ability to manage **processes and services** efficiently. Administrators can view a list of running processes, sort them by various parameters like CPU or memory usage, and terminate any that are misbehaving or consuming excessive resources. Moreover, background services, which may not have a visible interface, can be started or stopped directly from the **Services** tab, offering full control over the system's operations.

Task Manager also includes a **Performance** tab, which displays real-time graphs showing how system resources are being used over time. This can help administrators detect trends, such as increasing memory consumption, which may signal a potential issue that needs addressing. Additionally, the **Startup** tab enables administrators to manage which programs automatically launch when the system starts, helping to optimize boot times and reduce unnecessary resource consumption at startup.

For Windows Server 2025, Task Manager remains a critical tool for daily server management tasks. Whether you are troubleshooting a slow server or just maintaining smooth operations, Task Manager allows administrators to drill down into the performance metrics, helping to ensure that applications and services are running efficiently. To launch Task Manager in Windows Server 2025, complete the following steps:

1. Right-click on the taskbar and select Task Manager from the Context menu.
2. Once launched, the **Task Manager** will display the **real-time status** of processes and services and provide various performance metrics in an easy-to-understand format.

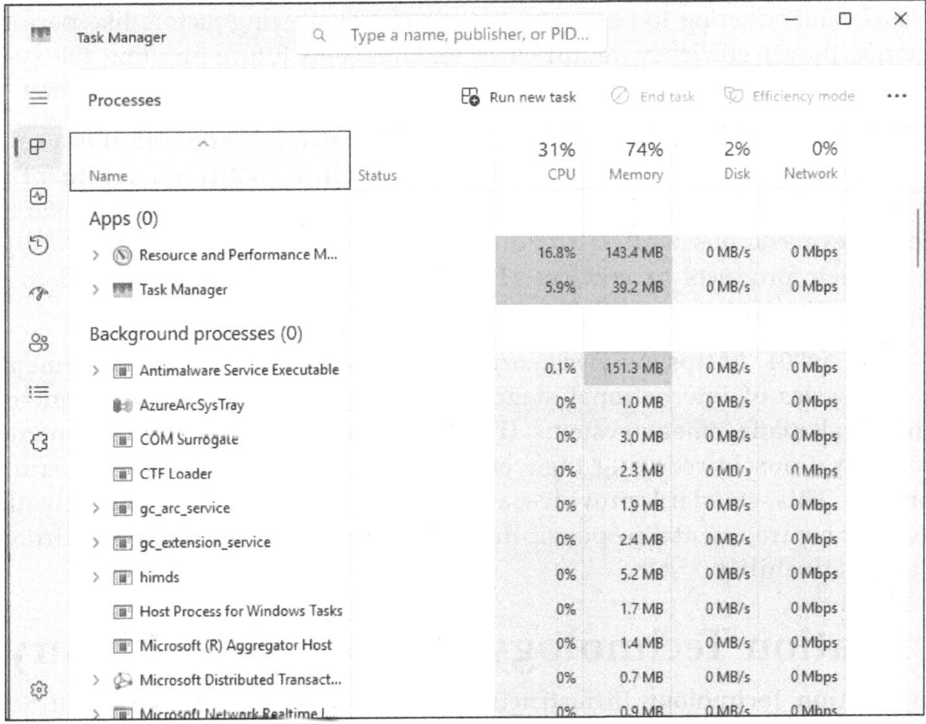

***Figure 11.8:** Task Manager in Windows Server 2025*

Best practices for server hardware setup

Best practices in server hardware selection and configuration represent the most effective strategies for solving technical challenges and managing IT policies. These practices are recognized as the most efficient methods to optimize performance, reliability, and security within an organization's IT infrastructure. Adhering to best practices ensures that servers are not only running efficiently but also that network services remain dependable, client/server applications are secure, and the infrastructure can scale as the organization grows. In the world of information technology, such practices are often aligned with internationally recognized management standards like *ISO 9000 and ISO 14001*, which emphasize continuous improvement and operational excellence. These standards provide a framework that helps organizations maintain quality and environmental management, ensuring optimal server and network performance.

In contrast to best practices, **guidelines** offer recommendations for achieving compliance with policies but are more flexible in their application. **Procedures**, on the other hand, are detailed step-by-step instructions that break down how to implement specific policy components in a consistent and structured manner. Following these best practices, along with proper guidelines and procedures, can help organizations mitigate risks, enhance performance, and create a robust, scalable IT environment. For instance, when selecting server hardware, adhering to best practices means considering factors like performance benchmarks, power efficiency, redundancy features, and future-proofing the system to handle potential expansions, ensuring that both current and future needs are met.

Note: ISO 9000 (https://www.iso.org/iso-9001-quality-management.html) is a collection of international standards that define the criteria for a quality management system (QMS). These standards are aimed at assisting organizations in fulfilling customer and stakeholder expectations while also adhering to statutory and regulatory obligations related to their products or services. The ISO 9000 family is structured to ensure consistent quality and continuous improvement across various industries.

Note: ISO 14001 (https://www.iso.org/iso-14001-environmental-management.html) is part of a series of international standards that offer guidelines for implementing environmental management systems (EMS). The ISO 14000 family is intended to assist organizations in reducing their environmental impact while still maintaining profitability. This standard provides a structured framework for organizations to manage their environmental responsibilities effectively, supporting the environmental aspect of sustainability.

Information Technology Infrastructure Library

The **Information Technology Infrastructure Library (ITIL)** was developed in response to the increasing dependence on computer technology and networking within businesses during the 1980s, as organizations recognized the critical role of IT and communication systems in enhancing productivity and efficiency. ITIL provides a robust framework that assists IT organizations in effectively designing, implementing, managing, and operating IT services to meet the ever-evolving needs of their business environments. Its best practices are encapsulated in a series of publications, with the latest iteration being ITIL v4, released in 2019 and 2020.

The **core ITIL framework** focuses on several vital areas, including:

- **Service strategy**, which defines the organization's objectives and how IT services can deliver value;
- **Service design**, which emphasizes creating services that meet business requirements;
- **Service transition**, which manages the process of deploying new services into the live environment;
- **Service operation**, which ensures that IT services are delivered effectively on a day-to-day basis;
- **Continual service improvement**, which promotes an ongoing cycle of enhancement to optimize service quality and efficiency.

By adopting ITIL, organizations can tailor their IT services to align with business objectives, streamline processes, improve communication and collaboration among IT teams, and ensure a high level of service quality. Furthermore, ITIL's structured approach not only helps organizations reduce costs and risks associated with IT service delivery but also positions them to adapt to new technologies and market demands more rapidly, thereby establishing a competitive edge in today's fast-paced digital economy. Through these practices, ITIL contributes to the overall success and sustainability of organizations, fostering a culture of continuous improvement and innovation.

Note: The official ITIL website (https://www.axelos.com/best-practice-solutions/itil) serves as an extensive resource for understanding ITIL, outlining its advantages and the latest developments within the framework. It offers a wealth of materials, including guidelines, articles, and training opportunities tailored for both individuals and organizations seeking to implement ITIL best practices effectively. Users can explore various resources that facilitate the adoption of ITIL methodologies, enhancing their IT service management processes. Additionally, the website provides detailed information about the ITIL certification program, which acknowledges individuals who have showcased a comprehensive grasp of ITIL concepts and principles. This certification can significantly benefit professionals looking to advance their careers in IT service management by validating their expertise and commitment to industry standards. Overall, the website is a valuable tool for anyone aiming to deepen their understanding of ITIL and its application in real-world scenarios.

Windows Admin Center for centralized management

Windows Admin Center (**WAC**) is a sophisticated management tool developed for server administration, originally known as *Project Honolulu* when it was launched in 2018. Since its inception, WAC has undergone significant enhancements and is now fully integrated into Windows Server 2025. This versatile tool enables system administrators to oversee both on-premises and cloud-based Windows servers through a user-friendly web-based interface. As a locally installed application, WAC serves as a modern replacement for traditional management tools like Server Manager and Computer Management, offering a more streamlined approach to server management. Administrators can download it for free from Microsoft's website, and it supports various operating systems, including Windows Server 2025, Windows 10, Windows 11, and earlier versions of both Windows Client and Server.

WAC is equipped with a comprehensive suite of management tools that facilitate the administration of Windows servers, hyper-converged infrastructures, Windows 10 and 11 PCs, and clusters. Its interface mirrors the Azure cloud management platform, allowing for a smoother transition for administrators who are familiar with Azure. Within WAC, users can manage and monitor essential components such as virtual machines, storage, networking, and security measures. This capability ensures that administrators can effectively oversee both on-premises and cloud environments, maintaining a cohesive management experience across different infrastructure setups. Overall, Windows Admin Center is a powerful solution that simplifies server management and enhances operational efficiency in today's hybrid IT landscapes.

Windows Admin Center tools and features

Windows Admin Center (**WAC**) serves as an all-encompassing platform for the administration of Windows servers and various devices within an organization. This versatile application enables remote management, allowing system administrators to oversee their server infrastructure through a user-friendly web-based interface. With WAC, administrators can monitor server health, manage updates, and configure settings without needing to log in to each server individually.

WAC includes a wide array of **tools and features** that facilitate the monitoring and management of multiple facets of the server environment, thereby streamlining the administrative process and enhancing system performance. For example, the Virtual Machines tool allows administrators to create, start, stop, and manage virtual machines directly from the WAC dashboard. This makes it easy to allocate resources, perform backups, and manage snapshots, all from a single interface.

In addition, the **Storage Management** feature enables users to monitor disk space usage and health, set up storage pools, and configure storage spaces for optimal performance and redundancy. Administrators can visualize storage configurations and make adjustments based on current usage trends, which can be crucial for preventing downtime due to storage failures.

The Performance Monitoring tool provides **real-time insights** into CPU, memory, and network usage, allowing administrators to identify and troubleshoot performance bottlenecks quickly. For instance, if an application is consuming excessive CPU resources, administrators can investigate further and take necessary actions, such as reallocating resources or optimizing the application settings.

In *Chapter 2*, you were guided to download Windows Admin Center, and now we will delve into some of the essential tools included in the WAC toolkit. These tools are designed to provide insights into system performance, simplify task execution, and ensure that administrators can effectively optimize their server resources for better operational efficiency. Overall, WAC empowers IT professionals by offering a centralized management solution that enhances visibility and control over server infrastructure, making it a vital tool in today's IT landscape.

Azure Hybrid Center

Azure Hybrid Center is a powerful tool designed to integrate on-premises infrastructure with cloud capabilities, enabling organizations to leverage the advantages of cloud computing while still capitalizing on their existing investments in local resources. This platform enhances connectivity between local servers and cloud services, facilitating seamless management and operation across both environments. Key features include Azure Automanage for automating server management, Azure Arc for extending Azure services to any infrastructure, Azure Backup for securing critical data, and File Sync to ensure that files remain consistent across locations. Furthermore, it supports disaster recovery solutions, allowing organizations to prepare for unexpected outages while maintaining business continuity.

Azure Kubernetes Service

Azure Kubernetes Service (**AKS**) acts as a management panel for orchestrating Kubernetes clusters, providing a robust environment for deploying and scaling containerized applications. This service simplifies the complexities associated with container management, enabling developers to focus on building applications rather than worrying about the underlying infrastructure. For example, using AKS, a company can effortlessly scale its application during peak usage times, automatically adjusting resources to meet demand without manual intervention.

Azure Monitor

Azure Monitor offers a centralized solution for tracking the performance and health of Azure resources and applications running either in the cloud or on-premises. With its intuitive dashboard, administrators can visualize real-time metrics, set alerts for critical issues, and gain insights into system performance. For instance, if an application experiences latency, Azure Monitor can provide alerts that allow IT teams to respond promptly and investigate the underlying causes, thereby reducing downtime and enhancing user experience.

Microsoft Defender for Cloud

Microsoft Defender for Cloud is an essential security solution that provides comprehensive visibility, protection, and incident response for cloud workloads. It actively identifies and mitigates threats across multiple cloud platforms, including Azure, AWS, and Google Cloud. Integrating machine learning and threat intelligence helps organizations recognize potential vulnerabilities and block malicious activities, thereby safeguarding their data and applications in a multi-cloud environment.

Remote Desktop

Remote Desktop is a versatile tool that enables administrators to access and manage Windows servers and desktops remotely from a centralized location. This feature streamlines server management by allowing IT professionals to perform administrative tasks without needing physical access to the hardware. For example, an administrator can troubleshoot a server issue or install software updates while working from a different location, significantly improving efficiency and reducing response times.

The secured-core server

The *secured-core server* is a security feature that incorporates multiple layers of protection across hardware, firmware, and operating systems. Utilizing **Trusted Platform Module (TPM)** 2.0 and System Guard ensures that Windows Server boots securely, significantly mitigating the risks associated with firmware vulnerabilities. This approach provides an added layer of defense against sophisticated cyber threats, making it ideal for organizations that prioritize security.

Storage Migration Service

The Storage Migration Service simplifies the server migration process by offering an intuitive **graphical user interface (GUI)** alongside Windows PowerShell capabilities. This tool enables IT professionals to inventory existing server data and efficiently transfer configurations to newer server versions. For example, when upgrading from Windows Server 2012 to Windows Server 2025, administrators can use this service to ensure a smooth transition, minimizing downtime and maintaining service availability during the migration.

Exercise 11.2: Installing Windows Admin Center

This exercise offers a step-by-step guide for installing Windows Admin Center, an essential tool for managing and monitoring Windows servers efficiently. To successfully install this application, please follow the steps outlined:

1. Open the downloaded file `WindowsAdminCenter2311.msi` by double-clicking on it to launch the installer.
2. Click the Next button in the Windows Admin Center Setup wizard to install.
3. Examine and approve the license terms, as shown in *Figure 11.9*, and then click Next.

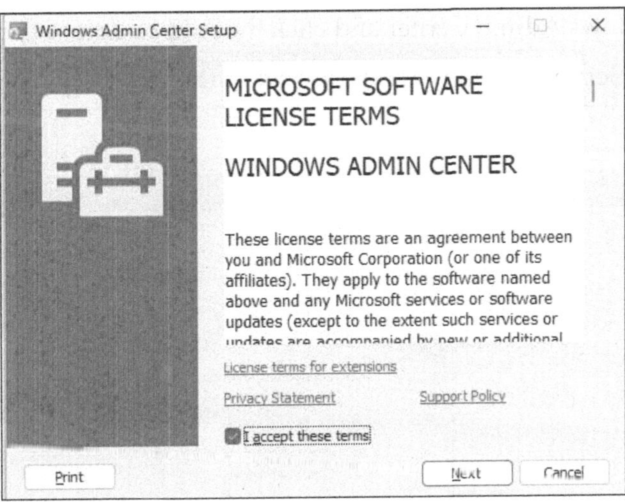

Figure 11.9: *Installing Windows Admin Center*

4. Choose the installation location and select **Next**.
5. On the Send diagnostic data to Microsoft page, choose the option that is most appropriate for you.
6. Select **Use Microsoft Update** when I check for updates, then click **Next**.
7. Accept the Install Windows Admin Center defaults on the Windows Server page and click **Next**.
8. Select the features you want to install, and then click **Next**.
9. Choose between a self-signed certificate or a certificate from a certificate authority, then click **Next**.
10. Review the installation summary and click **Install** to begin the installation process.
11. Wait for the installation to complete, then click **Finish** to exit the setup wizard.
12. To access Windows Admin Center, open your web browser and go to **https://localhost:6516.**

Exercise 11.3: Connecting to a server from Windows Admin Center

This exercise outlines the process for establishing a connection to a server using Windows Admin Center, a powerful tool that simplifies server management through a web-based interface. By following the steps provided, you will be able to connect to your server effectively, enabling you to manage and monitor its performance and configurations seamlessly:

1. Open Windows Admin Center and click the Add button in the top-left corner.
2. Within the Servers section, select the Add button, as shown in *Figure 11.10*:

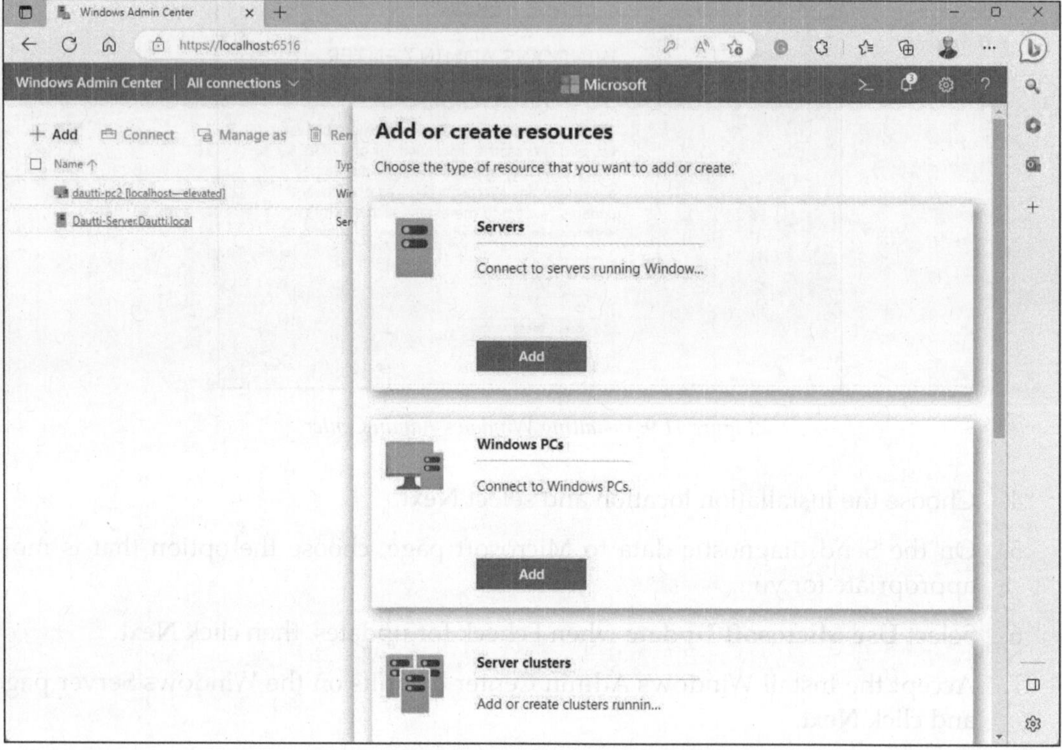

Figure 11.10: Connecting to a server through Windows Admin Center

3. In the Server name field, enter the IP address or hostname of the server you want to connect to.
4. Enter the credentials for the server you want to connect to.
5. Click on the Add button to add the server to your list of connections.
6. Please select the server from the connections list to manage it using the Windows Admin Center.

Importance of logs and alerts in monitoring

This section highlights the critical role of **Performance Monitoring** in ensuring the smooth operation of servers, emphasizing the dedication and meticulous attention required from system administrators. Utilizing the right tools, particularly logs, and alerts, is essential for maintaining server functionality and preemptively addressing potential issues. **Logs** serve as invaluable resources for conducting detailed analyses and preserving historical records, which can be crucial for troubleshooting, compliance audits, and performance optimization. For instance, if a server experiences unexpected downtime, logs can help administrators trace back the events leading to the failure, such as spikes in CPU usage or memory exhaustion.

On the other hand, **alerts** notify system administrators promptly about significant events, enabling swift action to mitigate potential disruptions or performance degradation. For example, suppose CPU usage exceeds a predefined threshold of 85% for a sustained period. In that case, an alert can be triggered, prompting the administrator to investigate running processes or applications that may be consuming excessive resources. This proactive monitoring helps prevent system slowdowns or outages.

One effective tool for this purpose is Performance Monitor, which empowers system administrators to gather and log performance data automatically while also configuring alerts for critical thresholds. Administrators can set up alerts to notify them of high disk usage, which could indicate that a server is running out of storage space. In practice, if the available disk space drops below 10%, an alert can be configured to send an email notification to the IT team, enabling them to take immediate action, such as archiving old files or expanding the disk capacity.

Additionally, the logged performance data can be analyzed for trends over time or exported to tools like Excel for deeper analysis and comprehensive reporting. For instance, an administrator might export performance logs to analyze CPU and memory usage patterns over a month to identify peak usage times and adjust resource allocation or scheduling for tasks during off-peak hours.

The following section will detail a recommended approach for configuring performance logs and alerts in Windows Server 2025, providing practical guidance to enhance server monitoring capabilities and ensure robust operational efficiency.

Exercise 11.4: Enabling performance logs and alerts service

This exercise details the procedure for initiating the performance logs and alerts service in Windows Server 2025, a crucial feature for monitoring system performance and identifying potential issues. By following the steps outlined, you will learn how to activate this service effectively, enabling you to collect performance data and receive timely alerts regarding the health of your server. This proactive approach is essential for maintaining optimal server operation and ensuring that system administrators can respond promptly to any performance-related concerns.

1. Press the *Windows key + R*.
2. Type in `services.msc` and hit *Enter*.
3. Locate the Performance Logs & Alerts service from the list of services and check its status, as shown in *Figure 11.11*.

4. If the service is stopped, right-click on it and choose Start.
5. Close the Services window.

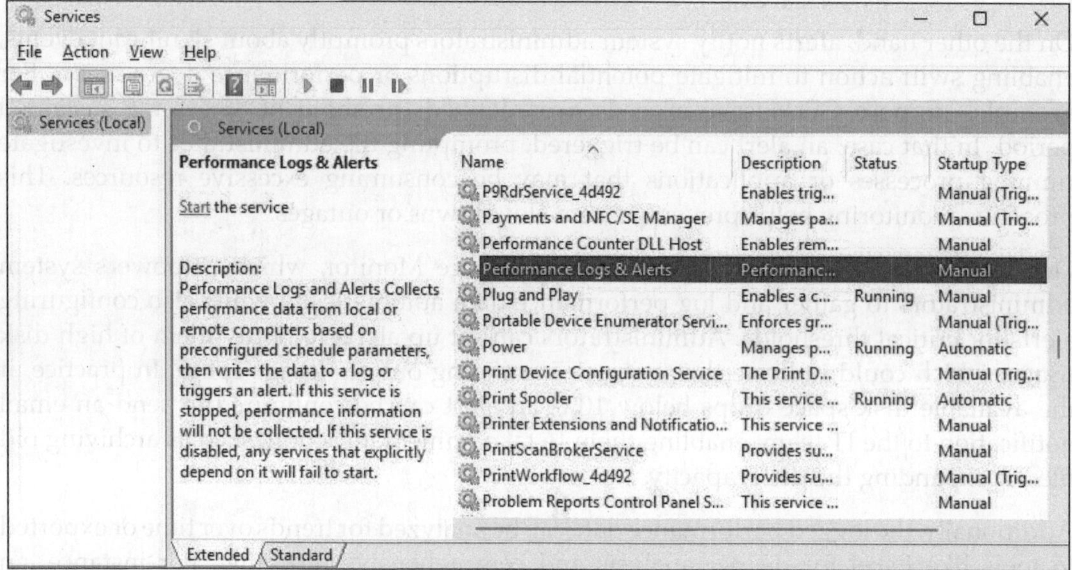

Figure 11.11: Performance Logs and Alerts service in Windows Server 2025

Exercise 11.5: Exploring the PerfLogs folder

This exercise outlines the procedure for accessing the PerfLogs folder, which houses the Performance Monitor logs in Windows Server 2025. Understanding how to navigate to this folder is essential for system administrators who need to analyze performance data for troubleshooting and optimization purposes. By following the steps provided, you will be able to locate the PerfLogs folder efficiently, allowing you to review logs that detail system performance metrics, resource usage, and alerts generated by the Performance Monitor. This capability is crucial for maintaining the health and efficiency of your server environment.

1. Press the *Windows key* + *R*.
2. Type **C:** and press *Enter*.
3. The **PerfLogs** folder will be displayed, as seen in *Figure 11.12*:

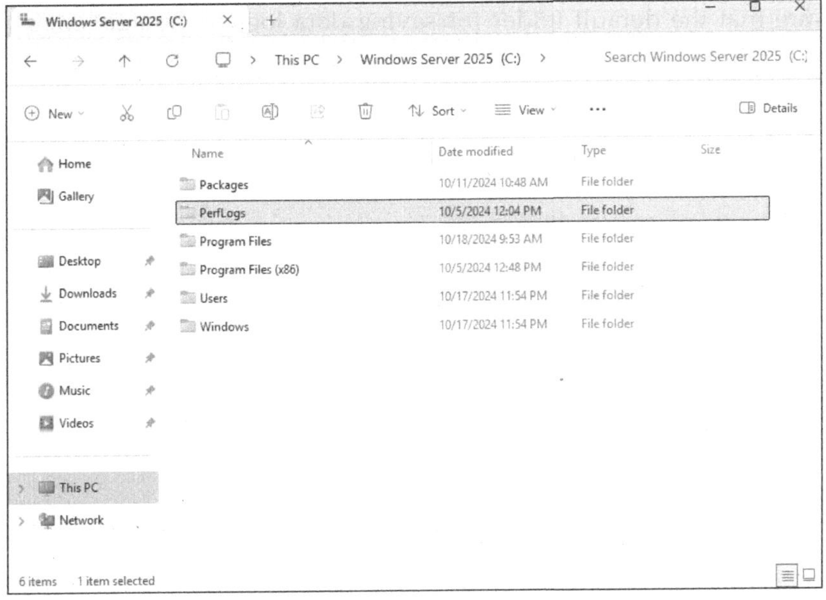

Figure 11.12: *PerfLogs folder in File Explorer of Windows Server 2025*

Exercise 11.6: Creating and configuring performance data logs

This exercise details the process of creating performance data logs in Windows Server 2025, a vital task for monitoring system performance and resource utilization. By generating these logs, system administrators can capture critical metrics that provide insights into server operations, enabling proactive management and troubleshooting. The following steps will guide you through the creation of these performance data logs, allowing you to systematically track key indicators such as CPU usage, memory consumption, and disk I/O, thereby enhancing your ability to maintain an efficient and responsive server environment:

1. Expand **Data Collector Sets** and select **User Defined** in Performance Monitor.
2. Right-click **User Defined** and select **New | Data Collector Set**.
3. Enter a name for the Data Collector Set.
4. Select the Create manually (Advanced) option and click **Next**.
5. Choose the Create data logs option and the Performance counter sub-option, then click **Next**.
6. Click the **Add** button to add counters, as shown in *Figure 11.13*. Specify the time interval, and click **Next**.

7. Ensure that the default folder for saving data logs is the **PerfLogs** folder, and click Next.

8. Set the User in Run and select the **Start this Data Collector Set now** option.

9. Finally, click **Finish** to complete the process.

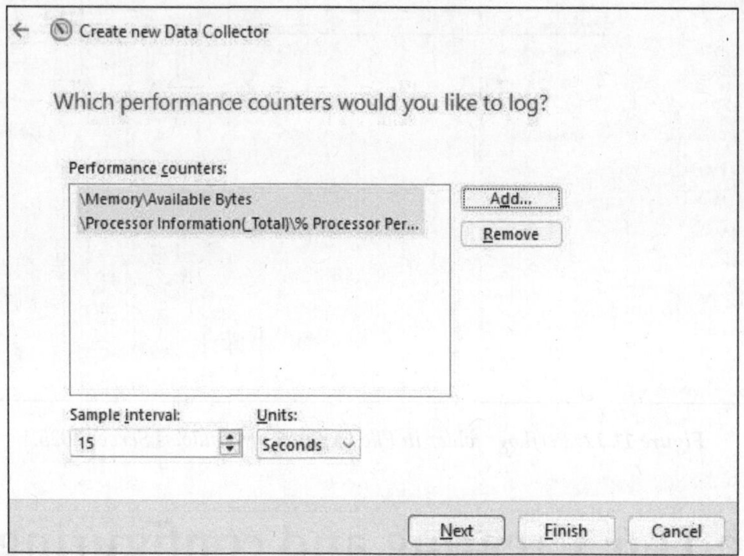

Figure 11.13: *Logging the performance counters*

Exercise 11.7: Performance counter alert configuration

This exercise outlines the procedure for configuring a performance counter alert in Windows Server 2025, an essential capability for monitoring system performance in real-time. By setting up these alerts, system administrators can receive immediate notifications when specific performance thresholds are breached, allowing for prompt action to mitigate potential issues. This proactive approach helps maintain server stability and optimize resource utilization. The following steps will guide you through the setup process, ensuring that you can effectively monitor critical performance metrics such as CPU load, memory usage, and disk activity.

1. First, follow steps 1 to 4 from the *Creating Performance Data Logs* section.

2. Choose **Performance Counter Alert** and click on **Next.**

3. Click the **Add** button to add counters, specify the limit for the alert, and click **Next.** *Figure 11.14* shows how to do this.

4. Set the user in Run as and select the Start this data collector set now option.

5. Click Finish to complete the setup.

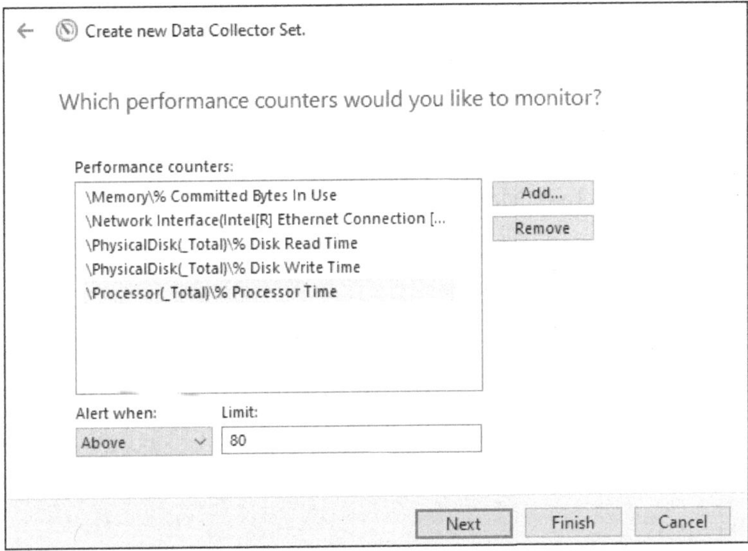

***Figure 11.14:** Joining a domain using Server Configuration*

Conclusion

In this chapter, we explored the essential hardware components of a server and methods for maintaining and monitoring its performance using the built-in tools and utilities of Windows Server 2025. Key components such as the CPU, RAM, storage drives, and network interfaces were discussed, highlighting their significant influence on overall performance; for example, a powerful processor can reduce processing times for complex tasks while sufficient memory ensures smooth operation during peak workloads. Various Performance Monitoring utilities, including Performance Monitor, Resource Monitor, Task Manager, and Performance Counters, equip system administrators to effectively track performance metrics, with Performance Monitor visualizing trends over time and Task Manager providing a real-time overview of active processes and resource utilization. Additionally, we discussed the Windows Admin Center. This robust management platform allows remote management and monitoring of servers through an intuitive web-based interface, centralizing tasks for administrators overseeing multiple servers. The chapter concluded with a hands-on exercise guiding you through setting up performance logs and alerts, including starting the service, navigating to the Performance Monitor logs folder, creating logs for specific performance data, and configuring alerts for critical performance counters, skills crucial for proactive server management.

As we transition to the next chapter, the focus will shift to updating and troubleshooting Windows Server 2025, equipping you with the knowledge needed to ensure your server remains efficient and resilient in a dynamic IT landscape.

Questions

1. What are the four primary hardware components?
2. What does the Performance Monitor do?
3. How does the Resource Monitor function?
4. What role does the Task Manager play?
5. What is the purpose of Windows Admin Center?

CHAPTER 12
Maintaining and Troubleshooting Windows Server 2025

Introduction

In this chapter, we will explore the essential yet often complex tasks of updating and troubleshooting Windows Server 2025. As you look into the content, you will find that with a well-structured plan and clear strategy, these tasks become more manageable and less daunting. Effective troubleshooting, regular updates, and proactive monitoring are key to maintaining high levels of business continuity, an essential factor for the success of any organization. This chapter will cover various critical areas, including the server startup process, advanced boot options, Safe Mode, and creating a robust backup and disaster recovery plan. We will also walk through the process of updating Windows Server 2025, server hardware, and third-party software to ensure optimal performance. Additionally, we will discuss the use of the Event Viewer for monitoring logs, which can help identify and resolve potential issues, reducing downtime and minimizing financial losses. By the chapter's end, you will have the practical knowledge to manage server logs efficiently, use the Event Viewer for troubleshooting, and ensure your Windows Server 2025 is consistently up to date, thereby maintaining high standards of business continuity.

Structure

The chapter covers the following topics:

- Server startup and recovery tools overview
- Ensuring business continuity and disaster recovery
- Exercise 12.1: Configuring folder redirection in Server 2025
- Exercise 12.2: Adding Windows Server Backup in 2025
- Updating OS, drivers, and applications for security
- Understanding troubleshooting errors and problems
- Understanding and utilizing the Event Viewer
- Exercise 12.3: Central monitoring configuration
- Exercise 12.4: Event Viewer log filtering
- Exercise 12.5: Log location configuration

Objectives

This chapter aims to equip readers with a thorough understanding of key tasks related to troubleshooting, updating, monitoring, and maintaining Windows Server 2025. It introduces practical strategies to make these essential activities more manageable. The chapter explores the server startup process, advanced boot options, and Safe Mode as critical tools for diagnosing issues. Additionally, it covers the creation and implementation of backup and restore disaster recovery plans and the process of updating Windows Server 2025 to ensure system security and stability. The Event Viewer is highlighted as an invaluable tool for monitoring system logs and diagnosing errors, helping to reduce server downtime and prevent potential financial impacts. By the end, readers will have a firm grasp of these concepts and the confidence to apply them effectively in real-world server management scenarios.

Server startup and recovery tools overview

A solid understanding of a server's hardware components and startup process is essential for effective troubleshooting, minimizing downtime, and ensuring smooth operation. Although highly technical, this knowledge is critical for service technicians to diagnose and resolve issues that may arise during startup. The startup process begins with the **Basic Input/Output System** (**BIOS**), which is responsible for initializing hardware components and performing a series of checks for errors before the operating system is loaded. By gaining a clear understanding of how the BIOS interacts with the server's hardware, technicians can quickly identify and address any startup issues. This proactive approach helps reduce downtime and ensures the server remains operational. A detailed comprehension of both the hardware components and the startup sequence is key to efficient server management and troubleshooting. Now, let us explore the systems involved to understand the server's startup process better.

Basic Input/Output System

The BIOS is a foundational component that becomes active as soon as a server is powered on. Located on a ROM chip embedded in the motherboard, the BIOS, as depicted in *Figure 12.1*, initiates a series of processes that are essential for setting up and configuring the server's hardware. It serves as the intermediary between the hardware and the operating system, allowing users to access and adjust critical hardware settings such as CPU configuration, memory settings, and device priorities.

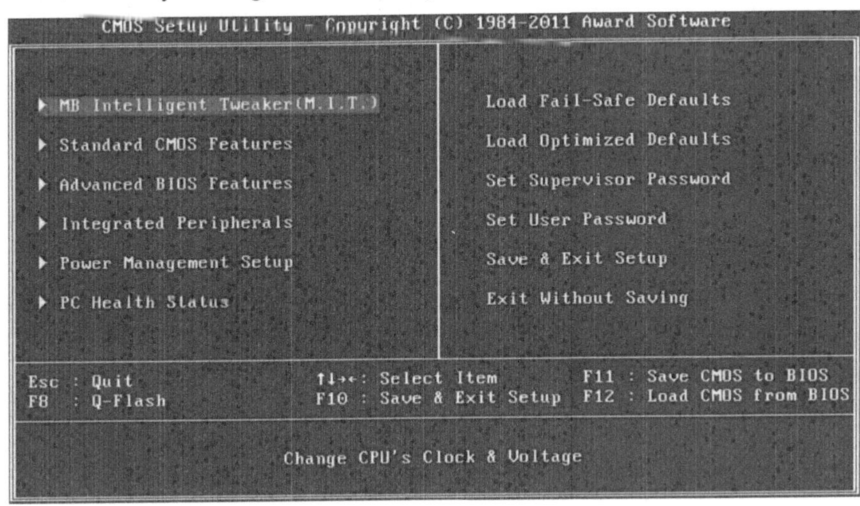

Figure 12.1: *BIOS in a computer system*

The BIOS is responsible for performing the **Power-On Self Test** (**POST**), which checks the server's hardware components, like RAM, hard drives, and network cards, for errors before the operating system begins to load. It also identifies and configures all connected hardware, ensuring they are ready for operation. One of the most critical roles of the BIOS is to establish the boot sequence, which determines the priority of devices (such as hard drives, SSDs, or network boot options) from which the operating system will be loaded.

Beyond basic configuration, the BIOS is instrumental in hardware troubleshooting. For instance, if a server fails to boot or hardware malfunctions, the BIOS may generate error codes or beeps that help technicians diagnose and address the underlying issues. This level of control and insight into the server's hardware makes the BIOS a crucial tool for both daily management and technical troubleshooting, ensuring smooth operation and minimizing downtime in the event of startup problems. A solid understanding of the BIOS and its functions is essential for any server administrator aiming to maintain and troubleshoot servers effectively.

Unified Extensible Firmware Interface

The **Unified Extensible Firmware Interface** (**UEFI**) is the modern successor to the traditional BIOS, offering enhanced functionality and flexibility for today's servers. Unlike BIOS, which is limited to 16-bit processor modes and can only access a small portion of system memory during the boot process, UEFI supports both 32-bit and 64-bit processor modes, allowing it to fully utilize the server's memory and provide faster, more efficient boot times. As illustrated in *Figure 12.2*, UEFI's architecture allows for greater versatility and improved system performance.

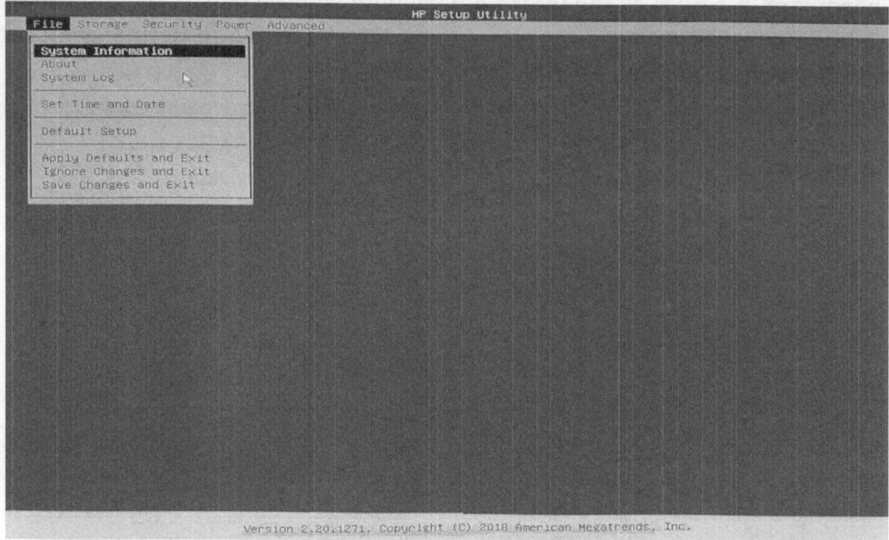

***Figure 12.2:** UEFI in a computer system*

One of UEFI's key advantages is its use of the **GUID Partition Table** (**GPT**) instead of the older **Master Boot Record** (**MBR**). This shift enables UEFI to support larger storage devices, allowing servers to boot from disks greater than 2 TB in size, something that is increasingly necessary as data storage demands grow. This makes UEFI especially valuable for modern servers that need to handle massive volumes of data and storage.

Another significant feature of UEFI is its ability to be easily updated. Unlike BIOS, which often requires manual updates through more cumbersome methods, UEFI firmware updates can be conveniently downloaded from the manufacturer's website and installed directly on the server. This ensures that administrators can quickly apply security patches, bug fixes, or feature enhancements, helping to keep the system secure and up to date.

UEFI also offers better security features, such as Secure Boot, which helps prevent malware from loading during the startup process by ensuring only trusted software and firmware are executed. As servers become more critical to business operations, understanding and utilizing UEFI's full capabilities is essential for server administrators aiming to enhance both performance and security in their IT environments.

Trusted Platform Module

The **Trusted Platform Module (TPM***)* is a specialized security chip embedded in the motherboard that plays a critical role in securing modern servers by enabling hardware-based encryption. As shown in *Figure 12.3,* TPM is particularly important when used in conjunction with BitLocker, Microsoft's disk encryption feature, to safeguard sensitive data. By storing cryptographic keys securely in hardware, TPM adds an extra layer of protection, ensuring that encryption keys are only accessible if the system's integrity has not been compromised.

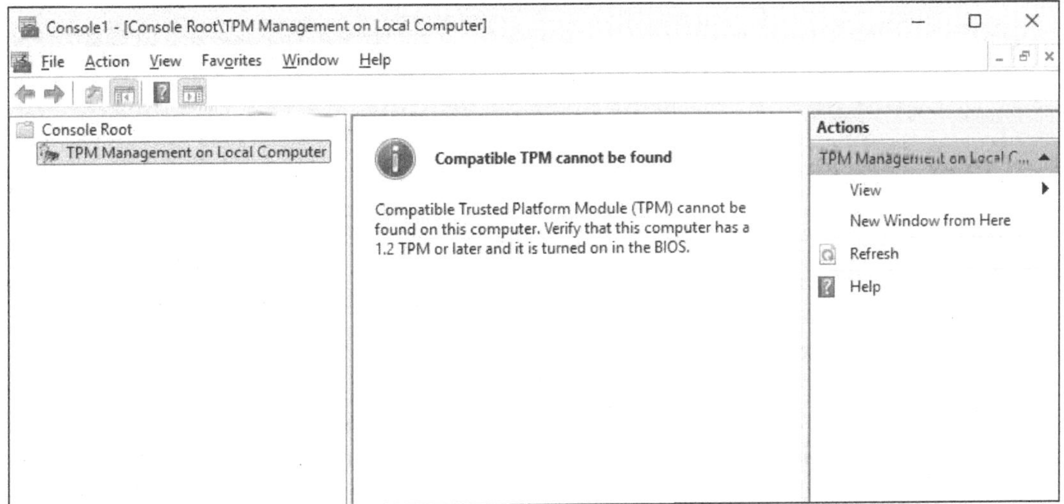

Figure 12.3: *TPM in Windows Server 2025*

One of TPM's primary functions is to verify the integrity of key startup components, such as the BIOS, boot sector, and boot manager. During the boot process, TPM checks these components to ensure that no unauthorized modifications have been made. If everything appears unchanged and secure, TPM releases the decryption key to the Windows operating system's bootloader, allowing the system to start normally.

However, if TPM detects any alterations, such as unauthorized changes to the BIOS or boot sector, it will withhold the decryption key, blocking access to any volumes protected by BitLocker. This mechanism ensures that even if malicious actors try to tamper with the startup process, the disk remains encrypted and protected, preventing unauthorized access to critical data.

This combination of hardware-based security and encryption makes TPM an essential tool for organizations looking to secure their servers and sensitive information. It provides robust protection against attacks targeting the startup process and helps maintain the overall integrity of the server environment. TPM's role in ensuring secure booting and protecting against physical tampering makes it a fundamental component of modern server security strategies.

Power-On Self-Test

The **Power-On Self-Test (POST)**, as in *Figure 12.4*, is a crucial diagnostic process initiated by the BIOS when a server is powered on. Its primary function is to ensure that all key hardware components are functioning properly before the operating system begins to load. During the POST, the BIOS performs a series of checks on essential hardware, including processors, memory, and graphics cards—these are typically the first components examined. If any issues are detected, the system will generate specific beep codes or display error messages, alerting users to potential hardware failures.

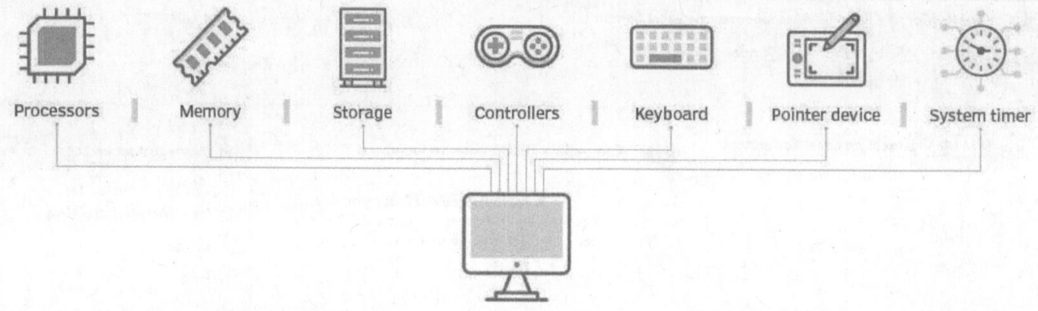

Figure 12.4: *POSTs hardware diagnostics (Source: TechTarget)*

These audible signals, often referred to as **POST beeps**, serve as diagnostic clues that can help users and technicians quickly identify hardware problems during server initialization. For instance, a specific beep pattern might indicate an issue with memory, while another could signal a problem with the graphics card. Being familiar with these beep codes can be invaluable in troubleshooting hardware issues early in the startup process, potentially preventing more significant problems down the line.

It is particularly important for users to pay close attention to the POST process, as it provides a clear indication of the system's health. A successful POST, without any beeps or error codes, confirms that the server hardware is in good working condition and ready for operation. On the other hand, any irregularities during POST should be addressed immediately to avoid further complications. This proactive approach not only minimizes downtime but also helps maintain the overall stability and reliability of the server environment.

Master Boot Record

The MBR plays a critical role in the server boot process after the POST confirms that the server's hardware is functioning correctly. Once POST is completed, the BIOS transfers control to the first boot device, which could be a hard drive, SSD, or other bootable media. The MBR, located outside of the disk's partitions, is responsible for identifying the operating system and initiating the boot process. It is created during the partitioning of a disk and contains essential information for locating and loading the OS.

In practice, the MBR holds key components such as the **NT Loader** (**NTLDR**) or **boot manager** (**BOOTMGR**), which work together to launch the appropriate Windows operating system installed on the server. The specific BOOTMGR depends on the version of Windows in use. For instance, older versions of Windows might rely on NTLDR, whereas more modern versions utilize BOOTMGR.

Understanding the MBR's structure, as illustrated in *Figure 12.5*, is vital for server administrators, as any corruption in the MBR can prevent the operating system from loading, resulting in boot failures. To safeguard against such issues, administrators often use disk imaging or backup tools that can restore the MBR in case of failure. This is particularly important when managing critical systems where server uptime is a priority.

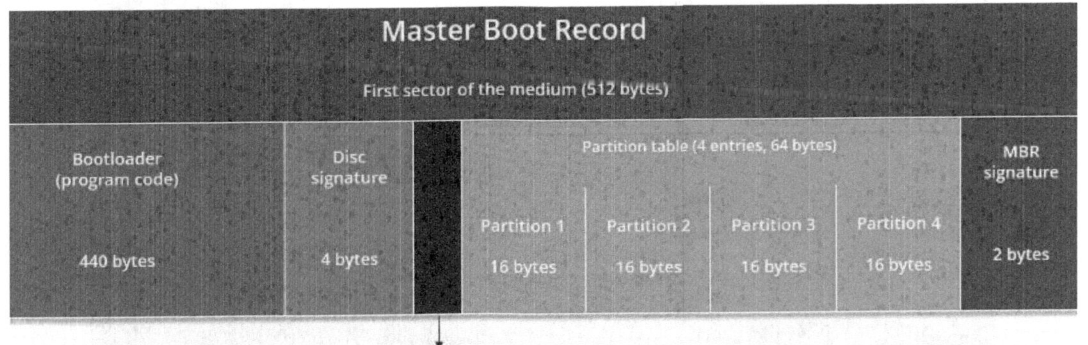

***Figure 12.5:** MBR structure (Source: IONOS)*

Boot Configuration Data

The **Boot Configuration Data** (**BCD**), as illustrated in *Figure 12.6*, is a vital component in modern Windows operating systems, functioning as a repository of files that dictate how the operating system boots. BCD provides a unified interface for managing boot options across recent versions of Windows, ranging from Windows Vista to Windows Server 2025. Unlike older boot mechanisms such as Boot.ini, which was specific to BIOS-based systems, BCD operates independently of the underlying firmware, making it compatible with both BIOS and UEFI.

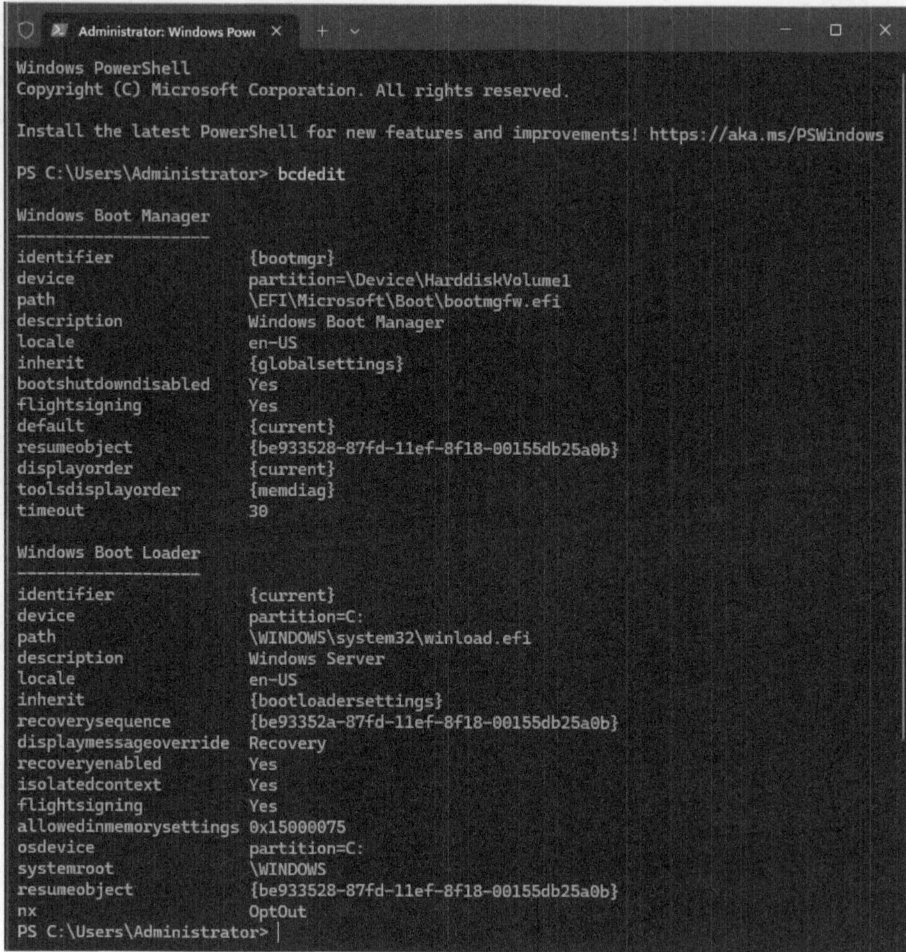

Figure 12.6: *BCDedit.exe in Windows Server 2025*

One significant advantage of BCD is its enhanced security features. Unlike Boot.ini, BCD allows administrators to assign permissions for managing boot options, ensuring that only authorized personnel can modify critical boot parameters. This added layer of protection is essential for preventing unauthorized changes that could disrupt system startup or compromise the server's security. Administrators can utilize tools like BCDEdit to modify and manage BCD settings, which can be particularly useful in scenarios such as dual-booting or troubleshooting startup issues.

For instance, if a system fails to boot properly due to a misconfiguration, an administrator can use BCD to adjust the boot sequence or repair corrupted boot files. This flexibility ensures that the boot process remains secure and adaptable, helping to minimize downtime and maintain smooth server operations. Therefore, understanding and managing BCD is crucial for maintaining server uptime and preventing boot-related failures in Windows Server 2025.

Bootloader

The **bootloader**, commonly referred to as a bootstrap loader or BOOTMGR, is a crucial software component that initiates the booting process of a computer following the successful completion of the POST, which checks the functionality of the hardware. Once POST confirms that the hardware is operational, the bootloader is activated to load the Windows operating system kernel into memory, enabling the system to start up properly. In the Windows ecosystem, there are two primary types of bootloaders: NTLDR, used for versions ranging from Windows NT to Windows Server 2003, and BOOTMGR, which is utilized in Windows Vista through to Windows Server 2025. The transition from NTLDR to BOOTMGR marked a significant advancement in the boot process. BOOTMGR offers improved functionality, including support for newer technologies like the BCD store. This allows for enhanced management of boot options and increased security measures, ensuring a more robust startup experience for users and administrators alike. Understanding the role of bootloaders is essential for IT professionals when troubleshooting boot issues or configuring multi-boot environments in Windows Server 2025.

Boot sector

The **boot sector** is a critical component located on a server's disk, housing the essential information needed to initiate the boot process for that server. Specifically, it resides in the first sector of the first track of the disk. This sector typically contains the MBR, which includes the bootloader responsible for starting the operating system. On a disk, tracks can be visualized as concentric circles, each divided into smaller units called sectors. The number of tracks can vary widely, and the size of each sector is determined by the file system employed by the server's operating system. Understanding the structure and function of the boot sector is vital for IT professionals, especially when configuring systems, troubleshooting boot failures, or implementing disk management strategies. For instance, knowing how to access and modify the boot sector can aid in recovering a server that fails to start due to boot configuration issues.

Boot menu

The **boot menu**, depicted in *Figure 12.7*, is an essential feature for systems configured for multi-booting, where multiple Windows operating systems are installed on a single computer. Each time the computer is powered on, a boot list is presented, showcasing all the installed operating systems, allowing users to choose which one to load. In earlier versions of Windows, this functionality was managed by the boot.ini file, located in the root of the primary disk partition, typically designated as `C:\boot.ini`. This file outlines various boot options, including the bootloader and the operating systems available for selection. However, in Windows Vista and later versions, the boot.ini file has been replaced by the BCD, which provides a more robust and flexible method for managing boot options. The transition from boot.ini to BCD not only enhances security but also simplifies the management of complex boot scenarios, making it easier for IT professionals to configure and troubleshoot multi-boot environments.

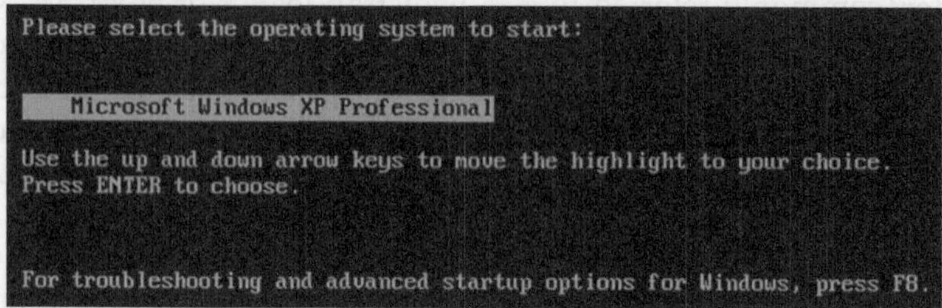

Figure 12.7: Boot menu in action

Safe Mode

Safe Mode serves as a critical diagnostic feature in Windows operating systems, allowing users to start their system with a minimal set of drivers and services. This mode is particularly useful for troubleshooting when users encounter malfunctions or issues that prevent the operating system from functioning correctly. In earlier versions of Windows, users could access Safe Mode by pressing the *F8* key during startup, which brought up the Windows Advanced Options Menu, from where they could select the Safe Mode option. However, starting with Windows Vista and continuing through to Windows Server 2022, this method has changed. Instead, these versions use the Advanced Startup Options menu for system recovery, which includes the option to boot into Safe Mode. As for Windows Server 2025, the *F8* key is no longer a viable option for accessing Safe Mode; instead, users can access recovery options through the **Windows Recovery Environment** (**WinRE**), as shown in *Figure 12.8*. This environment can be initiated by selecting the appropriate option during the boot process and offering various recovery tools, including Safe Mode, to help diagnose and fix issues effectively.

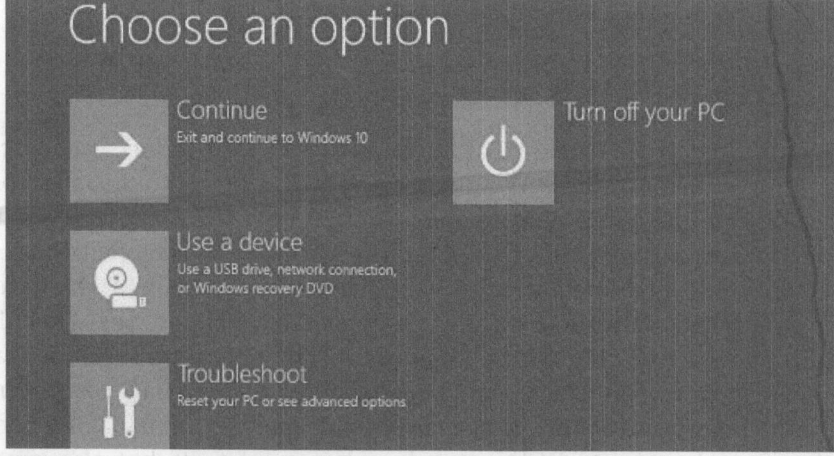

Figure 12.8: WinRe in Windows Server 2025

Ensuring business continuity and disaster recovery

In today's technology-centric landscape, system administrators must understand the significant impact downtime can have on a company's finances. Thus, one of your foremost responsibilities is to minimize any potential disruptions. To accomplish this, it is essential to evaluate the various components of your systems that may be vulnerable to failure and implement strategies to mitigate these risks. By proactively identifying these weak points and instituting preventive measures, such as regular maintenance checks, system redundancies, and robust backup solutions, you can significantly reduce the likelihood of downtime. This not only enhances system reliability but also contributes to the overall productivity of the organization, ultimately minimizing the financial losses associated with unexpected system failures.

Understanding the disaster recovery plan

A **disaster recovery plan** (**DRP**) is a comprehensive strategy designed to help businesses quickly recover from unexpected events, such as cyberattacks, hardware failures, or natural disasters while ensuring that essential services continue with minimal interruption. Although disasters cannot always be avoided, a well-prepared DRP can significantly reduce the impact on business operations and financial losses. For instance, if a data center experiences a fire, a solid DRP would include steps to switch operations to a backup site, minimizing downtime and allowing the company to resume critical functions.

Several practical steps are necessary when developing a DRP:

1. First, creating an inventory of all hardware and software ensures that all vital systems are accounted for. For example, if an organization's customer database is hosted on a specific server, this must be included in the inventory with details on its recovery plan.

2. Threats and vulnerabilities, such as power outages, cyberattacks, or human errors, should also be analyzed. An e-commerce company might prioritize the recovery of its payment processing system over less critical functions like internal email during an outage, setting clear recovery priorities.

3. Organizations must also define their tolerance for downtime, often referred to as the **recovery time objective** (**RTO**). For instance, a financial institution may tolerate only 15 minutes of downtime, while a smaller business may allow for several hours.

4. Reviewing how past incidents were handled provides valuable insights for improvement. For example, if a previous server crash took too long to resolve, the DRP might now include enhanced server monitoring tools or quicker failover mechanisms.

5. Regular testing of the DRP is essential. Conducting DRP **dry runs** ensures the plan works as intended in real-world scenarios. A company might simulate a ransomware attack to ensure its data backups are accessible and functional.

6. Involving staff in the testing process and ensuring they are trained to respond effectively can make a big difference. For example, IT teams should know how to activate backup systems, while communication teams should understand how to notify clients of the disruption.

7. Management approval is vital to ensure resources and support are available for executing the DRP, and frequent updates are necessary to accommodate changes in the company's IT infrastructure, such as new cloud services or software updates.

By implementing these steps, organizations can better prepare for unexpected events. System administrators play a crucial role in executing the DRP, ensuring that data is restored, systems are operational, and business operations can continue without significant disruption. For example, in the event of a server failure, the administrator would follow the DRP steps to switch to backup servers, restore lost data, and notify key stakeholders of progress, ensuring the organization returns to normal operations as quickly as possible.

Understanding data redundancy

Data redundancy involves storing identical copies of data in multiple locations to ensure availability and continuity in the event of hardware failure or data corruption. This method allows for automatic updates across all storage locations, but it is essential to consider the potential risks when these updates fail. If updates do not propagate successfully, data inconsistency can occur, where different versions of the same data exist in multiple locations. This inconsistency can lead to more severe problems like data integrity issues, where the accuracy and trustworthiness of the data are compromised.

For instance, in a financial institution where transaction records are mirrored across different databases for redundancy, a failed update could result in conflicting records—one showing a completed transaction while the other does not. Such inconsistencies can undermine the reliability of business-critical data, potentially causing operational delays, regulatory non-compliance, and loss of trust from stakeholders.

To prevent these problems, organizations must carefully design and monitor their data redundancy strategies. This includes using reliable replication technologies, ensuring that backup systems are regularly tested, and implementing mechanisms to detect and resolve inconsistencies as they arise. Additionally, having a solid contingency plan in place, such as procedures for data reconciliation or restoring from a known good backup, can mitigate the risks associated with data inconsistency or integrity failures. For example, if a cloud storage update fails, the system could revert to a previous backup while the issue is resolved, minimizing disruptions to business operations.

Understanding clustering

Clustering is a crucial technique that enhances service availability and reliability by harnessing the collective power of multiple servers. It combines the processing power, memory, storage, and network resources of these servers to work as a unified system, ensuring services remain uninterrupted even when individual components fail. This method is essential for critical applications where downtime can have severe financial or operational impacts. There are two commonly used types of clustering:

- **Failover clustering** is typically used in back-end services like databases, file servers, or email servers. In this setup, at least two servers are configured in an active-passive arrangement. One server (the active node) handles all requests, while the other (the passive node) stands by, ready to take over if the active node fails. For example, in a SQL Server failover cluster, if the primary node encounters a hardware failure or software crash, the secondary node immediately takes over, ensuring users experience little to no downtime. This is crucial for services that require high availability, such as banking applications or enterprise email systems, where even minutes of downtime could lead to significant losses.

- **Load-balancing clustering** is often used in front-end services like web servers or application servers, where multiple servers are grouped into a virtual pool to share the incoming load. Each request from users is distributed among the available servers to optimize performance and prevent any single server from being overwhelmed. A practical example is an e-commerce website during a sale event. Without load balancing, one server could become overloaded with thousands of requests, slowing down the site or causing crashes. In a load-balanced cluster, the traffic is intelligently distributed across multiple servers, ensuring that users can continue browsing and making purchases without delay. **Amazon Web Services** (**AWS**) or Microsoft Azure often employ this technique to maintain uptime during high-traffic periods.

For users accessing these services, the clustering process is invisible—they interact with what seems like a single server. However, behind the scenes, failover and load-balancing mechanisms ensure that the service remains uninterrupted, even if a server fails or traffic spikes. For businesses, this means greater uptime, reduced risk of service disruption, and enhanced user satisfaction. In high-stakes industries such as healthcare, financial services, or large-scale e-commerce platforms, clustering is a critical strategy for maintaining operational continuity, regardless of server or network failures.

To further improve reliability, organizations may also combine both clustering types, using load-balancing for the front-end web services and failover clustering for the back-end database, ensuring a robust, end-to-end high availability system.

Understanding folder redirection

Folder redirection is a valuable feature for system administrators, allowing them to move the contents of a user's local folders, such as Documents, Downloads, or Desktop, to a different location, typically a shared network folder. This setup enables users to access their files from multiple devices or workstations, as the data is stored centrally on the network rather than locally on their machines. For example, if an employee saves a file to their `Documents` folder, instead of being stored on their computer's hard drive, it is redirected and stored on a secure server location. This has several practical benefits:

- First, it enhances **data accessibility**, employees can log in from different workstations and still have access to their files as if they were saved locally.
- Second, it significantly improves **data security and backup processes**. Since user data is stored centrally on a secure server, administrators can quickly implement regular backups and security policies. For instance, in the event of hardware failure or a lost device, critical documents remain safe on the network, reducing the risk of data loss.
- Lastly, folder redirection helps with **resource management**, as large amounts of data are stored on the server, freeing up storage space on individual computers, which can improve performance.

Overall, folder redirection simplifies file management for both users and administrators by centralizing data storage and enhancing accessibility, security, and disaster recovery capabilities. It is a particularly effective solution in environments where employees frequently move between devices or where data security is a priority, such as in large enterprises or educational institutions.

Exercise 12.1: Configuring folder redirection in Server 2025

This exercise outlines the process for setting up a **Group Policy Object** (**GPO**) to configure folder redirection in Windows Server 2025. Folder redirection is a valuable feature for centralizing user data, enhancing accessibility, and improving data security by storing important files on a network location instead of local machines. To do so, complete the following steps:

1. Press the *Windows key + R*, enter `gpmc.msc`, and press *Enter* to access the Group Policy Management Console.
2. Expand User Configuration, then Policies, then Windows Settings, and finally, Folder Redirection.
3. Right-click on the Documents folder and choose **Properties** from the menu.

4. Select the Basic - Redirect everyone's folder to the same location setting, as shown in *Figure 12.9*.
5. In the Target folder location section, choose Redirect to the following Location.
6. Enter the root path to your redirected folder.
7. Click **OK** to close the **Document Properties** window and complete the folder redirection process.

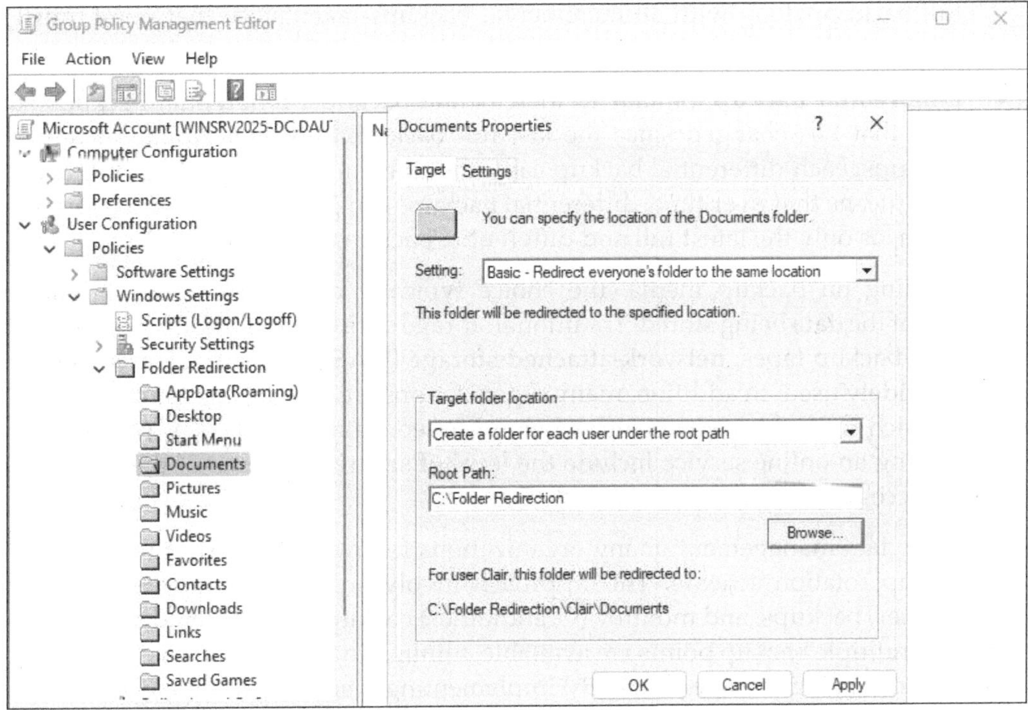

***Figure 12.9:** Setting up Group Policy Folder Redirection Setup in Windows Server 2025*

Overview of backup and restore

Ensuring the protection of data on servers is one of the most critical responsibilities for system administrators. The primary safeguard against data loss is implementing regular **backups**, which involve creating copies of data that can be used in case of hardware failure, corruption, or accidental deletion. Equally important is the ability to restore data effectively, which means recovering lost or corrupted data and returning systems to a functional state. Organizations can use various types of backups, depending on their specific needs and recovery strategies.

- **Full backup:** A full backup involves making a complete copy of all the data on a server. It is the most comprehensive form of backup, as all files and configurations are captured. Restoring from a full backup is straightforward because only the latest set of full backups is required to recover the system, making this approach the fastest to restore but the most time-consuming to create.

- **Incremental backup**: This method saves only the data that has changed since the last backup, whether it was full or incremental. For instance, incremental backups are typically scheduled Monday through Thursday, with a full backup on Friday. While incremental backups are quicker to perform and require less storage space, restoring data can be more complex. To restore to a specific point, the most recent full backup, along with all incremental backups taken since that point, must be used, which can extend the recovery time.
- **Differential backup**: Similar to incremental backups, differential backups store data that has changed since the last full backup. However, unlike incremental backups, each differential backup captures all changes since the last full backup. This means that over time, differential backups can grow in size, but restoration is faster, as only the latest full and differential backups are required.

When deciding on backup media, the choice typically depends on the volume and importance of the data being stored. Traditional storage options like CDs, DVDs, removable hard drives, backup tapes, **network-attached storage** (**NAS**), and **storage area networks** (**SAN**) are widely used. In addition, many organizations are now opting for online backup services, which offer the convenience of cloud-based data storage. Key considerations when selecting an online service include the level of security, the cost of the service, and the ease of access.

For effective data management, many organizations follow the **Grandfather-Father-Son** (**GFS**) backup rotation scheme. This approach involves creating daily (Son) backups, weekly (Father) backups, and monthly (Grandfather) backups. This layered strategy helps ensure that multiple backup points are available, minimizing the risk of losing critical data while also optimizing storage usage. By implementing a solid backup and restore plan, system administrators can significantly reduce the risk of data loss and ensure business continuity in the event of a disaster.

Exercise 12.2: Adding Windows Server Backup in 2025

This exercise guides you through the process of adding the Windows Server Backup feature in Windows Server 2025 using the Server Manager tool. This feature is crucial for system administrators to perform routine backups, ensuring data integrity and allowing for recovery in case of system failures or data loss. To do so, complete the following steps:

1. Open the Run dialog box by pressing the *Windows key* + *R*, typing in `servermanager.exe`, and pressing *Enter*.
2. From the Server Manager console, select **Add Roles and Features**.
3. In the Before You Begin option, click **Next**.

4. In the **Installation Type** step, select Role-based or feature-based installation.
5. Select a server from the server pool in the Server Selection option and click **Next**.
6. Skip the Server Roles step by clicking **Next**.
7. In the Features step, scroll down the list, select Windows Server Backup (refer to *Figure 12.10*), and click **Next**.
8. In the Confirmation option, click **Install**.
9. After the installation, click **Close** to exit the Add Roles and Features Wizard.

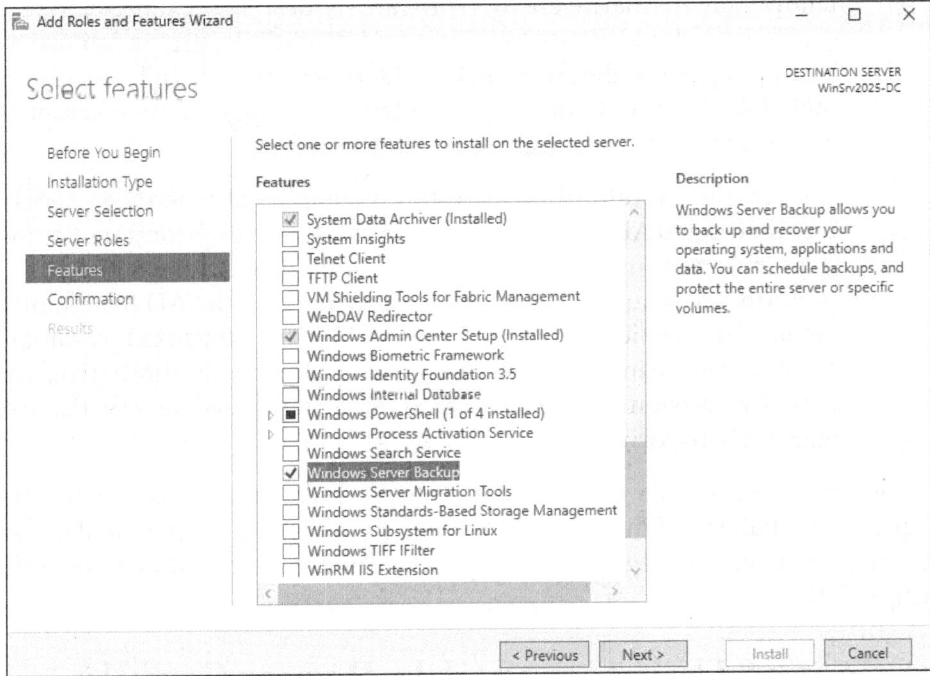

Figure 12.10: *Adding Windows Server Backup feature in Windows Server 2025*

Understanding Directory Services Restore Mode

During the **Active Directory Domain Services** (**AD DS**) Configuration Wizard, you will be prompted to set a **Directory Services Restore Mode** (**DSRM**) password, which is essential for restoring **Active Directory** (**AD**) when issues arise. Similar to Safe Mode in Windows operating systems, DSRM is specifically designed to troubleshoot and recover AD. There are two primary methods for restoring replicated data on a **Domain Controller** (**DC**):

- The **first method** involves reinstalling the operating system, reconfiguring the DC, and then allowing normal replication to occur from another DC within the network. For instance, if a DC fails due to a hardware malfunction, such as a hard drive crash, the administrator would reinstall the OS on the affected server, re-promote it as a DC, and then wait for the system to pull the necessary data from a backup or another operational DC. This method can be time-consuming and requires careful planning to ensure service continuity, especially in larger environments with multiple DCs.

- The **second method** leverages a backup to restore the replicated data on the DC. This can be performed through either a non-authoritative or an authoritative restore.
  - A **non-authoritative restore** is typically used when a DC has experienced failure due to hardware or software issues. For example, if a DC is compromised and needs to be restored, the administrator can use a recent backup to restore the AD structure. Once restored, it will synchronize with other DCs in the environment to update any changes made after the backup is taken, thus restoring the DC to a functional state.
  - Conversely, an **authoritative restore** is employed when it is necessary to recover deleted AD objects or restore the system to its prior state. For instance, if an important user account is accidentally deleted, the administrator can perform a non-authoritative restore to bring back the AD to a point in time before the deletion occurred. Then, using the **`Ntdsutil`** command, the administrator can mark the specific user object as authoritative, ensuring that this version of the user account is replicated across the network, effectively restoring it to all other DCs.

Understanding these methods is crucial for system administrators, as it helps maintain the integrity and reliability of the AD environment. By preparing for potential failures and having a clear recovery strategy, organizations can minimize downtime and safeguard their critical data.

Overview of Uninterruptible Power Supply

The **power supply** is an essential component of any server infrastructure, regardless of its processing capabilities, memory size, or data storage capacity. Without a reliable energy source, servers become inoperable, leading to potential data loss and service interruptions. To guarantee a continuous and stable power supply, an **Uninterruptible Power Supply (UPS)** is indispensable. A UPS is a battery-operated device that provides immediate backup power to the server during outages, allowing for a seamless transition and preventing abrupt shutdowns. However, it is important to note that UPS devices are designed to support systems only for a limited duration, typically ranging from a few minutes to a couple of hours, depending on the load and the battery capacity.

For extended power outages, electric generators serve as a viable alternative, ensuring that critical operations can continue without interruption. For instance, in a data center where uptime is paramount, combining a UPS with a generator creates a robust power management system. UPS can provide immediate backup power during the initial moments of an outage, while the generator can be activated to sustain power for a more extended period. This layered approach is essential for mission-critical servers that cannot afford any downtime, such as those hosting financial transactions or healthcare systems. By investing in both a UPS and a generator, organizations can effectively mitigate the risks associated with power disruptions and maintain operational continuity.

Updating OS, drivers, and applications for security

Following the installation of the Windows operating system, it is crucial to utilize the Windows Update service to check for and apply any available updates. This practice not only safeguards the system against potential cyber threats but also addresses existing bugs and vulnerabilities within the operating system. Windows Server 2025, like its predecessors, requires regular updates to improve its functionality, introduce new features, and ensure that drivers for specific hardware components are current. For example, if a server is running outdated drivers for its **network interface card** (**NIC**), it may experience connectivity issues that could hinder overall performance. By consistently updating the operating system and its associated drivers, users can enhance system security, improve stability, and optimize performance. Therefore, keeping the OS up to date is one of the most vital tasks to undertake after setting up a new or refurbished server, as it lays the foundation for a secure and efficient operational environment.

Windows Update explained

Windows Update is a crucial service provided by Microsoft that ensures the operating systems and applications, including Windows Server 2025, are up to date with the latest features, security enhancements, and critical fixes. Microsoft typically releases these updates on the second Tuesday of each month, a schedule referred to as *Patch Tuesday*. These updates are designed to address vulnerabilities, improve system performance, and introduce new functionalities that can enhance the overall user experience.

Updates are distributed through Microsoft's Windows Update server, which can be easily accessed via the Windows Update feature on the server or through the official Microsoft website. Users will receive notifications about available updates in the system tray and Notification Center, allowing for a proactive approach to system management.

In Windows Server 2025, users can manage updates by navigating to the Update & Security settings, mirroring the process found in Windows Server 2022. The Windows Update page, as shown in *Figure 12.11*, has been refined with a new theme and additional options that provide users with greater control over the update process. For example, users can get the latest updates as soon as they are available, pause updates for up to seven days to avoid interruptions during critical operational periods, review update history for transparency, and select advanced options to set delivery optimization, optional updates, active hours and other update settings.

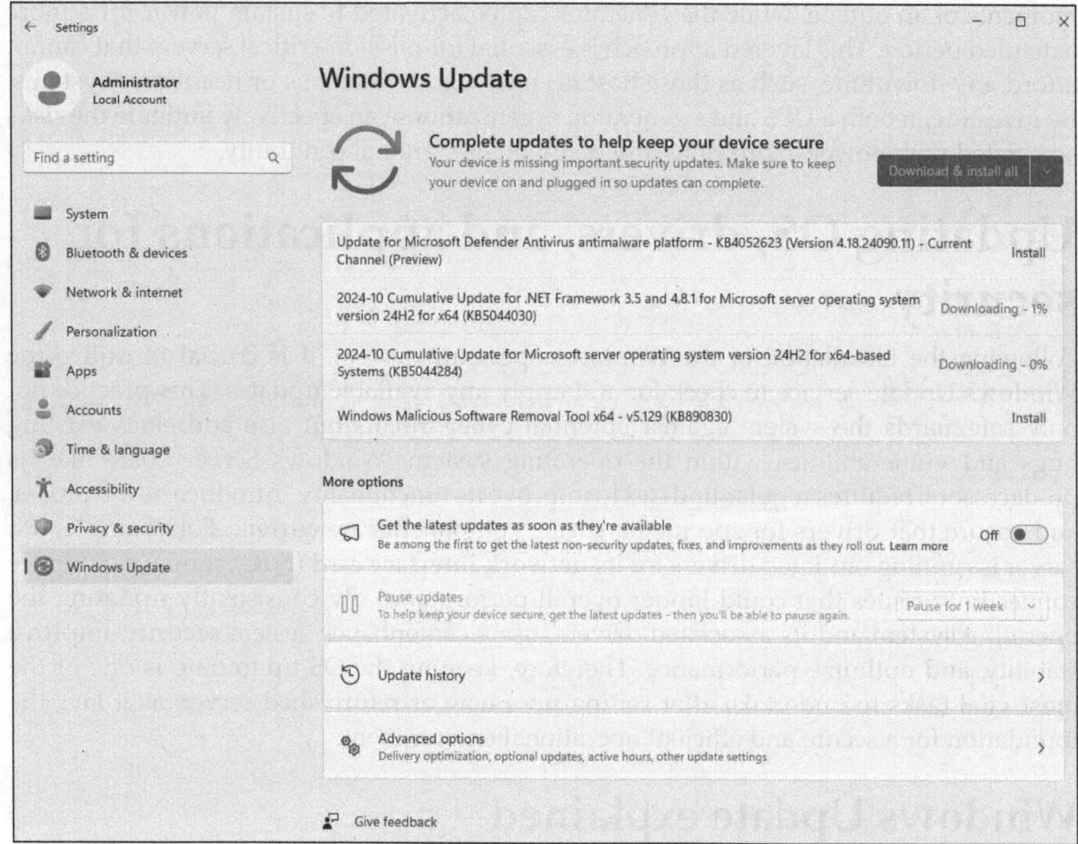

Figure 12.11: Updating Windows Server 2025 through Windows Update

Moreover, users can receive updates for other Microsoft products, such as Microsoft Office or Windows Defender, during the Windows update process, ensuring that all aspects of the system are secured and functioning optimally. It is also possible to defer feature updates, allowing organizations to maintain stability by controlling when new features are implemented in their environment.

Regularly installing updates is not just a matter of convenience; it is a fundamental aspect of system security and operational efficiency. For instance, updates often include patches for recently discovered vulnerabilities that malicious actors could exploit. By staying up-to-date, organizations can protect themselves from cyber threats, improve system performance by resolving known bugs, and take advantage of new features that can enhance productivity. In a practical scenario, a business that promptly applies updates may find its systems running more smoothly, reducing downtime and ensuring that employees can access the tools they need without interruption. Windows Update plays an indispensable role in maintaining the integrity, security, and functionality of Windows Server environments, making it an essential task for system administrators to prioritize.

Updating Microsoft Programs guide

Updating Microsoft Programs, illustrated in *Figure 12.12*, on a server running Windows Server 2025 is a critical aspect of maintaining system performance and security. Various client/server applications, such as Microsoft Exchange, SQL Server, and SharePoint, serve distinct functions like managing emails, handling databases, and facilitating team collaboration. Regular updates for these applications are vital as they not only introduce new features and functionalities but also address vulnerabilities that cyber threats could exploit.

***Figure 12.12:** Updating Microsoft Programs in Windows Server 2025*

To update these programs, system administrators can utilize the built-in update features available within each application or manage updates through the Microsoft Update service. For instance, Microsoft Exchange includes an **Exchange Admin Center** (**EAC**) where administrators can check for updates and apply them directly, ensuring that the email system remains secure and performs efficiently. Similarly, **SQL Server Management Studio** (**SSMS**) provides options for updating the database engine and its components, which can enhance query performance and improve overall database management.

In addition to in-application updates, it is advisable to regularly monitor the Microsoft Download Center or the official Microsoft website for any patches or updates specific to these programs. For example, SharePoint updates might include important security fixes or performance improvements that enhance user collaboration experiences.

Furthermore, organizations can implement automated update solutions for their Microsoft programs to streamline the update process and minimize downtime. By scheduling updates during off-peak hours, administrators can ensure that critical services remain available while still keeping the software current. Staying proactive with updates for Microsoft programs is essential for safeguarding systems against vulnerabilities, optimizing performance, and leveraging the latest features that can drive business efficiency.

Importance of updating non-Microsoft programs

It is important to update third-party programs running on a server powered by Windows Server 2022, in addition to Microsoft programs. Examples of such programs include Oracle database, Apache web server, and VMware ESXi. The article highlights that while Microsoft programs are usually updated through the Windows Update feature, updating third-party programs can differ. That is because each software company has its unique way of developing software, which means the procedure for updating such software can also be exceptional. As such, system administrators need to understand the differences between Updating Microsoft Programs and third-party programs to ensure the server runs smoothly and securely. Regular updates to third-party programs can help improve performance, address vulnerabilities, and ensure compatibility with the latest OS updates.

Understanding Windows Server Update Services

Windows Server Update Services (WSUS) is the modern successor to **Software Update Services (SUS)**. It provides system administrators with a robust platform for managing the distribution of Microsoft product updates within their organizations. As illustrated in *Figure 12.13*, WSUS streamlines the update management process by allowing updates, patches, and fixes to be downloaded directly to an organization's server. This server acts as a central distribution point, pushing approved updates to client computers throughout the organization.

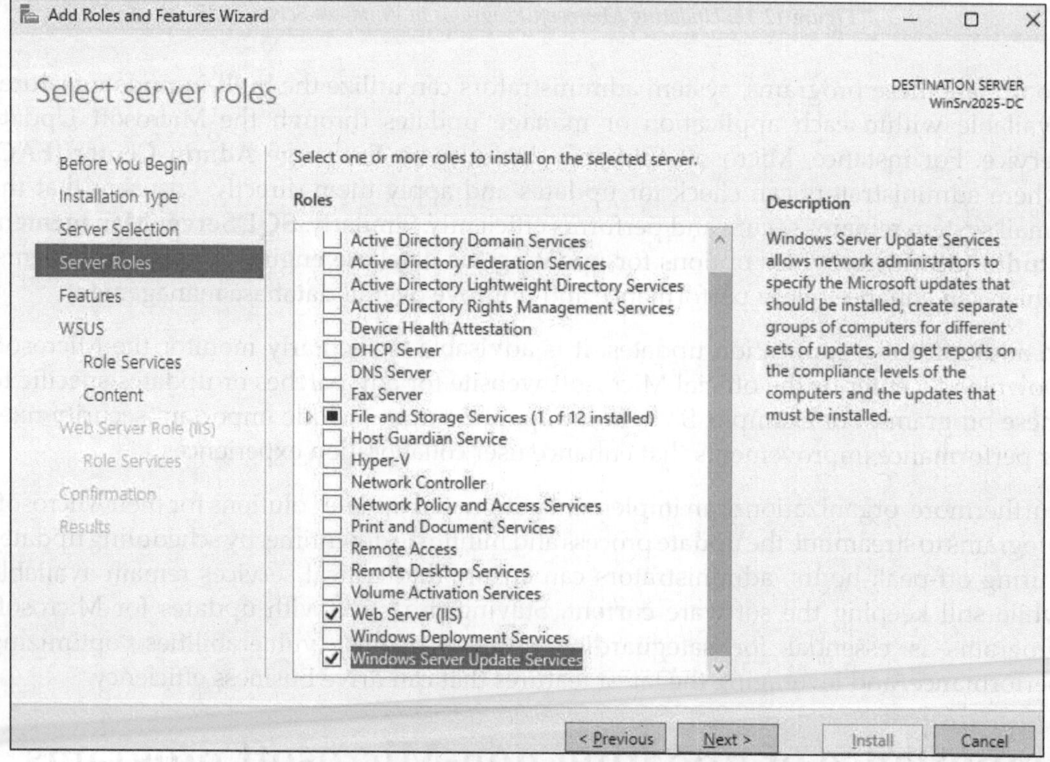

Figure 12.13: Adding WSUS in Windows Server 2025

With WSUS, administrators gain significant control over the update process; they can approve or decline updates based on their relevance and urgency. For example, if a critical security vulnerability is discovered in Windows Server 2025, the administrator can quickly approve the corresponding patch through WSUS to ensure all servers are protected. Additionally, WSUS enables the scheduling of installation dates to minimize disruptions during peak usage hours. For instance, an organization might choose to deploy updates overnight when users are not logged in, reducing the impact on productivity.

Moreover, WSUS allows administrators to generate detailed reports to assess which updates are pending for each machine, enabling them to identify systems that may be out of compliance. This is particularly useful in large environments, such as a university's IT infrastructure, where numerous devices need to be monitored. By utilizing WSUS, organizations can also ensure that their computers no longer need to connect directly to Microsoft Update, which reduces external network traffic and enhances security.

Note: Microsoft has announced plans to deprecate WSUS in future Windows Server releases. While WSUS will still be available in Windows Server 2025, organizations are encouraged to transition to cloud-based tools for managing updates. Microsoft Intune and Windows Autopatch are recommended for client management, while Azure Update Manager is suggested for servers.

This shift toward cloud-based solutions not only aims to enhance the update management process but also aligns with Microsoft's broader strategy of integrating more features into the cloud ecosystem. Transitioning to these modern tools will enable organizations to take advantage of more automated and streamlined update processes, further improving their operational efficiency and security posture.

Understanding troubleshooting errors and problems

Troubleshooting is an essential skill in the IT field that demands both practice and experience to become proficient. It involves diagnosing and resolving various issues that may arise within computer systems, networks, or applications. Each time an IT professional successfully addresses a problem, it not only boosts their confidence but also expands their knowledge and expertise. For instance, when troubleshooting a network connectivity issue, an IT technician may identify misconfigured settings or faulty hardware, learning valuable lessons along the way that they can apply to future challenges. This ongoing cycle of learning and hands-on experience is vital for developing proficiency in troubleshooting. By continuously honing their skills, IT professionals significantly enhance their ability to tackle complex issues efficiently, thereby improving system reliability and user satisfaction.

Understanding troubleshooting process

As highlighted previously, mastering the troubleshooting process is essential for server technicians. To facilitate this learning, CompTIA has introduced a widely adopted six-step troubleshooting model, which engineers in Microsoft product support also utilize. This structured approach includes several key steps:

1. **Identifying the issue:** The first step involves gathering relevant technical information. For instance, if users report that a specific application is running

slowly, the technician may utilize performance monitoring tools like Task Manager or Resource Monitor to check CPU and memory usage, looking for processes that are consuming excessive resources.

2. **Evaluating system configuration:** After identifying the symptoms, the technician assesses the system configuration by inquiring about recent changes. For example, they might ask users if any software updates were applied or if any new hardware was added recently, such as installing a new printer or a network device that could potentially cause conflicts.

3. **Listing and tracking possible solutions**: After a better understanding of the problem, the technician compiles a list of potential solutions. For example, if a server is experiencing intermittent connectivity issues, the technician may consider solutions such as checking network cables, reviewing switch configurations or assessing firewall rules. Each potential solution is documented, along with any relevant observations, to track progress effectively.

4. **Executing a plan and having a backup plan:** After formulating a strategy, the technician implements the chosen solution while preparing a backup plan to address unforeseen complications. For instance, if they decide to update the server's network drivers to resolve the connectivity issue, they should ensure they have the previous driver versions available for rollback if the update does not resolve the problem or introduces new issues.

5. **Checking the results:** Once the solution is implemented, the technician checks the results to evaluate the effectiveness of the fix. In the example of the application that was running slowly, they might run performance tests to compare metrics before and after the solution was applied, verifying that the application's response times have improved.

6. **Documenting changes**: Finally, adopting a proactive stance by documenting all changes made during the troubleshooting process is crucial for future reference. This documentation can include logging issues, resolutions, and any system changes. For example, suppose a misconfigured firewall rule was corrected to allow proper traffic flow. In that case, the technician should document the original rule, the changes made, and the subsequent effects on system performance. This creates a knowledge base that aids in quicker diagnosis of similar problems in the future.

By adhering to these steps, technicians can troubleshoot server-related issues methodically and efficiently, ultimately enhancing their likelihood of successful problem resolution. For instance, if a server is experiencing frequent downtime, following this model allows the technician to investigate and rectify the root cause systematically, be it a misconfiguration, a hardware failure, or network-related issues, thereby minimizing disruption to services. This structured approach not only builds the technician's confidence and skill set but also leads to a more reliable IT environment overall.

Understanding troubleshooting approaches

The effectiveness of the troubleshooting process largely hinges on the approach employed to address the issue at hand. Two primary methods can be distinguished: the systematic approach and the specific approach:

- The **systematic approach** follows a structured framework designed to tackle problems methodically. This methodology can be effectively applied to a wide range of situations, making it a versatile troubleshooting technique. It encompasses several key steps: first, identifying the problem by defining the symptoms; next, gathering relevant information to understand the context; then analyzing the data to pinpoint possible causes; followed by developing a detailed action plan; executing the plan to implement the solution; and finally, verifying the results to ensure the issue has been resolved. For instance, if a server experiences frequent crashes, a technician using the systematic approach would collect logs, analyze patterns, and test various components systematically until the root cause is identified and addressed.
- In contrast, the **specific approach** relies heavily on the technician's prior knowledge and experience with similar issues. This method involves using intuition and educated guesses to diagnose and resolve problems quickly. It is particularly beneficial when dealing with recurring issues or when the technician possesses specialized expertise in a particular domain. For example, suppose a technician has previously resolved network latency problems caused by a specific router configuration. In that case, they may quickly implement that same fix without needing to perform extensive diagnostics each time the issue arises.

Both approaches possess their strengths and weaknesses. The systematic approach ensures a thorough resolution process, reducing the likelihood of overlooking crucial factors, but it can be time-consuming. On the other hand, while the specific approach allows for rapid resolutions based on experience, it may lead to oversights if the technician encounters an issue that does not fit previous patterns. Ultimately, the choice of approach will depend on the nature of the problem and the technician's familiarity and expertise in the area, allowing for an informed and effective resolution strategy.

Understanding troubleshooting procedures

Effective troubleshooting requires a blend of expertise, experience, and a methodical approach to problem-solving. For server technicians, adhering to established guidelines and procedures is essential for efficiently diagnosing and resolving issues related to computers and servers. Several key techniques should be employed during the troubleshooting process:

- First, checking **documentation** related to the server and its configurations can provide insights into potential issues. For instance, reviewing the server's configuration documents may reveal mismatched settings that could be causing connectivity problems.

- Additionally, reviewing logs and the **Event Viewer** helps identify error messages and system events that could point to the root cause of a problem. For example, if a server crashes unexpectedly, technicians can investigate the Event Viewer logs to identify any warning messages or critical errors that occurred just before the crash, which can lead to a faster diagnosis.
- Another valuable resource is the wealth of information available in **knowledge-based articles**. These articles often contain solutions to common problems encountered by other users and can provide effective troubleshooting steps. For example, suppose a technician encounters a known issue with a particular version of the software. In that case, they might consult the vendor's knowledge base for patches or specific configuration changes that have resolved the problem for other users.
- Furthermore, utilizing specialized utility programs can significantly aid in diagnosing and resolving server issues. Key utilities include the **Advanced Boot Options** menu for troubleshooting startup problems, such as selecting **Safe Mode** to troubleshoot driver issues. **Windows Repair** can be employed to fix corrupted system files, while **Memory Diagnostics** checks for RAM-related issues that might be causing system instability.
- Other helpful tools, such as **System Information**, can provide a comprehensive overview of the system's hardware and software configurations, which is crucial when diagnosing compatibility issues. If a specific application is crashing, using **Device Manager** can help identify if there is an outdated or malfunctioning driver for a critical component. In cases of high CPU usage, **Task Manager** can be utilized to pinpoint which processes are consuming resources and take action accordingly, such as terminating a rogue application.
- Additionally, **Performance Monitor and Resource Monitor** can be used to track system performance over time and analyze resource allocation. For example, suppose a server is consistently running out of memory. In that case, technicians can use Resource Monitor to assess memory usage by different processes and identify which applications might need optimization or additional resources.

Ultimately, the success of the troubleshooting process hinges on the technician's ability to remain organized, systematic, and efficient throughout their problem-solving efforts. By employing a structured approach and leveraging various tools, technicians can effectively address issues, ensuring that server performance is maintained and downtime is minimized.

Understanding and utilizing the Event Viewer

The Event Viewer is an integral tool within the Windows operating system that enables system administrators to monitor and analyze server events effectively. It serves as a crucial resource for diagnosing issues related to software, hardware, and network performance that may affect the server's operation. Importantly, even in a system that is functioning correctly, the Event Viewer may display various warnings and errors, a reality well-understood by seasoned administrators. Therefore, system administrators need to grasp how to utilize this tool and recognize its potential applications in different scenarios.

The Event Viewer categorizes events into five distinct types of logs, each serving a specific purpose:

- **Application log**: This log records events pertinent to applications or software programs, helping administrators identify issues that may arise during application execution. For instance, if a critical business application crashes, the application log can reveal error codes or stack traces that assist in diagnosing the underlying problem.
- **Security log:** The security log captures security-related events, including failed login attempts and access denials for sensitive files or folders. This log is instrumental for monitoring unauthorized access attempts and ensuring compliance with security policies. For example, a sudden spike in invalid login attempts may indicate a potential security breach that requires immediate attention.
- **Setup log:** This log tracks events related to application installation and configuration. It can be especially useful during the deployment of new software, allowing administrators to review any issues that occurred during the setup process. If an installation fails, the setup log provides details that can help identify what went wrong.
- **System log**: The system log documents events generated by the Windows operating system components, such as driver failures or hardware malfunctions. This log is vital for understanding system-level issues. For instance, if a server experiences frequent crashes, examining the system log can reveal patterns related to specific hardware components that might need replacement or further investigation.
- **Forwarded events log**: This log is used to monitor events triggered by remote computers, which can be beneficial in environments with multiple servers. To utilize the forwarded events log, administrators must create an event subscription that specifies which remote events to monitor. This feature allows for centralized logging, making it easier to keep track of issues across multiple systems.

By effectively leveraging the Event Viewer and its logs, system administrators can gain invaluable insights into their server environments. This allows them to address potential issues proactively and ensure optimal system performance.

Exercise 12.3: Central monitoring configuration

This exercise guides you through the process of utilizing the Event Viewer in Windows Server 2025 for effective system monitoring and troubleshooting. The Event Viewer is an essential tool that allows administrators to review and manage event logs, providing critical insights into software, hardware, and network-related issues that can impact server performance. To do so, complete the following steps:

1. Launch the command prompt as an administrator on a remote server and enter `winrm quickconfig` to grant administrative rights to local users remotely.
2. Right-click the **Start** button and select **Computer Management**.
3. Expand Local Users and Groups and click on **Groups**.
4. Add the central server to the administrator's group.
5. Launch the command prompt as an administrator on the central server and enter `wecutil qc`.
6. Press *Y* when prompted to confirm the action.
7. Open Event Viewer by entering **eventvwr.exe** in the command prompt.
8. Right-click **Subscriptions** and select **Create Subscription...**
9. Enter the subscription name and description.
10. Select **Forwarded Events** as the destination log.
11. Click the **Select Computers** button to choose the remote server.
12. In the **Subscription Properties** window, click **Select Events**... and select **Edit**.
13. Set the event log filtering criteria in the Query Filter window.
14. Click **Advanced**... to make sure the machine account is selected.
15. Click **OK**, as shown in *Figure 12.14*, to complete the subscription setup.

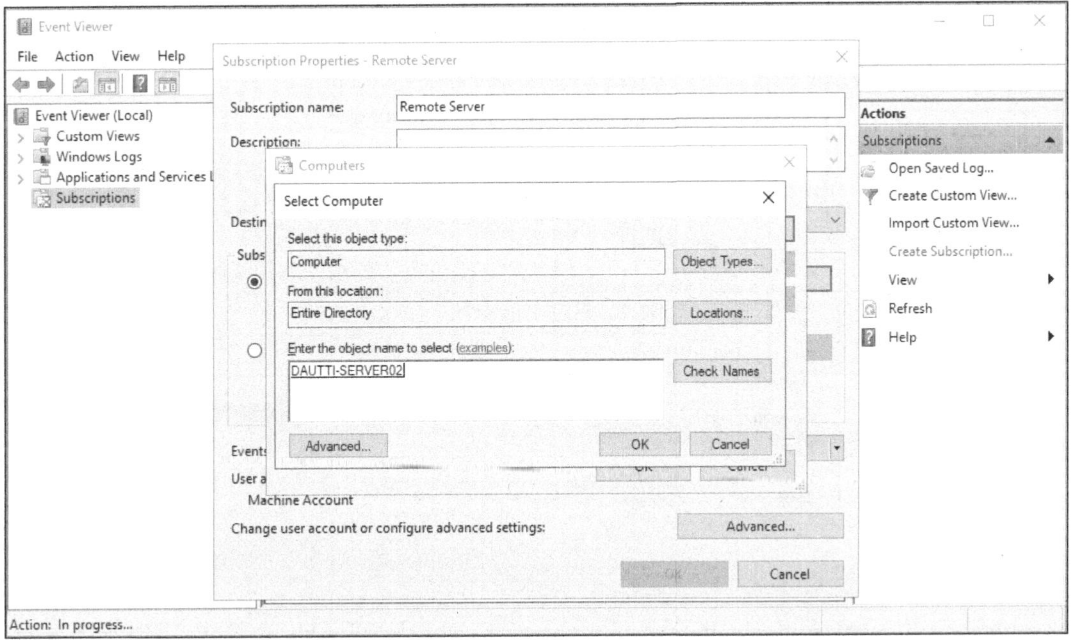

Figure 12.14: Central Monitoring Configuration over Event Viewer

Exercise 12.4: Event Viewer log filtering

This exercise outlines the procedure for filtering Event Viewer logs in Windows Server 2025. Filtering these logs is essential for effectively monitoring system events and isolating specific issues, such as application errors or security breaches. By focusing on relevant logs, administrators can streamline their troubleshooting process and enhance system performance. To do so, complete the following:

1. Press the *Windows key* + *R*, type **`eventvwr.msc`**, and press *Enter*.
2. Choose the type of log you want to filter from the expanded Windows Logs section.
3. Click on the Filter Current Log... option in the Actions pane, as shown in *Figure 12.15*.
4. Set the filtering criteria in the Filter Current Log window to get the desired results.
5. Click on **OK** to close the Filter Current Log window.

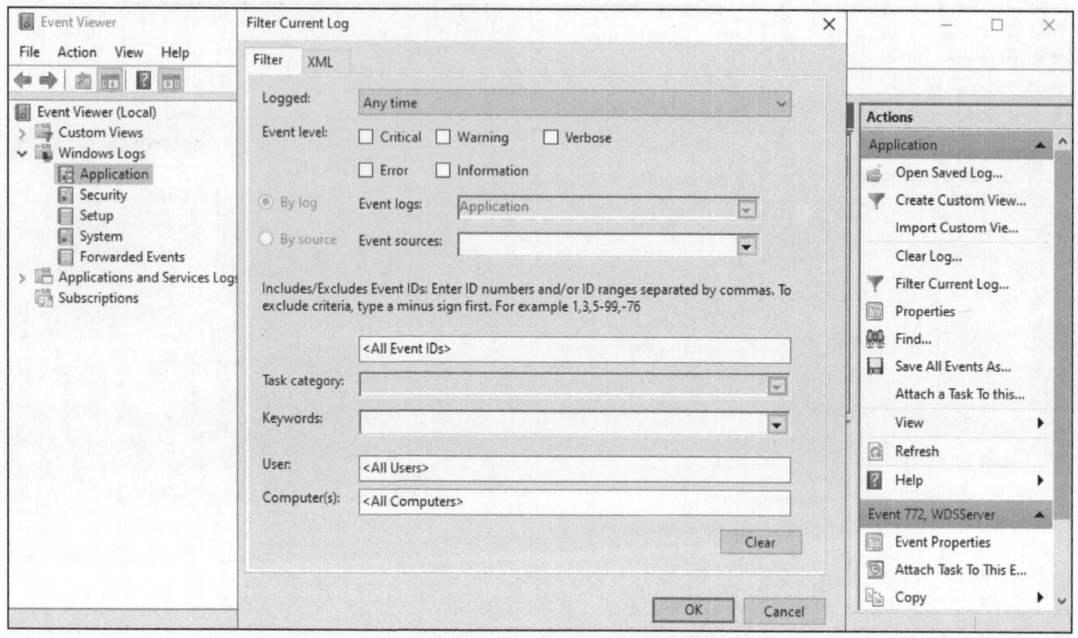

Figure 12.15: Event Viewer log filtering

Exercise 12.5: Log location configuration

This exercise guides you through the process of changing the default log locations in Windows Server 2025. Customizing the log storage location can enhance organization and accessibility, especially in environments with multiple servers or applications generating extensive logs. To do so, complete the following:

1. Press the *Windows key + R*, type **`regedit`**, and press *Enter* to open the Registry Editor.

2. Navigate to **`HKEY_LOCAL_MACHINE\System\CurrentControlSet\Services\EventLog\System`**.

3. Double-click on the File value, which is located inside the **`System`** folder.

4. In the Value data text box, enter the new path where you want to save the log files, and then click **OK**, as illustrated in *Figure 12.16*.

5. If you want to change the default location of application logs, navigate to **`HKEY_LOCAL_MACHINE\System\CurrentControlSet\Services\EventLog\Application`**.

6. If you want to change the default location of security logs, navigate to **`HKEY_LOCAL_MACHINE\System\CurrentControlSet\Services\EventLog\Security`**.

7. After making the desired changes, close the **Registry Editor** window.

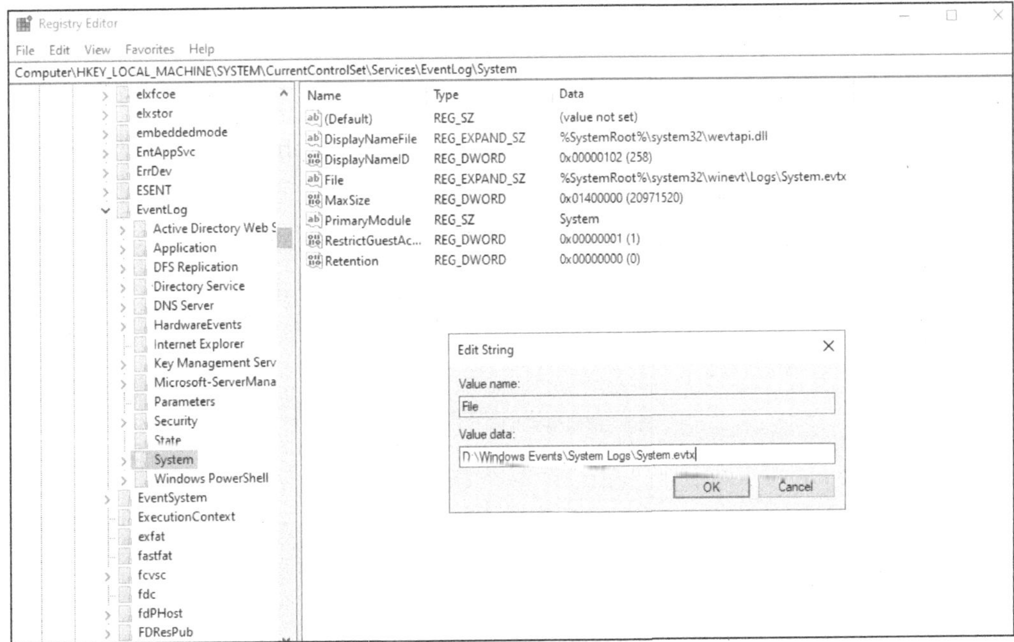

***Figure 12.16:** Log Location Configuration*

Conclusion

This chapter provided a comprehensive overview of updating and troubleshooting Windows Server 2025, beginning with the essential processes involved in starting up your server and familiarizing yourself with recovery tools, which were crucial for addressing unexpected failures and ensuring swift recovery. It emphasized maintaining business continuity through effective disaster recovery strategies, highlighting the importance of planning and preparation to minimize downtime during crises. Additionally, the chapter covered the significance of regularly updating the operating system, drivers, and applications to enhance system security and performance, ensuring that vulnerabilities were patched and server functionality was optimized. Various troubleshooting methodologies were introduced to help you effectively resolve potential issues, equipping IT professionals with the necessary tools to maintain a stable server environment. Moreover, the chapter underscored the importance of utilizing the Event Viewer, a critical tool for monitoring server logs, aiding in the identification and diagnosis of server-related issues to facilitate timely corrective actions. By mastering the topics covered in this chapter, you become better equipped to manage your server environment effectively, ensuring high availability, security, and performance.

Next, in *Appendix A*, you will discover strategies for studying and preparing for the Microsoft certification exam. It could significantly validate your skills and knowledge in Windows Server 2025, enhancing your marketability within the competitive IT industry.

Questions

1. What steps are involved in the server startup process?
2. What strategies are implemented to ensure business continuity?
3. Can you explain what a Windows Update entails?
4. How would you define troubleshooting in the context of IT?
5. What is the purpose of the Event Viewer, and how is it used?

APPENDIX A
Navigating Microsoft Certifications

Introduction

This chapter is a comprehensive guide to Microsoft Certifications, focusing on Windows Server 2025. It covers the essentials of Microsoft Certifications, detailing the skills evaluated in the exams and highlighting the importance of role-specific certifications in the professional world. Starting with the basics of certificates and certifications, it explains their significance and value to professional credentials. The chapter also provides practical tips and advice for passing certification exams, ensuring adequate preparation. Additionally, it simplifies the exam enrollment process by outlining the steps required for registration, making it more approachable for candidates. It also offers a range of valuable resources, including study materials, practice exams, and community forums that support candidates and share experiences. This information ensures individuals are well-informed about Microsoft Certifications and the steps needed to succeed in the exams. With proper preparation, individuals can acquire the necessary skills to become **Microsoft Certified Professionals (MCP)**, opening doors to a successful career in IT. This chapter aims to guide candidates on their path to certification, helping them leverage the latest advancements in Windows Server 2025.

Structure

The chapter covers the following topics:

- Importance of Microsoft Certifications
- Microsoft role-based certifications overview
- Microsoft Certification exam audience
- Microsoft certification exam skills
- Microsoft certification exam success strategies
- Study resources for exam preparation
- Microsoft Certification exam registration guide
- Exam day guidelines for Microsoft Certification
- Microsoft Certification validity and renewal rules

Objectives

This chapter aims to thoroughly understand Microsoft Certifications, specifically in the context of Windows Server 2025. It will cover the fundamentals of certificates and certifications, detail the skills assessed in the certification exams, and offer practical tips for adequate exam preparation. Additionally, the chapter will equip professionals with the necessary resources to succeed in these certification exams and achieve the MCP status. The ultimate goal is to guide professionals toward a successful career in Microsoft technologies by leveraging the latest advancements in Windows Server 2025.

Importance of Microsoft Certifications

Microsoft Certifications, illustrated in *Figure 13.1*, hold significant value in the IT industry. They are globally recognized for validating an individual's skills and knowledge in specific Microsoft technologies. These certifications prove the holder's expertise, confirming they possess the necessary technology skills, knowledge, and experience. CompTIA's president and CEO, *Todd Thibodeaux*, noted that certifications are reliable indicators of current and advanced knowledge.

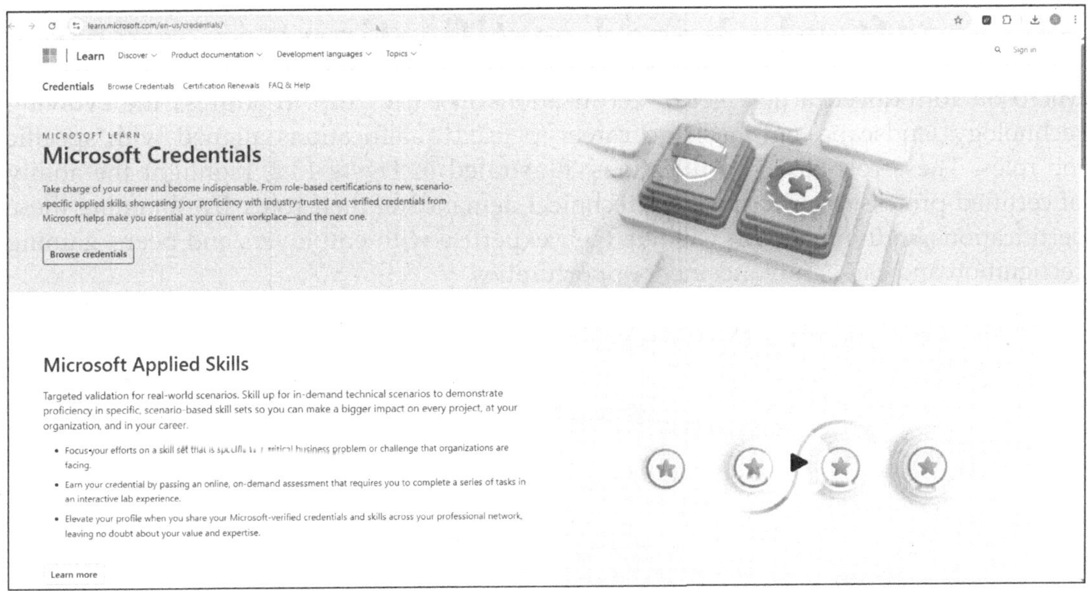

***Figure 13.1:** Microsoft Certification website*

However, it is important to distinguish between different types of Microsoft-related documentation. Not all certificates imply completion of a formal Microsoft Certification. For example, attending training at a Microsoft Learning Partner may result in an attendance certificate, which does not equate to a Microsoft Certification unless tied to a specific certification exam.

So, what exactly is Microsoft Certification? It is a comprehensive process where participants undergo training to acquire technical skills and prepare for the certification exam. Successfully passing this exam and earning the corresponding credential or title marks the completion of the Microsoft Certification cycle.

Attending training and passing the certification exam are essential steps to receiving a Microsoft certificate and achieving the status of an MCP. This certification process ensures that individuals meet the industry's skill and knowledge requirements and enhances career prospects by opening doors to numerous opportunities within the IT field.

Note: For detailed information on various Microsoft Certifications, visit the Microsoft Learn Certifications page at https://docs.microsoft.com/en-us/learn/certifications. This resource provides comprehensive details on certification paths, role-based and specialty certifications, skills measured, and required exams, and offers exam preparation materials, study groups, and certification renewal information.

Microsoft role-based certifications overview

Microsoft introduced a new set of certifications in early 2019 to address the evolving technology landscape, emphasizing career-focused qualifications aligned with specific job roles. These role-based certifications, illustrated in *Figure 13.2*, highlight the ability of certified professionals to meet the technical demands of their roles. By obtaining these certifications, individuals can validate their expertise with employers and peers, gaining recognition and career advancement opportunities.

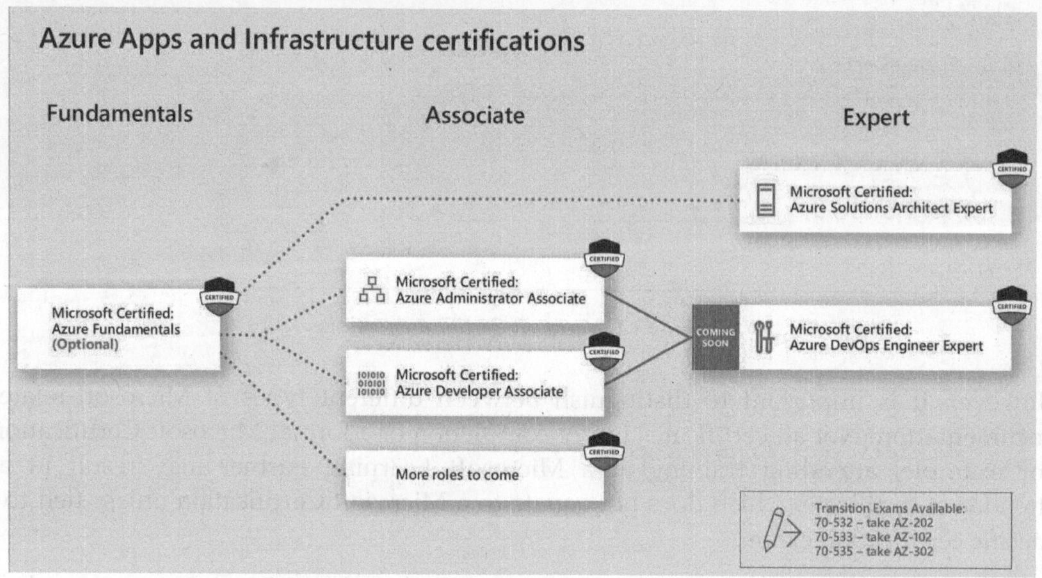

Figure 13.2: Role-based certifications for Azure Apps and Infrastructure

The increasing specialization and niche orientation of IT roles drove the shift towards role-based certifications. Traditional, broad IT roles such as system administrator or system engineer are becoming less common. Modern job titles often include specific subcategories, such as Azure Administrator or Azure Security Engineer, with some roles being further specialized. Recognizing this trend, Microsoft developed certifications that target these precise career roles, offering focused and job-specific training that surpasses a general overview of the industry.

In summary, Microsoft's role-based certifications equip individuals with the skills and knowledge necessary to excel and adapt to the industry's changing demands. By concentrating on the competencies required for particular roles, these certifications enable professionals to demonstrate their expertise and maintain a competitive edge in a rapidly evolving field.

Note: The link provided, https://learn.microsoft.com/en-us/certifications/posts/new-role-based-certification-and-training-is-here, directs to a blog post on Microsoft's website, announcing the rollout of their latest role-based certifications and training

initiatives. This post outlines the modifications to the certification program, underscores the benefits of the role-based approach, and details the availability of new courses. It also includes a list of Microsoft's newly introduced role-based certifications and a link to the certification roadmap for further information.

Microsoft Certification exam audience

The Microsoft Certification program testifies to an individual's technical acumen, rendering them highly sought-after by organizations and businesses alike. This section is a valuable resource for both current certification holders and aspiring candidates, shedding light on the revamped format of Microsoft Certification and outlining the pathway to obtaining it.

Certified professionals are apprised of the updated Microsoft Certification framework, while those yet to obtain certification can glean insights into the certification process and its potential career benefits. Microsoft Certification offers many advantages, as depicted in *Figure 13.3*, encompassing heightened employability, validation of expertise, practical application of theoretical knowledge, adaptability to diverse work environments, and avenues for professional advancement.

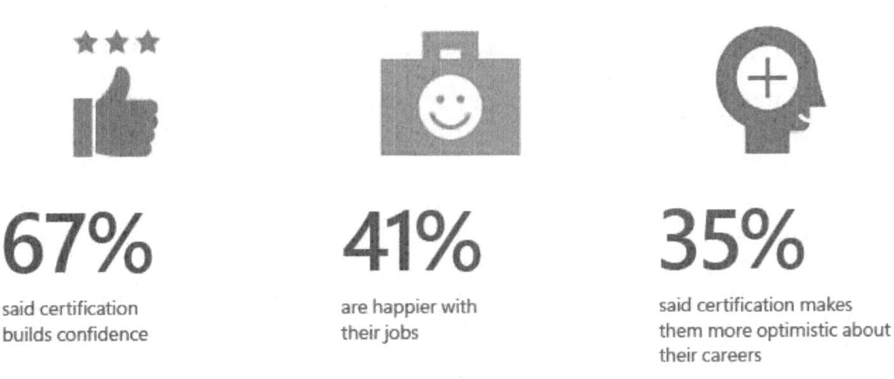

Figure 13.3: *PearsonVUE survey on the value of IT certification*

Microsoft Certification bestows a competitive edge by furnishing globally recognized, industry-endorsed validation of skills proficiency, signifying an individual's readiness to embrace emerging technologies. A thirst for knowledge is paramount in the pursuit of technological proficiency, and Microsoft caters to varied learning preferences through a spectrum of training and certification avenues, including:

- Microsoft Learn offers accessible, self-paced learning paths, comprehensive training materials, and hands-on product exploration at no cost.
- Microsoft Learning Partners provides instructor-led training sessions.
- MeasureUp furnishes official practice tests to aid candidates in exam preparation.

Upon completing a certification exam, candidates are notified via email of their certification status and receive instructions to claim their certification badge. Even for individuals with prior certification achievements, badge claiming is facilitated through the *Credly* portal (**https://info.credly.com**), housing all Microsoft-issued badges earned through past certification endeavors.

Note: The link https://query.prod.cms.rt.microsoft.com/cms/api/am/binary/RE2PjDI leads to a comprehensive PDF document on the Microsoft website. This document offers an extensive overview of Microsoft's certification program, detailing its benefits, available certification paths, and various certification types. Additionally, it outlines the certification process, required exams for each certificate, and available resources for exam preparation.

Microsoft Certification exam skills

Certification exams are crucial assessments of candidates' technical proficiency in specific domains. Organizations like Microsoft continually update the skills measured in these exams to reflect the evolving landscape of technology, ensuring their relevance and validity. For example, the AZ-800 exam assesses candidates' capabilities in administering core Windows Server workloads across on-premises, hybrid, and cloud environments.

Aspiring candidates for the AZ-800 exam are expected to demonstrate proficiency in implementing and managing various solutions, encompassing identity, management, computing, networking, and storage. Additionally, utilizing administrative tools like Windows Admin Center, PowerShell, Azure Arc, and IaaS virtual machine administration is essential for success.

It is important to note that certification exams undergo regular updates or retirement to align with industry trends and technological advancements. For instance, Microsoft retired the MTA 98-365 exam, focusing on Windows Server Administration Fundamentals, on June 30, 2022. Staying informed about these changes empowers candidates to adapt their preparation strategies, accordingly, ensuring they possess the requisite knowledge and skills to excel in their chosen field.

Note: The link https://query.prod.cms.rt.microsoft.com/cms/api/am/binary/RWKI0r leads to a PDF study guide on the Microsoft website. This guide is tailored to assist candidates in preparing for the AZ-800 exam, which evaluates proficiency in administering core Windows Server workloads across on-premises, hybrid, and cloud environments. The study guide offers comprehensive insights into the skills assessed, exam structure, and scoring criteria. Additionally, it features sample questions, case studies, and valuable exam preparation strategies to enhance candidates' comprehension of exam content and format.

In preparation for the AZ-800 certification exam, it is paramount to acquaint oneself with the skills evaluated during the assessment. Delving into the skills measured, as depicted in *Figure 13.4*, clarifies the exam's scope, facilitating targeted preparation. For instance, the AZ-800 exam scrutinizes proficiencies in conceiving and executing solutions spanning diverse Azure services, seamlessly integrating them with on-premises technologies, discerning trade-offs, and strategizing for public and hybrid cloud environments.

Refer to the following *Figure 13.4:*

Skills measured

- The English language version of this exam will be updated on January 28, 2025. Review the study guide linked in the preceding "Tip" box for details about the skills measured and upcoming changes.
- Deploy and manage Active Directory Domain Services (AD DS) in on-premises and cloud environments (30–35%)
- Manage Windows Servers and workloads in a hybrid environment (10–15%)
- Manage virtual machines and containers (15–20%)
- Implement and manage an on-premises and hybrid networking infrastructure (15–20%)
- Manage storage and file services (15–20%)

Figure 13.4: *Skills measured for AZ-800 exam*

Furthermore, candidates are assessed on their ability to analyze requirements and constraints, propose suitable Azure services, and architect solutions addressing identity, security, and compliance considerations. Beyond technical acumen, the exam also gauges project management and governance proficiencies, encompassing familiarity with project delivery methodologies, budgeting, timeline formulation, and risk identification. By grasping the skills assessed in the exam, individuals can streamline their study efforts, ensuring comprehensive readiness for the certification assessment.

As cloud technology evolves and integrates deeper into business operations, the need for experts in cloud solutions will significantly increase. That underscores the significance of obtaining certifications like AZ-800, which validate proficiency in contemporary cloud technologies and position individuals advantageously in the competitive landscape of IT roles.

Deploy and manage AD DS in on-premises and cloud environments (30–35%)

To complete this exam objective, it is essential to have a solid understanding of several key components. Firstly, you must have the knowledge and skills to deploy and manage domain controllers and configure and manage multi-site, domain, and forest environments. Additionally, being familiar with AD DS security principles and effectively implementing and managing hybrid identities is crucial. Finally, it would help if you had a good grasp on how to address the Windows server using group policies. You will be well-prepared to accomplish the exam objective by mastering these critical concepts. It is worth noting that being proficient in these areas can also prove beneficial in real-world scenarios, as they are fundamental components of effective server management.

To deploy and manage AD DS domain controllers:

- Deploy and manage domain controllers on-premises
- Deploy and manage domain controllers in Azure
- Deploy RODCs
- Troubleshoot FSMO roles

To configure and manage multi-site, multi-domain, and multi-forest environments:

- Configure and manage forest and domain trusts
- Configure and manage AD DS sites
- Configure and manage AD DS replication

To create and manage AD DS security principles:

- Create and manage AD DS users and groups
- Manage users and groups in multi-domain and multi-forest scenarios
- Implement **Group Managed Service Accounts** (**gMSA**)
- Join Windows Servers to AD DS, Azure AD DS, and Microsoft **Azure Active Directory** (**Azure AD**), part of Microsoft Entra

To implement and manage hybrid identities:

- Integrate Microsoft Azure AD, part of Microsoft Entra, AD DS, and Azure AD Domain Services
- Implement Azure AD Connect
- Manage Azure AD Connect synchronization
- Implement Azure AD Connect cloud sync
- Manage Azure AD Domain Services
- Manage Azure AD Connect Health
- Manage authentication in on-premises and hybrid environments
- Configure and manage AD DS passwords

o manage Windows Server by using domain-based Group Policies:

- Implement Group Policy in AD DS
- Implement Group Policy Preferences in AD DS
- Implement Group Policy in Azure AD DS

Manage Windows Servers and workloads in a hybrid environment (10–15%)

To successfully achieve this exam objective, you must be proficient in managing Windows Servers on-premises and in the cloud. That includes a comprehensive understanding of managing workloads in the Azure environment, an increasingly important area of focus in modern IT. Being well-versed in server deployment, configuration, and maintenance tasks is essential when managing Windows Servers. Additionally, you will need to be able to monitor and troubleshoot server performance and effectively manage server storage and networking resources. In managing workloads in the Azure environment, you must master several key concepts. These include effectively deploying and managing virtual machines in Azure and understanding how to leverage Azure services such as Azure AD and Azure Storage. Additionally, you should be familiar with monitoring and optimizing Azure workloads for performance and efficiency. By demonstrating proficiency in managing Windows Servers and workloads in the Azure environment, you will be well-prepared to accomplish this exam objective and succeed in real-world scenarios. It is worth noting that as more and more organizations move towards cloud-based solutions, having a solid understanding of cloud-based management will become increasingly important in the world of IT.

To manage Windows Servers in a hybrid environment:

- Deploy a WAC Gateway server
- Configure a target machine for WAC
- Configure PowerShell remoting
- Configure CredSSP or Kerberos Delegation for 2nd Hop Remoting
- Configure JEA for PowerShell remoting

To manage Windows Servers and workloads by using Azure services:

- Manage Windows Servers by using Azure Arc
- Assign Azure Policy guest configuration
- Deploy Azure services using Azure VM extensions on non-Azure machines
- Manage updates for Windows machines
- Integrate Windows Servers with Log Analytics
- Integrate Windows Servers with Microsoft Defender for Cloud
- Manage IaaS VMs in Azure that run Windows Server
- Implement Azure Automation for hybrid workloads
- Create runbooks to automate tasks on target VMs

- Implement Azure Automation State Configuration to prevent configuration drift in IaaS
- Machines

Manage virtual machines and containers (15–20%)

To successfully achieve this exam objective, you must thoroughly understand managing virtual machines using Hyper-V Manager. That includes performing tasks such as creating, configuring, and maintaining virtual machines and managing virtual machine resources such as storage and networking. Additionally, it would help if you were well-versed in setting up and managing containers, an increasingly important aspect of modern IT infrastructure. That includes understanding container architecture, configuring container environments, and managing container images and repositories. Finally, it would help if you had experience working with Windows Server virtual machines in Azure. That requires knowledge of deploying and configuring virtual machines in Azure, as well as being able to manage virtual machine resources such as storage and networking. Additionally, you should be familiar with Azure tools such as Azure PowerShell, which can be used to manage Azure resources, including virtual machines. By mastering these essential concepts, you will be well-prepared to accomplish this exam objective and succeed in real-world scenarios. As virtualization and cloud-based solutions become increasingly prevalent, a strong understanding of virtual machine and container management will be critical for success in IT.

To manage Hyper-V and guest virtual machines:

- Enable VM Enhanced session mode
- Manage VM using PowerShell remoting, PowerShell Direct, and SSH Direct for Linux VMs
- Configure nested virtualization
- Configure VM Memory
- Configure integration services
- Configure Discrete Device Assignment
- Configure VM resource groups
- Configure VM CPU groups
- Configure hypervisor scheduling types
- Manage VM checkpoints
- Implementing high availability for virtual machines
- Manage VHD and VHDX files
- Configure Hyper-V Network Adapter

- Configure NIC Teaming
- Configure Hyper-V Switch

To create and manage containers:

- Create Windows Server container images
- Manage Windows Server container images
- Configure container networking
- Manage container instances

To manage Azure Virtual Machines that run Windows Server:

- Manage data disks
- Resize Azure VM
- Configure continuous delivery for an Azure VM
- Configure connections to VMs
- Manage Azure VM network configuration

Implement and manage an on-premises and hybrid networking infrastructure (15–20%)

To succeed in this exam objective, it is crucial to have a strong understanding of deploying name resolutions and managing IP addressing and network connectivity both on-premises and in the cloud. Deploying name resolutions refers to assigning names to network resources such as computers, printers, and servers. That can be accomplished through **Domain Name System** (**DNS**) and **Windows Internet Naming Service** (**WINS**). By understanding how to deploy name resolutions effectively, you can ensure that network resources are easily identifiable and accessible. Managing IP addressing and network connectivity involves configuring and troubleshooting IP addresses, subnets, and network gateways. That includes understanding the various types of IP addresses, subnet masks, and default gateways and how to configure them on network devices such as routers, switches, and firewalls. Finally, in addition to managing network connectivity on-premises, it is also crucial to manage network connectivity in the cloud. That includes understanding how to configure virtual networks, network security groups, and load balancers in cloud environments such as Azure and AWS. By mastering these key concepts, you will be well-prepared to accomplish this exam objective and succeed in real-world scenarios. It is worth noting that as organizations increasingly rely on network connectivity for their day-to-day operations, having a solid understanding of network management is becoming increasingly important in IT.

To implement on-premises and hybrid name resolution:

- Integrate DNS with AD DS

- Create and manage DNS zones and records
- Configure DNS forwarding / conditional forwarding
- Integrate Windows Server DNS with Azure DNS private zones
- Implement DNSSEC

To manage IP addressing in on-premises and hybrid scenarios:

- Implement and manage IPAM
- Implement and configure the DHCP server role (on-premises only)
- Resolve IP address issues in hybrid environments
- Create and manage scopes
- Create and manage IP reservations
- Implement DHCP high availability

To implement on-premises and hybrid network connectivity:

- Implement and manage the Remote Access role
- Implement and manage Azure Network Adapter
- Implement and manage Azure extended network
- Implement and manage the Network Policy Server role
- Implement Web Application Proxy
- Implement Azure Relay
- Implement site-to-site VPN
- Implement Azure Virtual WAN
- Implement Azure AD Application Proxy

Manage storage and file services (15–20%)

To achieve success in this exam objective, it is essential to have a strong understanding of configuring and managing file synchronization in Azure and file shares and storage in Windows Server. Configuring and managing file sync in Azure involves understanding how to enable Azure File Sync. This cloud-based service allows organizations to centralize file services in Azure while maintaining local access to files. That includes understanding how to configure synchronization policies, manage conflicts, and monitor sync activity. Managing file shares and storage in Windows Server involves creating and managing file shares, assigning permissions to users and groups, and configuring storage options such as quotas and replication. That includes understanding how to manage storage resources such as disks and volumes and using tools such as Storage Spaces to optimize storage utilization. Finally, in addition to managing file shares and storage on-premises, it is also crucial to understand how to manage these resources in the cloud. That includes understanding how to use Azure File Storage to create and manage file shares in the cloud and using Azure Blob Storage to manage unstructured data such as images and video. By mastering these key concepts, you will be well-prepared to accomplish this exam objective and succeed in real-world scenarios. As organizations continue to rely heavily on data and file storage, having a solid understanding of file synchronization and storage management is becoming increasingly important in IT.

To configure and manage Azure File Sync:

- Create Azure File Sync Service
- Create sync groups
- Create cloud endpoints
- Register servers
- Create server endpoints
- Configure cloud tiering
- Monitor File Sync
- Migrate DFS to Azure File Sync

To configure and manage Windows Server file shares:

- Configure Windows Server file share access
- Configuring file screens
- Configure FSRM quotas
- Configure BranchCache
- Implement and configure **Distributed File System** (**DFS**)

To configure Windows Server storage:

- Configure disks and volumes
- Configure and manage Storage Spaces
- Configure and manage Storage Replica
- Configure Data Deduplication
- Configure SMB Direct
- Configure Storage QoS
- Configure file systems

Microsoft certification exam success strategies

When aiming for a Microsoft Certification exam, anticipate encountering various questions, typically between 40 and 60. The exam's duration varies depending on its type, with additional time allocated for introductions and surveys. Achieving a passing score necessitates attaining 700 or higher. You can flag questions for later review throughout the exam, provided effective time management is exercised. Navigating the exam is facilitated through intuitive features like the previous and next buttons, enabling review and modification of answers before final submission. Leveraging these functionalities, including flagging questions for review, is paramount to maximizing your performance and ensuring thorough exam completion.

Refer to *Figure 13.5*:

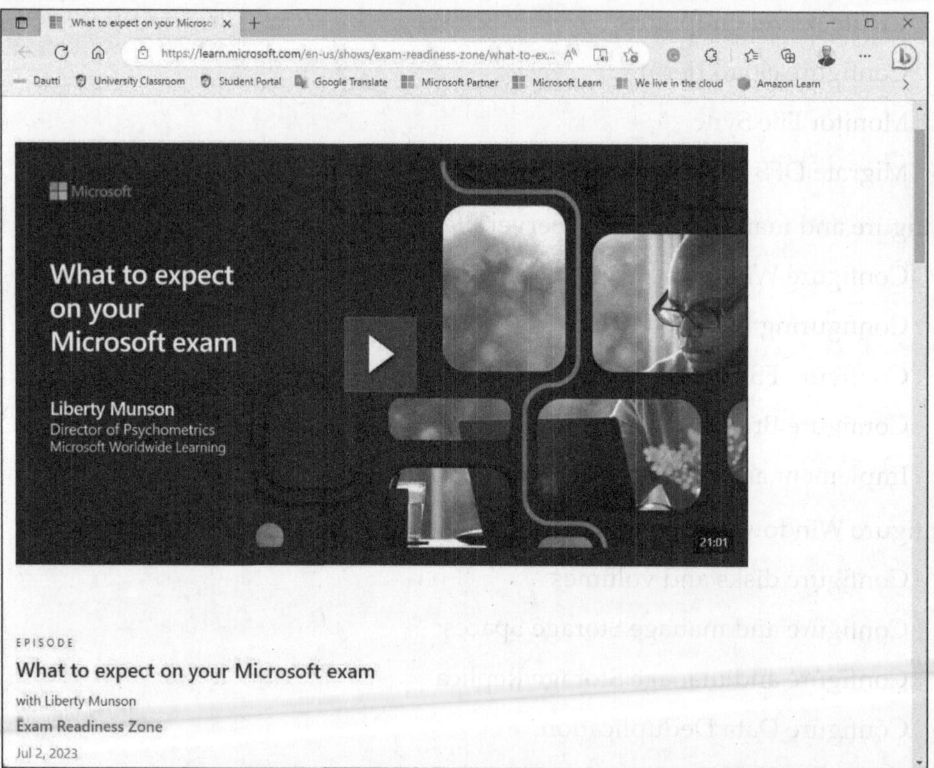

***Figure 13.5:** 'What to expect on your Microsoft Exam" by Liberty Munson*

Note: The link https://docs.microsoft.com/en-us/learn/certifications/exam-duration-question-types offers insights into Microsoft Certification exam durations, passing criteria, and question formats. It elucidates the options for reviewing and flagging questions during the exam and the ability to navigate back and forth within questions.

Study resources for exam preparation

Preparing for Microsoft Certification exams involves adopting effective strategies tailored to individual learning styles and exam requirements. While there is no one-size-fits-all approach, certain best practices can significantly enhance preparation efforts:

- **Industry experience:** Actively working in the ICT industry for 6-12 months provides practical exposure to Microsoft technologies and concepts, reinforcing understanding and skills.
- **Training at Microsoft learning partners:** Attending Microsoft training sessions conducted by authorized Learning Partners offers structured guidance and insights from experienced instructors.
- **Utilizing learning resources:** Leveraging resources like books on Microsoft technologies and the Microsoft Learn portal offers comprehensive study materials and interactive learning experiences.
- **Hands-on practice:** Hands-on practice with Microsoft technologies through labs, simulations, and real-world scenarios enhances proficiency and confidence.
- **Exploring other certifications:** Pursuing certifications from complementary vendors like CompTIA broadens knowledge and skill sets, contributing to a well-rounded expertise.
- **Practice tests:** Attempting practice tests familiarizes candidates with the exam format, types of questions, and time constraints, facilitating better exam readiness.
- **Seeking guidance:** Interacting with peers, both online and offline, who have successfully passed Microsoft Certification exams provide valuable insights, tips, and advice based on their experiences.

By incorporating these best practices, as shown in *Figure 13.6*, into their study routines, candidates can effectively prepare for Microsoft Certification exams and increase their likelihood of success. It is essential to recognize that each exam assesses specific skills, requiring tailored preparation strategies to address unique exam objectives and requirements.

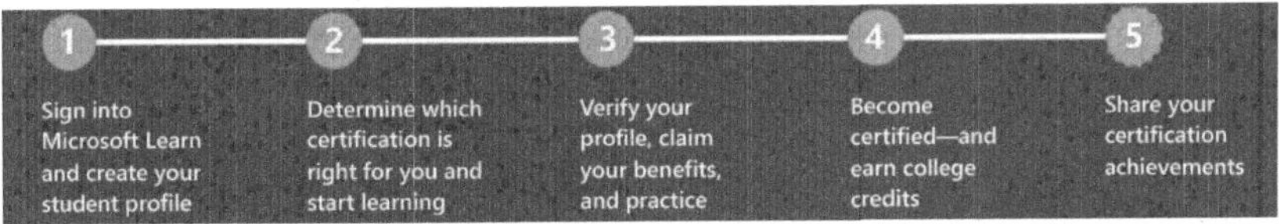

***Figure 13.6:** Microsoft's strategy for getting certified*

Note: The link https://aka.ms/examdemo offers access to a Microsoft Certification exam demo. This resource lets users familiarize themselves with the exam format, interface, and sample questions. It is a valuable tool for candidates preparing for Microsoft Certification exams, allowing them to assess their readiness for the test and become acquainted with the exam environment.

Microsoft Certification exam registration guide

When registering for a Microsoft Certification exam, candidates have two options available:

- The first option is to register online through the PearsonVUE website, requiring a web account.
- Alternatively, candidates can register by contacting a nearby PearsonVUE-authorized testing center.

Both Certiport and PearsonVUE, as in *Figure 13.7*, offer Microsoft Certification exams, providing two delivery methods for exams:

- The first method involves proctored exams delivered at a designated test center. These centers are authorized facilities that administer certification exams for candidates.
- The second method allows candidates to take self-administered online exams at home or in their office.

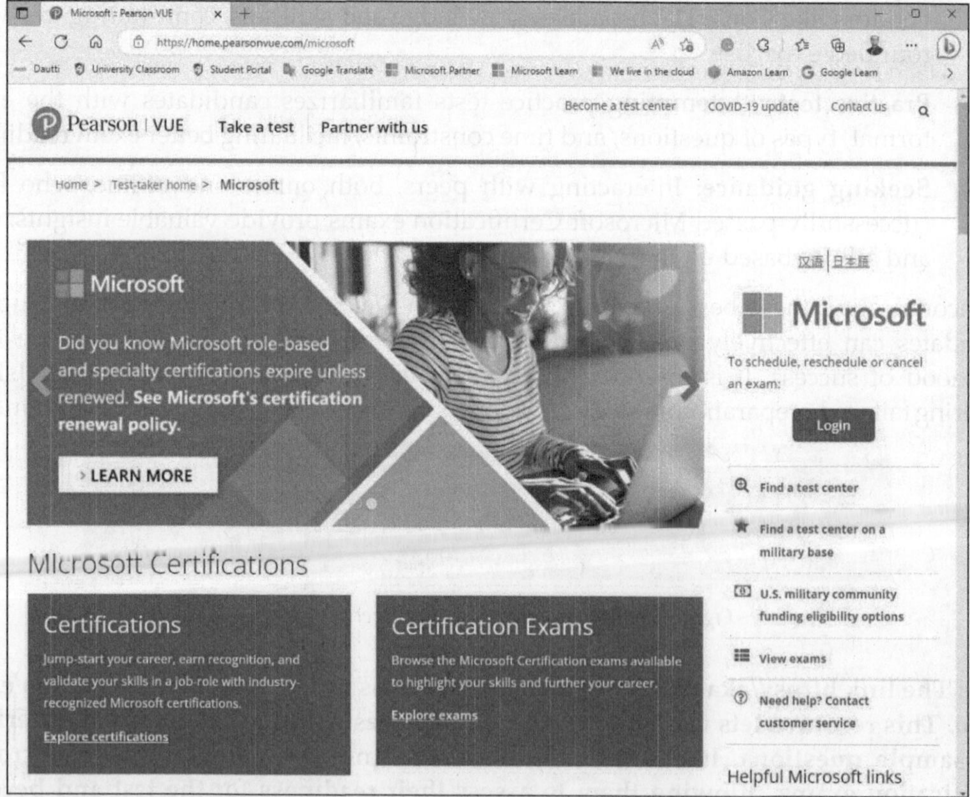

Figure 13.7: Pearson VUE website for registering for Microsoft exams

The online examination format gained significant traction during the COVID-19 pandemic, prompting many vendors to offer online exam options. However, it is worth noting that Microsoft had already provided online exams through PearsonVUE before the pandemic, demonstrating a proactive approach to embracing digital advancements in certification processes.

Note: The link https://home.pearsonvue.com/microsoft directs to the Pearson VUE website's Microsoft Certification page. Users can access comprehensive information about Microsoft's certification exams, including available certification paths, exam formats, and registration and scheduling procedures. Additionally, the website enables users to locate nearby test centers and offers valuable resources for exam preparation.

Exam day guidelines for Microsoft Certification

Preparing for a certification exam extends beyond studying and practicing. Mental and physical readiness for exam day is crucial. Ensure you have had ample rest the night before and manage stress levels. Arriving at the test center or beginning the online check-in process 30 minutes before the exam is advisable. Bring the necessary identification and adhere to the Pearson VUE Candidate Rules Agreement.

Once seated at the delivery workstation, take a moment to relax, breathe deeply, and carefully review the exam instructions. Approach each question attentively, avoiding rushing through them. If uncertain about a question, mark it for review or revisit previously answered questions using the Previous button. Effective time management is essential, so allocate time wisely to answer all exam questions.

Refer to *Figure 13.8:*

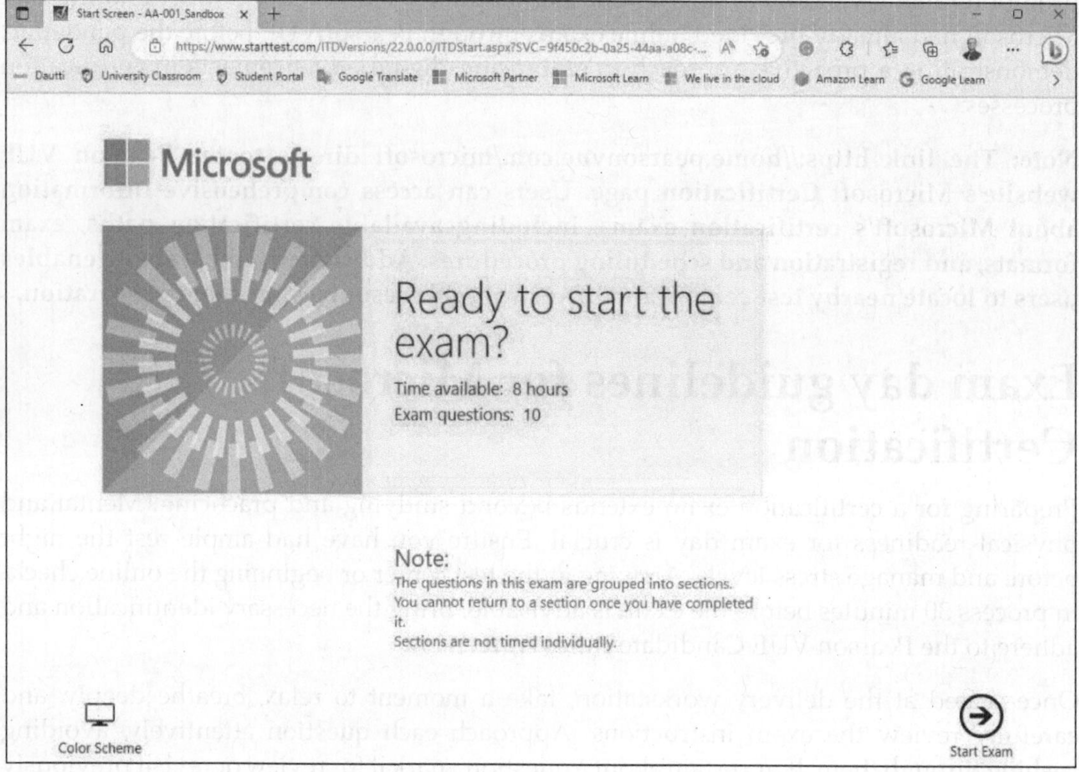

Figure 13.8: Microsoft demo exam

You will receive your exam's result upon completing all questions, which may evoke joy or disappointment. Passing warrants congratulations! However, if unsuccessful, do not lose heart. Acknowledge the outcome and begin preparations anew by pinpointing areas where improvement is needed. Recognize that exam experience enhances preparation, increasing your chances of success in subsequent attempts.

Note: The link https://home.pearsonvue.com/candidate-rules-agreement offers insight into the Pearson VUE Candidate Rules Agreement. This document delineates the rules and protocols candidates must adhere to during exam administration, whether at a test center or online testing. Familiarizing yourself with this agreement before exam day is crucial to prevent potential complications or disqualifications.

Microsoft Certification validity and renewal rules

In response to rapid technological advancement, Microsoft continuously updates its certification formats to ensure candidates stay current with the latest skills. An example of this is introducing a new certification validity period and renewal format in spring 2021, depicted in *Figure 13.9*. Under this format, Microsoft exams, excluding those in the Fundamentals track, remain valid for one year. The renewal process, which is free of charge, can be completed via the Microsoft Learn portal. Additionally, Microsoft sends candidates an email outlining the certification renewal process six months before their certification expires. This proactive approach ensures that Microsoft Certifications remain relevant and aligned with evolving industry demands, empowering professionals to stay competitive in today's dynamic technology landscape.

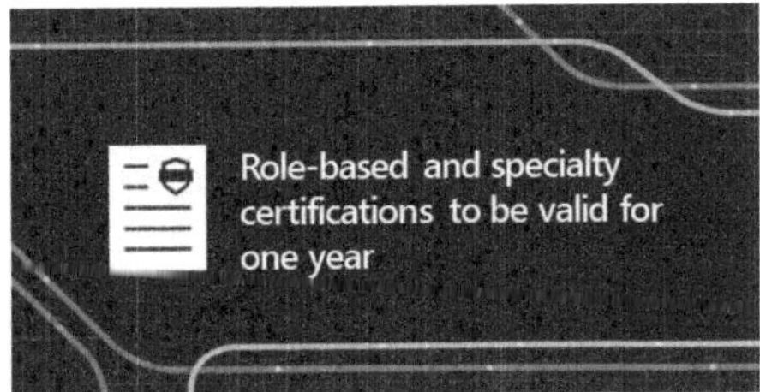

Figure 13.9: *New Microsoft Certification validity and renewal requirements*

Note: The link https://docs.microsoft.com/en-us/learn/certifications/renew-your-microsoft-certification provides crucial information for renewing Microsoft Certifications. With the implementation of a new certification validity period and renewal format, Microsoft emphasizes the importance of keeping skills current to remain competitive. The renewal process, accessible through the Microsoft Learn portal, is free of charge, with email notifications sent six months before certification expiration. Staying informed about these updates is vital for maintaining active Microsoft Certifications.

Conclusion

Throughout this chapter, you have delved into Microsoft Certification and its acquisition process. You have been acquainted with the diverse array of Microsoft Certifications and the sequential steps required to attain them, empowering you to discern whether pursuing a Microsoft Certification exam aligns with your goals. Leveraging the illustration of the AZ-800 exam, you have gained insights into the skill sets evaluated in Microsoft Certification exams and the structure of exam questions. Moreover, this chapter has provided expert guidance on exam preparation strategies and insights into the exam-day experience. Lastly, you have been informed about the recent enhancements in certification validity periods and renewal formats, ensuring your certification's continuous relevance and currency.

Appendix B
Review and Solutions

Introduction

This appendix serves as a dedicated resource to address questions posed throughout the book, consolidating the *Questions* sections from each chapter into a single, accessible location. Designed to clarify challenging concepts and provide deeper insights, this section is invaluable for readers who may encounter difficulties understanding specific topics. By exploring the detailed answers and explanations, readers can solidify their grasp of key ideas and reinforce their comprehension of the material. Beyond serving as a clarification tool, this appendix is a comprehensive review of the book's content, making it an essential resource for students, educators, and professionals. It benefits exam preparation, allowing readers to test their understanding and revisit core principles discussed throughout the chapters. Additionally, it provides a structured way to review and reflect on the material, ensuring that readers can confidently apply the knowledge in practical scenarios. Whether your goal is to resolve a lingering question, strengthen your foundational understanding, or prepare for certification exams, this appendix supports your learning journey. Its structured answers and thoughtful explanations make it a powerful tool for enhancing mastery of the topics covered in *Installing and Configuring Windows Server 2025*.

Structure

The chapter will cover the following topics:

- Answers from Chapter 1 questions
- Answers from Chapter 2 questions
- Answers from Chapter 3 questions
- Answers from Chapter 4 questions
- Answers from Chapter 5 questions
- Answers from Chapter 6 questions
- Answers from Chapter 7 questions
- Answers from Chapter 8 questions
- Answers from Chapter 9 questions
- Answers from Chapter 10 questions
- Answers from Chapter 11 questions
- Answers from Chapter 12 questions

Objective

This appendix is dedicated to answering the questions raised throughout the book, which are part of the dedicated *Questions* section in each chapter. Its purpose is to provide valuable insights and clarity to readers struggling with specific concepts or topics. The answers in this appendix are carefully crafted to help readers deepen their understanding of the material and ensure they have a solid grasp of the main ideas and concepts discussed in the book. By reviewing the answers provided here, readers can resolve any uncertainties they may have encountered and strengthen their comprehension of the subject matter. Whether you want to revisit key points, clarify specific concepts, or reinforce your knowledge, this appendix is an essential resource for enhancing your understanding of the content covered in the book.

Answers from Chapter 1 questions

Chapter 1, Understanding Network Components, provided a foundational introduction to the core elements of network infrastructure, tailored explicitly for IT professionals working with Windows Server environments. It began with exploring Windows Server's role within network architecture, providing a detailed overview of essential network concepts. The Computer Network Overview section clearly explained key terms such as hosts, nodes, peer-to-peer, and clients/servers, ensuring a solid grounding in network fundamentals. Additionally, readers gained insights into general concepts, including clients, servers, **Network Operating Systems** (**NOS**), hardware, software, and networking architectures.

By explaining these fundamental concepts in accessible language, this chapter equipped IT professionals with the knowledge to navigate and understand network components within Windows Server environments.

The answers are as follows:

1. A **computer network** is a collection of devices connected to share resources and exchange data. These devices communicate through wired or wireless connections, enabling collaborative tasks and efficient data sharing.
2. Types of computer networks include **local area networks (LAN)**, **wide area networks (WAN)**, **metropolitan area networks (MAN)**, **personal area networks (PAN)**, and **wireless local area networks (WLAN)**, each serving different geographical areas and communication needs.
3. **Network components** include routers, switches, hubs, modems, **network interface cards** (**NICs**), firewalls, access points, servers, and clients, all of which help in data transmission, security, and device connectivity.
4. **IPv4 uses a 32-bit address space**, offering limited addresses, while **IPv6 uses 128-bit addresses**, providing a much more extensive address range. Additionally, IPv4 uses decimal notation, while IPv6 uses hexadecimal. IPv4 often requires manual configuration or DHCP, while IPv6 supports auto-configuration.
5. A **Network Operating System (NOS)** is software that manages network devices and resources, providing services like communication, file sharing, and security to ensure the network's efficient operation.

Answers from Chapter 2 questions

Chapter 2: Introduction to Windows Server 2025 provided an essential introduction to Windows Server 2025, the latest server operating system developed by Microsoft as part of the Windows NT family. In the Windows Server Overview section, readers uncovered the fundamental aspects of Windows Server 2025, gaining insights into Microsoft's new server OS. Topics covered included an overview of Windows Server 2025, an identification of Windows Server 2025 editions, a comparison between Windows Server 2025 and its predecessor, Windows Server 2022, and minimum and recommended system requirements for installation. Additionally, readers learned how to obtain and download Windows Server 2025, ensuring they had the necessary resources to begin their journey with this latest iteration of Windows Server.

The answers are as follows:

1. The **four key hardware components** of a server are the processor (CPU), which handles calculations and tasks; memory (RAM), which stores data temporarily for fast access; storage (HDD/SSD), which holds data permanently; and the **network interface card** (**NIC**), which enables network communication.

2. Windows Server eras include:
   a. **Server for the masses era (1996-2000):** This initial phase focused on making server technology accessible to a broader audience.
   b. **Enterprise era (2000-2008):** During this time, Microsoft concentrated on enhancing features tailored for large organizations, emphasizing advanced management and security functionalities.
   c. **Datacenter era (2009-2013):** This era was characterized by resource optimization and improvements in virtualization capabilities, which are crucial for modern data centers.
   d. **Cloud for the masses era (2016-present):** The current phase emphasizes cloud integration, empowering organizations to utilize cloud services for greater scalability and operational flexibility.
3. **Minimum system requirements** are the basic hardware and software specifications for an operating system to function correctly, such as CPU speed, RAM, and storage space.
4. Three notable features in Windows Server 2025 include **enhanced security**, **better container support**, and **intelligent management tools**.
5. Windows Server 2025's most appealing aspects are its **advanced security features**, **cloud integration**, and **modern management tools** that simplify administration.

Answers from Chapter 3 questions

Chapter 3, Windows Server 2025 Installation, provided comprehensive guidance on installing Windows Server 2025, the latest iteration of Microsoft's server operating system. Through step-by-step instructions accompanied by easy-to-understand graphics, readers learned how to master the installation process of Windows Server 2025. Topics covered included understanding partition schemes, boot options, and the differences between Desktop Experience, Server Core, and Nano Server installation options. Additionally, readers explored various installation methods, including clean network installations, unattended installations, upgrades, and migrations, ensuring they had the knowledge and skills to deploy Windows Server 2025 effectively in diverse environments.

The answers are as follows:

1. The two primary **partition schemes** used in computers and servers are **Master Boot Record** (MBR) and **GUID Partition Table** (**GPT**). MBR is older and supports up to four primary partitions, while GPT supports more and larger disk sizes.
2. The **boot option** refers to the process or configuration determining the device or medium (e.g., hard drive, USB, network) from which the system will load the operating system during startup.

3. **Installation methods** include **bootable DVD/USB, USB flash drive**, and **network boot**.
4. Before installing Windows Server 2025, consider **hardware compatibility**, partitioning scheme, and **installation method** (e.g., Desktop Experience vs. Server Core).
5. A **virtual switch** in Hyper-V allows virtual machines to connect to the physical network, enabling communication between virtualized systems and the external network.

Answers from Chapter 4 questions

Chapter 4, Initial Configuration of Windows Server 2025, explained the essential steps after installing Windows Server 2025, focusing on post-installation tasks vital for server administration and maintenance. Readers learned how to manage devices and device drivers, check the registry and service status, and configure the initial server settings. Additionally, the chapter covered in-depth discussions on server device drivers, including installation, upgrade, uninstallation, and troubleshooting procedures. Topics also included managing services in a server environment, understanding **Plug and Play (PnP)**, IRQ, DMA, interrupts, driver signing, registry entries, service accounts, and dependencies, and ensuring readers had the knowledge and skills to configure and manage their Windows Server 2025 environment effectively.

The answers are as follows:

1. **Device drivers** are software components that allow the operating system to communicate with hardware devices, such as printers, graphics cards, and network adapters.
2. The **Windows Registry** is a centralized database that stores configuration settings and options for the operating system, software applications, and hardware.
3. A **Windows service** is a background process that runs on Windows Server to perform essential tasks, such as file sharing, print services, or security functions, without user intervention.
4. **Initial configuration** is essential for Windows Server to ensure optimal performance, security, and network connectivity. It allows administrators to set up necessary settings, such as IP addresses, user accounts, and server roles.
5. To run the initial configuration in Windows Server 2025, you can use tools like **Server Manager** and **Server Configuration**.

Answers from Chapter 5 questions

Chapter 5, Installing Roles Using Server Manager and PowerShell, provided comprehensive instructions for installing roles in Windows Server 2025 using both Server Manager and Windows PowerShell. Readers learned how to utilize the Server Manager interface and Windows PowerShell cmdlets to add roles to their Windows Server 2025 environment seamlessly. Through step-by-step guidance, readers learned to leverage both tools for role-based installations, ensuring streamlined deployment and configuration processes. Additionally, the chapter explored the purpose and functionality of each role, enhancing readers' understanding of role-based administration in Windows Server environments.

The answers are as follows:

1. **AD DS: Active Directory Domain Services** (**AD DS**) is a directory service developed by Microsoft for Windows domain networks. It stores information about objects on the network and makes it available to users and network administrators.

2. **DNS Zones:** DNS zones are distinct parts of the domain namespace managed separately. They contain DNS records for a specific portion of the DNS namespace and help efficiently manage DNS data.

3. **DORA in DHCP:** DORA stands for Discover, Offer, Request, and Acknowledge. It is the process used by DHCP to assign IP addresses to clients. The client sends a Discover message, the server responds with an Offer, the client sends a Request, and the server sends an Acknowledge.

4. **Hyper-V:** Microsoft developed Hyper-V, a virtualization technology that allows users to create and manage virtual machines on a physical server. It enables multiple operating systems to run concurrently on a single physical machine.

5. **IIS: Internet Information Services** (**IIS**) is a flexible, secure, and manageable web server hosting websites, services, and applications. Developed by Microsoft, it supports HTTP, HTTPS, FTP, FTPS, SMTP, and NNTP.

6. **PDS Role Services:** The **Print and Document Services** (**PDS**) role includes services like Print Server, Distributed Scan Server, Internet Printing, and LPD Service.

7. **Network Access Technologies of RA: Remote Access** (**RA**) technologies include **Virtual Private Network** (**VPN**), DirectAccess, and Web Application Proxy.

8. **Setting Up RDS:** To set up **Remote Desktop Services** (**RDS**), you need a Windows Server, RDS licenses, a Remote Desktop Session Host, a Remote Desktop Connection Broker, and a Remote Desktop Gateway.

9. **WSUS Connection Modes: Windows Server Update Services** (**WSUS**) can operate in two connection modes: Autonomous mode (where each server independently downloads updates) and Replica mode (where servers mirror the updates from an upstream WSUS server).

Answers from Chapter 6 questions

Chapter 6, Azure Arc On-Premises Hotpatching, delved into the innovative capabilities of On-Premises Server Hotpatching, enabled by Azure Arc, a powerful hybrid cloud solution from Microsoft. Readers explored the concept of hotpatching, a method for applying updates to servers without requiring a reboot, and how it could be seamlessly integrated with on-premises servers using Azure Arc. Through practical examples and step-by-step demonstrations, readers learned how to leverage Azure Arc to implement hotpatching solutions, enhancing security and minimizing downtime in their on-premises server environments.

The answers are as follows:

1. **Hotpatching in Windows Server 2025:** Hotpatching allows for installing security updates without rebooting. This method updates the in-memory code of running processes, minimizing downtime and enhancing security.

2. **Azure Arc support for hotpatching:** Azure Arc facilitates hotpatching by connecting on-premises servers to Azure. This integration allows administrators to manage and apply hotpatches through the Azure Update Manager.

3. **Benefits of hotpatching in on-premises environments:** Hotpatching offers several advantages, including reduced downtime, immediate application of security updates, lower resource usage, and simplified maintenance schedule.

4. **Configuring Azure Arc for hotpatching:** To set up Azure Arc for hotpatching, connect your Windows Server 2025 machine to Azure Arc, enable Virtualization-Based Security (VBS), and use the Azure Update Manager to manage hotpatch updates.

5. **Best practices for implementing hotpatching:** Best practices include testing updates in a staging environment, monitoring systems during updates, having a rollback plan, and ensuring compatibility by keeping systems and software current.

Answers from Chapter 7 questions

Chapter 7, Next-Generation Active Directory and SMB Enhancements delved into the evolution of **Active Directory** (**AD**) and **Server Message Block** (**SMB**) protocols in Windows Server 2025, introducing readers to the next-generation enhancements and features designed to elevate security, performance, and scalability. Readers explored the advancements in **Active Directory Domain Services** (**AD DS**) and the SMB protocol, gaining insights into new functionalities, improved security measures, and enhanced performance optimizations. Through practical demonstrations and real-world examples, readers learned how to leverage these next-generation enhancements to streamline authentication, access control, and file sharing in Windows Server 2025 environments.

The answers are as follows:

1. Windows Server 2025 introduces several new features for **Active Directory Domain Services (AD DS)**, including an increase in the database page size from **8k to 32k, schema updates**, an **AD Object Repair feature**, new **functional levels for domains and forests**, and **NUMA support for better performance**.

2. **AD security** in Windows Server 2025 has been enhanced with new *security capabilities,* including *protocols, encryption, hardening,* and *cryptographic support improvements*. These enhancements help fortify the environment against evolving threats.

3. **SMB over QUIC** provides a secure and reliable alternative to traditional TCP network transport. It uses **TLS 1.3 for encryption**, ensuring all SMB traffic is safe. This protocol is particularly beneficial for remote users and high-security organizations, as it creates an encrypted tunnel over **UDP port 443**, protecting SMB traffic from exposure to untrusted networks.

4. The **32K database page size** is an optional **Active Directory Domain Services (AD DS)** feature that improves scalability by allowing larger objects and more efficient data storage. This feature requires all domain controllers in the forest to support the 32K database page size format.

5. **SMB performance** in Windows Server 2025 is enhanced through several improvements, including SMB compression for more efficient data transfers, default SMB signing to protect data integrity, and an SMB authentication rate limiter to mitigate brute force attacks.

Answers from Chapter 8 questions

Chapter 8, Configuring Windows Server 2025 Services, provided comprehensive guidance on configuring client/server network services in Windows Server 2025 using **graphical user interfaces (GUI)** and Windows PowerShell. Readers learned to utilize multiple GUI wizards, tools, and Windows PowerShell cmdlets to efficiently configure essential network services in their Windows Server 2025 environments. Through step-by-step instructions, visual aids, and practical examples, readers gained proficiency in using both GUI-based and PowerShell-based configurations for DHCP, AD DS, virtual machines, web servers, DNS records, print servers, **Windows Deployment Services (WDS)**, VPNs, remote desktop users, and **Windows Server Update Services (WSUS)**.

1. **Domain Controller (DC):** A DC is a server that responds to security authentication requests within a Windows Server domain. It manages user access to network resources and enforces security policies.

2. **A Record:** An A record, or Address record, maps a domain name to its corresponding IPv4 address. A fundamental DNS record directs traffic to the correct IP address.

3. **IPv4 Scope:** An IPv4 scope is a range of IP addresses that a DHCP server can assign to clients on a network. It defines the pool of addresses available for lease and includes configuration settings like subnet mask and default gateway.

4. **Virtual Machine (VM):** A VM is a software emulation of a physical computer. It runs an operating system and applications like a physical machine but is isolated from the underlying hardware.

5. **Website:** A website is a collection of online web pages hosted on a web server and can contain text, images, videos, and other multimedia content.

6. **Print server:** A Print Server is a device or software that manages print requests from multiple clients on a network. It queues print jobs, manages printer settings, and provides centralized control over printing resources.

7. **Remote Desktop User:** A Remote Desktop User accesses a computer or server remotely using **Remote Desktop Protocol** (**RDP**). This allows them to use the resources and applications on the remote machine as if they were physically present.

8. **WSUS benefits:** WSUS provides centralized management of updates and patches for Microsoft products. Benefits include improved security, reduced bandwidth usage, and simplified update deployment across an organization.

Answers from Chapter 9 questions

Chapter 9, Enhancing Storage with NVMe SSDs & SAN, helped you understand the advancements in storage technology and integration in Windows Server 2025. It focused on leveraging NVMe SSDs and enhancing **storage area network** (**SAN**) integration for improved performance and scalability. By the end of this chapter, you have gained a deep understanding of the benefits of NVMe SSDs, including higher throughput, lower latency, and increased reliability. You also learned how to optimize storage configurations to harness their full potential. Additionally, you discovered strategies for seamlessly integrating SAN solutions, maximizing storage efficiency, and enhancing data management capabilities in Windows Server 2025 environments.

The answers are as follows:

1. **NVMe Protocol**: **Non-Volatile Memory Express** (**NVMe**) is a high-performance interface for accessing non-volatile storage media, such as SSDs, via the PCIe bus. It offers low latency and high throughput, making it ideal for modern storage solutions.

2. **Deploying NVMe SSDs in Windows Server 2025**: To deploy NVMe SSDs in Windows Server 2025, ensure your server supports NVMe drives, install the necessary drivers, and configure the storage settings in the server's BIOS/UEFI. Use Windows Server's storage management tools to initialize and format the NVMe SSDs.

3. **Tuning performance for NVMe SSDs**: Optimize NVMe SSD performance by updating firmware, enabling TRIM, adjusting power settings, and configuring write caching. Regularly monitor performance metrics and adjust as needed to maintain optimal performance.

4. **SAN integration in Windows Server 2025**: Windows Server 2025 supports integration with **storage area networks (SANs)** using protocols like iSCSI, Fibre Channel, and NVMe over Fabrics. This integration provides high-speed, low-latency access to shared storage resources.

5. **Software-Defined Storage (SDS)**: SDS is a storage architecture that separates storage software from hardware, allowing for creating a virtualized storage pool. It uses commodity hardware and centralized software control to provide flexibility, scalability, and efficient resource management.

Answers from Chapter 10 questions

Chapter 10, In-Place Upgrades for Version Updates, delved into performing robust in-place upgrades in Windows Server 2025 environments. This enables administrators to seamlessly update their systems to the latest version while minimizing downtime and disruption. Readers learned practical strategies and best practices for planning and executing in-place upgrades, ensuring a smooth transition to the new version of Windows Server. Additionally, the chapter explored tools, techniques, and considerations for validating compatibility, managing dependencies, and mitigating potential risks associated with version updates.

The answers are as follows:

1. **In-place upgrade:** An in-place upgrade is updating the existing operating system on a server or computer to a newer version without removing the current system or applications. This method retains existing settings, applications, and data.

2. **Preparing for an in-place upgrade:** To prepare for an in-place upgrade, back up all critical data, ensure compatibility of hardware and software, update drivers and firmware, and review the system requirements for the new OS version.

3. **Validating compatibility before an upgrade:** Validate compatibility by running the upgrade readiness tool provided by the OS vendor, checking hardware and software compatibility lists, and testing the upgrade process in a non-production environment.

4. **Mitigating risks during an in-place upgrade:** Mitigate risks by performing a full backup, creating a recovery plan, ensuring sufficient disk space, turning off non-essential services, and monitoring the upgrade process closely.

5. **Optimizing performance after an upgrade:** Optimize performance by updating drivers, applying the latest patches and updates, reviewing and adjusting system settings, and monitoring system performance to identify and address bottlenecks.

Answers from Chapter 11 questions

Chapter 11, Tuning Windows Server 2025 for Peak Performance, provided readers with best practices and strategies for optimizing the performance of Windows Server 2025. By understanding the significance of server hardware selection and performance monitoring, readers learned how to maximize the efficiency and reliability of their server environments. Additionally, this chapter covered essential maintenance techniques to ensure the ongoing health and performance of Windows Server 2025.

The answers are as follows:

- **Four primary hardware components:** A computer system's four primary hardware components are the **central processing unit** (**CPU**), Memory (RAM), Storage (HDD/SSD), and **Input/Output** (**I/O**) devices such as keyboard, mouse, and display.
- **Performance monitor:** Performance monitor is a Windows tool that provides real-time data on system performance. It helps administrators track and analyze system metrics like CPU usage, memory consumption, disk activity, and network traffic.
- **Resource monitor:** Resource monitor is a Windows utility that provides detailed information about hardware and software resource usage. It allows users to monitor CPU, memory, disk, and network usage, helping identify performance bottlenecks and troubleshoot issues.
- **Task manager:** Task manager is a system utility that provides information about running applications, processes, and services. It allows users to monitor system performance, end unresponsive tasks, and manage startup programs.
- **Windows admin center:** Windows admin center is a web-based management tool for Windows Server and Windows 10/11. It provides a centralized interface for managing servers, clusters, hyper-converged infrastructure, and Windows 10/11 PCs, simplifying administrative tasks and improving efficiency.

Answers from Chapter 12 questions

Chapter 12, Maintaining and Troubleshooting Windows Server 2025, delved into the critical aspects of maintaining and troubleshooting Windows Server 2025 to ensure seamless operations and high business continuity standards. Readers gained insights into essential maintenance practices, including the server startup process, recovery tools, and disaster recovery planning. Additionally, the chapter covered the importance of staying updated with the latest OS, hardware, and software updates to enhance system security and performance. Readers also learned effective troubleshooting techniques and utilized tools such as Event Viewer to identify and resolve issues promptly.

The answers are as follows:

1. **Server startup process:** The server startup process involves several steps: **Power-On Self-Test (POST)**, loading the BIOS/UEFI firmware, initializing hardware components, loading the bootloader, and finally starting the operating system.
2. **Strategies for business continuity:** Strategies to ensure business continuity include disaster recovery planning, data backup and replication, implementing high availability solutions, and conducting regular risk assessments and business impact analyses.
3. **Windows update:** A Windows Update involves downloading and installing patches, security updates, and feature enhancements provided by Microsoft. These updates help keep the operating system secure, stable, and up-to-date.
4. **Troubleshooting in IT:** Troubleshooting in IT refers to diagnosing and resolving technical issues. It involves identifying the problem, analyzing potential causes, implementing solutions, and verifying that the issue is resolved.
5. **Event viewer:** The Event Viewer is a Windows tool for viewing and analyzing event logs. It provides detailed information about system, application, and security events to help administrators monitor system activities, diagnose issues, and track security events.

Conclusion

In this chapter, you have learned valuable insights and clarity on questions raised throughout the book. The answers provided serve as a comprehensive review of the book's content, helping you deepen your understanding of the material and fully grasp the main ideas and concepts presented throughout the book. This chapter is a valuable resource for students, educators, and anyone looking to reinforce their knowledge of the subject matter. Additionally, this chapter can be beneficial for exam preparation or for individuals who wish to test their understanding of the material. Overall, the answers provided in this chapter are a valuable reference for anyone seeking to enhance their knowledge of the book's subject matter and achieve their learning goals.

Join our book's Discord space

Join the book's Discord Workspace for Latest updates, Offers, Tech happenings around the world, New Release and Sessions with the Authors:

https://discord.bpbonline.com

Index

T

STRENGTH OF MATERIALS